Collected Po

CHRISTOPHER MIDDLETON has lived in Austin, Texas since 1966, but, travelling far and wide, he has not ceased to be an English poet. For thirty years he has published poems, essays and translations with Carcanet Press. Born in Truro in 1926 and educated at Merton College Oxford, he retired from his Centennial Professorship in Modern Languages in 1998. Since 1972 he has been a member of the Akademie der Künste, Berlin. Christopher Middleton has received numerous awards, including the Geoffrey Faber Memorial Prize and the Schlegel-Tieck Translation Prize.

Books by Christopher Middleton

The headings in the Contents list give the titles of Christopher Middleton's books published by Carcanet Press since 1975, excepting *Of the Mortal Fire* (2003) and *The Tenor on Horseback* (2007) which were published exclusively by the Sheep Meadow Press, Riverdale-on-Hudson.

Carcanet Press also publishes Christopher Middleton's *Pataxanadu and Other Prose* (1997) and his selected verse translations *Faint Harps and Silver Voices* (2000), and his three books of literary-critical essays: *'Bolshevism in Art' and other Expository Writings* (1978), *The Pursuit of the Kingfisher* (1983) and *Jackdaw Jiving: Selected Essays on Poetry and Translation* (1997). In 2004 Shearsman Books (Exeter, UK) published his *Palavers and a Nocturnal Journal,* in 2007 his *If From the Distance: Two Essays* was published by Menard Press.

Prose by Christopher Middleton from other publishers includes *Serpentine* (London: Oasis Books, 1985), *In the Mirror of the Eighth King* (Los Angeles: Green Integer, 1999), *Crypto-Topographia: Stories of Secret Places* (London: Enitharmon Press, 2002) and *Depictions of Blaff* (Los Angeles: Green Integer, 2008).

His twenty books of translations appearing with other publishers include *Andalusian Poems* (Boston, MA: David R. Godine, 1993).

CHRISTOPHER MIDDLETON

Collected Poems

Signed for dear Leah

Christopher Middleton

June 3, 2008

CARCANET

First published in Great Britain in 2008 by
Carcanet Press Limited
Alliance House
Cross Street
Manchester M2

A CIP catalogue record for this book is available from the British Library
ISBN 978 1 85754 980 5 (paperback)

The publisher acknowledges financial assistance from Arts Council England

Typeset by Jack Grosskopf, Austin, Texas

Printed and bound in England by SRP Ltd, Exeter

CONTENTS

Nonsequences/Selfpoems

Our Flowers & Nice Bones

The Lonely Suppers of W. V. Balloon

Two Horse Wagon Going By

Silent Rooms in Several Places

Apocrypha Texana

The Balcony Tree

Intimate Chromides

The Word Pavilion

Of the Mortal Fire

The Tenor on Horseback and Work in Progress

xiv

TORSE 3: POEMS 1948–61

Definition

Torse[3].
[f.med.L.*torsus,-um,*
for L. *tortus* twisted.]
Geom. A developable surface;
a surface generated
by a moving straight line
which at every instant is turning,
in some plane or other through it,
about some point or other
in its length.

Shorter Oxford English Dictionary

1

Seven Hunters

1

On skins we scaled the snow wall,
seven hunters; roped, leaning
into claws of wind; we climbed,
wisely, for no fixed point.
There was no point we knew.

Staggered upon it at noon.
Drifts half buried it. The coils
horns eyes had to be hacked free.
We lashed, as the moon rose,
its black flesh to sledges.

It was dead as a doornail,
thank God. Labouring
the way down, by luck
we found a hut, beer and bread.

2

Some came in cars, some barefoot,
some by air, some sprang from ships,
some tore in by local train,
some capered out of bed
and biked there with babies.

Like flies they filled the hot square.
The cordon, flung round that heap
of black tubes, when the eye blazed,
could not see. The crowd did.
Then we heard the first shout.

Now in our town the streets
and houses have gone.
Here, underground, we
who were seven are one.

Amigos de Corazon

He's hard to make out, the old man next door.
All day he sits outside in his rocking chair,
Gap-toothed, in a blue shirt, and broken sandals.

About five times any day I pass him by;
He looks up from making his lobster baskets,
And smiles, but never finds anything to say.

He looks up and smiles, and nods his head
In a way that strikes me as having dignity.
He looks accustomed to tumultuous ovations;

But he isn't, he's like the goats hereabouts;
They're hobbled, but if you peer over their wall
And wait, they amble over to be amicable.

Sometimes this old gentleman takes a walk,
Around sundown, to the sea.
You notice he's not tall, on the contrary

He fits so well into the tiniest rowing boat
There could be room for something at his feet.
You wouldn't think it as he smiles over his basket.

One afternoon, a big new boat was being dragged
Out of the boat shed opposite. Quite a crowd
Had gathered; and how the people shoved and shouted.

The boat was so big two square feet of stone
Had to be hammered out of the boat shed doorway.
There the boat was, and everybody staring hard,

And the old man had run to the wall between
His dooryard and the street, and he was staring hard
And standing on tiptoe; and he had broken into a smile

That was different from any smile I ever got
As I passed him by, the usual five times a day,
Waiting for him to lift his head and nod.

Objects at Brampton Ash

The quick thrush cocks his head,
bunching his pectorals, halted.

Long holly shadows hone his shining claw;
you thumb its edge and grass gets grassier.

The tapered spire, at anchor in its ring
of tomb and cedar, has to quit ascending.

So you revolve in hearth-smoke's occult caves,
banished by touch of frost beading the roofs.

What increase, could these ends outlast
perpetual waste.

Oystercatchers

So luminous around them lay the air,
The wavebeat died; rocks in the bay below
Retrieved their shadows, shrank to nothingness.
And here they flew, unerringly as souls; it seemed
The body's beauty died and they remembered
Only the dazzling wrists that launched them once.
In upward vertical flight,
Black M upon white M the wings' twin boomerangs
Fought the full blast of western ocean wind.

In level flight their voices rose like flutes,
And imposed on the air a sudden shape;
Short cries, unshaded, liquid, lingering
An instant overhead and then clean gone.
That black and white, by phantom definition
Anchored in emptiness, gave, almost one supposed,
Gave off the calm so luminous around them.
As bodies they could shed all trammeling,
More eager with their shape's precision move
For having mastered so their own harsh element,
Mastered the shrouding armies of the wind,
And launched in space another, wilder song.

At Porthcothan

A speck of dark at low tide on the tideline,
It could not be identified as any known thing,
Until, as one approached, a neck was clear
(It is agreed that logs, or cans, are neckless),
And then a body, over which the neck stood
Curved like a questionmark, emerged
As oval, and the whole shape was crouching
Helpless in a small pool the sea had left.

The oval body, with green sheen as of pollen
Shading off into the black plumage, and the neck
Surmounted by the tiny wide-eyed head,
Were not without beauty. The head was moving,
So like a cobra it seemed rash to offer
An introductory finger to the long hooked bill
Stabbing the air. Danger had so
Sharpened what intelligence the bird possessed,
It seemed to pierce the mind of the observer.
In fact we were afraid, yes afraid of each other.

Finally though I picked it up and took it
To a quiet side-bay where dogs were rarer.
Here the shag sat, happy in the sun,

Perched on a slab of rock where a pool was,
In which I caught five fish for it
With a pocketknife, a handkerchief
And a plunging forefinger. But at six o'clock
It left the rock and waddled off seaward.

Though breakers came in high and curling
It straddled them, bouncing, buoyant,
Borne along the sealine sideways, with head up,
Slithering across the bay's whole width, and then
Drifted ashore again, to scuttle flapping
With webbed feet flat like a Saturday banker's
To shelter on a level rock. Here it studied,
With the air of one of whom something is expected,
The turbulent Atlantic slowly rising.
What could I do but leave it meditating?

Early next morning, on the bay's north side,
I found it cuddled under the cliff. The tide
Was low again. What hungry darkness
Had driven so the dark young shag to shelter?
It did not resist when I picked it up.
Something had squeezed the cobra out of it.

I took it to a cave where the sun shone in,
Then caught two fish. It opened one green eye,
And then another. But though I cut
The fish into portions, presenting these
To the bill's hooked tip, it only shook its head.
Noon came. The shag slept in the cave. At two
I hurried back. The shag was stone dead,
With its fine glossy head laid back a little
Over the left shoulder, and a few flies
Were pestering its throat and the fish scraps
Now unlikely to get eaten.

                    Ten minutes perhaps
I sat there, then carried it up the cliff path
And across the headland to a neighbouring cove
Where oystercatchers and hawks flew and far

Far below in loose heaps small timber lay, tickled
By a thin finger of sea. There I flung the shag,
For in some such place, I thought,
Such bodies best belong, far from bathers, among
The elements that compose and decompose them,
Unconscious, strange to freedom, but perceptible
Through narrow slits that score the skin of things.

Or perhaps (for I could not see the body falling)
A hand rose out of air and plucked the corpse
From its arc and took it, warm still,
To some safer place and concealed it there,
Quite unobtrusively, but sure, but sure.

The Suspense

'senza speme vivemo in disio',
Inferno, iv, 40.

You are too light, blonde, to bear much hardship.
Slight bones cannot carry much weight of weariness.
Bowed skin leaks, the long mouth voids a fountain;
Bitter as lemons then, your stocked heart shrivels.

How, fair frail body, can you pour out such holiness yet?
I mean this measure, being, where nothing was or shall;
I mean this body, grafting space to heal chained chaos.
Yours, the grave glance, belly's target, level smile:
You, pure injury to the poured blood, shouldering veins'
    weight,
Base flesh you hoist up (how?) into the blue-peaked eyelash.

Number may vanish there. Blind hence your levity brings
A calm of visions into the puckered face of things.
Even that world's elision into a wrung tear;
Even this radiance you wrench clear of the world.

Edward Lear in February

Since last September I've been trying to describe
two moonstone hills,
and an ochre mountain, by candlelight, behind.
But a lizard has been sick into the ink,
a cat keeps clawing at me, you should see my face,
I'm too intent to dodge.

Out of the corner of my eye,
an old man (he's putting almonds into a bag)
stoops in sunlight, closer than the hills.
But all the time these bats flick at me
and plop, like foetuses, all over the blotting paper.
Someone began playing a gong outside, once.
I liked that, it helped; but in a flash
neighbours were pelting him with their slippers and things,
bits of coke and old railway timetables.

I have come unstuck in this cellar. Help.
Pacing up and down in my own shadow
has stopped me liking the weight it falls from.
That lizard looks like being sick again. The owls
have built a stinking nest on the Eighteenth Century.

So much for two moonstone hills,
ochre mountain, old man
cramming all those almonds into a bag.

Yes, Mr. Brecht

> 'Wie anstrengend es ist, böse zu sein',
>   Brecht, *Die Maske des Bösen*

A Persian princess hangs on my wall.
In her white turban, robe of orange,
yellow slippers and white drainpipes,
I find her strange. She is alone.

A flower is in her left hand; with her right
she fingers the fan in her embroidered waistband.
On a slight hill, with deep blue sky behind,
she is musing. She may be in a paradise.

What slender symmetrical toes she too had,
that Indian girl long ago at the greengrocer's.
And even now, staring at such hopeless grace,
I have to fight to quench a yawn.

A Bunch of Grapes

Michelangelo's Sybilla Delphica, upon what
    hard times wistfulness has fallen!
The faraway look is called a foolish thing,
    and even Rilke's girls may be lying all tousled and
tubby in bed, longing for lunch. Once though
    wistfulness meant knowing what others don't
but highly regard, seeing from a distance
    that something one contains cannot be touched.
So Goethe, coming into Italy, stopped a night
    by Lago di Garda, where he remarked
waves scrolled by south wind clutching the water
    exactly as Virgil had described them. And your
amberhaired unawakened girlchild playing
    in the park by water, in water, with a coloured ball,
was plumb constancy, in being precisely herself,
    not broken by oblivions of now and then.
Yet seeing from a distance that now and then
    can telescope, to magnify one instant into
a lilac light suffusing consciousness
    from its very ground of animal exhilaration—
this is wistfulness. One's world is multiplied,
    to share in what, the time before, was not itself,
or seemed not so. You best exist in things
    outside, are faraway, though they may not look it.
Wistfulness then is a luminous corrosive working
    through all immediate, objective, enveloping stuff

10

which has little or no regard for us. Suddenly
    you wake up, you swam like a fish in starlight,
and it meant what it was, the mountain pool,
    the balloon with a skin of gold that another child
hugged at your huge and crumpled bedside. And as now,
    in the panic instant, skimping responsibility,
even at wits' end, or just arranging for a journey,
    wistfulness remains, and puts the welter of things
for a time into order. It is a stillness
    nothing can sunder. It bears comparison
with a bunch of grapes on a plate on the table
    in a whitewashed room among wrinkled olive boughs
where the sun beats, and it is not yet time
    to be gone from that place.

Aesthetics for Benetto Gulgo

(IN MEMORY OF EUGEN GOTTLOB WINKLER, 1912–36)

Old men, forgotten, mumbling, all alone,
Must rage with visions, of dark dazzling skin;
Fair Helen's tumbled hair, her body pressed
Under their mouths, but soft, in shared surprise.

Husbands athirst, again, when the great noon slackens
Over church and garden, being only half aware
Their fruit is falling, begin to stare and tremble
At wishlike breasts on schoolchildren walking past.

Shall the face that shows no reason for disguise
Make dodderers forfeit wisdom and atone
For sins undone by going fast demented?

Is there such harm in dispossession, that we crawl
Backward through being, mindless, nothing done,
Heart-hollow drab, the whole house unfrequented?

This rose-dissolving wind, this doddering one,
Bequeathes a radiance, absence unconfined.

The line that breasts the form must be like steel,
Dread handling all we have that's beautiful.

The Thousand Things

Dry vine leaves burn in an angle of the wall.
Dry vine leaves and a sheet of paper, overhung
by the green vine.
From an open grate in an angle of the wall
dry vine leaves and dead flies send smoke up
into the green vine where grape clusters go
ignored by lizards. Dry vine leaves
and a few dead flies on fire
and a Spanish toffee spat
into an angle of the wall
make a smell that calls to mind
the thousand things. Dead flies go,
paper curls and flares,
Spanish toffee sizzles and the smell
has soon gone over the wall.

A naked child jumps over the threshold,
waving a green spray of leaves of vine.

German Ex-PWs (Russia)
   at Münsterlager, 1948

Shadows mass, feet stamp the black earth,
Metallic sun
Streams down across the compound. Here they walk,
As if kneedeep in something. Where the roofs stretch,
Their eyes like thrushes' eyes flicker and hunt for shade.

Questioned, they suddenly shrink, timid, and blurt out
The stock responses.
Fluids rise from choked bends in the mind and coat
Their tongues with a bitterness. A heavy lid
Slams in the throat, bows head and shoulders, legs
Shaking. This prisoner has a penknife, opens it and sees
Seven winters uncongeal in the blade,
Sunrise of steel unhinge embracing armies.
Wan, he looks up, as if a door had opened and they said,
'Here is the land: we have come back to it.'
Only the knife is his. The transport is waiting.
When they embark, they wave their sleeves
With the levity of men who have ceased to live.

The Hedgehog

Hot March came with the hedgehog;
by the coal bin he crouched, first,
nibbling milk, mackereling
snoutmarks on the saucer's brim.
Then three successive nights he came;
came later the last night, dumped
glistening in the saucer
one small amorphous turd. Why?
In gratitude? We just laughed.
Scorn? Or some offence he took?
How hurt a hedgehog's feelings—
human he's not, though shut in
by belly and genitals,
like us,—or the isle untucked,
some blanket sliding off its
back, and he gone for he knew?
Southern wind this morning veered
crushing to cottage size high
cumulus and thicker grass,
warm as this child's hand, which tugs;
for Quick, she said, and Quick, Come,
and we found the path cracked, ants

rushed from the crack all around
the turd freshly planted there.
I think she knew the plain cause,
for Now! she said, then exclaimed:
Better not hurt these sweet ants!

Hotel Linde, Zürich-Oberstrass

Finkslin, mastercook and king of the Linde,
A man compact and hard of head, requires
For each fresh guest a white embroidered napkin,
A toast, for regulars, or a gesture of the hand.
In his soup may be perceived no fishbone.
Within his doors, the wine pours with a difference.

His combed helmet of silver has logic in it,
Roofs over smiles to goodevening various
Grotesques gathered for meat and talk at his tables.
Champions in skittles, Gygax the gallowbird,
Cannot bruise his aplomb. How calm, how warm
His consort comes annealing, to adorn his order!

Red beams aglow beneath fog in January;
Red lattice, blown loose, beat under wind;
Snow silted up all little lamps and orifices;
At six, frozen, beds divulge their bleary forms.

'Your bookcase you shall have. I have ordered it.'
He walks bolt upright when he walks upstairs.

Montagnola

A fan with five peaks cools his door
in the hot hill. Forked paths lead there.
Under chestnut you pass caves for clear wine;
swerve over gradients of changing green;

14

float through woody dark following the bird-note
sung by two birds. His windowsill
showed white trousers; on the balcony
a lanky hawk stared and stooped. That afternoon
he stirred, with a silver spoon, his coffee backwards,
because of rheumatism; you could have sworn,
as he spoke to unspeak every word he spoke,
that his freedom was a way to deny nothing.
His only memorable remark was an afterthought:
a butterfly with open wings
clung alive to the minute-hand of his study clock.
He did not allude to his lyric on the subject;
and on reflection it was hard to tell if paradox
or wisdom lay, inextricably veiled,
in the churning limpid well of his senescence.

Alba After Six Years

There was a winter
            dark fell by five
four noses ran
            and shouting children
she got so quickly in a rage.

Now when I wake
            through mist and petrol
birdsong cannonades
            blaze open-sighted
at a climbing sun.

Hopeful but prone
            I turn to face a wall
between me and that wall
            surprised to meet
wild arms which did not hold this way before.

Abasis

Walking docile as you do down the empty street
The shadow-crowded granite, glow of sodium seas
It may shake the pavement under your feet
May drum with fists on air beside you
Mirage at your back may corrupt the clarity before you
May knock on your door when guests have turned and gone
May trouble your dream in the house (angel or monster
Figures recoil then into the cavity of the dream)
Dissolving bastions you had made sure were solid
Dispensing the life that is casual (not good but average)
May issue a spectre out of the throat of morning
Mask of sweat at noon
Forbidding the ecstasy that rides the noon's brow
Perplexing the cool that lays the dust at evening
Hollowing the tranced hill where you squat at sundown

Happy with friends to watch the turning of the stars

The Ant Sun

The ant sun rams
Its ivory egg.
Grinding gears
Mix: it trundles on.
Slow river loomed,
A barge bellows;
Exhaust oils
Banked cloud of stone.

Sleep and waking
Swop lefts:
Old men, tenderly,
Thrump their brides
Of decades gone:
For white robes
They wait and stew,
The crowding misty girls.

And a day comes
And a day comes
With brisk birds.
A swab slops
Over dud marble.
Harder day comes
(Purity. Purity!)
With sweetly reeking coins.

The Forenoon

All the long forenoon, the loitering of insects;
Their invisible wings, whirring in choir and alley,
By lemon pyramids, in domes of organpounded air,
Over golden loaves that cool on glass in Greek Street.

One has flown to the vine slopes of a gated city,
One is crushed in a tube; one is a foreign king,
Stern in his carriage, popular, waving;
One with a whip stumbled after office girls,
And woke smiling. In iron shade
To one on a bench his nostril's curlew pipings bring
Concomitant visions of vacant moors.
One has dwelled among the springs and heard
A throbbing in the ark above their mountain.
One sidesteps a banker with a beak
And a dead baby dangling on a string from it.
One wisecracks. One darts giggling under a hat,
To munch a matchstick. One reads words
ARBOGAST FACTION PACT BUT HEAT RISES

One: severed from the great root the strong shrivel
One: the voluminous black fire answers their cry of terror
One: the plumed waves have burst long enough on this shore
One: scattering the blind swarms that drink at the carcass.

The Dress

Her blue dress lightly
Is all my care.
Nothing I am
When not beside her.
Not every day,
Not any hour she passes,
Not always when she passes
Am I enough eager.

Not enough the streetcorner,
Nor the quiet room,
To take her body in.
Not enough the colour
Of patience, of murder
To draw her down
From the balcony she leans upon,
Highcrowned

And in the nighttime turned
Pale into amber over arch,
Inviolate sun.
Not enough the table
Under the awning, nor the elbow
Moving for me to see her,
For she must come
Unseen, without wanting:

Then I shall lightly
With all my care
Have my hand under
Her blue dress when she is there.

The Greenfly

I am in the train. It is a summer afternoon.
I am in the corridor. A bar of warm aluminium
Cools my palms. The greenfly on the window
Is making an effort to move across the glass.

But six legs each with a claw at the end of it
And each claw groping in turn while the other five
Try to grip—but two feelers fencing with air—
But two tiny trellis wings of brinded fire—
It's not much help to a greenfly on a pane of glass.

Between me and the ruined plots rushing past,
Between me and the new blocks and dumps of brick,
Between me and several consecutive cranes
Fencing with air, clawed to earth, the roofs and halts,
This greenfly is an inquisitor.

You'll eat my one or two roses, is what I think.
Mine or someone else's. Some evenings I squirt
Swarms of your kind with a reliable poison.
Here it may not be the same. Here you are a most ravishing
Insect. Your six legs—they take the breath away.

No, here it is different. But what can I do?
We are rushing toward some constellation, so they say,
Onhurled by bricks and poisons, claws to grope and probe,
Gardens that contain a rose or two with any luck,
And I have no notion what to do about the killing now;
I have no notion why it starts, how it can end.

The Sniff

Beak nose, bug eyes, almost bald head,
Drumskin over cheekbones, drawn in slack,
Wry over jawbones, flesh sucked into a mouth
Where pursed lips poise, to spit out evil taste,

He sniffs, with skidding jaw, and nose pinched,
Gills rise, then fall, and then he sniffs again,
Coughs up such snot as dropped back in his throat,
Till nostrils gaze again, eyesockets empty, and disclose
Darkness inside, where of small hairs undergrowths glisten,
Tricked with the stinted light this economic café gives.
He sniffs regularly, ravenously, glaring about himself;
Not picking, not blowing, he sits and sniffs; perhaps
To dislodge some crumb derelict after a choked meal?
To dull memories of cooking he loved as a little child?
Or to shake off desire, roused in a fragrance wafted over,
So that swallowed lust mysteriously glides into the dew drop?

A too hard sniff culminates in a sly gurk.

Ode, on Contemplating Clapham Junction

All day rain fell. Morning:
one dusky liquid nymphless cave.

By noon the cave was crammed with ocean.
Two trains, full tilt, great whistling mackerel,
raced in an X under whale-shaped shadow.

Umbrellas, propped in halls, by tea,
behaved across the floor, like puppies.

All fall, by day, had rained. As late
as nine now moist sun
ushers a fearful agitation in

through curtain after lifting curtain.
Some thrush or other aches to sing.

Joy. One thrush. One overhasty . . . ? No.
The sun mistaken, rising upside down?
Washed clean, no, space begins, unfolding

a million brilliant swishing fans
of bluish nothing.

Draughts of tomorrow
drawn slow
into empty lungs.

Tenebrae

Enter my discourse as you dared and stood
Between your doorway and the dark and easily
The halflight curled into the hood of your hair.

Then you might have been
Other than what is ordinarily shown.

Shaking the timbers of the compatible world
Wisdom along her veins and her eyes withdrawn
One instant from her dream on the obedient stair,
Night seas unfurled through glory into her form.

Now among flaring things, now moving in the mist,
Their element in distress, might they not
Might they not have drowned in error for tenderness?

No fragrance fell, no motion troubled the air.
Back and gone in thickets of unbreakable glass,
Large-eyed, upright, indubitably gone she has.

This might have happened long, very long ago.

Waterloo Bridge

The rolled umbrella on my wrist,
How much air, crushed in the folds,
Aches for expulsion? What is starved,
Between my hat's crown and my own,
Of angering freshness deep deep down?

Chimney and sailor, ship and star,
Strangely belong. The cobbled lanes
Rib the long river; wet flint mounds
Tug at its roots; and cranes that inch
Athwart thick roofs, suppose this freedom.

Horns blast the ear, like anchors flung
By fluke through sludge to block
Derision riding seaward with the sun.
A meal of rats, doled out by love,—
Crushed by the silence, bolt it down.

Pointed Boots

At three in the morning,
A quietness descends on central railway stations.

A mail van, or an ambulance, may be there;
A man in pointed boots, a Miss Carew.

Quietness keeps them apart,
The quietness that descends on central railway stations.

It is not meant for me.
It is not meant for you.

3

Male Torso

Before I woke, the customed thews
Alighted on strangeness.
Crammed over booms of vine,
The once buxom canvas quilled.

From his hot nest, before I woke,
The snowgoose flew, in skyward rings;
And funnelled air that filled my mouth
Rang with his wingbeat.

The customed eyes, before I woke, were glass;
A bleating queen whose legs were sheaths
Of hammered moon fed swill to pigs;
With needle oars they swept her bark

Through floes of starfruit, dolphins cutting
Under her eyelid's bow blue arcs in air;
And the beat of their oars like drums
Fanned my hushabye head.

Before I woke, no savour was;
But three birds sang that song they piped as girls,
Of sweetness, golden-rinded, and the fountaintree,
For mortal grapes cooled in my hands.

Then down the quartz-walled galleries of ears I coiled,
Before I woke; cymbals clashing sliced their hill,
And there with bulls my skew-wigged mother trod
Her crocus dance around its axle;

Counterwheeling Horn and Bear
Shared in her coronal the thud of fingertips on flutes,
Until my customed silence dipped and rose,
And gall was mine and darkness was.

I live now in a hutch of mud,
Without a floor, nailed by the sun,
Now for the interminable writhing sea
A fair food housed in roofless marble.

But if I wake to sniff the air of clustered stars,
I'm clothed in dew, for babes to drink,
The snowgoose moors her nest on light,
And the small horned worms walk high with hope.

Southern Electric Teddygirl

Politer
And less dull than I, gazing,
Since ribs which mackintosh plates
(Belt on the ninth hole) must make,
For ease, one vertical
Brief tube, topped by a face
Eye-staring at a moon—
So Pomona, worn thin by fish and comics,
Hair yet
Bushes of torchlight
Bounding over hills through whose glades
Cool surf burrows—
Here knees and nose going
No particular way
Back, insistent, toward
Algae, plasm in pools that Pomona inched
Her million years from, now
Leaning back, on springs,
She peers for huts flash by,
Blinks with blued condescending
Eyelids over roof seas
And yellow skies that roar,
Recrossing the ankles
Her winkle-pickers bruise, to resume
Into Orpington
Her airy trail.

24

Absences

On either down a wreath of plume
Carved clear on the hill, her spent
Body aroused in a cedar dream,
She lay the warm day long,
And there a wraith he lay.

Their feathers swim as each breathes
Undone by slumber, and half-askance
They stare away to the other eyes:
They see nought of the night,
Though an emerald semblance outward goes.

A double sleep uncovers them,
Body abounding, drowned now,
And the stiff limbs athwart the sands
Hollow the light their glow gives up:
Entwining lie, nor drowsing doubt
Though time divides, the earth amends.

On neither one the wild grows,
No wheaten acres wave their smile,
No bramble on their ankle is:
For whole is the body if spent at all,
Just as she lay the day long,
And he a wraith beside.

[1949]

China Shop Vigil

Useful these bowls may be;
what fatness makes the hollows glow,
their shadows bossed and plump.

Precisely there a wheel whirling backward
flattens them. Knuckles whiten on copper:
headless men are hammering drums.

Cup and teapot may be such comforters:
small jaws mincing chatter
over the bad blood between us once.

When baking began, the air in jugs frothed
for milk, or lupins. Now mob is crushed
by mob, what fatness but in wild places,

where some half dozen dusty mindful men
drinking from gourd or canvas huddle,
and can speak at last of the good rain.

Nightlabourer

FOR GUY DAVENPORT

Reclined the body of the world:
    No hill whiter with olive,
Hair burned gold by the sun,
      Target of fair skin,
Head of a traveller, to pity turned,
With kingcurled hair and hat of fire,
        Pity upon the near hill,
With roseate staff and silver shoon,
    Brown body, bent like a sail,
Shoulders bound to the treesap:

Now pity will suffer of love,
Yet dries its acreage to a chart
Where crouched the leopard sings,
    No watercourses move;
Will bless the leopard for his thirst,
    No tempter offering
Cavebearded king or saint
No fruit more gold than his encircled head:

No hill whiter with olive:
Will watch on,
    Though the night fall,
Will to the earth his suppliance commit,
    As head bows to the knee,
    Body curls in the hill,
Leopard kneels in the end at the gate of the city:

For though the thorn
    Press needles through his palm,
Pity too near is entered still unseen:
    Beast, curltongued at the cave's mouth,
But to the head laid down under the hill,
To the eye, brushed by sleep's silken sleeve,

Will bring the light the leopard watches by
So that the olive springs from his blood's overcast
And seeds ring the bright blind bone:
    No sail, no land, more curled in amethyst
    Than pity's silence in the stone,
Than the grave hair risen to a golden country.

[1949]

Rhododendron Estranged in Twilight

'Und kommen muss zum heil'gen Ort das Wilde
Von Enden fern . . .'
    Hölderlin, *Friedensfeier*

It crests this tunnelled London hill,
Growing a little space behind this house.
It stands aloof. It is contained by calm.

A blaze of bloom in May now, no hunched bush,
Gawky it is, and stands as in deep water
With slender boles akimbo, coral horned;
Then mutely swayed by undulating wind.

Sky's porcelain inclines, unplaceable,
For each taut cave of flame a shifting margin.
Roots rustle underground, make arch advances.
Red grows oblivious, fat, on eating shade.

Air sweetly rinsing it, the image floats
Into its own reflection imperceptibly.
A slotted mask with one mind's eye divines

Through emerald tropic, ruthless dream,
Lust at meridian, unclenched energy rising:
The sylvan slattern, bawd bedaubed with flesh
Drawn off some lurching drunkard's feline whim,

Green windgod of the hill in hot pursuit,
Those olive shoulders, wrenched back, risking all,
Then, unresisting, thighs from bark unsheathed.

Yet nature's needle teeth bite off what wrong
Reflection cries in them. Quicksilvered man,
Turn you estranged to risk unbaffled more:

This rose unfolding in the air's clear volume
Scents out its own lost womb of origin.
The shown form whispers of the invisible one.
The hill's firm headstone marks the shrine this was.

Without Shoes

'. . . unbeschuht.' Mörike, *Peregrina*.

One goes lightly
    down ignorant rays
across history buoyant
    with fruit and shade

One goes lightly
   mother and father wave
from dormer windows
   of the dove-starred house

Happy anthems—
   owls make naked
women laugh
   in the dark orchard

Babies chirping
   girls of cork
and moonboys quiver
   nailed by the bowstring

Perhaps an orange
   tastes of Padua
an alien chord
   spits visions

But one goes lightly
   over echo-dancing shores
up wrinkled lightning
   surges a friend

yielding tombs of air to trumpet wings
   along whose colonnade
without shoes
   one goes lightly.

News From Norwood

Professor Palamedes darts down Westow Street.
Nothing explains how he avoids
Colliding with mutton, plastics, pianos.
Professor Palamedes, darting down Westow Street,
Tunnels through petrol fumes and tundra;
Rhomboid oysterbeds under his rubbers,
Sparrows and sandwiches scatter before him.

Where is he going, Professor Palamedes?
It's well past three. What has he forgotten?
What can he have forgotten, Professor Palamedes,
Who stood with Agur by Solomon's elbow,
Who flogged the sea, full of nymphs and sheep,
Whom meat moods or helpful harmonies do not perplex?

Let us say he is going toward the stranger.
Again: he is going toward the stranger.
No matter who. The stranger. Who showed his face.
Who showed his face over Solomon's shoulder;
Who saw at Salamis, as planks buckled and the nymphs
Cheered, how sheep just went on cropping grass,
Side by side, to a tinkling of bells.

Matutinal Adventures of a Third Person Illustrating the Untold Agony of Habit

Anachronist or no, he was not one
    to disregard for long the unhurt daffodils'
rosarium, chrysanthos, quills
    plucked from the prancing porcupine sun
their holy circle slew. And soon, as though
    in nature metaphor now faced a match,
rounding his periplum arose
    a second sanctum: snowblue dorsum of nuthatch
winding a six-clawed wedge of sky up a hawthorn put
    a knife like brightness through his eyeball, moderate
as bodies flighted perfect to their purpose.

    How come then so soon the immortal had forsaken
its habitat on this last holy London hill?
    Some scrubbing housewife, had she put them wise,
who had been angels in the suburban sunrise?
    Or had six hundred intervening heartbeats shaken
the three directions time can choose to travel
    into one crooked labyrinthine shadow?
For on his countermarch he found them gone,

found them, but only found them flower and bird.
So brushed his hair at home, then ate his bacon
   with the air of a being invisibly injured,
yet strangely relieved not to have to be saying so.

Cadgwith: 6 PM +

Alternate light and shade englobe
the chimneyed hill. Silver shafts slip
mute under heaven's rib, and open bars.

Four cardinals astride the public bench
dip their noses deep in the grogpots.

Gulls wheel clear,
to skirt the corpus mysticum flung taut
in ribbed gold from swart cliff to winged horizon.

Bloodshot
the venerable sea shifts
one drunkard eye, and wipes its white moustaches.

Gulls turn on their heel.
Night blots the conqueror out.

Climbing a Pebble

What did it mean (I ask myself), to climb a pebble.
From the head of a boy depends a very thin cloud.
A red speck shifting on the Roman Campagna.
This sea-rubbed pebble has no cleft for toes.

It is simple, the ant said (my Nares and Keats).
You start low down, with caution. You need not
Slash your soles for lime like medieval Swiss.
No, but with spread arms, easing up, imperceptibly
Colluding with the air's inverted avalanche.
This cushions, O, the aching spine.

A very thin cloud is falling from the sky.
A shot, a shifting robe of crimson,
Whiffs of powder on the wind—
The sidelong buffet slams. And still you cling,
Still easing upward; giant glades, they creaked and shone,
Fresh mown, now small below—you do not smell them.

And you begin to know what it can mean,
Climbing a pebble. The paradise bird
Drops, dies, with beak fixed in the ground.
An urchin made off with its cloudthin tail.
A cardinal, with footmen to load his fowling pieces,
Peppers Italian larks a glass held spellbound.

The glass was tied to an owl, the owl to a stick.
I struck the pebble, digging, as the sun went up.

Thinking of Hölderlin

(HILLS NEAR HEIDELBERG)

Never mind avarice; the hills
squander at least a sprawl
of steep oak. Speak
of the moroccan green
pines that fetlock them; of rumps,
rutted by axes; of bristling stung flanks,
flushed by puffs of cloud—

for first and last
who saw them crammed the air
with hawk and temple;
and what fetched them avarice, in the interim,
cannot change their green
bulk and butts of sandstone,
let alone rot the wits, killing,

as hawk and temple, his, for the crime
of being put, by them, wise to the least thing.
No, not in his name
do I join these crooked words, lest I miss
for him, more than temple, his hawk,
now lofted by their hot gusts, now
plucking the crowded vermin from their folds.

Antiphon, After Laforgue's *Stérilités*

There torridest lagoons decant
    steeple cool and star
in jugs ophelian orphans drain
    haunting springs
    with oh and ah
    in father-want
    in mother-pain.

Coagular cloacal jig
    the cicatrice
feline ophelias christen itch—
    it robes the gnat
    in candle grease,
    it hogs the fat
    in fuller fig.

An oval-torsoed swan we saw
    furrowing air
and the air shook and clung for joy;
    that duple egg
    we swallowed raw,
    routed for Troy,
    her shambling dead.

What phantoms reign when gods ascend
    our haunted springs?
Quaffers of cloud, we do not know
    ah from an oh
    nor a nailed hand
    from fists of blood
    lambasting things.

Then if a wise Ophelia found
    tarantular
the moon domain, its milken hills
    a serpent ground,
    and chose to shun,
    shaken with tears,
    the dogged sun—

Her caryatid dream conjures
    (if dream it be)
ophelias more fool than she
    to prophylax
    against the swan
    in horizon-
    tal parallax.

Occipital, precipitous
    though hungers drive
moonshine in schisms round the skull,
    no phantoms fuss
    their seraph lull
    from solar rose
    to honey hive.

And man, misty history man, for all that,
    identifies
his shadowshapes with seraphim.
    The garb of him!
    And hopes disguise,
    ellipsoid, slim,
    a Cheshire Cat—

Kedge-anchored in the axletree
   (immortal moon
feline ophelias catechize)
   mortally afraid
   of being free
   from once and soon
   from whats and whys.

A bubble moon we saw, we saw
   a cloven tree;
and phantoms thronged the threshingfloor
   and orphans came
   and did not dance.
   Eyeless, and lame,
   they did not dance.

There too we heard the dew's descent
   on acid hills
and shade elide with sliding shade:
   what image made
   them so lament,
   sobbing through space,
   that were innocent?

Thirst

Should wine and melon, jug and wasp
break from their images, their single sense
shine in the air, burn in the wind:
then were the ripe within grasp—
this axle of the mind.

In cooler cisterns frogs decide to sing.
How morning sun
silvered their throats in your battered pail.
How long since the dragon heard, on waking,
your footstep, heavier, cross his hill.

The Lake of Zürich

(FOR ROBERT WALSER, SWISS POET, IN HIS MADNESS)

Than sky, the lemon, dredged, more dark this liquid.
Fluminal violet, in a lockjaw littoral, swings
Wind-swathed, wind-cradled.

                    Asunder the scooped rays
With fanged spire sentinels at last unbend
Over slender moles, where pedalos are harnessed.

Dazed, mad or dumb unscented gaze, but ladies
Emit, by twos and threes, conspicuous shadows
In a suave star-acre, hum in the voids they leave.

Sickle through throats of cloud the moon drops rustling
Down, as for a day forgotten. Configures heaven,
Curved luminous, in concord, over this brain's trim bed.

Loll, where the rat stalks, the gowned fish and breed.

Air glabrous, may taste of acid, beast uncoil
Cocked like an abandoned eyebrow over
All ease, dark arbour, armoured there, his tail.

Time runs thick as thieves this iron way of water.

Art Machine

(the automatically rotating epidiascope at the exhibition
of Brazilian art, Paris 1960)

There are needles lancing disks
a saint soared across a crowd
I saw tormented women
whirl down a tall hill

a prairie lobster
polyps in a wedge and bronze
twin birds that claw their combs
then boots with sieves in black pools

of beams and winds
the silver fruit

harpoons have been plunged
through grinding millstones
Saint Paul shook his fist
at packed cafés
three pairs of trousers
float from a window
being women whose
rumps must weigh tons

in rice fields
negroes prowl

as shadows ooze from hills
horn pincers wrung
quit their cactus paternoster
plasm flashing wings
a nude candelabra
tilts the tricorn
to allure at that angle as
her image pounces

negroes prowl
in rice fields
rinsing silver fruit
of beams and winds

Intrusions

On rare mornings
    a man at my table
gazes into the left-hand sun.
    Huge heat arriving
snuffles glass and bars, against
    his doubtless smile.

Seas come crashing, horned waves
    airing their volume;
bull-roarers
    make brave men tremble; pitch
flops on gorgon shields as yelping
    gnomes flit batlike by
through cactus stars to holy laughter.

I stand on the threshold, barefoot;
    boosted by half a plank, having guessed
its place by rule of suns,
    as on some thick fly throng
a bone Electra, royally gaoled,
    I print my footmark.

It is a room
    of rod and exit; taller weeds
dry in the jar on a plinth of blue.
    Yet not in fear
this lone loon starts on my intrusion,
    waves in vacancy, with dwindling
hands held to an old old friend.

Five Psalms of Common Man

'Je n'aime pas le dimanche'

1

Whisky whipping g-string Jaguar megaton
sometimes a 'purely rational human being'

it's me they tell of yonder sea devoid of amber
it's me they tell of column and haunting song

noncommittal me my mumble eaten
by the explosions of clocks and winds without routine

not fountains not millennia of light inextinguishable
ebbing through column and throat with its
    wombwombwomb

come my pet my demagogue excruciate me watching
yonder fountain douse the yolky dunes

2

The creatures of coal have looked for you all over;
the creatures of tea heard a snatch of song, it was not you.

The creatures of smoke have looked for you all over;
the creatures of tar saw a tree, it was not you.

The hand was not you, nor the hairy ear;
the belly was not you, nor the anklebone.

The eyeball was not you. Tongue and teeth
and jawbone were not you. The creatures of hair

have looked for you all over; the creatures of snow
touched a locked door, it was not you.

The creatures of paper have looked for you all over;
the creatures of steel smelled thick wallets, it was not you.

These creatures wanted to be free to look for you;
and all the time you looked to be free of their want for you.

3

W. N. P. Barbellion (pseudonymous)
March 1915
sees 'on the top of an empty omnibus
a little heap of dirty used-up bus tickets
collected by chance in the corner'

felt sick
the number of persons
the number of miles
the number of buses

at all times
the number of voices
the number of voices not speaking to one another
perplexity without surprise

Avenues Madison Shaftesbury Opéra
the number of heart beats
without number

the sick one is he on whom his desire advances asking why
the sick one is he who has begun all over again
not waiting not
'waiting that hour which ripens to their doom'

he speaks (Adolf Eichmann April 1961)
'in starchy, clerkish language
full of abstractions
pedantry
euphemism'

4

My blind wife kicking in her flesh of flies.
My blind wife in her ring of ribs beating me flat.
But no shard of keg shall cool my last bones.

The flies were dancing in their ring.
Their ring was dancing in the flies.
The ring desired by the nature of flies.

Stomach eyes packing it all in tight.
Knotted wings kicking in a glue film.
Ghosted in glue was the nature of eyes.

Revolt severe if sieved for its ghost of motive.
Air without motive rubbing in the arid throat.
My blind wife I warm to the coolness of bones.

5

Order imagined against fear is not order.
Saith man. Fear imagined against order
only negates or does not negate existing order.
Out of a rumbling of hollows an order is born
to negate another existing order of fear.

Nights broken before they end, interrupting
the millennia of my vigilance, saith man.
The nights of past time never slept to the end
re-enact themselves in the existing order of fear.

Another order of fear is chaos.
Images of chaos variously coordinated
by disparate imaginations accord or do not accord
to their seasons in time enacting the indeterminations.
The orders revolve in the ring or do not evolve.

The orders revolve as improvisations against fear,
changed images of chaos. Without fear, nothing.
Let me, saith man, take another look at the sea again.
And in his ear begin the rumblings of keels again.

NONSEQUENCES/SELFPOEMS

One inscription for the Berlin Wall

Red earth
of the mountain
red earth dark bodies
twisting and leaping
in their mantillas
of silver and green

Up the staircase
and down
massive accordion
red earth
dark bodies
the walls of stone
hewn fitting

Level to level
weeper-holes
proof
against the burning cloud
erosion breaking
the heart
of a generation

Cabal of cat and mouse

He has a way, the cat, who sits
on the short grass in lamplight.
Him you could appreciate, and more —
how the musky night fits him,
like a glove; how he adapts down there,
below boughs, to his velvet arena.

His, for playing in. A shadow
plodding past his white paws
could be a swad of anything;
except that, as it bolts, he retrieves
and has tenderly couched it,
and must unroll alongside, loving.

His paws dab and pat at it; his
austere head swivels at an angle
to the barrel neck. Prone, he eyes
its minutest move; his haunch relaxing
parades tolerance, for the pose entreats
doubly to play — it is energy

involved, if you like, in a tacit exchange
of selves, as the cat flares up again,
and has seized what he seizes.
And acts proud, does a dance, for it is
his appetite puts all the mouse into a mouse;
the avid mouse, untameable,

bound by so being to concur,
in his bones, with the procedure.
Even the end cannot cancel that.
The shift from play to kill, measured,
is not advertised. He has applied
a reserved gram of tooth power,

to raise this gibbering curt squeal
at last, and now glassily gazes down.
Plunged, barked as if punched,
and has axed his agitator. You heard
soon the headbones crunch; and you shrank,
the spine exploding like a tower in air.

Gaunt man striding

FOR JONATHAN WILLIAMS

Asperity. This rock
pins this hand; from
the other's palm air

spirits a cactus. Rock
heavy as habit. Cactus
throbs and shoots —

it is the pain, love
elemental, gnawing us
animal stars. Clamped,

from shoulder to toe
the body still can
thresh round, wrench.

To rise! You want
man striding, gaunt,
but nimble, dropping

gods in his furrow, now
his famous mushrooms, nights
bruising his great bones

on the desert grains. His
defiance! That being so,
here there is only a hand

under the rock and a hand
the cactus grows from.
To free these — how

burrow the one down
beyond the rock's root,
haul the other up, hose

the whole cactus through it — :
Jonathan Jonathan
keep your pain alive.

The cyclops

Since the bellowings
off that hill
predicated some size
above normal

and a vision,
undeflected, deep
and more broad than
ours in our hollow,

our tribute, one beam
from his brow, to scan
our corn, fish, us,
seemed not improper.

We were wrong; drawn
by that monolithic
stare its blank
fondly swallowed

our lies. And the thing
done, we fingered,
as we scoured the hill,
think, from a crevice,

the eye, like a slug,
and it clung, as a slug
clings on a decaying
carrot.

What would you have made of it, Kavafis

What would you have made of it, Kavafis —
he must be standing, in that top room,
the one knee flexed a shade, hand on the sill;
on a table by the window, coils of thread,
needles, patches and other tools of his trade;
but his hair and his nose make him a handsome one
as he glances back, to the peeling door.

All around him, the street below —
in his mind, porters bloom in round caps,
policemen stick their thumbs into their armpits,
linking fingers across silver jacket buttons
as they move along, but gaze at the notices.
A smile passed from a porter to a policeman
is worth his living — or the power of government.
Let them expel his nature, he'll return

to drift above the bar stools,
evenings, when his shop shuts and all that thread
has done its trivial and benign business. Or then
he may saunter down the same street,
to admire, once more, his notice pinned
in the glass case outside the tobacconist's,

not pausing, but smiling, with the grace,
the killing grace of one who keeps a secret,
keeps it (why not)
even from himself when he buckles, offhand, to the task
its message tells of: 'Minute adjustments
to gentlemen's clothing'.

Disturbing the tarantula

The door a maze
of shadow, peach leaves
veining its wood colour,

and cobwebs broken
breathing ah ah
as it is pushed open —

two hands
at a ladder shook
free the tarantula, it slid

black and fizzing to a rung
above eye-level,
knees jack knives,

a high-jumper's, bat mouth
slit grinning
into the fur belly —

helpful: peaches
out there, they keep growing
rounder and rounder

on branches wheeled low
by their weight over
roasted grass blades; sun

and moon, also, evolve
round this mountain
terrace, wrinkling now

with deadly green
emotion: All things
are here, monstrous convulsed

rose (don't anyone
dare come), sounding through
our caves, I hear them.

The runner

She ran to him
   from the ticket barrier
      saying,
         in her language, Are you angry,

are you angry?
   In her blue coat and white
      lambswool cap-
         comforter, cheeks flushed by the

snow, she ran to
   him. So let her run,
      eventually, just
         as late, with just that question

to the one who
   cannot help gathering her
      either
         from the thin night crowd.

In some seer's cloud car

Eyes of slain stag,
Borges the Argentinian,
62, being blind,
flew up to Austin
on tiger's breath, I think,
in some seer's cloud car.

Borges' mother
is 86.
She can't darn or cook.
She feeds him canned soup,
with what tenderness,
and sends the laundry out.

Borges the poet,
by her escorted, steered,
quotes by the yard in living rooms
English saga, German song.
He has it all by heart.
He's honeycombed.

And robust bread
browns in our oven.
We zoom down streets to shop
detergent, checked by signs.
And behold, way below,
the dark town sparkle.

Me, my table groans
under Arp and dictionaries.
60 ungraded exercises,
treatises, a score — when
Borges asks 'What was that word?'
there's not one I remember.

By whale I came here, it seems.
On whale back, past Labrador.
On the nth day,
spotted dawn over Dallas
in skies of purple steam,
and ate an egg.

Navajo children Canyon de Chelly, Arizona

You sprouted from sand,
running, stopping, running;
beyond you tall red
tons of rock rested
on the feathery tamarisk.

Torn jeans, T-shirts
lope and skip, toes drum
and you're coming
full tilt
for the lollipops,

hopefully
arrive, daren't
look, for our stares
(your noses dribble)
prove too rude

in your silence,
can't break, either,
your upturned
monkey faces into smiles.
It's no joke,

as you grope
up, up
to the driver's door, take
them reverently, the
lollipops —

your smallest, too small,
waited three
paces back, shuffling,
then provided,
evidently

by a sister on tiptoe who
takes his hand, helps
unwrap the sugar totem.
And we are swept
on, bouncing,

look back,
seeing walls
dwarf you. But how
could you get any
more thin, small, far.

Lenau's dream

Scares me mad, that dream;
wish I could tell my-
self I slept without

a dream! But what of
these tears pouring down
still, loud throb of heart?

Waking, I was done up.
My handkerchief wet
(had I just buried

someone?). Don't know how
I got hold of it,
and me fast asleep —

but they were there, the
visitors, evil,
I gave them my house

for their feast, then got
off to bed, while they
tore the place to bits,

the wild, fool ele-
mentals! Gone out now,
leaving their trail, these

tears and from tables
great wine pools dripping
slowly to the floor.

Three Brixton gardens

In this one a boy
engages brickwork
bouncing a football —

the one-eyed house
has one, the soil just
turned for planting

a prairie, there the boy's
friend saddles up, hugs
a black twister

of hoofs at any sound
of leather
bouncing; in a third

the smell of tea,
the smell of washing make
a bit of a man

happy, happier
without vistas
of wheat or longhorn,

happiest without
the mist and its
immense animals.

Songsheet song about Liebknecht in Brixton

When Liebknecht walked in Brixton
He asked a coloured man:
How long can you live
On bread and jam?

When Liebknecht walked in Brixton
He asked a coloured child:
What happened in school,
Did they say you smelled?

When Liebknecht walked in Brixton
He asked a coloured girl:
Which staff manager said No
Because customers will?

When Liebknecht walked in Brixton
White cabbage vendors grinned:
No flies on that bastard,
Talks them into the ground.

Generations

On his oblong
blotting pad, indelible,
indecipherable,
a sum short of a total,
the signature doubling back —

In no hand of his, but
his father's, dead: must,
let him conjecture, identity,
here or recollected, come
to this — what sons

at the panicking
from his mouth of a call
or figure would not recoil,
all nerves,
unknowing,

or: older, needled, none
dare read in the mirror what
matter the remote
index of a will
jabbed at, dwelt on.

Never the solar track, merely
its similitudes, a rain of dreams
clubbing the gory hue
into substance, these
puzzled records of his goings-on.

The monsters

They slide from rooms,
trees, tunnels, and gleam
in the airy halls, diffusing
round their bulk the stale
room-stench, tree-glue, tunnel-twinklings.

Bodies, bearable to themselves, chairing it
down the airy corridors, a
mutual shoving, a sedate
crush, happy, crashing the stillness,
bored, they pick

and mull it over in their shaggy
stomachs, the music, as emotion
to be recognized, figuring
its flesh to be
their lightest repast.

A time is coming for the monsters.
They begged their helpings of it,
the music, and we lent them
our ears, played into
their hands our instruments.

In the light

Sitting in the light by the fireplace,
she held her daughter's nightdress up.

It would have fitted a girl of sixteen,
but her daughter is less than half that.

All the same, she said, if the girl wants,
let her wear it — the hem warms her feet!

Then she began to pin a strong patch
across the shoulders of the thing.

When the hem comes up to the knees,
her daughter will think of marriage.

As the feet vanish in it, I enquire: why
start always at nought and move along?

It's the lack of any alternative;
like being born with ten thumbs.

Stony old men, it's no wonder
you kept on willing the utterly other.

Soon made adaptable its cruel machines.
Round whizzing absolutes ranged your needs.

Yet someone here can stitch the garment still;
and it must be evil to forgive such things.

The snowy bed, ha, this dead of winter,
she'll not let little feet go down it bare.

Sitting in the light by the fireplace,
she held up her daughter, the way it is.

Penny pastorals in Texas

1

MUD-DAUBER

On yellow shanks which slot into black thighs,
hoisting his behind he crouches,
nose down, sipping mud.

Look long enough, if you can, to
measure the waist. The wings have spread,
or they fold up for poise.

Somewhere in that machine the grains
of mud get stored, once truly munched.
He licks the rock clean;

then bounces off, as if air were cushions,
hangs dazed, in mid-air, to spy out
some fresh crevice,

drops hard on it, and stoops again, quaking
in the static dive. His flight mimics
the buzzard's drift

along whatever warm current may offer,
over the barnyards and the airports,
creeks and turtle backs;

but is blinder, a black mist solidified
into the floating leggity tube
that lolls as it steers.

Then under eaves he mouths the pulp out,
to the shape his trowel nose and hundred
voyages aimed at.

His colonies cluster; each nest shall hug
its dry egg by October; and the house
must wear that necklace,

while smoke of cedar scents our room,
and we lug by hand strong logs home,
for the few cold days.

2

A bayed wall of red brick,
pillars white and squared;

south a roof like a prairie
schooner balloons and rolls.

Their shrubs lap the pecan shade;
the mechanic plugs in, whistling,

and slopes off, elsewhere.
Grass gnaws old local news,

and four cans decompose,
then across a jack on wheels

an ant headed full pelt
for their torn canyons.

In roasting yards coloured
men hack the hard dirt down

with shovels. But here,
a shelf for the crisps,

and a shelf for the fram,
the sign saying . . . CHARGED,

even coke bottles caught it,
and at shoe height a can's alm

of copper rain had —
not pounding sun but a dense

lustre mounting the spine,
a cool in the body, recoiling

from the same cans, and again —
it was exultation for the way

they came to propose to be,
in a slow regard, so long

the pouring down of air
among minerals had lost cause,

and left none for alarm.
This might be perceived

after forty minutes
of standing still;

for once not able, not
needing, even, to move on.

3

NIGHT SOUND IN JUNE

It begins
at dusk — with a ping
the overbaked
bowl of night begins
to craze,
and a snaky cool —

strongest in the hills,
it may succeed
chuck-will's widow's
rippling treble —
least
explicable its prickling
the foreign ear —

soda sparks
into perpetuity — drummed
phosphorescence
as quartz beams fizz
fork lightning
from their gangue's thick dark
crisscross
through scores of holes —

then to the bleat, shrilled, of lambs
round bronchial ewes
entire kibbutzim of gnomes begin
grinding wee scythes —

midget grannies
knitting on clickety cactus spines
breech clouts for wizen brats
jabber
sforzando snippets of news
and slurp quick
gins without cease —

                    now dark

chafe dark

                              fill

night

sightless in

              mummystiff

muslin —

        Llanorian —

Hermit pot

Down that steep valley, west
of the old town, a brook
threads one plantation.
By peach, bean and marrow,
in that plantation —
bean poles arching over —
an old rotund
earthenware pot is lying.

Passing on down —
it was only the rim shone.
Returning,
it was not there.
Who would have taken thought
of this pot
at that precise moment
as the middle of the enigma of the world.

For a future

Your camping lantern shone among
the cottonwoods. It was then
I should have come. Watching —
the way your lantern swung —
I could have told you from anyone.

Again, now. I shall bar no holds
but surge to you across darkness.
Fluffy as the owls, firm as ready apples,
under your window I shall stand.
Your wall's chimney bricks do for my toes.

It was long ago, in the mountains.
Such deep snow all tracks were gone.
When you slipped I caught you,
pushed you upright with a hand.
Then you were light, and still you are.

The cottonwoods, the antique canyon,
what a place, of tamarisk and sand.
You stood on the sand among rocks,
and stared the sun's way. The truth
was moving so fast I could not stop.

Now there are these cottages, tonight.
Between them, the beans and the cauliflowers
make an odd place, to be sure, for us
together to come to. And perhaps,
after all, it will be too cold,

or our moans will disturb the cows, then
they'd wake the others, coughing;
or the chimney bricks under the appletrees
will not support now the toes unskilled
from being denied you, for so long.

Difficulties of a revisionist

All day fighting for a poem. Fighting against what?
And for what? What, being its own danger, wants
to get rescued, but from its rescuer?

So many voices. So much silence. The air, thickened,
reeks of tobacco, hints of blood; still the thing
gibbering somewhere takes no hints at all.

Up the road in the rain someone stopping a car asks
the way to the next estate. I find myself
giving instructions that will get him lost.

In praise of the functionary

The apple tree cannot trap
                his attention. Buds
begin to uncurl; sky,
                to turn blue,
liquidates a cloud;
                soon fruits evolve,
on long wands flourished
                by the bole.

For all that, little he cares.
                The apple tree
cannot trap his attention.
                He sticks to the bugs,
working madly in the bark,
                as usual; to the woman,
darning his sock
                at the heel;
to the child or two,
                who scream in its shadow.

There are processes which are
                not to be bothered with:
these at least illustrate
                the effort it takes,
being a bug, darning
                a sock, emitting
a scream. Tomorrow he flies
                to New York with papers,

neatly typed, important; the sums
                are already worked out
in his head. Tuesday
                he will convince the steel
collective that the party commands
                the wisdom of experience;
that individuals have no
                access to this; that errors
must be rooted out.

He builds on dry ground
                for us a dwelling.
We thank him that his attention
                was not trapped by the apple
tree. Nor by the sea (since
                the apple tree only
distracts), the sea
                which we behold with wild joy,

also with fear which gnaws
                the bones of the bronzed head
he marks human as it steers
                a speck through the boiling
salt verticals, the sea
                which he ignores
and its crunching
                in the bronzed head's
blank marrow.

For a junior school poetry book

The mothers are waiting in the yard.
Here come the children, fresh from school.
The mothers are wearing rumpled skirts.
What prim mouths, what wrinkly cheeks.
The children swirl through the air to them,
trailing satchels and a smell of chalk.

The children are waiting in the yard.
The mothers come stumbling out of school.
The children stare primly at them,
lace their shoes, pat their heads.
The mothers swirl through the air to cars.
The children crossly drive them home.

The mothers are coming.
The children are waiting.
The mothers had eyes that see
boiled eggs, wool, dung and bed.
The children have eyes that saw
owl and mountain and little mole.

Octobers

They watch the big vats bubbling over.
They walk forward, fists dig
into hip bags and sweep in silver arcs
the seed. They put ready
files that will rush from room
to room when the crisis breaks.

They rake the pear leaves into piles
on lawns. Among square mounds
of air bricks they prepare foundations.
They return, with faint tans, to renew
their season tickets. They are giving
again the first of last year's lectures.

They remember Spring. It is the walk
of a woman otherwise quite forgotten.
Wondering if it is for the last time,
they drive through the red forests.
They control the conference tables
with promises of mutual destruction.

They put the cat out with unusual caution.
They clean the flues. They fall
flat on their tough backs off mustangs.
They visit the rice and the apple barns.
They man the devices with fresh crews.
They like the o in the middle of the name.

Celestial déjà vu

(AFTER A POEM BY WILHELM KLEMM)

I woke up to find, if you please,
a horde of pumpkins battering the door.
What sort of a child's was this nightmare?
Their big pot, just who did he think he was?

You should understand:
it was the whole mob. Toad man, jabber man and mushroom,
kicking up such a stink of rostrum,
all quodlibetterers of my mankind!

I might have looked back, for the laugh that comes
when a thing's done with;
but clapped a hand to my mouth —
remembering, so help me, all their names.

Sketch of the old graveyard at Col de Castillon

To get there from here you have to drop
over a dozen or more broken terrace walls;
it is the absorbed oblong far below,
sole plane on the grade of the green mountain.

*

There is no path down to these predictable dead
cabined in their parallels. The way up —
a track rolls off the road, and forgets itself;
antique cars chugged among the grasshoppers once,
or there were twelve shoes to shuffle under each box;
but you arrived jumping, almost out of the sky.

*

Their photos preserve the staring aunt;
grandpapa with a crooked smile like a locust's;
Mimi who looks beautiful and died at 17,
happy in a frock whose narrow v whittles
boneless white to the shape of a weevil's nose.

*

The red-backed grasshopper stuck his head,
shining, through a leaf's hole, shifting it,
little by little, the leaf, beside the blue flower.
Blue flower burying the carpenter bee.

*

The things one imagines of the dead,
who cannot see: broom like green porcupines,
and, higher, the crab-apple tree; cold shrapnel
on the abandoned terraces; the one rose
meandering in through a wire octagon;
and cannot hear the immense murmur now,
floating behind the silence in the air.
Oval photo, dryness of the plastic rose;
hollow chapel sprayed with bullet scars.
Picking the father's bones, his flesh

tastes rotten, sticks between the teeth;
different echoes, tomb and the blue flower's bell,
thicken to old screams in the houses you explode.

     *

And the marrow starts to itch for the sting.

And the fat daughter wore on her finger
a snail, its body transparent almost,
starry wetness, the knobbed horns taut,
pointing to the rosy mound, the tip of the finger.

Harrar

Dawn, for some reason,
last night, or a sundown,
and it appeared, the house
of Paul Verlaine. In a gray glow,
here was the dockside it stood on.

A room, full of bunks
and benches, then children,
scores of them, women, age,
faces — uncertain. Round their faces,
stolen through a window, light hung.

And a great cry was
gathering itself, ready
to go, pounding my ribs.
Once I turned from the window, said,
inside the cry, 'Whose, whose house is this?'

What else to do with
the cry but help myself.
It was rock. Here they were
with nothing to eat; I was there, having
to eat my rock cry, piece by piece.

The ancestors

When they come, we begin to go;
it's the ancestors,
they walk into the warm rooms,

eye our women and food, hear out
the good words. Then for words
and rooms we no more exist,

once the ancestors have come,
than a little dust on a vase,
than the breath wasted.

How do they come? They make no
parade of moans and winds;
they borrow no fears, none.

I am persuaded they have come
by the strength of shoes,
by the one shirt extra,

but if most by the bloody love
my shoes and my shirt need
to be seen that way,

I tell myself this is a thing
they'd far better not know,
who have lost the knack,

and only accuse, by the malice
they march us out with, from one
to the next lost place.

Old bottles

It must have been long
I lay awake,
listening to the shouts
of children in the wood.
It was no trouble, to be awake;
not to know
if that was what I was.

But I had to buy
old bottles, barter
for steerage, candles too,
each stamped with my name.
It was hurry hurry
racing the factory canal toward
the town of the kangaroo.

Up the street I came
across a knot of dead boys.
In the room with a flying bird
on practising my notes
I found its lingo;
my body knew
those torsions of the cat.

She came by, that girl,
she said it's to you, to you
I tell what they are doing
in South Greece and Germany.
My parents killed, brother gone,
they read this letter, I'll
not be here, you do not understand.

In my striped pyjamas
I was not dressed for the journey.
I changed into padded zip
jacket, boots, canvas trousers,
my pockets bulged with the bottles,
I was carrying the candles,
and I ran and I ran.

Notable antiquities

Cooling
in the Valley of Marvels
I could see the contoured silver

prehistoric disc
of a cloud below, shaping to propel
dews into the faint folds of corn and plum,

and recall how
in Peckham where the beatle boots cost
thirty suppers of frozen cod

and shoppers
happily slice through cars and shocks
of nobody's noise,

was unearthed
some centuries ago
a Janus head, in character notable

considering
the girl's face quarried from curls one way,
the man's hard with a marble beard the other,

is no common alloy
among the models of time
so constituted, hell, the complexion rivals

even the tree
Blake surprised in Peckham, wearing
in lieu of leaves

an angel, it is said —
though how the tree took all this
is nowhere recorded.

Amour fou

The hand taking the hand holds
nothing. And look: the trouble
with two sets of eyes
is that each wants out.

Islands. But we float. If face
to face we sit down in bars,
our space acquires us —
orphans of blue dust.

There is a call for help, milking
an older silence than can give suck.
Me, I shall not resist.
An owl should adore the empty air.

So make your body from the heap
of shadows down my mind. Nothing's there
for you to resist. Today, dear house,
you've not a thing that's mine.

Mirrors — not needed, we
are detached otherwise.
Chairs and shoes, our
dependants — gone.

To the call the one perplexed
voice calling replied less
and less. Darkening our room,
these are the mountains we roll.

Old man, looking south

Old man, looking south, you saw
these trees with pleasure; from

your toecaps their field began
rolling slopes into the hill behind.

At this gate, you said, I shall hear;
I know quite well when it's coming.

You'd even tell yourself Let's go;
and left the cottage before time.

*

What you saw from this gate was only
oak trees in a hollow. Not a screen:

not the old man, inoperable, mouth
a hole for air to go in and out of.

Not this tortoise mouth of a time,
pulp between the pounding gums;

at best the blades, green and jolly;
perhaps the shell's ambiguous old gleam.

*

Comas of the last years. Once,
sweating and naked, opening the divan

to lay the moon in white linen,
you babbled of love. Whom did you accuse?

And that you should ever refuse to refuse,
benign, some book or the special talk

of work and country people, when the racking
worsened, can make me wonder still.

*

What hosts of things we found to say.
At this gate, looking south, up the hill;

or breakfasts in the Spring, you by then
drinking your eleventh cup of tea.

That was the same pleasure trees gave
or listening, just, for the due sound.

So one day we walked these thirty paces;
you waved and went, not looking round.

Skins and bones

One thing but one
   only comes all at once,
      and almost came, when,
         little red hands,

your tweaks and hits,
   husky drummings,
      drove to my throat
         dark gobs

of blood — more I could
   not honestly afford.
      All I thought and thought
         was Lord, what has living

been anyway, it's too soon,
   my hollow clothes! what am I
      doing, dying? Now
         should I shrink again

to scan so the blank
   wall, wishing, too late,
      I had known how skins help,
         or can, me and these folk

ripen the wiser for living,
   I shall try still not to say
      O black food, un-
         predicted as this afternoon,

you would taste,
   had the realities, those,
      those, eaten my knowing
         bones whole,

the same,
   the same,
      the same,
         the same.

Rentier fantasy

Tonight we shall be content.
An old life is ending.
We and they shall be there,
dancing under the plane trees.
We shall have gone through the gate
of a golden horn and a song.
The horn is gatepost and lintel,
the song in huge foreign letters
opens through the middle.

Shooting bullets, we shall hit nothing.
Buying numbers, ours will be wrong.
We shall be dancing like crazy,
a guitar tune floating the time.
Someone will fall off his chair,
backwards, just from laughing.
The girls with their dark triangles,
tumbled from old broken houses,
will refuse only our money.

Under a silver half moon,
a mountain sky whitening,
the old goat road shall see us home.
In the time to be silent
we shall start remembering.
How much of it all will have gone.
How much that had gone shall return,
hatched into our brilliant new ships, the swoop
of spacious bridges, and cool blue buildings.

Sanity

After bolting my supper,
    eggs, sausages, bacon and chips,
I see this photograph in the paper:
    it is a crowd of ordinary people,
the Jew cocking his thatched head, the old
    vocal woman, the mechanic.

Two hold the middle of the picture:
    a young man, whose face, head-on,
has the symmetry of a dark Ajax;
    a young woman, hair anyhow,
high cheekbones, the lips parting,
    her remote eyes look straight at you.

They are walking beneath many banners.
    These they uphold casually.
The whole crowd is coming at you.
    I walk across the room, for the first time
can raise my face to the black trees,
    a silver sky of Spring.

Dangers of waking

Waking has dangers. When children
stride into the room, one by one, with reports
and messages, you shout and roll over;
but back they come, with more news,
a slamming of doors, a sound of breaking.

Like a friend you meet — what he
confides to you, you, with your empty look,
turn against him: enmity of others
who can confide nothing to anyone.
They were always the aliens,

ignored or savaged by racier children,
regretfully refused a place
in useful professions. Desirable
dead or mute or not at all,
soon every sound they heard,

voices or wheels or waters,
or wind in the barbed wires,
was the sound of a key turning in a lock.
But these dangers of waking —
well, you'll roll over, shout, do nothing,

as when the children strode in,
one by one, like Greek messengers,
to declare the killing of this or that
man, thousand, or million
on the good green sward.

Itinerary for the apparent double

With you the lane winds uphill,
by day, hatching schemes;
by night, cockshut memory overhauls
your brooding mobile mind.

It steepens for you, on splay claws,
feeling the weight of eggs not engendered yet;
up the incline a lost day
floats its faint rose of shadows.

It is dark from the hill's foot to halfway up.
Boys with stones have smashed the bulbs; some shinned
corkscrewing up the posts, to rob them, furtively.
Morgue of maidenhead, *nigredo,* always foots the hill.

Here, for girls, black men come jumping
big from the ditch with naked choppers.
The mewing of owls armours them as they bolt
with goosepimples and their foretaste of moans on beds.

Yet with you the path can be picked out
from the furrow of hushed and curving space
dividing oak bough from oak bough on either side.
On the upturned face a breath of cloud and two stars.

All for you, who edge forward into the dark,
who have no mind to harp on foreterror,
trust these rounds of light, crossribbed by shade,
to be bodies, nameable, loafing against the fence.

Among them you mount the curve to the one lamp.
Here foliage hoards the spray of beams;
myriads of leaves have multiplied occult dawns.
So the beetle steals through moss in the summer night,

locked in his portable house, which he cannot enter,
and is overwhelmed by the cresting forests of chrysoprase.
You'd find it harder going, to their Cold Mountain;
always the snow cone with its ice flanks recedes,

brands in muscle the black joy of the primal motions —
mystery of effort, this seeming barely to move,
till the body, twice-born, swells with tender power,
raging afresh to expel the last stride.

It might be something, to have lived like this,
with a vacant air, behind those blessèd eggs.
Yet you crossed the ridge. You have begun to drop,
free, from the zone of calm that is gorged with nothing.

Or does another day convict by the death of so many,
the slope sucking you under as you run to the choked town,
through shrieks of birds that flash in the sun like axes?
What pain you have to bring, from ignorance, always.

You flail the earth with it, you track the sun's wheel,
either way, up or down, following everywhere the hill;
the child of ashes has it for a spoon;
it domed the round Iberian tomb before Carthage came.

So you are continuous, and might have been noble;
but you will forget and I forget what you have forgotten:
how deep the hill shines under its shade of tall trees,
and when no stars come, goes to them darkly upward.

Crossing

This is the unknown
        thing beside us. We
cross the street, walking
        together. We walk
across the street,
        and this unknown
thing surrounds us.
        It happens: to
be saying only what we mean.

Many people are
        crowding past us. This
unknown thing surrounded us. Now
        it is in us. It must have
claws, for the words
        claw their ways from
our bodies. Unless
        these are hooks we feel,
this being tenderly
        pulled against the huge stream.

We shall ignore it,
        this unknown thing. No,
do not give it a thought.
        Not now, or it cannot
keep us here, being this way
        while we can. Or it may heave
through the crowd,
        like a hope,
very destructive
        in its ebb from us.

An Englishman in Texas

FOR DONALD HALL

First he sees the sky. It is the one thing
not making as if to move. Far south
its blue excites the long spine
of hills. To fetch him
home from that higher tangle
could take years.

Coombs below those hills detain him. Sheep jaws
munch on berries which now ripen through
low thickets. A creek appears,
whose yellow weed foam
ephemerids populate.
Limestone belts

polished by bursts of huge rain will occur,
across trails leading him from nowhere
to nowhere. The lizard gapes
beneath a boulder,
and admits, magenta-mouthed,
the baked air

crusting some inveterate scarab. Twirl
of cardinal bird song and blue jay's
retch sculpt on space distincter
verges. Heat becomes
inhabitable, fresh fanned
from their throats.

His haze diminishes, too, when one roof
of rusting tin has topped a hollow,
as if its apparition —
manhandled — had let
at last the estranged eye in
on something.

It hardly exists. Has stuck it out by
a mere stronger irrelevance than
the horned goat skull's candid gaze
levelled at his gaze
across curly miles of scrub.
Prickly pear

looks like a telling friend for time's cripple.
Dwarf cedars thronging undulations
balk grass and buckwheat between
those hills and his place;
so each dawn, like milk, they leave
his new wish

to be present, now, to drop character,
its greed for old presences, its dirt
fruiting demi-selves in groves.
Yet there still he prods
that suture of hill and sky
for ways through . . .

Help him, tall shades, Wallace and Westfall, whose
addresses, inconspicuously,
changed as men flocked round and round
your cockeyed cabins,
bleating and sad, agog at
the gun's wit.

Or do not help him. But let him move once,
free, of himself, into some few things.
Sky, after all, meets nothing.
And with my snake axe
I'll trudge to meet him, should he come
without you.

OUR FLOWERS & NICE BONES

1

Three Microzoic Nonsonnets

FOR HANS VOGT

1

    Failing: to sit
by the knotted hands
       the night through,

    all
       meaningless, as
the backs of words, the black
      cream of moments —

    then, on the feet,
to approach
       a door, before switching
off,

      to put straight
a picture on the wall, the hand
    opens . . .

2

    Then Goethe, he
says: The old story —
      sea-bed (from

    this
      height down upon
Weimar), the whales playing,
    villages now;

what thought of us,
our molluscs,
        had the sea-mew then; yet,
    think,

        hear him cross
again this mountain, his wingbeat
    not far.

3

. . . vines, thick with fruit,
moons of pollen &
        the wild rose

    cling,
        I make them, to
the archivolts; lion,
    cathedral snail,

    camel, my loves
make in me
        a room, growing; as light
    swells,

        propels all
night old ribby shadows up red
    curtains.

Radiation Motif 1

afloat in the windowpane, stuck
in the visible section of tree trunk

like a circular sawblade
the oval breakfast table

supports again objects: the tall
milk bottle, only half full

& a banana, a bunch of grapes
behind the coffee jug, two cups

flanking half a small flower vase —
three globes of blown delicate glass

to bounce, out of the sun,
three windowpanes back to the first one

The Burrow

Room fanned cool, this curtain
is white, blown to the rondure
of a shell,

they are in me, but anywhere —
tacked to the wall
diamonds
of angry rose, the woollen
god's-eyes, torn from a book
magic fish, a north unicorn:

they feed on the eyes I do not trust,
hearing the air jag
with cicada wings, the latest
day thinly sings out,
old glass —

& with the squeals
of men dying, young,
anywhere, on the highways, old maps,
under helmets,
thinking: Hanoi.

Day Flower

Sectioned green
stalk, the few
finger-long leaves crinkle

tiny blazon:
four yellow stars
make a lozenge

peopling the silver
membrane
curl
three blue feelers

& all spring
from an ostrich head
jowly green

remote:
blue rounds
the two petals

are palms upped & flat —
why now
bear the weight
of some other universe:

you bring the day flower
the crucified

& leaves flap hallo
as I hold it up.

A Topology of the First Telstar Faces

FOR THEIR RECORDER, R. B. KITAJ

Nylon knee & more
a heavenly tan —
calf, ankle, toes dwelling
precious in a boot
of white kid
substitute:

knee & more — not so, curses!
white, a dead
white & thin, pulpy
chicken —

so much hidden
looking
& ascertainable
the dreaded legs

vomit

your syntax of essence
mine as time rolling
unrolling —

a solar
wave, tapering
to spray, filtered
for the skins (infinitesimal)
through the blue
dust-gauze

Woodpile

Yucca, sheaved
standing blades

& singular
the full moon

shone
this

destruction of green
It is veinless

tough grass
It supports my

shadow kneeling
Woodpile

neat
human oblong

heavy
with flame

Lecture Notes

white shirt dovewhite flapping clockwork
past through vents in the venetian blinds

voice of the lecturer never to return
baritone white neon overhead in this semi-cellar

voice from under his very particular horn rims
never to return he said & it was Alexander Blok

silver cantaloup back
of Fania's braided head laughs on the other shore

(Blok) crooks of arms pressing doveshapes also
on armrests grained landscape of yellow grandfather

a poem made of everything in the world of fact
I see with my eyes in one instant of time

sunset mystery over the church fence meant symbolic
boundary the model model of his world

even the colour white or was it collar he said
a different something blizzard shirts & ice

spectral changing city Peter the Great I heard
these yellow days pass between the houses & NAZHAKHA

& gulping October 1912 there is a pharmacy
he sighed between every house & the next a pharmacy he said

crowds bloodstain sunset ooze in unstressed ees
composed in dovewhite January 1918

green wicker handbag on the lino with diffuse vowels
eternal battle dream of peace

mathematics on the armrests for skin & swastikas
the whole fragment describing a consonance

my time I will spend I will spend
with a knife I will slash I will slash

died August 1921 in great torment
blackboard Greek triangles

blackboard of chalked Greek triangles

Edwards Plateau & Elsewhere

The joy these objects echo: to be at grips
with nothing. Upland curlew spans
from Venus to an ear his sporadic
radar treble. Space

rippling through corrugated volumes
of Spanish oak flows & flows
round boles of the black smooth persimmon.
Greyfox through the night barks his lost long cry,

immense sky
floods personality, making all
magnitudes infinitesimal. Ego
(asphalt crawling with vertebrate stunned bees)

a frostflake
cathedral, half
one millimetre flat & two across
blots out webby organisms in the fluting of elm trees:

lavishly, though,
ignoring such phenomena,
pioneers in bed
pumped from the vacuum the genus pinhead,

with laughing hats, big steaks & automobiles:
Jerusalem — Jollyville, built
with powdered mountains in pursuit of ranch-truck wheels
under the eyelid of a foreigner.

Avebury: The Temple

What these stones are,
stone by stone,
their circle, the road
bisecting it, and the heavy
green earthwork

Night here, gradual stars,
the dew keeps rising
in a mist till the blue
and dark beeches go
for another time another green

We sleep under a mountainous
parsley stick, its rosettes and fans
catching the dew light, and darkening
with the dreams we do not have

All night a murmur and the feet
freezing soundlessly, sleeping bags
damp, not with the tears we do not shed

And at dawn we are walking
under the sweet lime trees, we climb
a gatepost of granite and sit up there

We gaze for horsemen to come,
girls with bacon,
and among grasses for the small flowers,
the far stones touching a remoteness
which is our remoteness, stones
we ask nothing of, as they are revealed

We are revealed in our hands
holding other hands

For once not scared they will come
up the road,
others who do not know what this night is,
who do not care what comes
when the night goes, the night goes

Nudes

1

Ah what have the bunnies & playboys done to us

on a postcard of yore
round moon bottom all naughtiness
nude of yore
I see I see
your big smile of yore
& your rolling eyes wondrous

2

In the centre of the room
a vacant cage.
To its bars from walls & comers
jungle grows.

Rubber trees are rising from the floor,
rustling fronds rotate
a web the light sifts through,
becoming copper.
What throbbing eggs assemble
the sonatina of the vines!
And in their midst an old machine-gun hangs,
manned by a parrot.

In the centre of the cage
a boat appears,
and in the boat a girl, asleep,
a nude.

3

Absolute altitude
of the golden hairs
planted &
wide

clearings

> underfoot
> the skin
> a bronze
> flows touching
> no horizon

4

When moving
surfaces become spaces.

When moving surfaces
become spaces

who lives in this house?
Groin Smile.

5

No one killed this nipple yet;
happy nipple.

Shoulder, no one broke you;
shoulder white repose.

Peace concave. No one slit
this belly with a bullet.

Sweet to climb, spine, many-turreted:
no one burned you down.

Hopeful woman, like a lake, no,
a sky of smells & wild

ideas balancing
on little toes.

Radiation Motif 3

Now begins
the straightening of the house

book on the ironing board
bathtub cluttered with shoes
washing a white heap for hours

on the bed &
passports in the icebox
brushing hair

eye in profile absorbs
a torn print column yellowing
horoscope

the head cocked smiling
across crumbs & apples
barefoot

blue air grisly still
with plucked hearts, incessant
harp Mexico

balloons & temples wait for us
our mouths crave
your shape of dust

Merope

Don't let me
chase
the big stone
down the mountain

your laughter
wells
here,
little spring.

96

2

Birth of Venus

Computer's Karl Marx

". . . how does . . . this reorganization of
production relations actually proceed . . . ?"
N. Bukharin

production relations
class consolidates
rioters plot
patriot sailors
pelt iron captains
soldiers postmen
loot old arsenals
rotate tripods
capture police

conscript prostitutes
rusticate prelates
cut pop opiates
stop past increments
start national product
poor labourers
proud as lions
note price reduction

popular action
protect red capital
nouns are tools
stone duct latrines
replace palaces
true cloud snailports!
pleasure in creation!
nice proletariat
not proletariat!

Lausdeo Teutonicus

monstra
skandalaus
auslös
demonstra

kandala
demondial
ösende
monstrandalaus

onende
dadalaus
skandalos
ionen

mondala
mandalaus
ödelösende
mördermaus

domlose
demonstrata
astralende
monstradom

mondlos
lauslos
lauslösende
skandalauslösendedadademonstrationen

The Joke

nun found nude on dunes
nun found stunned on dunes at noon
nude nun found stunned at noon
nude nun on dunes had been stunned & screwed

who saw nun stand scanning dunes?
who stunned nun?
who denuded stunned nun?
who screwed nude stunned nun on dunes?

what had nun done from nine to noon?
was nude nun heard humming tune?
what tune did stunned nun hum?
was nude nun turned on?

stunned nun not screwed: was queen
nude nun smiles: I am a queen
stoned queen stunned self on dunes
queen staged nude stunned nun come-on

Armadillo Cello Solo

didl   dodl   dadl
o   aro   ma
miomar miodaar
a   dio   da

    oom   oom

a   mor   id
odlm   mamdl   id
o   mal   or
a   dio   ia

```
        oom
    didl   dadl

dodl   dadl   didl
a       dio       id
miomar  miodaar
malamormalamor

        oom
    malamor
```

A Concert 1866 (Found Poem)

After the overture were performed successively
    several pieces, well adapted to display
    the talent of Mr. B and Mrs. S.
The duet in the first act
    was very beautiful.
It was encored
    from every part of the house.
We also had the pleasure of hearing Madam P.

The second act began
    by a grand symphony of Haydn.
The adagio was eminently
    well executed.
The violin concerto was deficient in melody, but
    it was executed with great brilliancy by Mr. ....

Finally, after the most admirable of all overtures,
    the master-piece of the human mind in that kind,
    I mean the overture of the Flauto Magico, of Mozart,
The concert concluded by a chorus of Glnck,
    which produced a sensation I cannot describe.

3

Mysterious Still

Mysterious still
how the first
warm spring wind

deepens
the town
lanes & doorways

recede toward
caves
of light beyond them

The Armadillos

You suddenly woke and saw
on the bedroom hearth an apple green
puddle of moonlight. It was the armadillo,
sitting on top of the chimney, put it there;
with his long snout for a siphon, I suppose.

More often the armadillos
perch in the trees. They stare
at each other, count the rings
which buckle them in; or —
they discuss things.

Don't fall, Harriet! Arthur, don't fall!
We can't help it if the armadillos
drop like bombs and catch only
in the lower branches with their claws.
Falling like that, they can't be lonely.

Winters, they leave the trees and trundle
to the end of the valley. In twos and fours
they cluster there and comfort each other.
The frost feels them under their bucklers;
they taste it happening in their jaws.

But in the trees where they build hides
of cardboard boxes and paper bags,
their main concern is believing summer.
For my friends broken by special committees
I hang out armadillo flags.

They run fast and go underground
where silence is, for sending signals.
Or they climb to the tops of telephone poles
and jam the exchanges of political assholes
with the terrible sound of knitting.

If you wake again, do not scare,
but wonder at the armadillos;
they'll be watching us from up there,
winking their neat eyes, arranging their faces,
hoping that something shows.

Radiation Motif 2

Tree-roach, mantis, moth
cannot come in; huge throbbing sun,
this lamp is not for them —

cling to your window screen,
tremendous extinct immortals:
owl mask & friendly elm
distort our features —

it is long since they came in
(on earth a little space
to bear the beams of love) —

invaded palms discovering the swell
of buttocks, the slow tongue thrust
into the sex, another mouth
open holds the shining phallus —

their terror. We blind it
with a kind of pleasing. No
heavier joy.

The Arrest of Pastor Paul Schneider

Together, from
    the bed they hear
        footsteps; it
must be (he thinks, today
    and she:) a dream

my sinews legbones
exploding head
        changed into
    powder, then
cloud, whitest, the gate
    clicking, now
who's there? He can
        hear them

further
    down the hill (& the cloud

a cool in summer,
        roasted) she

to the window

nothing
but the road (yellow curl) stabbing
        to his church

wakes
    him
        the knock
Why (he says) wait
        we're surrounded

Found Poem with Grafts 1866

To the north-east
    is the park of Mousseaux.
The Baths & Gardens of Tivoli
    & the slaughter-house du Moule must be seen.
Tivoli, near the Chaussée d'Antin
    contains forty acres of ground.
It is quite equal to your Vauxhall by night
    & is much superior in daylight.

But who is the man in the rusty black shapeless felt hat
    pointing south-west?

The walks are ornamented
    with roses honeysuckles & orange trees.
Amid the copses are seen
    rope dancers & groups riding at the ring or playing at
                       shuttlecock.

All around are arbours filled with people
    enjoying the sight of the various amusements.
There is in the middle of the garden a theatre
    on which two hundred couple might dance at the same
                       time.
There are also artificial mounts from which people descend
    in a species of car with incredible velocity.

But who stands in the huge overcoat that had once been brown
    & now is stained with large green patches?
Who is this in the trousers that are too short,
    revealing blue socks?

There are many canals
     in which the public amuse themselves in boats.
In the evening
     the illumination presents a lively spectacle.
All sorts of dances
     commence then,
& after the vocal & instrumental concert the evening concludes
     with the exhibition of splendid fireworks.

Is he not the man who cooks
     hideous mud in the Rue Beautreillis?

Who says: The day will come
     when a single original carrot shall be pregnant with
                                             revolution.
Whose wallpaper groans with addresses in the childish script
     of nudes he throws downstairs cursing through his teeth?
And I am aglow, he says,
     with all the hues of the infinite.

TV Masts in Central Texas

Two webs, tall,
soaring up, straight & thin,
beyond juniper miles,
and spun,
the distant structures,
so fine what is seen
is the blue
rotunda
which encases them.

This wanes
to black
but their beacons, all night,
slide winking
up & down in line:

beads
of crimson dew,
heads on a totem pole.
The dark intervals pump,

O you lost dream-Indians,
through cathode tubes
our sog of doings: golden
bombers & grins bracketing
soap-brands, always
the mouth will explain them,
the bald
ranked faces watch on,
filling in the time.

Victoriana

In the gardens of Windsor Castle
walks a philosophic owl;
wingtips clasped over his coccyx,
stooped he stalks, pondering much.

Meanwhile the moon puts pale fire
in the turrets of Windsor Castle:
shut windows halt its gleam,
the queen is pulling her boots on.

The moon is evident also
on the buttocks of stallions grazing,
in the lake without any holes,
in the blood that drips from the owl.

For certainly blood drips down
the philosophic owl:
he leaves a pool on the turf,
wherever he stops to think.

106

Now the queen comes riding, sag-jawed,
down the long moonlit avenue;
her dead prince gallops beside her
on a very noble ostrich.

Radiation Motif 4

Toward evening I switch on the sprinkler.
The calyx of springwater frays into silver drops.
Red bird & yellow bird
people a bush the water beads with stars.

Drinking the stars, fluffed-out throbbing bodies,
I can smell you, the wet dust you shiver off.
Your silver whistles come to shape my hearing;
the touch of your claws
tinkles on the leaves.

Absurd. To be so possessed
by the nature of things. What claws,
what creatures of air can take & give
the old gentleness.

The Last of Mexico 1967

Roadsigns are cleaner,
Most people are taller.
With first-class loot
From a second-class people
We arrived here happy.

Our bowels itch
For the red-roofed house,
Whiter than ice-cream,
Hopefully cooler,
And perfectly certain.

In the long tube flying
Dick wore a wild hat.
Squirts of insecticide
Guarded our genes,
Flagons of Kahlua,

Big pottery doves,
The chocolate crunchers
And genuine gods
Near busted the seams of
Our bags in the hold.

Our profiles are realer,
Our pictures prove it.
Here's one we stopped for:
A cracked old woman
Holding her hand out.
Oaxaca was cute.

We have done our stuff.
Our money is more.
Our President is nicer.
Our c - - ks are longer,
Our c - - ts are homier
Than in that lost land.

Bonnard

Does the body rest against his eye, the cool
changing its colours: rose, purple, silver
framed in a door, the enamel of a bath

their life the elements dream through,
figures all facing at different angles
do not touch, they include one another —

dwelling on a thing, the eye feeds its boutons
energy sprayed from a few co-ordinates: loaf & horse,
each its own dimension in the starred dream

shields the colours! blue skins,
cocooned girl's crotch, or aloof apple,
a buffoon child, flowers in a bowl

& her face everywhere, turning from a cup
to smile with a mouth like a slice
of baby watermelon, celestial clown girl

or bored, sprawling bare on a rumpled bed,
brown arm thrown across her ribs,
the left hand tilting a small breast —

but where the skin starts it is the idyll
playing out any boundary to scan
throbbing ascensions in the space around,

street dappled with skirts & metal,
woodland blue with edible branches,
crimson billow of a kitchen cloth

it is where the dogs do battle,
canaries roast in evacuated rooms,
the history-makers unload their dead,

hack it to pieces. To pick it up again,
restore it, whole, a lifetime on fingertips
grinding a rainbow from the ignorant dew.

The Children at Longboat Key

We have gone to the sea at evening.
We float over waves in a rubber tyre.
Your legs are glistening your hair is wet.
My shoulders are cool I hear the ripples.

Orange cloud swells over a thin black line.
We gaze at the water wheeling with rainbows.
We lean back with upturned faces.
Your hair hangs down it darkens the water.

We are floating out to sea we are happy.
On the far white sand are two black dots.
White sand curves a warm banana.
A swept and sharp banana a sword.

We see the two black dots are waving.
Bigger it grows all the sea around us.
They wave and shout we wave and wriggle.
We beat the sea with our feet and hands.

It is a very old man and a very old woman.
Far off he is jumping on the hard sand.
Far off she is brandishing a parasol.
He wears a black hat and she white stockings.

We have ridden the billows and watch the foam.
Soft crystals cling and spit on the rubber.
There are two voices shouting and mixing.
We stand in the water we feel its pull.

It is pulling your knees and you go under.
I catch your feet it is hauling you away.
The little old people walk toward us.
The sand nudges between our toes.

His black hat rim sits level over his eyes.
Her white stockings cover two sticks.
They are saying to us their big worries.
They make their hands go up and down.

We hear the voices we hold the tyre.
Its cool ring slaps to the sand between us.
They walk away in their twiggy skins.
The shrunken faces will speak no more.

They meant it well the old people.
The sea pounds the beach behind us.
Its blue roar begins like a shiver.
We watch them vanish into thin air.

Wire Spring

I saw the wire Spring come,
the first clock beclambering the redbud;
out of a marble cloud thrush-legs fell
hitting the grass with a twang.

Like a rose through muscle,
like flesh through a wire web,
through the cities & sewage meekly
aromas of bluebell bubbled, coffee & cod.

O the tender new vibrations
of radar marines attentive in airports.
O the nuzzling of sweet electricity
along the intricate barbed fences.

A huge oak harp began to moan & sway,
a phantom ocean of green navels.
The marble cloud was hanging low,
with numerous strikings of twelve.

The first clock said: it is time we killed.
The second clock said: it is time we told.
The third clock said: it is time we have.
The fourth clock said: it is time we kept.

Phalloi enamelling the round of roots,
white & orange & purple, each
with a spring coiled tight in its tucket:
the air shook with their slow tremolo.

Vivaldi

In the bird-throat,
silence.

Venice glacial dome,
in the dawn-light, rippling.

Delicate moving labyrinth,
plucked by the temperatures:

transfix it.
The canals

blacken; this oval
whirling, whirling

in the palace of air; this
lidded minim

hopes, like a child,
for snow.

O, the dark
day.

4

Pavlovic Variations

1

I came to the sea shore to hear speeches about beauty.
Nobody's here.
It still gives the pebbles gooseflesh
merely to think of the metamorphoses:
driftwood sparser, modesty
after all the big words.

I came to the city, back
to the wise & their logic.
Fish met me on the way,
we walked along together.

Sea roads & city roads all lead to the same banquet.
On the table the cuts of sun are transparent & cold.
I keep watch at the gate, to discover who makes the changes in
                                                    things.

I raised my hand, to make sure of the sky:
I touched the breast of a giant bird,
dead, only it had not hit the ground.
Through its eye I saw ships travelling in circles;
an ancient way to bury the sails.
What day of creation is it?

The chair I sit on sinks deeper and deeper into the sand
under the weight of the city I am clasping.
I preserve it in the hollows of my hands like a sip of water,
with few words,
& shall surrender it to someone with fewer
tomorrow.

More & more one loves
the man beneath the sea.

2

Senator Dogface demanded a complete bomb
to rub out the problem on his agenda.
Professor Quorum, on efficient feet, strides outdoors,
behind him a trail of neatly beheaded pupils.

I numbered the pebbles: there were too many.
The sea keeps coming at me, with confusion but no change.

Moving my chair back I turn to the gate:
brown city with choked arteries; a thousand
died on paving stones under four inches of snow,
under four miles of Senator Dogface's blotting paper,
under Professor Quorum's electric pyjama cord.

I keep watch at the gate. Who makes the changes in things?
The cuts of sun thickening multiply,
young pigs & cows go gallivanting —

a summer fish patrolled its pool.
                    What night waits for them
with its dioxide oven? On what day
will their creation come?

3

Shining yellow:
                    cyclones
        polish the sea.
                Bald clown
down there, it put a stop
        to your wrinkles.

I was discovering your games:
                    temple columns
shuffled by artillery,
        floating hair of the dancers;
                    flute note remote foghorn
calling through surf-thunder.

114

The sea from its pocket
    has taken papers: unstamped,
portraitless.
        These tongues are torn from our heads, we pound
at the gates with ammunition & whiskey.

He
walks because he is not stopped by anything.
He considers things
as points breaking the light for his amusement.

4

Over a splintered pine these blank pages riffle.

From foam the orbiters rising; later, keel tracks,
fisheries; last, the naming of stars. With newborn mouth
a tablet sucked holy milk: I understand

the central nervous system of Alexander. I collect
25 different vine-tip sections in the camote patch. I interrogate
the quiver of needles tracking Mars.
                    I can peel
an orange in 11.52 seconds. I know

nothing. The beat of a heart tears it from the breast
of the giant starry bird. Nobody
is here. Nobody knew

what to do with it.

5

To what space do they belong, the figures torn from a fog
    & what are you? A cathedral. I woke to the silver trickle
from one tap in one hut the twenty of us

    & stood up another day
lidless brimming excrement bucket
        columns & motes tearing asunder the stored deluge of light

200 metres to the bodies we dug out with bare hands
    a snowy braid was widow Lautmann
Pavel's child came to pieces in my hands

    To what realm do they belong, rays modelling
the chevelure of stone, pierced volumes which walk
    my body through transfigurations of the rays, 200 metres
                                                    more

carting the flesh in barrows
    flesh peeling from bone as we dragged them ghostless
out of the earth to the furnace

    To what region where the forms dwell all day another day
for dragging by the hair we had stroked
    ghostless bundles of flesh bulletmarks in the neck

silhouettes: to what space will the trickle from one tap scrape
    from our eyesockets the memory of that flesh, washing
the smell from our gums with a sip of water

6

There is one who shouts with the shape of himself
last seen
feeding on garbage in the camp near Voronezh

Now I shout with the shape of myself to hear
in the new light the flap of old timetables
platforms I spent the better part of my life on
a solitary overcoat among broken signals
& shall bleed to death on a street between the painted lions

I came to the sea shore to hear a different rampage

The city cupped in my hands I drink its terrible child gaze
Balls of foam blown inland
I found the marble head, butchered its eyesockets
& stare back at the abyss closing & opening
its immense sex

But it is now, at the table, as we whisper with things
under the old lamp that hangs

It is now
over the glass blue pepper-pot that stands, Pavlovic, stands

When we see a grass blade bend in the new light
When we can hear
someone playing a saw over the hill.

Note: the first section is a translation via German of a poem by the Yugoslav
poet Miodrag Pavlovic.

5

Lucky Caesar

Lucky Caesar,
epileptic,
bald,
the last man
to know
you were crossing
the fish-filled,
Latin-speaking,
real river Rubicon.

Found Poem

Tommy Phelps traded grunts
& groans for prayer &
Scripture quotations.
Mr. Phelps, once known as "Nature Boy",
had long blond hair
& wore tights &
wrestled for a living. Now
his hair is black
& he wears a suit &
he is an evangelist.

The Hero, on Culture

Shit
On
You,
Mother.
All I wanted was out:
To be free
From your festoons
Of plastic
Everlasting
Christmas cards.

118

Hans Christian Andersen

Sweet amazing marginalia
to a Denmark as dead
as its parsons. What gloom,
the nineteenth century,
dripping Hamlet's
corpse-fluids. Snowy forests

he entered in a golden submarine;
pale aurora desire,
a sunken god
in tight black boots —

up crowded streets he sped
in Prague,
across the cobbles
bobbing about in a tiny carriage,
shouting, waving & shouting:
"Beautiful girl!
Stop! I love you!"

The Measure

She is going down to the water
restless
& the long hair on her shoulders

the arches of her feet
skinned roots of olive, as delicate,
shape small hollows of air across the sand

Clambering towards her
the sea that knows nothing
the young form, aerial, always cool hands
how do I know her

crossing with swift transition
sometimes, Ionia, your hills

it is the measure
outpacing prediction, we must go
ten thousand miles to the broken statues

The Find

What to do
here, now
but write

how it is
to wait, in the body
a thing keeps

pounding, biceps
grind,
almost, with

the load of it, no
need to say
who, ever.

To shed it into
an image,
how pathetic. Look:

the hero, no
bigger than
a pin, so far,

he leaps horizons,
triggering acute
crises in nature,

e.g., a man who eats
bats,
the fleas & all,

or a mountain
of a man,
with his ores,

off him cascade
in chaos
glorious adventures.

This table keeps
my legs buckled,
I am hungry,

I am rock,
useless, altogether
useless, but

for waiting.
When you come,
you'll find me

gone, waiting
elsewhere, in
some brooch pin,

or in the glass
you have filled
to drink from.

Nothing

Nothing
as it is, you come
from the bath, barefoot
& I see how barefoot

every time
I say this, say that
what goes wrong
is it the time

O barefoot
to hold on
in the silence
you understand

Shoreham Walk

We walked
up through the wood
nettles & oak
a dark green

fall of light
leading us
past soft
erect wheat

then the white
potato flowers
& flints, a few
rusty can tops

it is the shining
June day, warm
as seldom
in our country

on our skin
a south wind
silver barley ears
are swaying

swaying us
& a lark
less visible than
the flower, blue

big, no bigger
than your pupil
under crusty
oaks again, ferns

they smell of salt
curved seawaves
& a place
we found

called the kingdom
of children
you said, because
nobody frowns

as you climbed
vanishing up
a giant beech, red
as old blood

tall as the sky,
so many strong
branches it
was easy

Concerning Revolution

All summer the jasmine bush
was billowing
between the house & the forest.
Winter trotted the beercans out, hung
rusting in its ribcage; bedsprings & aspirin bottles
sprinkled under the oak trees.

Why curse
the previous people. At my back door
a scarred enamel pot,
rickety boards:
there is a sea coming in
hides nothing.

In the forest I left a toy
for the spirits; a diminutive
tricycle. By the hole
an armadillo dug I put a warped picture book.
Lest all the old life be wasted
I have kept one tabasco bottle, bent, of clouded glass.

Man on the Wall

up there, climbing the wall
where he is, we see him
flex the left knee
right leg straighten, right arm
sprung from the shoulder blade
left hand like a fist
of ribs

the flat body so taut
its tallness, all reek & sinew
ignores the feet his
bloody finger ends
& gasps cannot reach

but the wall
neither smooth nor rough
neither brick nor glass
horizon of schist
upright in a reversed
world not a world

there being no roof for it
to taper into
there being beyond this place
which is no place
nothing

124

& the legs & the arms
slip at the ultimate
tension, like liquid
the whole body subsiding
without thunder
the head out of sight
flipping back, just once
has hammered on something

we have fitted him
into the black bed the black bed
a soft whistling
as the body threshes
under the wool & the linen

Memory

Hard plank hurting the bones in your bum,
but between them and the Caribbean:
indigo undertow, fanged barracudas.
Sun like sandblast & the stink of shrimp.
Salt fret gnashing the left eyeball.
Endless blue gush the boat chugs through;
unplaceable blaze that aches in the head.

Six yards off, a tiny rose-pooped caravel
always floats alongside
with five proportionate people.
A life contained, sweet music
of sea-harps faintly heard,
swept past the coconut island,
while her soft long hair
rippled over your face, not tickling.

Who

Who is she,
dressed
all in black, the woman
who floated from your naked waking body,
whispering Remember me Remember me

Now she comes
at us,
now, with her soundless pigskin
telephones, running in dreams down roads,
& as we wrestle with our shirts off

Cloudy bird,
perched
on my shoulder & piping she is
the tunes & words I cannot compose.
This dragon-keeper, who travels

with guitars
& cobras,
whose drumming tightens around us
her moss of blood & 3 A.M. kisses,
burns with exhilaration our unique bones

Dark Venus
under the golden hair,
be
merciful to her, & if torment you must,
torment me

6

Curbaram

Curbaram says: At present they are encamped outside the walls, and we shall drive them back into the city. From this hill you can count their horses, unsaddled, in the enclosure to the left, also their tents, including the storage tents, which are not round but square. One thousand four hundred and thirty two men spread over an area of one mile: by eleven thirty they will be concentrated at the city gate, a tumultuous mass of armour, horses, elbows and heavy feet. At that time you will stop firing and save your ammunition. They will kill one another as they try to press through the gate. By noon we shall have them inside the walls, and they will see us, crowding these ridges with our camels and artillery. The rocket batteries will be positioned at these three points, northwest, south and east of the city. You will maintain a heavy and constant fire from shortly after noon until the sun sets.

Some of these men will plan to escape from the city after nightfall. They will lower ropes from the parapets, and arrive at the foot of the west wall one half hour after midnight. Probably they will be called Guillaume, Albric and Wido, but you need not concern yourselves with that: besides, there will be others, of whose names I am not yet certain. Well now, these men, about twenty in number, having reached the foot of the wall, will move stealthily westwards, making for the sea. The terrain is not easy. By three thirty their exhausted boots will have given up on them, the soles torn away by the rocks which carpet the entire area west of the city to within half a mile of the sea shore. They will continue to move forward barefoot, then on their hands and knees. By dawn, their hands, feet and knees will be lacerated down to the bones, but they will keep moving, for at dawn they will, at last, get a first sight of the ships. The ships are manned by their own people, sailors from Akra Korakas, Archangel, Florida and Plymouth. Then they will be standing, kneeling and lying on the shore, perhaps even feeling the sea as it cools their wounds and stings their eyes. At that moment, the sailors will up-anchor and cram on sail, for they will be subjected to a concerted attack by our air and sea forces: the galleys from coves north of Port Saint Simeon, carrying archers and cannon, and aircraft loaded with bundles of our widely read literature. The ships will attempt to escape, while they, for their part, will stand on the shore, shouting and waving and weeping with the pain of their wounds and their worstedness. Their ships will consequently be destroyed, as soon as their sailors have seized the opportunity to study our discharged literature.

The men on the shore will then retreat to the low dunes, where, human strength being not easily exhausted in times of stress, they will build a defensive wall of sand, rocks, seaweed and rotten fish. The wall will be fifteen yards long, three and a half feet tall, and two feet wide. It may, even at noon, provide them with a modicum of shade.

The Interrogators

It is some time ago now. The pines are wedges of silver, on either side of the road. Fresh snow crunches under the tyres, with their thick tracks, while the road keeps turning and descending, through a country of frozen lakes, a buried country. We left the main road ten minutes ago. Now we are filtering through these layers of green, silver, and air.

There are a few houses, with small windows, hunched under their loads of snow; a smell of woodsmoke, after we have stopped by the low wooden house with the notice outside. These houses cannot be empty, yet we are not being watched, it is too cold at the windows. The people are presumably huddled around their stoves, burning wood, papers; the insignia were the first things to go. They eat from the pannikins on the dresser, a cold potato, sometimes the leaf of a discovered vegetable. Always they carry these pannikins with them, hoping to discover something edible as they walk around. In mittened hands, or attached to belts, knocking their buttocks. The wooden houses, gashed by snow, are scattered under the pines, as if hurled apart by an explosion. The village has no centre, unless this house with the notice is the centre.

There is a desk, with green blotter and an inkwell, several neat bundles of printed forms. On the blotter lies a yellowed sheet of paper inscribed with some lines in sloping gothic script. The room smells, warm, woodsmoke and faint local tobacco, a suspicion of rum, doubtful, but stale, it invades first the nostrils, then the folds of the thick blue material of our clothes. The windowpanes are opaque around the edges, steam inside and frost outside. The transparent centre reveals the road, churned with tracks, hanging boughs of pine, and then the nearest two houses, their dark walls quite suddenly facing away, as if just caught in the act; and the door creaks as a little man steps in, takes his green hat off, and is seating himself at the desk.

He is as trim and brittle as an elf. The green forester's jacket and trousers, the black knee-boots, belong exactly to this body. His face is wrinkled, the white pointed beard wags as he speaks, his eyes are blue ice. The officer facing him is immediately ashamed of his stomach, so large, shamefully large, and he cannot draw it in. Yet he makes the effort, now that he has to draw breath to speak.

Outside, somebody is there. The black shape against the snow, a head enveloped in a scarf, whoever it is he moves to the window, peers in, then abruptly clears off, into a silence disturbed first by his boots, then only by the sifting sounds of the snowflakes falling against the glass.

The forester has little to say, in fact. No, there never were any batteries here. But 35 kilometres north. No, these forests are empty, there was nothing hidden here. We never saw anything like that. The people who live here have always lived here, only one refugee family, from the east. No accumulators. No searchlights. The lake is that way, it is frozen.

The Birth of the Smile

There are three legends about the birth of the smile, each relating to a different epoch. It is the custom to tell these legends in a reverse chronological sequence, as if this might hopefully point toward an ever-receding antiquity with secrets which may one day be told in legends that still have to be discovered.

The first legend concerns the Sumerians. These people came down from the mountains to the plains, in search of food and water. After several centuries of food and water they became bored with the flatness of the plains, pined for the ancient exertion of striding up and down mountains, and decided to build a mountain of their own (there could be no question of returning to the old place). For ten years the men laboured at the mountain. It was the priests who put the finishing touches to it — drilling weeper-holes, planting a tree on top, fashioning chambers inside, near the base, for library materials and, inevitably, a toilet. While the priests were getting busy, an enormous sheet, woven during these ten years by the women, was draped around the mountain. Finally, everyone assembled; and then the mountain was unveiled with due ceremony and with a great beating of gongs. As the sheet sank to the ground, the strings having been cut by some excessively large pairs of Sumerian scissors, the mountain stepped fresh and naked out of its veilings, and all the Sumerians smiled for the first time. This was a short smile, all the same. The Sumerians had built a mountain to walk up and down, a mountain of the heart, a mountain of despair, a mountain of pain; but their smile disappeared when the officiating priest, from under the tree at the top, declared: "This place is a holy place; for whom it is intended, do not ask. And do not enter or climb around on the outside either, or you will die."

The second legend tells that the smile was born on the face of the first woman when she stood for the first time before the first man and perceived the silence with which his phallus grew and rose at the pleasure of her presence.

The third legend tells of an epoch which must have preceded that of the second, if only by a few days. This is what the legend

130

says. When the shaper of life was making men and women, he was careful to give them strong contours to contain the spirit in them. There was always the danger that these forms might dissolve into the flowing which goes through all things. The spirit raged in the new beings, wrathful at being contained, and after mighty strainings and heavings it burst out in fire. The fire streamed from the bodies of the creatures and all creation might have been consumed, had it not been for a cool god who took the spirit in hand. Suddenly he was standing there, in front of a girl. As they faced each other, an island of coolness was created in the midst of the burning. As he gazed at the girl, he began to marvel at her lightness and grace, and at the diaphanous body from which the fire was spreading in great lashes. The god spoke divine words to her body, as he gazed in wonder. While he was speaking, the spirit overheard these words and for the first time began to grow content in such a dwelling. That was when the girl smiled. In those times, a smile was simply the consent of the spirit to dwell in us.

If older legends are ever discovered, they may explain to us the terrified smile of Kafka; or the smile inserted at the corners of Ché Guevara's mouth by the thumbs of his murderers.

7

Isla Mujeres

1

On one deserted tip
a temple
indelible tanned people
                        Ocean
                              Ghosts

At the other, Mexico
of guitars
         revolutions
                camelias

Reek of urine & fish
            the great garbage tub upended
over a powdery mile.
                 Fishing smacks

Leak essential oil & men living
off hunger.
          Under the coconut palm
            pointed boots
               of a guitarist

Can't get the tourists to pay him anything
                      for a voice
sobbing of love
           and the spiderwork
of ten
delicate fingers.
             Caribbean
blue rippling hot
           fat mammas
folded into hammocks

And nothing
happens except
Americans

Depressives inspecting the silence
or skindivers festooned
                              with cameras & gum.

2

Well before nightfall
El Circo Modelo, with bent gramophone records
& six tons of static the devil's fart
digs into your skull its permanent icepick

                    Run to the sea
with split ears (in the sea
there is no silence), to the garbage can
& clap the lid on (there are no garbage cans).

In hell I appoint a place for Mexicans
where the silence is holy & perpetual

And the slow trapeze
act of Norma Ramirez repeated
repeated *ad*

nauseam will not haunt my more exacting dreams:

for the guitarist
one hundred pesos to get out of the place
with breakfast:
                    magical kick
in the devil's ass, or a cork
to blow him skyhigh when the pressure mounts
(there is no pressure). Juan Manuel

                    Time you were gone
down the dead straight road
past squat brown cottages
of stick & thatch & Indians rotting
in the ocean of Coca Cola.

3

Ramirez bellowing for ever
sensacion olimpica parte artistica
de la programa, was he
        holding his nose? It sounded
like all 27 veins in his cabeza
                        would explode

                Gusts from stars
Pythagoras,
great heaps
of broken triangles
        block the doors,
                        nothing

Nothing doing murmur VIX KABAAL / what
is your name: & the hammock

                grotto rocks
                a small cobweb
                hole through emptiness

What, though, if these
dragon organs, trumpets, yelps gushed
                                from radios
        to lure back the grim
discarded gods, crush
                        the solar fruit
        silence
                        between galaxies & this disc:

Yucatan innocent dream
a different people, eyes
        in their chins, gull-wings flap
for ears, a people
            of dancers whirled fins
drumming
ovations for everyone. And always

the same human wave grinds
down the shores with its blood & sputum

                    Inert norm
invading every grain of antique caracol
& pore of puffing skin.
                    The same hands
grab, the same guts
        to be filled—
                    your ghost

fat Guillaume

Porthole blue zero.

THE LONELY SUPPERS
OF W. V. BALLOON

Nun seh' ich die Ebene und die Rauchklumpen, die die brennende Hölle auftreibt. Wie mich hineingelüstet! Mein Wind läuft gerade über das dunkle, breite Sterbebett der Völker; und da will ich mich in den entzündeten Schwaden senken und mitschäumen wie der elende Mensch.

Jean Paul, *Des Luftschiffers
Gianozzo Seebuch*

1

In Balthazar's Village

Voices in the night
        voices below begin
                wind rising orderless too
rumbles & howls

upstairs a silver light
        falls
                on collected rocks
& new maroon espadrilles

in another room
        Rampal's flute is
                Bach who breathes for these
elementary propositions

odd as it is to care
        anyhow for things
                their mass & contour
& all beginnings

A Cart with Apples

In the blue shadow
alone with its rose
and full of fields
round ones and yellow ones
an apple stands

a blue apple stands
in the field of yellow
alone with its cart
and round of roses
full ones and shadow ones

and full of yellow
the shadow stands
alone with an apple
a rose one a round one
in a blue field

and in the apple shadows
blue ones and yellow ones
a cart stands
alone with its field
and full of rounds

but in the field of roses
and full of apples
yellow ones and round ones
a blue cart stands
alone with its shadow

Roya Valley

Down green slopes
    rock wings, wrinkles
the sun
    beams lower
       circle & circle

  mort pour la patrie
  mort pour la patrie
      puff, perforate the tall
    grass tufts, radiant terraces
      mort pour la patrie

      How
    yellow the broom flower
on peagreen quill, still
    for petals
      the streaming air
has holes

in & out
     plenty of holes
  are there, the mountains flock
& fly, fly
          & breathe

Cantabria

     'a tradition of art
in that region'
             20,000 years of
  tingle

     ibex horn swept
to shape the human
  vertical
     shoal of pollen

     tectiform
          red & antlers
focus the pristine
          God's morphemes

     motifs lapsed
erode the heavy
          silhouette Galba
     Wellington Franco

     as writ blent
  in dark holes blows
               the solar
pulse through mountains

     reappear
          a bull guffaw
  a nameless
box whirling bowmen

        down floats a star
(Miro) to caress
                'le sein
    d'une négresse'

Petrarch's Country

This peak infuriating the winds
this valley fluting down the foothills
these crabby oaks & soon apple trees & blue grape

at the valley's other end a slope of roofs
this maze long abandoned by the tinkling animals
old stone room inhaling all the winds

antique prayer book this decrepit bible
black dented bowler with a cracked brim
a lexicon of place names coming to pieces

dead or alive someone forgot the sunday trappings
but the bowler fits I clamp it on my head
under this peak a thousand weathers flow from

books in hand & looking solemn enter the Café Pons
now my full glass of wine I raise for silence
now I drink to all the winds

Oval History Poem

Stalking the deep
seashell
twists of a cavern below ground
he longs for an arrow
paradise capsule
flaked as the blue intact
sphere of day
outside

142

Puzzle
floors impenetrable rock
green breves
dapple rump to rump
these horses in a frieze
two like toy
star charts yield
not a one he can detach

Attractive
holes repulsed each pointing
finger tip
the bloodcoloured
bison lift
flighted hoofs
in a shower of earth sweat

But
thwong
the shaft still
is shivering — watch him redhanded
pluck at it
the fresh cleft
drilled in his brittle
nobody's head

Holocaust

Here were the huts
here the granaries
here were the clocks
the wigs & harps
the loaves were there
& the long bottles
here were the bells
& there dogwood
here from the froth
amphibians oozed

cave paintings here
a radio telescope
here was a bridge
here the volcano
flea market moon temple
& there the airport
here were the hills
a flop house there
here was the post office
& the Foreign Office
the Gobi was here
there the Appomatox
here was the backbone
here the skin
there the fingers
the flowing hair
here were the spoons
a windmill here
the flutes were there
here were the elephants
& here the tombs
mice & cylinders
the first map
here were the ships
& there the hands
budding weapons
here were the snails
the weeded vegetables
& a lake was here
here was the
here was
here

Snake Rock

Tall snake without strut or buttress
snake which talks in the rhythms of chemicals
snake with legs

tell me where the spyholes are
come between my sheets and just be yourself
snake with two breasts which look at me

snake with hair and very tender armpits
show me the moon
show me the moon or must I split your skull
tell me

tell me animal with fruits
animal of cellulose and lignin come into my house
animal with leaves
cambium animal come into my house

animal which sucks minerals out of the dirt
tell me animal drinking the sun
dead centered animal shaping sugar into wood

drinking lakes also towering flower
tell me how you can change the sun into yourself
flower with a snout
rock with claws come into my kitchen
tell me how you can cook the air and crunch its bones

flower with fur
flower with padded feet smelling of incense
snake who stands in the suchness of silence
come to my table of wood and wickerwork

flower with white teeth
calcium flower teach me the revolution
rock with jaws which bite the flies and all flesh
tell me tell me the rain

snake with a wet nose tell me the lightning
tree which snorts and twitches
umbel snoozing with bristles of soft wire

flower which runs across the street suddenly
tell me how you die
tell me how you die without having to think of it

Mandelstam to Gumilev 1920

The word, you said, stars in terror of it
Clung to the moon; eagles folded their wings;
Men ringed it with number, dreading its radiance.

Our sounds, woven of that radiance, were sacred,
You said — but now what a stink of dead words:
Dead bees, old hive deserted.

So take from me, I ask you, for the joy of it,
A drop of sun, a drop of honey: this
Persephone's bees ordain that we should do.

There's no unmooring the same boat twice over.
Fur-shoed shadow, certain things not a soul can hear,
Or overcome — the fear we live in, thick forest.

What's left to us? Only kisses,
Little bees, all shaggy, in their hives;
They fly into the open — their flight is death.

Night, forest of glass, the space they swarm through.
Taygetos, mountain forest, there they are born, bees
That feed on moments, honeyflower, and mint.

So take this gift, for the joy of it, this
Necklace, unassuming, made of dead bees:
They wove the honey, wove it back to sunlight.

Holy Cow

No, you never give us
a thought. Indifferent, down
to your codes imprinted
in fractions of mud, or up,
for that matter, to your commotions
calving new stars.

146

How long
and still entranced we are
by your surprises, we
believe you a body, perfect somehow
as a woman racked
with love, haloed by
her own heat, but offered, as it goes,
to any takers, you made
each brace of shadows twist
and shake.

Believing also
our bodies different
from yours, we were lost
in whatever thoughts
we robed you with. White
on the mountain, rivers the swish
of your tail, laughing harsh madame, free
with your earthquake favours, bellowing
death-songs we have sought
strange means to dominate you:
bridges, violins.

Naked
you might have appeared
to the old hunters. Should
I wear my shoes because
their masks and antlers,
fantastic forms invented
to contradict your moo, sprang into space
not without hope of wringing
from your bloody udder
drop by drop the pure milk.

In strawberry light
dancers and sorcerers
rose from slime to outwit you.
Wise men watching the sea
chewed the lightning bolt. Cultures
built of their bones
crystallized

in tongues, in architectures, but
the great dome of imagined
destiny sat
capping the dreams that sweated
from spinal column and skull
our deadly chemicals.

Now, song, where
shall we go? No more to suppose
we can arrive at any
complete explanation; possibly
to live in truth apart
from paroxysms of the One; we have
a place in mind
offers the grip
to strip off not her hide
but the inedible crusts caking her,
their weight the imponderables
of history:
so like a moon her variety
sank, her wholeness
we instructed
in our oblivions, the clenched fist,
the frightened man's
mindless standard, death camp, swollen
the veins of orators convulsing
her whims into purpose.

Do not go back
to the swamp where, row on row,
the idols point. Rather to her,
at sixteen asking me
in the ice-cream parlour
how many dips, then dishing them out
with a flash of banded teeth. To someone
reading near dawn at some
ramshackle desk, aware
of the light reflected shaping itself
on a stone or piece
of an apple.

Go where I cannot,
anywhere the animals
are punished, with iron whips,
for our iniquities, and stop
voracity's fictions,
vengeance in its
continuous gathering
momentum, stop them
with a glimpse of her radiant
free
ongoing creation.

Also go to me,
who am answerable,
but walk a street through ruin
without so much
as the faint torchlight
of dejection.

Briefcase History

This briefcase was made on the Baltic coast
in 1946
some prize pig was flayed for the leather
metal stripped from a seaplane
silk for the stitching picked from parachute cord

People say where did you get that singular briefcase
and then I notice it
people ask how much did it cost
and when I say fifty cigarettes not many understand
once the leather was flying wrapped
around seaplane fuel tanks the space between
wadded with two inches of rubber
this briefcase might stop a bullet I wonder

For twenty-five years I have carried in it
books of poems battered or new
cosmic mountain notebooks plays with broken spines
bread and cheese a visiting card from Bratislava
and a pliable cranny for anything to be pocketed
at the last moment

The handle ribbed with stitches of parachute silk
anchored by clasps of seaplane metal
is worn shiny and dark with sweat
the whole thing has an unspeakable gray colour
running a fingertip over a surface
leprous one might say
various tones of gray flickering mould green
the scored leather looks to me like the footsole
of an old aborigine bowman earth in a space photo
nerve webs of a bat's wing

The two side pockets have their seams intact
two straps happily slip through buckles and hold there

Furthermore this briefcase has contained
a dynasty of shirts mostly now extinct nothing to declare
my Venus relics old stones believed
animal figures carved back of beyond in France

Everywhere
this briefcase has been with me somehow
I find reason to celebrate it today

Briefcase helping friend
ploughshare beaten from the sword
briefcase bag of tricks peaceful seaplane spirit
ocean wanderer
you have never contained an explosive device
never have you contained an explosive device
yet

150

Opoponax

A blue field for summer
Rib curve the dotted lines of lavender
Discontinuous flesh beating a signal out
And a man
Lifts a heart on his knife point
High

Possibly
He was hunting
He could be sacrificing
A squirt of cloud mixed in slow time
Would you believe it
With peace
It comes in a little bottle

In a little bottle
Knife in hand
A man stooped now he turns his terror
Like a fruit in the market
Palpitation of quanta
Like bomb bursts the line of lavender tufts

Now the tin cap sits tight
Rubber bung beneath
So the flashing knife will split
Memory down the middle
Mist of dawn on roofs multiform mask of cities
Moist chasm of spit and smells
Remembers the man

Now he strikes and again
But with five hundred baskets
Of flowers on its arms
Dew is calling out the names and prices
In a little bottle

Mountain throbs with rockfall
All its years at any moment
Distilled at a touch
On a fingertip fathoming the knife gash
Might balance or be crushed
Such crystal stars
Vast infolded systems
Index of man

Tenderness
And a great wet shroud
Catching the yellow blood of lavender

Extract the years of carnage
Touch your face

2

Curling Form for Olga Korbut

This moment none too early in the day
sitting by myself
at the circular kitchen table —

and a section of the other room is opening
it appears aslant thanks to the sun
a tawny oblong with bright slits and trefoils
being framed (adjectival but exact)
in the kitchen doorway

Now I see the blue armadillos of Pablo de Jesus
build their nests in air
I see pinned to the wall panelling
the chevron of barley stalks hung with two bushy ears
beside the light switch

and above the blue armadillos a white oblong
cardboard field with a splotch in the centre
I know it is a throned figure
upward gaze
cow-eyed and captioned 'König der Angelsachsen'

and below the blue armadillos which are frisking
Kaspar Hauser engraved in steel
identification doubtful never mind beside it
an oval photo of cardplaying officers
Lilo in Suzette (Vaucluse) inked other features in
now bottle noses tilted bowlers have encompassed me
I flourish at French professors wearing them
a prehistoric stone

The base of the section
an old oak chest of drawers
like rippled mud at the mouth of an estuary
the horizontal graining or fan vaults
in a cathedral take your pick there are two drawers
four brass handles

On the chest a black telephone
dangling cord it looks like an enormous pubic hair
or a plain one
crossing the lens of a radio telescope
take your time certain objects look beyond words
scrolling what is it called at the base of the chest
in what curling form does emotion ravish it
and a pair of binoculars
and so on

and so on
lest I let out a whoop of joy
for in fact I exalt a space ripening and continuous
very rare under these rooftops
naming some elements I hoard a little of it
hoarding it I alter a little
the time I have taken the continuous time I stole
to be writing about it

Uschi's Epistle 1949

'. . . *como una pompa de jabón al viento*'
   Antonio Machado

    Y *todo*
          in Bamberg   the square
opens
  a cathedral and the tombs
        after spring drizzle
among tombs

154

A little boy his head all shorn
the shape of it Roman
            plucked from marble
snails and many snails
            from the grass blades

And stood beside me
            la memoria se perdía said
        would I help him
so we fill his old meat can
            touring the tombs
and you come to supper he says

Down winding golden lanes *y todo en la memoria*
        my high heels make such a clatter
                slow going
slippery wet cobble snails no quicker
            his eyes meet mine sidelong

Huge knotted oak door then the song
    of hinges
                but we stop
and in my face he flicked several cool
    drops of holy water

So we can go
in
recoiled interior things
        in his world of snails are we shells?
His grandmother
            deaf   cooking the soup of snails
rare salt
so he tells me the tale of a straw
                murmury dark
            the *mär* of a straw he tells
so dass ich nichts verstand

And the soup
        y todo the taste of it
wonderful and all and afterward
    she held to my lips a little wooden cross
open door

Open door everything outside rose to my lips
        aleph globes and jewels I kissed
                the five wounds *todo se perdía*
was this rain
I kissed I had forgotten
        it was Friday

Le nu provençal
(photograph by Willy Ronis, 1949)

The wooden shutter hanging open,
sunlight commands the shapes around the room.
A jug has left its ovals on a flagstone,
and tilts a little, as if listening in
to a kneecap or a buttock.
                Not so the chair
with one leg out of touch with everything,
about six feet away across the floor.

If a round mat covers several flagstones,
what of the swirl of shadows all around,
tipping the chair, invading the towel that hangs
from the rail of an iron washstand, burrowing
into the armpit poised above the bowl.

The bowl is luminous enamel and contains
two hands, from one of which an arm sprouts
rounding into the gleam across a shoulder.
The mat, woven of rushes, also supports
the lines of feet mounting past the ankles
into calves that curve up into little pits
of light back of the knees.

Above the bowl
a mirror on a string, and where the frame
swooshes down to complete another oval,
a smudge of hair, a flit of shoulder show.

And the hair itself is tucked against a nape
never to be seen because the back's ellipse
conceals it, with a ripple of its flesh
and muscles held in tightly to the backbone.

Least mysterious of all a nipple charms
the bowl of white light with its bud, which echoes
across delicate dark waves of flesh and is there again
in the round bottom and its dusky cleft.

Watch as you will, the mystery is elsewhere.
Perhaps between the things, distributing tensions.
Perhaps in the diagonals which cross, from chair
to shutter through the body, from the mirror
downward across the body to the jug.
Or in the volume of the space they occupy,
for such a little time sifting the silence,
buttressed at one end by the puckered wall
of stone and plaster, at the other end
by the gaze exploring all without distress.

Third Generation

For two old immigrants
who do not speak the language
I drag this wooden dog
over the bending floor
of a corridor in their attic

It circles the town and crosses it
from one end to the other
many doors are swinging
open and shut as I pass
and the dog behind me clicketyclack

They lent me their plank
and played me the Mass in B minor
I lost the plank in a park somehow
or it turned into this dog
I am dragging for ever and ever

The Monk of Montaudon

1

Wife-loving types, they
get my goat, even if the lady is
Our Lady of Toulouse. Beneath contempt:
simpering chaplains chockful of lies,
monks with beards.

               A pox on
those hawks always reconnoitring another
likely shore. Cripples I trip over
on my morning trot, God
rot them, and any wretch who flaps
Our Flag: pig, him, to snaffle
my horse's oats.

               Hell! How can anyone
ungrumbling munch hard tack and curse which way
the dice falls? Bad again,
bad as no guitars in a dance hall:
to be hugging yourself on a highway in winter,
then catch a whiff of roast
from some tavern kitchen.

               Devil take
a stormy port, the dirty whore
I had this noon, I hate
the likes of both. But, even more so,
a young buck making eyes at his
muscles in a mirror; no less a woman

158

fat-paunched with spindly legs. Bad too,
to be tired out with never
a wink of sleep coming.

2

Best of all, friends, I like music,
knockdown fights, uproarious parties,
and a woman with a terrific body.
Sparkling talk, how the words whizz out and up
like daggers, and
this I like: a good fellow
with money on him, also one who spits
in his enemy's face.

             Praise I like,
wherever it comes from; forty winks
out of doors, just so long as
no hailstones hit me,
a salmon steak at 9 p.m.

             And this,
glorious: in summertime
to be lying down
beside a brook, the fields
are green, flowers new, birds
keep singing, high overhead, and in the haze
I spy my girlfriend, there she is,
and I go hump her.

The Pogroms in Sebastopol

All night she wept,
Fania, ten
at the turn of the century,
this afternoon she saw
the tsar
in his karieta,

taking the curlers out
she had combed
her hair, long and blond,
she had washed her face, the tsar
waved
in his karieta
at everyone,

but in particular
the hand waves
cupped and white, feeling
its hollow through the hot
horse flanks,
inflexible dragoons,

at Fania freshly combed, noticing
her clean face, he waves
who is god-on-earth,
who for the good of his people
wishes
the Cossacks could make less noise
about it, a tidier business
next time,

and
besides
who waves his hand
at me, at me
all night she thinks,
weeping for joy, tsar, we say it
the same in Yiddish.

Old Woman at the County Dump

Sitting in her cracked hutch,
beneath trees, hidden from the road,
she is the guardian of a torrent
of burst mattresses, rust and rubber,
bodiless lids of objects without present function.

One tooth and a hank of hair,
a form of speech that spits and babbles
like the nerves of a scorpion in a jamjar.

Junk, mounds of it, from dark hollows
little dogs erupt, sniffing, stretch and disappear
like stars that fall in August. All the stuff
people have left, beyond and behind,
marching toward a world of absolute deodorants,
infallible laxatives.

                    What if she died?
Who'd notice? She might be found,
a few ribs and shanks, hardly smelling at all,
at home among the vacant basins. Her apocalypse
the O all these unbolted toilet lids
trumpet to the skies.

At night, I imagine,
stuck to her rocking chair, she dreams,
dreams of being guarded by the garbage.
A block of rusty bedsprings at her door,
plucked by rat claws, gives off
intermittent echoes of an old serenade.
With all its worms a portly wardrobe,
her protector.

I think of the lightning,
if it was lightning lashed from the waters,
the hiss of it, a sort of red
veined quaking cream, and frothed ashore
the whiff, a first, of space and time.

And I think of the women who floated
out of the forests, hard on the tracks of vague men,
thud of their feet, the wind's cry,
tall savannah grasses bending:
some carry in hollow logs
a yellow flame.

Puffs of smoke
struggle up from her heap of clapboard.
Still she is the guardian
of an element that signifies
a good roast crackling, a legend to live by,
of power tamed and change.

History
has beaten most of the life out of her body,
but still the days flash on,
nights blossom with new moons, the people
burst through time, breaking things like toys,
and leave her the rubble.

Football Players, U.S.A.

                            behind frosted glass
a linebacker, lilac spray
                   rock liquid shot
        from earth oven: fire
                       lilac roar
   growls
behind the lens
          oneway sun is this the orange bowl
I can't
    speak with authority what are
                   the elementary propositions

         but the name of the game is money
disc sun to pocket
          inaudible inedible electrons
    stick in my throat
            safetyman
               tomorrow
      sees with a microscope
        or with a telescope he
                  does he

spirit in lightning strike spirit in tree
                              red sumac & the green
          is a cedar: these are life colours
black smoke 1000 mouth zoomorph
             tough scales like a lake of quilts:
blockpoint
                                        But these
be not those paired
           four jockeys trim paint hair moustache
                              ginger & black

come jumping ride the beast
                  his body is air: naked eye
gaze
      at the serried blue
             treetrunks bark split near the root
into a smile
         oval pendulous
football tobacco brown punching fist

                         a nimble game!
      particular leaf
           tiger stripe
             everyone planting
in unquenched dust his very slender feet
                              the silence
             of a flute in a pumpkin.

Idiocy of Rural Life

FOR KOFI AWOONOR

Where
begin: often it is
the disposition of objects
on a table:
             tall tin coffeepot,
blue saucepan, a membrane
of milk in it

163

Or: 'what a gulch,
Texas . . . ,' the buzzard pecks.
your politic racoons, gas
millionaires
            and smoke
machines horizon
the shadow of your smile

That
motel: fake pine panels,
over the interstice
            it is mulcted
Rainbo bread, a power
nails you: gaze
of a vacuumed stag head

Or: what finger might,
black or any, moonflower or toad,
make the infinite effort,
write 'Thy kingdom . . .' on the wall

Or: what voice
in a deep cavern echoed this
antlered dancer's rigmarole,
bucking and twirling;

            the void has drunk
bloodfoam, spun from the void, look,
a glittering web, spun by his dance measure . . .
my people have chosen

Dull demons:
first iron, then dynamite, painful
transformations, the peanut
gouged out of Africa, epochs like 1215,
1634, 1933
            (Himalayan
tigers, what
new deceit, fanned by your breath, cooks
in the pot of spleen and okra)

164

Or: when electric
zeroes halt
the spate of babble, who shall decode
the alarm flushing from grass
goldfinch argosies,
                    palm leaves of Cumae,
who shall dance now
a sycamore in the wind

Or: the right verbs
here, and here, might relate
the things; then let these eyes
reap the sacred
space
between them

A Window

Oddly like a porthole
It contains a thistle

Someone with a hammer fashioning stories
Imagined a deep square hole

And placed it in the wall it was real
Light in the morning returns to roost in it

No sea for a hundred miles
Among these unforsaken mountains
The deep square hole is white inside

And a hundred years afterward
Someone trod across the stone floor

Someone holding a vessel
Old glass and in it a thistle

Now the waves of light come crashing through
The blue head of the thistle

The Ulcinj Postcards

Truly, it takes the breath away,
This 'view',
The Adriatic, opal,
Unpopulated, and the dark now

Absorbing it. No wind,
Said Xristic, after sundown. The beach
Shrugs off its mass
Of splendid flesh —

What tentative hand
Carries along the sea wall, like lamps,
These young flat-bottomed women?
A major stomach, grandpaternal,

Does it shudder a bit when filling itself?
All the dusky shapes
Of appetition tangle, mask even
Such space as boys on tiptoe

Flit through. Had you
Lost the thread? Found, for *sladoled,* a table;
Two jugs; look up, the fort, 'attractive'
Turco-Venetian ruin;

And a tomb is built
Into a wall, hollow, candles 'twinkle'
At the foot of
A real coffin.

Godlike brigands, all gone; vestiges
Of their abrupt
Brilliance a mosque, the 'Chinese' house, and these
Nine heads on a rock, nine

White shirts, 'fierce moustaches'
Float in a shadow,
It hangs heavy, the last rock, one face
Gnawed to a slit by its own

Teeth: these be
Aboriginals — elsewhere
Hand in hand the families cluster,
Collectives trample, unemployed,

Up ankle-cracking alleys, chew the fragrant
Mutton, grilled on prongs,
And there is music. Behind a drainpipe
Tapping, too, is heard

At intervals, 'windless' intervals,
A tapping, strangest: the lizard
Busy in there, likely
Also a cricket

'Aims'
To be eaten, shucking off
Carapace and universe,
Twitch by twitch.

Transit

Garden wall from this bed
Hollow square to support
                the faint harp sounds

In the acacia tree
                light flows and stays
It is filtering round arches
                        the gray spire

St. Germain from this bed of an early morning
It is an essence which breathes
                        or is savoured

An essence tasting of my entire time
My time clustering
                in the light which flows and stays

White curtain open window
         old harp to pluck
There are black cords
           a palisade of cypress trees

My time passing them by as I wake
And hew down the cords
        one by one with a free hand

3

The Fossil Fish

15 Micropoems
   (Vaucluse: July—September 1969)

1

village quote idiot unquote
look a walking often takes
long at you

       stops & slow hows
       he come through

           screwy? clutched in
his one scrotum hand the other
crumpled hugs a fingering book

                        2

                    them squads in
               helmets
                 burning
                the dragonfly's eyeballs
             out
           is just ants

      3

      & silver eggs on stems
          be nobbut topknots
of a grass — ah savage head
      see them caught
             nodding in the wind launch
  your airy
hundredfold
    parabolas of seeing

4

ivy around the capstone
starts to fizz:
early snailhorns are
sounding the systems
of their space

5

shorts white
at the sharp angle of
trim bronze legs
to a melon balanced
in one palm she subtends her
equilateral nose
deepening the hidden
rose of that sphere
between cone & cone

6

rock & bough
tumbled over slammed against
pluck out their fillets
of necessary flesh
mad pleasure
for once to bleed
on a hill groaning
with apricot trees

170

7

       inside the shell, fields:
          listen, lavender, wheat
   behind it, blue
           mountain behind
      the wheat, the sun
over the mountain, curving
    up, the wave murmur: it
      won't fall

8

storing its times
the body
learns weightlessness

space be skin
limit
my flesh of lightning

9

toad
crawls
up
boulders
always
dragging
his
ughs!

10

                    a place ribbed with quartz
           between
                soaring
                   rock wings here the wind
       swivels crashing sucked
                   back into its helix
        luminous flesh in which
           embedded far below beyond
               float mountains little
      mossy tuffets

11

feeling the leaf
a tree
wrote
spine
longwise it is not
chinese but crinkles

12

         calm in the face of nature
         •
               fearful in the face of nature
         •
         maggot, neither, holes
              up in a peach

13

to please a nymph
    sip at her spring
so her true voice told
    first a far cry
now sharper breaths
    moisten this rosy moss
& soon for sure
    she will be coming

14

coming also his long gusts tell me
the wind a river he roars
         in pine trees pounding walls of rock
      to destroy he scatters to build

speech a silver breath & seed once he scooped
         a whole man from a cave
            flicked him away
   like an eyeball

         with twisted clay
trumpets at dawn we call for him hopeless
         on the mountain

   he floats in the crested ocean eastward
      blue cattle waiting to drink
the first torrent of rays

      how else from his flowering
chiselled hollows
      could these bee snouts tap our honey

15

the fossil fish
hides in time
for now it is the season

& all the hunters come
with long clean rifles

4

Chanel Always Now

FOR FRIEDERIKE MAYRÖCKER & ERNST JANDL

1

by sir francis rose
     a combination of sheer poetic lust
hard work
and important artistic was fifteen. she had come
     like a slim youth.
       then when she moved
a small dark boat on water.

2

striped sails Chanel
but small and fascinating. flat figure
and great-smallness was at all costs. must reveal.
fragile greek faience mask
lying in a miniature nest of sawdust.

3

coins on cotton wool
in a small white tortoiseshell
   which he would twist around his neck several times
   it hung
heavily down to a pocket
     in his trousers. the goddess
   of mentally women
       and a woman of boni de castellane covered all
her large square sofas.
     poiret and bakst
the palely powdered women in their forties.

4

Chanel destroyed this very expensive boyish
little girls of the working class.
buses and aeroplanes.
boyish line of the sports field and english
public school
luxury except in the details. heads bare and sleek.
valentino
brilliantine hats were bullets. very solid.

5

kit wood who died admired
the great ivory negro nancy wore on her arms
but not the junk Chanel made fashion
for the first time.
hide bare skin up
to the shoulder. a pendant bosom
made for lady abdy toussaint a large blue
egyptian in gold lotuses
like a miniature temple.

6

much was simple. it was opposite.
it was essentially. nothing could have been.
she made that. taste abominable. square.
scent bottles. everything Chanel. black walls.
black *toile ciré*. kitchen tables. don antonio de gandarillas.

covering paris the power of the scottish mackintosh.
I forced my mother with shoulder straps.
it was one of the mysterious objects I have seen.

7

blue cape
in the french navy another time
labourers' gauntlets of coarse hide
dyed a pale sky blue
on the palms. now called pop. inspired.
shanghai blues by all the pimps
these cotton chinese colours
not forgotten.

8

peter blarney the greatest doyenne of proust in 1930
said: I adore her for the italian stitching the madwoman
of costume. jo dufy said: Chanel makes rounded horses.
andré hemingway said: I do not understand without sex
for literature in dressmaking. dolly sister jennings
said: they have always said

black velvet
but my fox terrier loved the chinchilla
so I made it into his bed. boni de cocteau
the most extravagant man said:
*la femme fait la cuisine avec les garçons de Chanel mais
c'est la bonne cuisine d'une paysanne.* thank god
in 1926: the machine lace
is far more important than clothes.

9

scot bibesco the russian virgil gertrude tchelichev
alice b lavery jean-gabriel serge and lifar thompson
said:

le tout paris are dreams
      a woman with a face
      an outline
         goes to your concerts
            she has destroyed beautiful hats
          magical creature

COCO

      Chanel a lovely dress one forgets it
    with going up to bed Chanel is politics
  after all Chanel stripped women
a date palm without dates Chanel

10

      her head a little boy in black tights
        for a masque by inigo jones
          a monument of palm leaves
      at the end of the party
this wonderful headdress

    I lost it in a gust of wind on the way home

Nine Biplanes

FOR RICARDO GULLÓN

   una vaga astronomía
   de pistolas inconcretas
     (Federico García Lorca)

Summer 1940: I opened the double glass front door of that
rambling country mansion, school, and saw nine biplanes flying low, in close formation, and slowly; the lower edge of what I
saw is a ruffled green mass of trees.

177

But I do not know what day it was, or the month, only that the summer had begun. And there may have been six biplanes, or twelve. Certainly they were biplanes, heavy ones, with two motors, and they were moving slowly, as if a great wind belaboured them, though the trees were hardly moving, there was no wind, or just a little. I opened the front door, was standing on the gravel path which looped a large flower bed, and then came the noise.

Now, looking out of the window, I see a low wall of rocks, a section of gray drainpipe stood on end as the base for a bird feeder, a green bush, and behind these, somewhat higher, a mass of foliage, and behind the foliage a sky, frameless, though parcelled into infinity by bird calls delineating territories, and beyond that, the real sky. A child looking the same way sees deep down, a window, and deeper, little pine tree, clear lake, another window, and deeper, little pine tree, its image, in a clear lake.

The noise is still loud and clear. Looking upward I saw the biplanes. I had heard about the war, but nobody had said much about it, except, now, that the Germans had broken through. They said it, yet one saw nothing; at any moment, they said, it might happen, the invasion. They, whoever they were, spoke of invasion, invasion, and there we were, eating toast, miles from home, running up and down the long corridors, and doing extra Latin. The schoolmaster went on smoking his pipe, whacking us with his slipper, and writing neat equations with his goldnibbed Onoto pen. It was an odd thing, so much noise, overhead, and rushing out of the house, more than a house, a country mansion, after crossing the immense panelled hall, and opening the door, and now to be standing there on the gravel, looking up, and seeing the biplanes.

Nine or six biplanes, already oldfashioned, as one knew from pictures in the papers, flying somewhere, to fight, in the sky, some how, the Germans, who had broken through.

Deeper still, a street in Hué or An Loc, no, this time Barcelona, and a little girl's head being sliced off by a bomb splinter, her

178

mother clutching at the body, two soldiers in bedraggled uniforms looking at the head, down at the head, which lay at their feet.

They were flying across Norfolk, toward the sea perhaps. Woods, the breckland, miles of wheatfields and dark barns, heading toward the sea. The Germans were not at sea at all. What were they looking for? How would they identify it when they found it? They had been told to fly. So they flew, airmen, wearing leather helmets, which are not blown off their heads because of the leather straps and the buckles. Signals from their home base filling the cockpits, determined looks on their goggled faces, the air humming among the wires we drew crisscross between the two wings when we made our sketches.

When people are blocking the French road, exploding steel mouths gobble their canaries, grandparents, and bolsters. Deep down, a clear lake, it reflects the sign to be seen in a certain Moscow elevator in 1937: It is prohibited to put books down the lavatory.

They sat in the cockpits, looking determined, with orders to fight the Germans, if they found them, knowing that their machines were rickety and ridiculous. Maximum speed 150 m.p.h. Down there on the gravel I heard the droning clatter of their motors. Type of armament: unknown. Range: uncertain.

Seeing German soldiers marching into the Saarland, they were marching on the front page of the *Daily Sketch,* made me ask one day in the basement kitchen, with the paper spread out before me on the kitchen table among jampots and knives and cups: So is there going to be a war? My mother at the stove, without turning around to face me, must have said Yes or No, probably No; but with the biplanes flying in close formation low overhead, I was not remembering this.

The men wearing helmets and sitting in the cockpits of the old biplanes were not twiddling their thumbs or drinking pop, but they were English. Perhaps they knew about the bombing in Spain, whereas I knew nothing, or had noticed nothing, ex-

179

cept the Crystal Palace Fire, the Abdication, the faraway deep throbbing at sea through late summer nights, before September, when German armies marched into Poland, and Polish cavalry with sabres launched attacks on tanks, I knew nothing about bombing in Spain but thought I must have heard fleets of submarines moving out into the Atlantic. So these airmen were setting out, on a summer's day in the fifteenth century, to fight the enemy, flying low, in close formation, and I had rushed through the panelled hall, had opened the door, and now stood and stared at them, my feet on the gravel, my head tilted back, mouth open, and did not realize that this was what was happening. A loud noise in the sky, continuous. Antique gesture.

A child, instead of looking downward, now looks outward, and still cannot awake, the inability to awake being, like an arm's reach or the tilting of a head, part of his condition. With hacked-off hands he constructs for himself someone else, old, scribbling. Amid the droning clatter of the motors, a bell of pink fire suddenly sounds. He listens to the long trumpet blaring tightly across the neolithic heath, on which he found flints during Sunday afternoons; he listens to the flying metal blare and does not see the girl's head rolling across the gravel to his toecaps.

The sounds are people running in plimsolls, knock of the red leather ball on the willow cricket bat. A smell of linseed oil in the thatched pavilion. But the pilot's head is wrapped in leather: the pilots are going to knock the Germans for six, if they can find them, behind the pavilion, between the pavilion and the woods, where you could hear the cock pheasant scream before any thunderstorm, or, in the evening twilight, quietly see rabbits feeding, their ears laid back along their little skulls.

5

Invisible Forces

Hot sun
and dripping with air
through blue sky the airship
sails

hooray hooray
suddenly everyone
is a clown
jumping tumbling

in the beauty of bulgey legs
here this girl's
gently walking and slow
difficult
with dark hairs

Luberon Story

Roasted gray & sunken
     shells but stones
          fitted blocks echo
the place high where the wind
          strikes

now ilex thickets & hairy
     thongs of ivy inside
          holes for grain here in time
I took a wrong turn
     three pretty maids
  came out dancing

                    over the grass
a white loaf
            jugs of mountain wine
      & who is this old man blowing
                  an ocarina
                            what is this foam
      clematis

bullets ripped across his chest
            women slither
                  screaming weeping
down the hewn steps I'm plodding up
            men grab hoes & running
      crumple in blood
stickbones
            crack & roofbeams everywhere
                        rotted falling

      dust a green
lizard
      that long
                  slid into a cistern
      there are birds now
a few sweetly
            flitting

Jindřichův Hradec

This is the chapel of the holy
      spirit he said and lifted
            the old yardlong iron latch

while in the castle courtyard
      outside raindrops were smacking
            old stone roses around the rim

of the fountain so in we went
      and from an organ loft with pious mien
            detected under the dust

182

a conference of upright chairs
   occurring in the chancel
      a leather sofa in the apse

and heaped around the font
   several curious brown closets
      so we ask him simply tell us

Who dismantled the organ pipes
   Who presided with a pen in his fist
      Who howls here when the moon shines in

A Serbian Motif

Snow unrolls over Scythia
Its blanket; Scythian bowmen
Put up their feet,
And a great stain smelling of shit and wool
Fills the huts.

     For the poem
Might have ended. The poet, in the amam,
As from her head he lifted up
Heavy sheaves of hair, holy banners,
Put his lips to the breast of a woman.

     The poem
Was a fault in time, a gulf
Wrought by centuries into a well shaft;
Its intricate pitched coping now took shape,
As tongue and teeth
Modelled the air, opening its limbs,
Tiny caverns torn in breath
Bled sensation.

     She had to answer for it,
Shook free the lifted hair, and slowly
The tree danced to the music of its moistures

And a river he was listening for, underground,
Still carving out in monastery suppers,
Mountain battles and the flesh of goats,
In cracked shouts at sunrise filling the baker's yard,
Those many domes and vaults,

        Rosy membranes linked
The folds, luminous web
Of sonorous rockwalled corridors, the flood
Purest, fretted with stars,
As it bore onward
Pools of shade for the village dogs
To sleep in —

        That moment, as it is,
Now the new earth, all of a piece,
Appearing —

        Up against a wall
The poet sees
Heaped and red the snow
At somebody's feet, hears the first
Arrow thud
Into his body,

One hoofbeat.

Two Water Poems

1

Swim in the spring
it's cold
and bites like
you slept with your daughter

184

At summer's end
glowing waters close
like silk over your shoulder

This time it's mother
such an evil hobby
envious
comparisons

2

Labyrinthine roots
of the water cypress
anchor
this green dove weighing
dozens of tons
this hairy cone haunted
by the cuckoo

and vanish
far under water
yours
my friendly purse
of blood fly up

through speech-
bubbles past
their faint boundaries
into thin air

Bishop, Rabbit, and Ducks

The bishop shelved among the cooking shapes
at a touch
a rabbit could be glistens in the grass

Conical cast
after rain how green and hidden for the rabbit
their sinister ovals

And ducks
by moonlight carry to roost across the grass
four different sizes of himself

So the bishop springs open
how come the ducks keep setting off at midnight
white explosions

But back of the house
his crook and robe encrusted a cold hollow
beam from a patrol car rifles the park

Even the rabbit must munch fright
a wad of tubes wet and spiky
every mouthful of beaded grass root

Fruit of moon
could be sacred could be solid snowy ducks
in heaven's name this bishop is not hot pellets

Anointed by neon does not scatterbomb with Honeywell
children peaceful cottage people
but with chocolate

Truly glistening rabbit come close
gobble if you will
the whole house

Avocado Plant

How good it was
to burst from the nut
now my roots dangle in clear water

white roots trailing gripped by little turrets
cockfeather cloud I plant in ears
a sting of wind

yet nothing shakes me from the split
nut held in the mouth of the bottle
and my sixteen leaves shot from the tendril

quilts pointed at either end
and oval
only hatch these tufts of shadow

flicked across the wall as I climb forever
out of myself on the sunbaked zinc
casing of an old water-fan

Tall Grass

Is it because I was ill
or just little, late
in summer we moved, everyone
else busy, I am put
into a garden, tall grass,
everywhere in 1932

tall grass, in the sky
a biplane puttering, whiff of coal
smoke from the station, smell
of the tall grass
I knelt in, hidden, building
a nest, this

was the place, this was the place
for me, at a touch
it creaked and whispered, low
overhead the biplane swooped as
in I go, chirpily
stretch out, look upward,
waving.

Essay on the Texas Panhandle

Absolute milage might be the same
Paris to Nice but road hits horizon
straight as a rocket
and between   and the next
not one polyphonous place   wind
whistling over the windshield   cows are
shorthorn   blowing in   somewhere
town is   briefly street   punctuate
tables of dark earth receding
every which way and for ever

As if anything recedes   no hidden places
as if this were a landscape, as if
punctuation fitted this kind of earthtalk
no corners
nothing secret
a sponge split open in every direction
drinking blank air

No place for such
folds in time as a form
sprouts from: sorghum
cotton
white puffs badge a tan stick
burst from the pod
pregnant with summer trousers

Estelline 5
Childress 21:   a curtain of gray
nothing bushes peeled back thereafter
by a green field

Elsewhere: splutter of empty shacks
at all angles   wonky porches   juniper
shade lives   Moon hat on this
old labourer   ghost of a black grandpa
he done got lost.   Definite article   noun
done got lost

188

Valiant misnomer
little billboard by a brick hut proclaims
Western Art
and who named the places and for what? Keep
going you grip the wheel at eighty-five
never look like getting anywhere
foutre foutre sans jamais partir
not a landscape
mystery
perhaps in the shudder of a grassblade

Blasted by cyclones and blizzards
the space you are crossing
an eyelid never opened
today with a blue edge its imperceptible
bulge the curvature only
of earth its veins
rivers
Red River Cimarron Wichita
Salt Fork and Double Mountain Fork of Brazos
did anyone ever watch them as
Bobrowski the Vistula

Winds
treeless levels
elsewhere rolling dunes toughened
by dwarf cedars
flatness
earth pulled to flatness by such gravity
the eye finds itself
hungering for verticals
at last intimate
with a telephone pole
embracing a flock of crows lofted suddenly
a grain elevator
less lovingly southward
squat black oil pumps pecking the ground
for Gulf or Phillips

Pulling up sharp for a piss
at the sign which says Get Right with God:
remember Buchenwald
stank in a billowy landscape famed for seeming
a mirror of the infinite:
wonder how else the wealth for wars
could have been extracted
to support
single vision   vested interest
the owners' all-falsifying consciousness
if not by force-feeding from just such
a placenta of panic
the grab into fingers brainless itch to annihilate
whatever deeply moves
like deer through a forest
or might promise
to be different

Idiocy of Rural Life (Variant 2)

There it is, in the window
Glass, blue
Oblong, blotting out
A bush in leaf, bald rock

Raised eyes, and a mask
Slips, there it is, near, 'easily
Destructible, a feeling of
Nearness', now four cornered

As Eli's blue Treblinka
Fire, public, the tormentors
Grunting slide bodies through
An iron orifice

Mine possibly, what was
Of me, my eclipsed
Future also, what core
Not rendering ash

But not sky, essence, for the asking,
Of a book reflected, open
As you place it, in terror, on
The table, so bring down

Not destruction, but
Fresh vacancy on it, and fight now
For the thought: bush, table,
Oblong, what can they mean?

Mérindol Interior 1970

Sheets of paper you wrap around me
Crucify me with a length of string
Tip me into the box and hopefully
I'm off by air to another place

There if it's blue the roof shores this ocean up
And a limestone kitchen hangs under our bed
My tappity spoon threads our bowls into a china harp
A glass of blood you stroke from the sobbing bottle

But we are branches now and I am thorned
For joy we prance in a whirlwind of quilts
Finches hopping from breath to breath we fatten
With kisses and nipples and cool cherries

Afterward your brown legs are not paper any more
I shriek for air entombed not in string
But in the furrows I have gouged all over you
My knife is tender truly it is a lamp you hold

Or in your town the houses are little orbs
With leaves eager to sprout and harsh beaks pecking
They circle the elms we sit beneath at night
Listening to drums beaten by maggots

Never can we reach a darker place than this
My hot oils drip on your belly and make us laugh
Again out of your looking glass I have come to you
Marked sender unknown return to addressee

The bringer of news has rushed through the gate
Without even the horror of a knock
He shows us the crop impaled on our prongs today
Naked children racing a sunburst of petrol

You wear the smile a lamb at pasture lives through
I touch the earth and regret my fingers
Several times I told you never turn your head
The bull roars in his cave the mouse in his pit of smells

Brightness thickens the names
Old fountains clogging and the rain harsh
Darkens all that is done for us — on crusts of blood
Torn from the back of the world we spread our butter

Untitled

When you got up at four to make pipi,
I walked to the window & pushed open the shutters.
Silver crescent moon in a sky of clear dark peach colour.
One star a thumb's length from it shot from the bow.

There was a silence, the kind you can hardly remember.
You came back to bed & I was in beside you.
To touch your breast was all a new day,
Warm & cool your legs were hitched around my waist.

Beginning slowly it is a violence creates mountains.
Now a moon & a star stand over the ridge quietly.
Here in this little mound between your legs I touch you;
So a star could begin to appear in another person's eyes.

Of that violence we make what we tenderly do,
Rock & moan, laugh & weep for the joy of it;
But the window is open, swallows tweet dotted quavers & cut
                                                            loose.
As the rooster calls I count the heads that will roll today.

The Gloves

A pair of gloves on the floor
of an empty spacious institutional john.

Quilted cotton gloves of a dun colour,
with wrist guards, irish green and orange

horizontal stripes, the orange thicker.
A pair of gloves, the right hand crosses

under the left, cupped like a mendicant's;
agony twisting the left one's thumb erect,

it seems, you'd think, smothering a giggle,
someone has been sucked down the john —

nothing left but gloves on gripless lino.
Can such jolts be just whims of nature?

Objective gloves, digits in thought space
adding up, sooner than seen, to real mutilation,

real, though few folks wear
gloves while sitting, normally, on the john.

It happens to stick out so, such
terror, no more than a question of timing, now

the telephones are silent, desks darken, everyone
has given up for the day, given up and gone.

On Mozart's Birthday

FOR TOM RAWORTH

Suppose a birth
& it is clarity
but what are the odds

or the way sudden words
of yours launch into a pure
unemotional space

now & here & by name
even these tasks
a referential bodymass

turned satellite
the Great Udder in orbit
fans through networks

trade cycles flashpoint
battle fronts
but few words from the quick

fleeting objectives
bring home
a faraway

figuration of earthglow
uncoop for some
the joy in a thing

altogether sexual
a high speed submicroscopic
impetus

& ever up against
that wall
before the blood be dry

gunners our lepidopterists
before they pin us down
we hear the wave

throb of Osip's
carbolic guitar
& clean through it

go the words go naked
steady torchbearers
to serve the wise unborn

first a spirit
listening for the ancestors
& then a rose

Autobiography

My father said the best time is early morning
A twig or two across the window and beyond them

All the stillness you could want in the world
All this clarity below in the garden

He stood in his dressing gown holding a teapot
Such white calves and feet like a sculpture's

Across the room he'd stroll singing and harrumphing
Settle at his desk and write six letters

This poem is solemn it has a bad meaning
All night confused whisky music and words

Miles I limped past blackening heaps of snow
Biafra bodies police pressure Britain Third Street

As head touches pillow eyelid traps a vision
My uncertainty is the soul of the weapons system

They say my daughters they say my son
At my age you'll not find any air to breathe

The Lonely Suppers of W. V. Balloon

Thank the thunderstorm, rain
Striking the mountain,

No light in the house, but a bottle
Of seadark wine,

Not yet the cold, not yet, and air to eat
Every night, popular air, a lonely supper,

Here we sit, love, listen,
Thumb in book, it is Balloon's, and believe

What floated past the window was Balloon's lasso,
His anchor was the lightning.

A Drive in the Country /
Henri Toulouse-Lautrec

Drawn out of the bones of light,
Definite figures, a few, ordinary.

As if in its bones the light had known them,
All: the horse, trotting away,
The yellow trap, and in their Sunday hats
Face to face, the man and the woman.

Properly, half a man and half a woman.
Come to that, only half a horse.
Locomotion, yet essential muscles
Are hidden in the picture; even the dog,

Athwart, running behind the yellow trap
Like the wind — not a leg in sight.

Gone any moment,
Beautiful creaking old trap drawn by half a horse.
No, not that. It is the way
A definite hat plume centers everything
On a still point in the sky.

Or the hatcrowns compose
One imaginary diagonal streaking off
Into the sky's oblong blue; and it is nice,
The way it slants against the lower
Green diagonal of the field's edge.

Not even that. The dog — great cool gush
Of the air across his nostrils. Not that:
Shot with rose, an undulation of shadow
Racing the trap, a feather's cusp,
Magnified, as dog, and sideleaping
Not from a hat but from the road.

Not so, not so; a presence, tacit,
Holds in place, for the eye to strike them,
Fugitive signs in their consortium: an egg!

Interior oval, its yolk,
A yellow trap, the crystal sun chariot —
Across the emerald cone, an egg, tilted,
That is what the figures make and are made of.

Parabola, it begins
At the tip of the horse's ears, it hugs
The hatcrowns, rounds the dog's tail,
Returns to base along the curve from wheel to hoof.

Even then, not so.
It never was an egg. If not, what else,
What else but the eye of Henri Toulouse-Lautrec:

And hiding it had spied
Upon itself, slicing itself
In half, had scooped up this other universe
Out of the escaping bloody mucus; now
The figures dwelling in it,

Healed, flawless, are the very nerve
That sees, and they retreat from you
Because of this,
When all the time it happens to be there.

CARMINALENIA

1

Anasphere: Le Torse Antique

kami naraba
yurara-sarara-to
ori-tamae!

I

Among the grains how small you were
Dry in the desert of your image

You did not hear the cries of love as you passed
Down the street, you did not see
The spittle
Fly nor the beads of blood on the axe blade

The naked masked woman
Twice she swung it & once more & high
By its long handle

II

Here we are travelling from place to place

Here I keep you hidden
Held by a great lightness
Body & voice if I could set you free

In my cage a castle rose to its turrets
Only for mice & a flock of ravens
Pure columns unbent by thought
Here they shall flower from our stillness
Voice their future dream
Of being trees

Plant them giving shade in a field
For five cows composing a sign for us
The diagonals of a dice
Or it is the pentagram—
Hidden in a bed the conversation of bodies.
Hidden I keep them

And still there is a voice
Whenever in sweet nakedness you nuzzle me
Voice I want you not only to say

A white cow is made of cream & fury

—Hathor

So your face took shape
It was in the boulders uphill before us
A movement of lines to the measure of a dance
A flashing of earth years Egyptian axes and eyes
No time at all in which it happens

One hundred thousand horses
Toppling off the crag were chopped into food
For the hands that peeled leaves of laurel
Out of the flint core
Now in a field of old rain goofily like a fortress
A red horse was planting his hooves
—Look how it is to stand there

Devastation
Marks no tracks of ours
Lightly now through these hidden places we shall walk
Where mouths collect & change to make expressions
Listen
A street with many twistings this one

Lightly you are here you had no weight whatever
Wearing your little cloak over so much nakedness
You leaned against me

III

1

Body of light
      Dwelling in a piss jet
Or particular cherry blossom

        Look, a spirit
Wanted something
     A sign, to be manifest
          In all directions

   Never
Sure, inhaling itself
         A whirlwind

2

       Desire, pressing
On silence
   To lure you, poem
One or two words

   Go
To the southern shore
       One flesh we pursue

3

     One, through Never—
A span, slightest across
        Perdition, horrible
   Deep, the gurgle

                    It is
Pepper behind my eyes, it fashions
            The eye of the hurricane
It fills
                    With snakes & stars
The liquid cathedral collapsing across
            Atolls, Florida keys

4

        World, great harp
Built of blood
                Now then
        What sounds in flight

What muscular forms of breath
        Never flow, leap
Up the torrent & restore

        To you
Your open tunes

5

        One flesh—
Other, another
                Horizon, ancient
        Unplaceable

Twitter your speech again
        Models
        Out of oblivion
The bud & the wave & the snowflake

6

        Your never is yes,
Out of nowhere the cry
                Gone & again
Cupola, welling, spiral, it lifts from

204

The bird throat

        Soon hushed

7

      But song, in
Some few broken
        Tombs

A touched sex

IV

Difficult
    Piecing the life together

       'like a supper in the wind'
How it comes, goes
         Exact from perception
Rhythm

        Not snatching
    It comes in waves
Not knowing me from you
  A spirit cannot be spoken
Or spoken of

Drums drumming the exact measure
Dancer to dancer the flower spray is passed

To build for you a space
    In this drain of being it is I
  Smash the heads & fix famine
A floor strewn with rock-orchid
         Lotus roof

In mid-air, air dangerous with heat
        Carbonic gas, beams of cassia
I have suspended
    A floorspread weighted down with white jades

Margins, like these
        Then at sun up to have leapt into
The blue fragrant living sea

Profit motive melts the poles
            Paris drowning, Bombay
Alexandria

I have hung strips of flesh at porch & gate
        The flesh of children

The time will not come again
                    It will not come again

Note: the epigraph, from the twelfth-century Japanese text *Ryojin Hissho,* means: 'If you are a god,/With a swing and a swish/Deign to come down.' See Arthur Waley, *The Nine Songs* (London 1955, p. 14), source for certain ancient Chinese shamanic motifs in sections III and IV.

2

Ginestra

What on earth makes it possible—
Over rocky slopes
Yellow explodes and replenishes itself,
With pulse on pulse an airy
Marine perfume floats and is
A robe of shivers around the mountain

It must be contained
In the chemical roots
Nothing explodes, the yellow simply
Unfolds; nothing,
Nevertheless, unfolds like this,
Metaphor and fact refuse to mix

And the plant hangs in such
Delicate balance the wonder is
Yellow shrank in us to a blazon
For jealousy. Here no
Body of self or doubt or fury bends desire,
Bolts a door or kicks it in

These great birds fly
Full stretch in their perfume,
Their talons fit the quartzy
Generous ground,
And in the slant

Light as night came, in sips
Of yellow pastis we drink them down,
Slow, all but
Rippling in the broom as in bamboo
One diligent Chinaman, long ago

In the Secret House

FOR ANN

Why lean over the fire, and who is this
Being
Vaguely human, who
Watches the steam float from wet boots
And regards the rose interiors

Various woods keep
Recomposing themselves; nothing holds
In the fire, the fire is always
Less than it was, the fire—

Expulsion
Of old smells, new intangible horizons
Does not hear through its decay,
Calling in the cold
Rain, the little owl, one note
Over and over

Nor, under its breath, does the fire give
A thought to the petrified
Print of a snail, its broken wheel—
Rays on a rock at the hearth's edge. Who
Is this, and who thinks

Through the fire, sees the rayed shell,
Solid axis, the whirling death
Of some incorrigible small thing
Before the ice came

Before the ice came carving out the mountain
And the fire took
Or took care of someone
And the house was constructed
In a cloud of goats, coming, going,
Before the cockerels

Put down their tracks, cry and claw,
Through generations, this fly
Settled on the breadloaf—

So stare, into the fire, and what for
The important
Citadel, towers of light, crepuscular
Tunnels, simply face
The black rain, blue wave
Of mountain birdsong

Mud on my hands, little owl, it is
No grief to share with you,
Little owl,
The one note, not lost, for nothing

Discourse on Legend

I hug to my breast
The green head of wheat
And I suckle it
    Forough Farrokhzad

Legend, you are the one, the who
The woman jumping out of the global box
The song the wave the blue in the veins
Which has no completion

Try as I may to decipher you
I find no text at all
When I riffle the book to find a rule
You escape, happily
Cleaning your teeth with a carrot;
Or a certain African king, for him
As you knot your hair and strip,
I hear you cough, ahem, in a vast
Green Sahara of hope and desire

Or you have cut the world's
Irascible droning
Throat and wallow, legend, you,
In the blood. You give yourself
To the hilt, yet
Every drop,
Your own undulant
Body drinks it back, freely the torrent
Returns, and you, legend,
Swing through the maze with never a blank
Drawn, from pulse to pulse. Speak

And you rip heads off
The cardboard
Categorizing men who try
To read you. Laugh

And you speak a song, I hear it
Far off as the wind
Sucks and guzzles
A single grain of sand and whips
The flesh of moons
Wicked habit tramples. Legend,

Do not be deceived
By the mechanical gesture,
Yours or any. Do not think
That you repeat yourself
To death.
You'll die more easily, with a croak
In a goatskin tent, in Italy a cough,
A flash of your laugh
May extinguish you
On a ship, but not this, not

You, anonymous,
Crosseyed
Kissing your knee, not
For fascination fingering your bush
All curled up in a madhouse.

But
But I could be wrong
I could be wrong, and when or where
It starts, the track of this
Incomprehension, I alone (this
I whom you
Provoked and
Must ignore) can ask. Of what? Ecoute,
O godforsaken oracle, écoute . . .

If it is in
A certain falsity, which bends all sense
When thought like twilight
Spirals up from its depth to meet
A promise of connection, legend, is it you

Multiplies and snarls the track,
Do all the flying
Jagged particles
Connect
By grafts drawn from the dark
Body of legend?

You, distinct, and
No other, but
Escaping
Autodestruct, so
Like a civilization bent on death
You might be a messenger, come
From the core of life with his tongue cut out,
Or a mirror
In the pure
Instant as it falls
To the stone floor, and

From the impact, shattering, has
Already arisen the wand of mimosa,
Yellow, without
Fracture, stillness in a room,
A melon is glad to be round like that,

Lips parting, listen, the first
Sound
Of a speech for an exchange
Of natures
Between things and people, a joy arises also
Giving this blue to the sea,
To the city its dawns and sacred statues

And in some, legend, among us
A spirit responds, not
So as to speak of it, with a longing
To be
Reborn.

Celeste

looks like them elementals just poured
a glass of blue champagne
and you look up
—silver fizz—
because your body
is
the stem

Caromb, Vaucluse

For the giant boy who plays
Alone
Pétanque in a yard

For the idiot girl
Who sings at the wrong time
Stone feet
Plunged in a dance of fish

For the white & yelping
Imbecile afloat
In the same old stream

Listen to the shriek
It is only the hirondelle

This rush of wings

Listen to the fly, it is not a fly
The buzz of weight
Is fattening a fig

Which you peel, as is right
They say
Never peel a peach
You need not fear

This blue tint on a vine leaf
The shivering part
Of sunrise

A Dark Line

Far off, a beach, the sea
Blue heat lives
In the sand, but far off
Real sea and she swims in it
The girl with Moroccan
Mysterious hair

Swims the long distances
A dark line traversing day discovers
Itself in her body
Swimming

Breath comes and goes
Body sheathed in cool salt
Separation and closure
Of the breasts as her arms
Have spread and again
She folds them

The long distances almost forever
Forgotten beach, the same talk
Over and over, swept toward
Unspeakable stars

By the arms and legs
By the breath going out and in
And out-
Spread on the sea floor far
Under her, far

An ancient ship
Crusts of shell and a coin or two
Beams half buried
Cargo of squid in figured jars
An old prow pulling
Once in a while
Like a curtain of moonlight
The depth aside

Night Blooming Cereus

The student has woolly hair
& a clear mind. He
is intent, he explains

the poem's genesis. In
certain terms,
a boot

being a boot, here
is deixis, there anaphora,
deleted

the entire predicate, glow
came to substitute
for green, & who

wrote it, someone? In a
hazel bush? Now suppose
you 'unexpress the expressible,'

these two parts
of speech, at random juxtaposed
make (something)

(new) having
begun with, or not, but what
was the link

it is jolly, a morning,
fog overnight devastated Austria,
clunk

of (pause) (deletion)
noun on (overmuch
consonance). Here the pen

scratches 'relation,' 'procedure,'
you have to feel it,
bones in the hand

remember a walk
uphill—battered cemetery—
the little one, lonely, a hand, the

notion of being
'fathered,' born, that is, first off,
then to find

a warm solid through the blur,
company ('helpless'),
so what is it

imagination, a
factory, grinding out, like
sentences, one by one,

ghost forms, they hover
back of each
(substitution) construct

we select, for instance,
filter & select
a basis, become competent

(variable, to be sure)
& identify
a scream, a star, this 'political'

system, that
vestige of a bird
in a woman. He did not,

someone, he did not
want it so, an
overwhelming otherness planted

'boundless space
in a square foot of
paper,' the work on words

begun, it was
a fragrance, dank, filling
the courtyard, then the laugh

a wind popped in his body
shells
of seed sounds, an alternative

universe is
composing itself in slow measure, not
as in Manhattan

walk, rapt, & listen
to the fire bells, repeat, fire
bells around the clock, but

these cups
of nameless flowers
had opened, once

only, white, a few hours
& heady
through the night, inside them

forty fifty filaments
drip
from tiny golden knobs pollen,

out it thrusts
from below that annual cupped mass
the pistil, a trumpet

split-mouthed, open, star,
avid this
reaches out, not a breath, all

insides, into the night,
& moistens
for something, something, promise

to the last drop. Now the moth,
fresh-hatched,
has to come to it.

Snail on the Doorstep

Snail on the doorstep
Is it rain or dusk
Plants giving off odour of sheep's fleece
So strong the curls cling
Wet between fingers

Snail on a doorstep far south
A radio knob you want to turn it
(Knees crack as you crouch to see it)
For news and think another catastrophe
News counts the decay
And substance of sacred things

Snail on the doorstep knees cracking
Light from nowhere
Point like a pyramid strikes the shell
Strikes the ultimate
Spiral centre

It is this expanse only an expanding
Centre of the spiral
The light stops where it started
But the snail on the doorstep
Uncoils in the light and blooms

The pyramid whispering expands
It follows the infinite curve of space
It ends where it started
If this were not a snail
There could be no universe

If this were not a snail
Another door would not let out
These children
They would not have crept
Under the mulberry on tiptoe
Fingers to their lips

All the snails would roll
Hightailing it away from them
Startled horns aswish to test
Cooler air
Not spirals like the sun

3

Miguel Unamuno

Spaniard
Call out
Over the centuries

Powerful angle

Skeletons roasting
The grip
Of what we said

Berlin / Wittenbergplatz

Something he said about a poem before getting into the 60
bus at Wittenbergplatz with five minutes to spare noticed the
iron frame with place names across it like rungs of a ladder
and could not see very well go closer they were the names of
places like Auschwitz Bergen-Belsen Buchenwald Theresien-
stadt in alphabetical order and off the square on a corner he
could see looking beyond the frame Sexpool a window and in
the window was a dummy woman wearing a black leather corse-
let chains and a steel studded collar and on her head jauntily a
military cap with several squat fir trees planted to commemorate the great undulant plains and forests where

Wax dummies were being pushed about in wooden carts like
this one coming up the street now it is perfectly true white and
thin and upright stiff

Without hair being pushed into a tailorshop I suppose a whole
bunch of them being liquidated cremated no he said they
were being pushed in a wooden evilaesthetic cart diagonally
across from the Sexpool Wittenbergplatz named after Luther

of course who was fanatical authoritarian and got everyone
spiritually standing to arms waiting for orders to be washed
down with big draughts of beer conformity was the thing after Luther saw what Münzer with his hungry peasants might
do so he called in the Gestapo actually most of them uptight
little barons wearing leather corselets and eyeglasses mad with
greed and shouting frightened mirrors of Luther himself with
his anal obsession like Wagner often painfully

Constipated needing purges in front of the Sexpool are two
trees quite large let's say lindens with shocks of foliage shaped
like breasts pointing upward in which case the Sexpool is the
head the squat firs pubic hair and the iron frame saying ORTE
DES SCHRECKENS would be the cyclopic twat that watches
over the system   If the poem got written I'd be surprised
you can't do much with too many loaded variables and it would
be inexact too he knew this when he thought it up or over sitting in the borrowed wicker chair by the open window not waiting for the Emperor's Message at all but listening to sparrows
in the courtyard and looking up at the green young chestnuts
the three soaring boles of acacia which are also berlinisch

Thinking also how many people in these rooms around the
courtyard I hardly know the archaeologist the doctor the
beauty parlour lady the apothecary the electropod plumber
the little Japanese wife and her baby and the lady of eighty giving private lessons in literature who does not mind when Jür-
gen Theobaldy upstairs switches on the rock music and Frau
Mortan too what a talker with her quadroon grand-daughter
growing up to be a thoughtful active happy person

The Right Note

A little bell tinkles
You hold it in two fingers

And change it
All at once it rings between the tips
Of your thumb and forefinger

220

That loop
Contains the whole force of hatred
Through the concertina sound you hold it
Inside the drums

The little brass bell from Senegal
Safe
The right note
Ringing in your fingers

Not the big mouth
A bell that boomed alarm
Across heathland. Not the bell
A body threshing in it, clapper
Of splintered bone

Here in a room, good, in a room, now
For a moment, anyone, can anyone
Hold it

A Small Bronze of Licinius I

His beard, clipped trim, looks like
A chin strap, but
Is broader, he meant it
To clamp for ever to his skull
The wreath of three spikes. Sixteen years
A small but stylish emperor—

This round eye gazed out, at home
Inside a circle
And the circle was made of letters
Telling the world his titles and his name.
Toga folds were clasped below
By a ring
Where neck joined shoulder

Ready to stab or sing
The spikes
An open beak with a tongue stuck out—

Not so the sportive
Actual profile, nose to nose
With the immediate, for flesh is total,
Power the rage, you bend
Every nerve on timing
Countertricks—Fortuna shifts
Her weight, another
Fist
Slugs flat the monstrous glory. When

When if ever did the true
Eye detect
The head of Constantine? Constantine
Pushed with his palm
Coins across the table, worn
Stockpiled silver, harvests of bronze
Mint as this one

And the troops of Constantine took
Such coins by the handful
And bit them, with Turkish yellow
Dog teeth hopefully
They bit them

Hearing Elgar Again

FOR D. M. M. AT 75

Not crocked exactly, but in a doze,
There I was, before supper time: Elgar,
Stop your meteoric noise, the glory
Leaves me cold; then it was
I woke to the melody—

Back, a place, 1939, and people
Singing, little me among them,
Fresh from a holiday
Summer, beside the Cornish sea, I sang
In chorus with a hundred English people.

You choose to live, as far as possible,
Spontaneously. So life is all
A wandering—curious orchestra, the whole
Sound of it accords with such
Invention of melody, song half-buried

By tympani, trombones, the glorious hot
Imperium. A life proceeds,
It is all, all of it, found in the instant:
Look, flowing, a friend shone, but wizards,
Drunken, forgot what I have to say

And underneath, in her garlic subway,
Busbied Persephone stands and waves
Her tambourine, a rabbit
Drums little feet on a village green, the snare
A moon halo strangling him.

Mother—we have gone on while others,
We remember, flew as ash into the sky.
To what? We have gone
On, dense trees, birdsong in cool petals
Never the ignored sustenance;

Rolling music is what deceives us, only
An appetite springs from the core,—
Melody, in a flash,
A harsh frog croaks in the creek now,
A bit of rain has touched my hand. Why?

The Palace of Thunder

(from *Calligrammes* 1918)

The outlet open on the trench in chalk
You see the opposite wall which looks like nougat
And the wet deserted corridor forking left and right
Where a shovel dies prostrate with a startled face
     two regulation eyes fixing it under the lockers
A rat retreats in a hurry as I advance in a hurry
And the trench runs off crowned with chalk
     and sprinkled with branches
Like a white hollow phantom putting a void wherever it goes

And aloft the roof is blue and quite covers the gaze
     enclosed by several straight lines
But this side of the outlet is the palace quite new
     although it seems to be ancient
The ceiling is built of railroad ties
Between them bits of chalk and tufts of pine needles
And from time to time chalk débris drops
     like bits of age
Beside the outlet closed by floppy cloth of the kind
     commonly used for packaging
There is a hole for a hearth and what burns there
     is like a fire in the soul
It whirls with such turbulence and clings fast to
     what it devours and is so fugitive

Taut wires everywhere serve as a frame to support planks
Also forming hooks and from them one suspends
     a thousand things
As from memory
Blue sacks blue caps blue scarves blue tunics
Pieces of sky tissues of purest memory
And sometimes in the air vague clouds of chalk
     are floating

On the plank are gleaming fuses detonators goldwashed
    jewels with enamelled heads
Black and white and red
Ropedancers awaiting their turn to move into the trajectories
An inconspicuous elegant ornament for this
    subterranean dwelling
Which six beds in a horseshoe embellish
Six beds covered with rich blue overcoats

On top of the palace a high chalk tumulus
And plaques of corrugated iron
Static river of this ideal domain
But dry for all that flows is the fire gushing
    out of melinite
The flower park of cartridge caps gushes out of
    sloping holes
Lots of bells with soft tones of glittering
    cartridge cases
Elegant and small pine trees of a Japanese landscape

Sometimes the palace is lit by a candle flame
    no bigger than a mouse
O tiny palace seen as through the wrong end of a telescope
Little palace where all is muted
Little palace where all is new nothing old
And where all is precious everyone clad like a king
In the corner a saddle mounted on a box
A daily paper drags along the ground

And yet in this new dwelling all seems old
So distinctly one is aware that the love of antiquity
A taste for junk
Must have come to men at the time of the caverns
Everything was so precious and new
Everything is so precious and new
That anything older or used there seems to be
            More precious by far
Than what is at hand
In this palace dug underground in the chalk so white
    and new

And two fresh cut steps
        Not two weeks old
Are so old and so used in this palace which seems antique
     but does not imitate antiquity
One sees whatever is more simple more new and
     whatever is
Nearest to antique beauty so-called
And anything heavy with ornament
Needs must age to have the beauty they call antique
Beauty which is the nobility the force ardor soul
     the abundance
Of what is new and useful
Above all if it is simple simple
As simple as the little palace of thunder

Setting the Breakfast Table

A cracked old cup or two
Will catch the sensitive
Blue

Bit of shadow as it shifts across
Woodgrain or tablecloth
—Provided

There is a table, and your guest
Not a fugitive. When
The girl appears, elbows up, repairing

Her braids, be sure all details give
Doubt the go-by. Her mind at rest
Perhaps will tell her

This one perhaps knows how to live—
Sun-up your double act, the world outside
For once in revolution. She'll really see

For joy the plazas
Leap out of their stone flesh,
And all the stupid statues, liquefied,

Compose the fragrance of some cyclamens
You've stuck into a wobbly vase,
Entwining

A lover's tact with mute intelligence
—This milk
Is fresh, this cold

Whiskey wild,
This knife
Shining.

Pollen

1

Sweet & bitter & unsolicited
The smell
Drifting up from inside my shirt
All of a sudden
Fresh cut pine log

2

Tug at the tangled string
I think
Therefore I draw this up

Steep roofs collecting snow
Perhaps Ratzeburg, the lake ice
Immense on a road
Broken back of a Holstein stallion

3

Alles kaputt. In 1946
Kartoffelschnapps. Loot:
A bellyful of turnip. Sludge caked
The Humber's axle when we clambered out
Hunting dynamos,
Parachutes, invisible nazis

4

Now southwestern daylight streams
Into an empty
Teacup, it has me
By the hairs, fresh cut log,
Pine log

5

Squadron Leader Butt blanketed in
Sheepskin
Barges through the door, with a shout
Scaring the guard shitless:
'I come from Vladivostock!'

6

Mexican buckeye forks
From stony ground, red flowers
Of the wild thyme
Nod across the interface, with bees,
They break nothing nohow

Tiny Butt I ask you
What are we to do with them
If we find the nazis

Now it's howdy

7

These winds
They bring you almost
Anywhere you never meant to go

The Prose of Walking Back to China

The poem began when I walked out,
Early, discovering forty minutes to go
Before the traffic would raise its roar.
It was nothing at all but the motion
Of walking, nothing at all
But the sight of a fish head in a heap
Of trash in a pail, a flower, an egg shell,
Until I began to compose it in my head.
And until
An amazed man with a beard scooped
Colour photos out of a cardboard box
Close to a wall, and a couple of doors away
A dog discovered a bone in a bin,
My skin thickened. A mouldy lemon
Took the first heat of day in the Rue Madame
As I turned to the left
And an old lady
Hosing the pavement said: 'Il faut
Arroser, hein?' with a laugh, and I
Actually found the words to say: 'La rosée même,
Madame, c'est vous.'
Was this the poem? Up Rue Vavin it went,
With shirts in a window, was
It this, the stacks of little magnetic cakes
In the patisserie where schoolgirls go,
And this, in La Rotonde, the waiter of
Two years ago not recognizing me?
The trash truck whines as it grinds
Rot to powder; the poem
Attacked by fleets of random objects

229

Had no purity or perspective whatever.
Ninety tomorrow Marc Chagall declares
You are nothing if you have
Materialist ideas. A capless man
Sponges down the glass walls of the bus shelter.
Again I scan the print, see: Nuclear reactors,
Negociations, a charge of treason,
Crucial support, failed to progress,
Emigrate to Israel, why do the words
Come in the plodding rhythm of the poem
If the poem isn't? Now the sun's heat
Goes up another notch, I gulp
The last of the coffee and trundle on,
Along the Boulevard Montparnasse,
Crisscrossing it
For a line of books, a cluster of lamps,
A Syrian store with distinctive
Waistcoats, coral and silver on display,
Suddenly arrive, walking the poem,
There where the chestnut trees in full leaf
Frame lawns punctuated by statues.
The sprinkler's long horizontal bar
Rotating flung the water up in a fan,
So that it fell
Far across the grass and over the wavering
Fronds (at least I thought
These were 'fronds'), it dripped from the beards
Of bronze lions topping the pedestal
Of an old lamp, this might be
A thing to watch, like the poem
You can't write, ever, this
Machine dispensed
Freshness, beginning
Everywhere it touched, for sparrows
And the grass at least. I
Sat in the sun which had risen
Above the long green wave
Of Indistinguishable Trees, in the dust
My boots were settling among
Delicate prints of the feet of birds,

A broken egg shell, also a naked
Razor blade. The blackbird
Is listening for a Worm, he
Can place it by a slight
Shift of his head, and I was listening
For the poem, but heard, placeable nowhere,
Pure low Bach notes on a flute,
The flute
Undulates, the dove's flight
Undulates, descending spray
Fans out like nervous wings from shoulder blades
And floats to earth as the flute again
Soars upward. A dog trotted across
The sunlit opposite street. A gnat
Glittered for an instant in mid-air.
From where I am the flute is clear,
I cross the grass to be closer, it has gone,
Almost, into the traffic's roar.
A woman in an open window says
'Yes, I hear it, sometimes, yes,
But I don't know, I live here, yes,
But really I don't know,' and on she went
With the ironing. Could she be
A scalded grandchild of one of those women
The musician took through a secret door
In Saint-Merry? Not for bewitching as
Her grandma had been? The flute
Plays on and on and I thought
Not the moon is seen but fingers pointing,
How could she ever tell me
What can't be matched by dharma?
Perspective makes a space intelligible,
But you only find the place to stand
By moving as you may, for luck, so nothing,
Nothing in the voice
Guides the poem but a wave
Continually broken,
And restored in a time to be perceived,
As the flute is perceived, at origin,
Before creation.

4

Old Kitsch Print

Something he cannot tell her,
The room emptied of light,
Almost and a distance, the shape
Of a halved fruit, swells between them.

A tree outside, gentle summer,
Edge of a cart, a horse buttock;
Elsewhere a wall glides through silver,
A chair makes no effort, simply
A wrestling of the lines, leg and back.

She wants it so. Her elbows beat
Grainy air that spills into the folds of her dress;
Her feet, defensive beaks, have trimmed
The intervening floorboards to a spike.

Radiance of the bodies, meaning battle.
His fingers, cupped, knuckle to eye, shore up
A hidden face, cannot now replicate
Animal indecision, the tiger, stripes
Shot into the wallpaper, behind her head.

Eight Elementary Inventions

1

Some kind of spirit
Being absent, one body
Is just another body

    But strip—
None more strange I ever saw
Nor one more lovely

2

Straight-limbed & tough-minded
Aphrodite of the Orange Socks

Dihedral eyes, colour of seashine
—Play for me
Space the colour of your veins

Golden dark thatch you are
Musician of Spanish Moss Croatian Milkmaid
Lay for me

3

In a freedom
A person.
I see you there, embrace you there, I
Did not put you there

4

Sometimes not one
The arc the wave the circle the swan

& your small left breast looking out
From the shelter of your arm

5

& a time we created
White
Midnight in a room
Lit by the black star

In a desert far
Stands a lion, claws, my love,
Grip the sand

Right before his nose
A quarter of an apple

Oddly the quarter apple is
Just as large & just as small
As the lion

Two pips for an eye in a fibre cocoon
Eye to eye the lion & the apple—
All this you see my love in time
As we leap through this black star

You with your wild hair over me
Swirling, me holding you
Night or day by the smoke
Colour of your eyes, your eyes

6

Now, now
I lean into your time

I have watched the sea
Many waves coming in small cry out
Slowly bring
The long one crests fly
Clean through us and we
Ride it

7

It is night
Where are we going
The wheels under us always
Try to say something

Shall we wake in a city on that shore
In one another's arms like this
Shall we walk out into sunlight
Saying it

8

What shall it come to, the hard
Imagined thing
What shall it be, the phantom

When they mix, how to account for them
A sand grain hot in the desert
The tenderness of your footfall

A music surpassing, a cold wind, like freedom,
Changing our shapes, death, and this, forgotten

Salami in Romanshorn

That salami in Romanshorn, so
good the taste of it, so
good,
a slice, the first, another, & the bread
white, not too much

donkey
gristle, nor smoke, a piece
of the best, a cut, she said, above
the human,
& set down the book, not

the greatest, right
there, opposite
the salami, so the book shall do some
eating too, no, I mean
be like it, kind of

admire the salami, maybe
read some. Where
was this? On the beach? Other stuff
going on
around the world? Lots, but shoot, if

anything mattered,
aside from
that salami &
the book, anything, sure why not,
she'd like to know of it

The Winter Poplars

seventeen
in a line, outside
your window, widen your eyes, but
still are shut, one by one, tight shut

ghosts
      upspring
            imagine
the first touch
of green, an alteration of smells, how it is
to wear a long leaf dress

what lightness
to grow from your good eyes
inward
a substance of bone & dream
                 out there
only what can be seen begins

but living is, & is, one of a kind,
faith, which makes
actual what should be there,
        felt on your pulse
the full tree, fluttering

it does the world
out of a death, for nothing then,
nothing can take hold of you

Or Else

As I went into the tabac to buy two boxes of matches, I happened to glance to my right. Or else, as I glanced to the right on going into the tabac to buy two boxes of matches, or else I had gone into a tabac to buy two boxes of matches, and glancing to the right I saw a small woman, not old, not young, perched on a chair, and she was eating what I took to be a tartine, or else the remnant of a tartine. She held the bread in both hands, like a squirrel, and her feet did not touch the floor. She was a very small person, and her face was round and white.

Then I asked for the matches, paid for them, and while turning to leave took a second look at the small woman. It was a small tabac, too, with only two or three tables and chairs lined up against the wall, and a mirror ran along the wall, reaching to the floor. The woman, perched on the chair, her feet not touching the floor, was half-turned toward the wall, she took a bite at her tartine, leaving behind a white streak of bread in her two clasped hands.

She sat turned away from the rest of the tabac. But she was so small that her round white face hardly appeared in the mirror. She ate like a trapped animal. She did not want to be seen. She did not want to see herself, yet, turning her face away from the space of the tabac, she almost had to be seeing herself, in the mirror, and also in the mirror the inescapable tabac space in which she felt conspicuous.

Or else: she was a very small woman with a round white face which nobody wanted to see, not even herself, but she had to be somewhere, in order to eat. Still, she was eating in such a way as to indicate that she wanted to live, hands clasping bread, even if living meant disappearing.

All around her, all around me, in that small space, the packets of cigarettes and the boxes of matches, the people walking in the street, on their way from the day's work, in their appropriate clothes, and the dogs going about their business, and the continuous roar of all the cars.

Or else: I cannot say all around us. No link. No common root, at best a rhizome, contrived by the other bodies and the noises, in their scatteredness, connected her particularity and mine, within a surface of observation more fleeting even than the last white shred of her tartine at which I saw her now sucking, not chewing, no, but sucking.

The question of her teeth had not yet arisen. Strong teeth, squirrel teeth, grow in straight jaws, but hers might be weak teeth, in such round jaws. She lacked the courage, or else the presumption, to use a good toothpaste, and this had been going on for years. Nor had she the means to visit a dentist. Or else she had once scraped and saved, had once made an appointment, but the dentist had sent her away the moment he saw her. A tartine has a strong crust. So many sacrifices, in such a life. The cheapest food, a tartine, with ham or jam, and a little butter. Even then, she had to eat the tartine in her particular way, by sucking, and in public, she had to turn her face aside and not look, she wanted to eat while being invisible, she had a passion of great force, dangerous, for the tartines of this tabac, and here the rhizome put forth another bud, because in her I saw another being who had to aim, straight-on, for the impossible.

Or else: I went into the tabac after spending an afternoon with a young woman, small and beautiful, with a laugh like the silver trickle of starlight seen in the water of a well. We had walked across bridges and along corridors, we had exchanged sweat from the palms of our hands, we had sat beside one another with mirrors behind us, gazing out into the world, or gazing at each other, in the envious ancient way of Assyrians, but who, now, among the ancient Assyrians would care to wonder about the small woman with the round white face, or who else, one century or two from now, in Paris, would want to know that she existed?

She might never have been touched. I saw her short legs, white and lumpy, because, the way she sat, twisting away from the world, her skirt was hitched up to her knees. Nobody had ever wanted to stroke them. With her weak teeth she had never bitten anybody. With her small and frightened mouth she had never sucked anybody. Or else nobody living one century or two from now, no ancient Assyrian either, would, unless I am mistaken, want or have wanted to be bitten, or else sucked, by the small woman with the round white face and the unstroked legs.

She was not a tiny soldier in the battle against chance, so by chance she had to be a nullity. When she looked in a mirror and saw herself, she might have found it hard to believe that this was all she was: not even worth a glance, but worse—a pretext for averting every glance. Round, small, white zero, with a circumference nobody would dream of stroking into place, thus not even, really, a zero. The continuous roar of traffic. The dogs going about their business. Perched on the chair, a blob of absolute anxiety. Blob—and there they go, the beautiful ancient Assyrians, and others, who can be seen, who think it is they who happen, not chance, who receive existence from a knowledge that they are to be seen; and there they go, the dogs, capering and sniffing, a blob in their track is a small woman with a round white face and wet-looking hair which nobody wants to comb or pat; a blob sucking a tartine in a tabac and looking aside, or else down, she wants only not to be there where everyone else happens to be going.

Or else I am mistaken, entirely mistaken, and what I see is a large and very beautiful flea. A star among the fleas. And the dogs, in holy terror, worship her? From flea to angel, the spectrum of perception bends and cracks under the buffetings of chance, as, in a changed perspective, a world of different objects comes into position. Lens-grinding Spinoza says to the small woman (she does not hear, and I may not have heard correctly): 'Every being which is made conscious of its interior power comes to persevere the more insistently in its particular nature.'

Never once did anything occur to the small woman such as might have shown her that plenitude of interior power. She perseveres because she has been doomed to do so, by the dogs in the street, or else like them, by the space of the tabac, by the mirror which has finally annulled even her capacity to despair of herself. Or else: A chair in a small tabac, her twisted body insisting on it, is this a likely perch for the Celestial Globe-Hopper, the Pure Flea Spirit? Passing from Spinoza's triangle to the cube, I put one box of matches in my coat pocket, the other in my trouser pocket, and could not say whether or not I was mistaken. Or else I had ground this lens not cruelly enough, for I felt mounting in my throat a galaxy of tears; or else I was grinding into the lens not this indelible presence but my own shadow, nicotine, idiotic.

Velocity

Flat on your back sometimes in the long
Summer grass
Thoughts come thick, eyes close,
Eventually images

Of this or that, far off, in, high
Liquid outline, then
Mouth, it rose to you, hers, pulling, still
Dear tongue, is it
Licking

Through the dark, a door panel
Bends, flash of a
Rifle butt, pig's head
Grins on a slab, and sand, sand is it
Trickles under your little footsole

You sit up fast, sweat
Flows, the field of rye
Just over there, has it gone wrong, become
Absolute distance,
So blue

How to Listen to Birds

Put no trust in loud sounds
Learn from the crystal
Ladderings of music

To listen: bodily. Slip
Through the rifts which model
Their notes. A moment, one, day
Or night, may be a more favoured
Time

For penetration: one tiny spool
Of the unseen
Unrolls from a chirrup. Feel

Feel again its formal flute alarm,
The wave creation—
A dancing woman's hair, it floats
Across your face—

A note or two, at last,
Concentrates the practised world
Into some new thing

Wake, otherwise, attentive
To such a call, you might
Inhale the first perfume on earth,

Touch the ghost,
Voluminous, of a howl tight coiled
In the plain tune,

Or find no way of your own
To speak
Belief, at a variance so fine
It modifies the whole

Machine of being: this
Is not unpolitical

The World First

Emptiness, the emptiness in you
Fill it, fill it with, I don't know,
Something, not with toys, not with

Mythologies, fill it
With something, no, you can't, with solid
Villages, or seas, bottle corks, desire,

Inconspicuous bent nails, almost anything,
Fury of enemies, whatever grips
Fill the emptiness for fear

Fill it for never ending
Fill the emptiness or it will tear off heads,
The heads you love, watch them, down the drain

Float like yours, the heads,
Howl and tumble, torn off, not much
Not much to hold on to

Fill the emptiness, facing it, raw grief
Now and really surrounds your face,
Fill it with that, if you can, the world first

And do not dwell on it, laborious, only,
Shapeless hole, seize it, can you,
Scattered curse, you can't blot it out

But clear figures, more than imagine
Other worlds, they spin with other feeling, fill it
Fill it with them, you can't, trackless

No map, impenetrable, specific, you
Can't, but make them dance it out, different,
Muscular and trim, repeat it over and over

Only to yourself, can you now, the emptiness,
Know it inside out, always there,
The great sucking emptiness you keep

Replenishing with towns, the birds, a river,
Roofs of old tiles red and wet with dawn,
You can't, it is always there, control

Impermanent in the timed flight of words
And with your interior animals refresh it,
In first light they do face one another, free

Not spellbound, not,
By the gaze of any remote Upholder,
When for them you invent an open deep indwelling,

Can you, and a secret air, for there you plant
Under the clocks and mouths, under the drums
No foundation without fault, emptiness

Not like this, a turning around, but to be made
Into the holy field of apple trees
If death itself be no more strange or final

History of Not Quite Everything

Slamming of a car door outside
Is it you
A burst of music like sea waves human feelings
Turn over and over
Is it you the silvery heat of thigh to thigh

Because my jaloppy was radioactive
They took me to the nut house for testing
The hooded lunatics happy as sandboys
Did their dance in a ring

Was it you
Beside me the air with your shape in it
Rustling was it you Hungarian girl with twelve grenades
Went under the tank and blew it to pieces

Between our bodies nothing but the moon stood
Nothing was ever wasted
There was time enough twelve years but was it you
Before I died under a tree we had fallen asleep
Was it you woke up and screamed for a hundred years

And forgotten words who spoke them
Head of a halibut who cut it off
A driftwood stick in sand
Who rammed it into the fish throat from under

Or the provision of justice under law
Is it you
Drenched in blood these were hungry babies
Old men froze by the roadside
Is it you very gentle fingers on the long march

Is it you very gentle fingers
Silent void
The voice
I must go on answering for ever

Lens

The book, blue
Small but thick

Glass ashtray
And the candlestick

A woman's face
On the matchbox

She wears a bonnet
Cypress tree, the tilt

Of a roof and a pink
Mountain peak beyond

Link vaguely
Smile of her mouth

To the curving porcelain
Shallow bowl

Of the candlestick
A swoop and the ashtray

Echoes with clefts to fit
A burning cigarette

As the bowl sits in the brass
Grip of a spindly base

Motions in the depth
Of unastonished stars

Hold such wanderings
Surface to surface

History of Nothing

A commonplace
It extends
Under us
Mistily obscured place

Clouds puff out of it
And great blue tears

Its wedge is driven down
Deep
It hurts

Always these globes
Float upward out of it

We fish in it
For decisions
And go hungry

The lines catch on rotten
Old bicycles

Clouds
And great blue tears

Ibeji

African figurine on a desk
This morning,
Polished with lemon oil, hoists
More high his furrowed hairdo,
Deepens his frown

Abstraction pulls from him a living
Crystal shape, distinct
From books he blinks at; dark wood
Sprang from a tuck in time, but lord
What loops one lives in—

Day's action crushes
The mulberry, then drink at seven,
With one kick bourbon the flamingo
Restores to its native
Air the toothless pink soul

Funny for once it looks, the pit
Of delusion. You wonder at
The skill: what intuition gouged
Three angled dents in his forehead, silver,
Even the tilt of this mouth

Cheek scars plummet to the corners
To force a smile. A nail gores
One eyeball. A sneeze
Might anytime explode. The belly
A column of root—it has returned

His ancient feel for trees
To the whittled beast, worm-eaten
Man. And it is good
When the door creaks open, to find him in
Still, only him.

A Very Small Hotel Room in the Key of T

Of a saying which
Came to nought
The gist   débris: une tonnerre totale

And after it
A sparrow on a parapet
Gingerly twittered

Room the pink of a strawberry wet
Ice-cream; cube; not even
The shape of a letter, and why today
Rack my wits
For its format

Too little for talk let alone a feast
A shaft   cracked walls peeling
Sole prospect   Siste
Viator   soliloquit (shall I?) All

The single people been
Such
Different bottoms put this
Precipitous dip in the strict

Vermilion bed. Might
One have thought
The sparrow   astonished
Still to exist?

Or did another ask
Is it all right? This bloody
Faint

Life, never yet
Quite what
I wanted?

How to Watch Birds

1

Nothing to it. Live your way
Into the magnitudes of
Their bodies. Breathe your way
Into their disappearing

Flight. Be
Silent, go with them, strip off
Opaque muscle, breakable
Bone. Unframe

Your speech, be tree, air, without
Winking fly
Clean through your eyeballs. Or slit-eyed
Glancing sideways

Catch them on the hop. Soon
Sleep with them, a branch
Will shape your claws,
Grip it.

2

Difference—touching it
You see solid life
'A hair's breadth aside from habit'

Said Thoreau: Snow, a blank, then
Redpolls flock
And ripen, 'glowing creatures,' through
The birch seeds they feed on
Significant

Hexagons glittered, secret
In a winter, the whole
Particular rainbow.

3

No signs but the sharpest.

Feather fabric, a certain call, a tuft
To make their difference legible
Cling to a limit, hardly more
Visible than your own. Action

Defines them, that's the thing: housed
In a time, stuck
In a slew of pointlessness, the right words yet—
Bib and hood, squawk, dorsal—
Reveal a gist,

No less, of non-possession. It is
Their maker's Have-Not. Never quite
The proverbial freedom, but
A giving.

Perhaps it is,
Transparent in
A warm pocket,
Gray or crimson, perching or
Propelled, of
Messages a universe.

So

All in all
You do not listen
If your voice
Had been speaking

As it climbed
So seldom so
Seldom up
And up its own
Sounds

Rung by rung as if
To an island
In the sky

Where nothing is
But in the centre
A well

Deep
Contained
Calm

Wild Horse

As a more or less literate person
Who writes down things that have
Some connection with the English language

What should I do with a wild horse
Suddenly presenting itself to my thoughts
In Berlin this winter morning

Under no circumstances would I write
About a wild horse in a manner approaching
That of the savage Mr Ted Hughes

I cannot recall that I have ever
Seen a wild horse in the flesh
Perhaps in films but I have not smelled one

Not once not even from afar I have not
Watched a wild horse glow in moonlight
I have never touched one who has?

I do not live in Marlboro Country
I have no spurs no saddle no skill
I cannot even ride a tame horse but this one

This wild horse has given me a shake
Bucking inside me   One moment it is
Chestnut brown like a cello

The next black as Pelikan ink
And white the next like nothing
On earth   Pitiful comparisons

The thing is all muscle and fury
It is controlled as a star is said to be
By certain magnetic conditions

The thing is abrupt   It hears
Who knows what and is off like the wind
In pursuit or going just anywhere

It stops to drink from a pool
Hoofing it over a hill   cropping
Prairie grass   Impulse grips it

This horse but in that grip it is free
Knowing in its bones a radiance
Which I ride like a speck of dust

Bareback   Can the reason be this belt
I bought from a junkstore north of La Grange
Texas?   Its oval buckle with a horse

Embossed on it was first prize once for riding
Bareback in a rodeo   Influences must have
Penetrated my guts gone to my head

Or does it just come at a gallop
This wild horse because a few friends
And loves these past months have

Irradiated my body with something keen
Intrinsic to the universe a power
I would not dream of questioning

Or putting a name to   Don't look down
Or behind   Fly in the fury of the horse
With wild love   They'll drag you off

Soon enough ordinary humdrum things
Is what I tell myself feeling it
And I'm up there all right this very moment

Thinking of you Ann Alberto Caroline
And you Tsëpë Rumanian clown my friend
And someone else I'll put no name to

I'm up there all right the world's force
Hits me bends back my spine but hell
Head up I'm going through the crosswinds

Clean with the perfume of Saint Elizabeth's Weed
Or what is it called over the hills and down
Uhlandstrasse   If this is a lion I say hallo

Raccoons fling me nuts which I catch
Reaching a hand up as I pass beneath
Cheerful pecans the looped vines the sweet

Sophora   Sun shines all day   Is this
An exaggeration? Probably it is
But this wild horse under me knows best

How to crash through hope the barrier
Shielding the helpless
And how best to help this blaze the universe

Propel itself by subtle shifts
And twistings of the shoulderblades
Onwards   Deep orange canyons then scrub

Flats tender tamarisk cactus towers whizz
Drumming   Its hooves are my heartbeats
Mine its flying sweat silken tail floats out

Into spaces which contract behind us
Bleeding shadows across the kicked dust
At moonrise   To the tinkle of waters

We listen listen the great crag blossoms
Indigo with a hundred faces cut by the ray
From horn and cleft   We watch watch

He appears the magician with his finger
Beckoning the sharp interior form unfolds
Across rock mass   Profile gaze upstream

To where the waters
We now stoop to drink
Have come from

5

Razzmatazz

δενδρέων δὲ νομὸν Διόνυσος πολυγαθὴς αὐξάνοι,
ἁγνὸν φέγγος ὀπώρας.
    Pindar, fr. 153 (125)

1

This
Very erect real tree
Sticks in my flesh
And follows it

Through
An eye-swivel
It has grown

A loss of contact
Cement
Wall a sudden house
Blurs

Beyond, perplexing—
All that meat, those lamps—

A heave of twenty branches
Now it shakes off the salt
Rough juice we enjoyed
Again the hole
The hole we pierced

(All heart, or is it)
Fills with a round
Of retreating fictions

254

2

       O the bleeding hole
Tom in the flesh
            Heart, the hungry people
Beaten down by the winds
   Bayonets, rifle butts

No figure can fill it
      No fiction has healed it
   Do you see them always

The broken souls for whom nobody speaks
And the great birds flying onward

Over the sands that choke
Over the streets that are pitiless

3

Petals of the sunflower, flames
Lick around
The hole's apparent limit:
A ring of air

Hugs the shivering shapes
Of heat. At noon
Beef starts to sizzle, a calf,
Elsewhere, opens his throat
For a bellow:

Soon the enormous whispering
Forest of fictions
Will assemble to eat:

Afterward, what a collapse: crumple
Sufficient words
Crawl back into your oblong
Nightmare meanings—

No, not so fast:
Inconspicuous
The picked ribs in a bucket
Still make sense, mean business

For our friend Flick Digit
The Flying Guitar

4

Do not lose track. These
Are exercises. Sleepwalking
I make a pattern, see what comes into it
A finger pattern for the smell
Of tree bark, an eye pattern to involve
A taste of gaps

. . . . distance, without focus or history,
I was groping in it
To remake a rainbow. Like that. Impossible
Now listen

What did they have to say
The bloodspeckled messengers always arriving
Why do they have to die
Messengers who also called the sun silk and yellow
And died gasping 'You don't have time'

In my pattern I wanted
Figures to point without mystification
At themselves, the messengers, on horses half-wild—

Because I am starving, all I can bite on
Are the gasps of messengers as they hit the dust
And I drink the negative stain fast spreading
All over Europe. I wanted

Not the rubber stamping
Punitive bureaucracy of words. The words
Ready in the mouth, what were they to do

On clear skins what act was traced
Simply what were the times they witnessed
What sounded through their veins
In a rhythm of perceiving, before they were told
'Take a chance, ride like fury—
One message is false'

5

What matters is not, I suppose
The hole a figure makes
With tree or sunflower
Through this contracting universe

But the
Hurt: wall, final, unfocussed
You can't push it back, nothing
Can't get me out of here

The human
Round: Who'll build a fruit trap? So many
Wasted works of love—libido's rebound—
Everyone encircling someone,
No air: what was it, space in the veins
Their colour: a joy
To breathe and let breathe

Space—
             Weltinnenraum
                          The flying duck
And lions advise me, also Caroline
In her letter:

             On dit qu'en Chine
People have begun to eat one another
Adding:—Paris, all that remains
Is
Remains—
             Of mountain? A rubbish
Pickup *stiften die Dichter?*
Old mountain circle hold up still
The sky's lid, higher

6

No go, that one, can't say
It as it is: the terrible shriek

Of escaping fruits, the numb
Forms, cannibal machines of time

Walking afterward
I was in the tracks we had created
In and out of places where we had stopped

Muse, help me to say what I mean
And this to survive

I entered spaces you had left,
Fitting my body into your hollows
I felt for your hands, your hair

—And me to survive, Muse, I'll need
Every scrap of the folly you've got

It was wild a weeping and a dancing

What is there to catch
But absence, a kind of
Being friends with it. In love's midst
Everything scatters, like birds
At gunpoint

7

        Quickly they age, the new spaces

          It was, there, the sleep
Mountain, planted with trees like bells
              Behind the house you saw
Expanding a plateau, in slant light
          Bear and elk and lion

Tall with legs the giraffe walked
As if a cloud cushioned its breastbone
And like hope or snowflakes
Five ibis swoop down crossing the blue
Screen of trees

Remote.
From the dust I pick myself up, a few
Specks of it
Come loose under a fingernail.
Again I scratch my head, this meat,
Feel.
How much can hurt in one lifespan

8

The tentative
Figures
Will not
Bind up the wound. They are part
Of the great heave, over and over inflicting it
The splitting of this mind
At that moment when flesh took:
Over and over the spasm
Repeating itself, birth
Foredoomed:
It is man, it is woman

9

I fish this wound out of time you give me your dream
Siberian midgets backflipping all over the tundra
I give you the wound
You give me a honey cake for my birthday
I give you the wound

You get up and dance when the moon shines in
I teach you the very quick step of the goldfinch
I give you a kiss I give you a wound

You give me a kick and I catch your foot
We twirl to this rhythm you beat out on my back
I give you the wound but whenever it hurts it is there
Where you are not

You give me a little breast I taste you
You taste of mango and Je reviens what a runaround
You give me all it takes I give it back in kind
I give you the first snow a slice of tropical ocean
A grief it was always there I give you the wound

Which suddenly with your fingers you rip open
I scream don't but it is there
The great laugh popping in the wound's root

It comes at us with white teeth
The great laugh shining all over it is truth
I give you wine flute music a flying guitar
Why do you tell me trombones have bald heads
Why do you tell me ghosts smell of egg
I give you the go-by
And if you want it take it, I love you
But what is your name and what name now is mine

I give you, no, this you can only give to yourself
It is a home-made contraption
It fits in nowhere
It is a fruit trap made of air and you

It is made of the wound with the laugh coming out of it
Now mind and flesh join in the song
A whole orchestra ascending
It plays for the fireflies it plays in the wound

You give me a tiny old conversation
It is a little girl in red lace pantaloons
I give you a glass photo of freedom

What I cannot give you call it what you will
By small names for it is passionate and without fear
When it goes out there to do it look it escapes
Because it is so passionate
It might multiply the infliction of wounds

It is not often at home among human concerns
It is not really at home on earth at all
Not in the Guadalupe Mountains not in New Orleans
Not in Calcutta not in South Dakota where is it

Where it is
Happens between, happens between names
When I call you by yours feel it
Call me by mine believe me back I shall come

TWO HORSE WAGON GOING BY

"A wagon went by. Two horses were in front of it, and on its high seat was a man with his hat on sideways and a woman with a big fascinator hiding her face. There was seven children in the wagon — two with sleeps upon them and a little girl with a tam-o'-shanter and a frown and a cape on her. I have thinks from the looks on their faces they all did have wants to get soon to where they were going to."

Opal Whiteley, *The Story of Opal* (1920)

Silent Rooms in Several Places

1

Old Water Jar

Like one of the old ideas
It won't hold water any more
But it is round in the belly
And has strong bladed
Shoulders like a good woman
Elegant even the curves
Run down from the mouth
In a long sweet wave
You can't help liking it so
Simply for the way
It stands there

Suddenly Remembering You Still, Cecile

No such owl
Might exist, who said I saw it,
Silhouetted against
A tangle of
Chimney pots and starlit

Down it swoops, the wings
Curve like shark fins up from its
Ocean
Blue body, for, having never
Flown so far

Out of sight, it clove
Through towers of whispering thistle,
Midnight potato garden,
Sensed a military
Silver button

To be pelts of mice, but
Has revived, peat
Vapour bubbled from the throat
Of an ancient whisky jar,
And now has heard them,

Now it hears them,
Lips,
Wrinkled lips of an old woman,
Insomniac, beautiful
Still, breathing

Jacob's Hat

The great boled oaks lift up their limbs
To paint the air

But Jacob's water bottle and his cloak
Are heaped beneath his hat

And the sheep and the shepherd on horseback
Have somewhere else to go

Is it not curious, Jacob's hat?
The crown is tall, of straw, the broad brim

Crumpled like the edge of a mushroom
No, the top lip of a madman

Take your eye off it if you can
To watch Jacob's knee

Ram the groin of the angel or gather
The muscle tension

Making a shadowy ocean of
The flesh on his back

You do not hear the sheep bleat
Or the river ripple

You do not choke on the dust kicked up
By the shepherd's horse

You might not even notice the painting oaks
Or the spear laid across

Jacob's bundle of belongings, or the sword
Dropped in its sheath

Only the hat absorbs the shock of attention
An old straw hat

For all the world like a skull fungus
Doffed evidently by Jacob

Who took time enough to put in order
His precious few belongings

And with his well worn hat crown the heap
Before he sprang at the angel

Shih-Ch'u's Magic Letter

On Footpath Mountain
Once I stayed as a guest;
Poems, brush, even now
Mountain colour drenches them.
Thirty years you've been there;
They fondle bones of rock,
Unfancy words of yours, I think.

Steam of cloud and water rises
Here, at Hsi-ch'eng.
Midges flit, intrepid, each
Quick as a painted hawk.
Your Buddhist cell, so help me,
I envy it, your snow cold —
In long glowing lamps
Motionless orchid oil.

I have arrived, look now,
Friends on the mountain know it;
What sort of a state I'm in,
All run over to see:
Calumniated as I am,
Worse off by far than others,
I have two eyes intact,
Can still write tiny characters.

Iphigenia Ingénue

Whole streets of new trees now she'll suppose
Carry themselves so lightly; dogwood —
Radiant branches
Lift no stranger fruit than waxy
Pink petals

Entirely opening their bodies to the light
Slow substances have ringed the earth
For any plum to splash
A burning white up. Those violet fleets compose
A sky, their cool discrepant
Fragrance melts
Boneheaded categories

What is this secret haunts the earth
To curb oppression? It is hers: kept
Dark in her silver box —
A flower, crisp, and a carnelian moon,
Two feathers touching brush her cares away

Also an involved sea shell she keeps
In her silver box, at least
So she says, but
That's about all — my voice
Escapes for singing and my eyes you said
Go misty when you say a thing to excite me, sad
Or happy

In Anatolia

Slit eye, so young, in your place,
I mean no harm, but see you
And am close, in this light, so
Close. Food, knives, a red floor peak
And are gone in your flesh glow. The curve
Of a bird comes back to me.

Yes, it was big, as birds go. Blue wings,
A throat, I think, rain-rose, and a crest.
All at once it flew out of no place.
It perched on a plinth of white stone
To flute the one song it knew.

Noon: heat in this old town spent
Long breaths on rock. Wells dry. A few
Cubes of shade. Candid weeds made sure
The song could last. Pure notes
Go well with dust; in the doom of that high place
Time showed its drift.

On that plinth it put down claws, a bird,
Spikes — it told the air
What it meant: *io dio,* it sang. *Io dio.*
You will not say it. Your hair is
Coiffed to fall, soft, across your face,
As if your face should not be shown here —

A wing, gloss, when
You shake your head like that you hide
Most, at least, of your face. Wax
Boys, they sit, one by one, dumb, with hands
They fold and twist, here, at this feast:
You do not foot their bill.

Rich you might be, or
Not, but are you here? Your place seems
Close to oak boards, wild rice, raw fish.
That blue bird, you are with it.
Still you have ways to resist
Dead mouths, our small norms, blood that froze,

So much heart ache. Why, white stones
Once were grooved, to hold up roofs. White
Stone, fierce hands hewed it
Into forms. Through the fresh
Stone robes a god flew, those days, a pulse
It was thought. Worse off by far,
We have none or put ours in the wrong place.

Stand there and speak. Tell
Why no springs flow there. Why no folks walk
The old streets. Did the no-good bird
Eat the gods up? Let your wing fall
To hide your face. We do not know
What now to fear most.

Pink Slippers

Pink slippers —
The voices
Return, the voices
From Antioch, Agrigentum, wherever
Return, clear

Splitting apart
The bottled, rotten
Remnant we
Dwell in, with a swish
Of clothes falling

From limbs radiant
The voices
Return. She stood
And shook
Off everything, stood

In the silver light
A moment,
In a forest, in
A city, ancient lamps
Marble paving —

And the pink
Slippers? Later they
Crossed
A road, other feet
Than hers in them,

But to death
He loved them. Pink
And voices, distinctly
They spoke, delivering the drift
Of old stories —

Wickedly
The swish, the dark
And silver joy, the arms
Holding, the perfect
Fit, immediate

22.XI.84 In Memory of Julius Bissier

FOR JOHN ASH

A happy skill, when first light strikes
Home on the peak —

Snowy, the light, a moment
Only, it came with horse hair,

A pernambuco bow.
Counting out the practice

Years it took, now a breath
So singular, off it floats

Parting branches, for a glimpse
Of heaven in the air

Another Village

— Atmosphere
Wrong: past noon a sunlight
Denser than flesh, across
A bowl of red

Berries women at the
Marbletop
Table
Softly talking —

And the wild, fingery
Garlic flanks
The ravine, apricots
Quicken to be bitten —

Old bell, one chime
Remote — wind down deeper
Ruffling vine leaves;
Muscular,

Gorged with heat
A pine cone prepares
To open, crack, the poplar
Shivering — bluer, there

And now a mountain
Lifts, the idiot
Framing a theme can
Sit up and write about it

Exercise for a Singer

1

     Certain songs —
Forests of light —
Belong to gods. Others propose
A shape of knowing. These retain
What comes from them.

2

     Yours, the songs
You make your own, are framed
Likewise: by fictions.
             Heavenbent
You quarry from the earth a curling sign
For joy, for despair,
With luck, a home.

3

You are
A cave. First a mouth. Then
A throat. Shallow breath in it. Not
So fast. Breathe deeper, roll
The hollow around.

                    It is filling
Your nostrils now, yours. Blow out the random
Unwanted air. The cave begins
To glisten. Silver snow,
                    Folds of fire, it is
Luminous, heart,
Now lungs, the cave is belly, sex, contract
Muscle to feel it.

4

                    The cave, a rose, in
Or out of you, is opening, large.

Larger still, like time before,
Time after you. No song in that time.

Only a sign, hollow, your body, universe:
A big clay pot in the making, on a wheel.

The wheel, you make it spin. The wheel
Darkness. Of earth now
No thought, no china
Crashing to the floor, no canopy
For heaven. Signs.

The cave is enormous with breathing.
See this bird come to live in it.

5

A bird, many coloured. Plumage
Glows in a perfume
You dash on air, fling through dark
Like a wave with its rainbow. Thumb pressed
On a latch, you pushed an old gate open:

6

Summer garden, flowers, many
Names near-forgotten. The bird is chamairis,
Wild strawberry, quadlin, in leaf
A white thorn, dammasin, quince;
Germander, the bird, bear's foot,
Monk's hood and water mint

The bird, it is musk rose, later in August
Melocotones, also musk melon,
But unattached
Always it dwells, the bird, in the fountain form
Shaping the cave. Walkways, galleries
Harbour its orderly manifold in a shimmer.

7

At home in the hollows, feel
The bird's delicate bone cathedral around you:
Flute bones,
Breast and shoulder bones, legbones
Tunnelled — conch, trumpet,
Hummingbird feather: passages,
In them the air is you. All of you
Rushing through feathery hollow silence.

8

When the bird flies out, at dusk, be ready.
Nothing tense, no
Effort. Spread (and hang there, lightly
From your eyebrows) finger and toe. Likely as not

The closeness of
Everything will stun the bird —
If it flew. Now, now
Or never, with one breath disperse
Clustered faces
To the boundaries of your universal hollow. Four
Walls cannot object, nor anxious
Roofs, abolished clouds.

9

Now fresh clouds and stars are in their places.
Demons, too, you put them in their places.

These
Bodies all compose a ring, singular
Each, with longing, each remote.

10

        Never or now
A song pretends to sing. You
Take your time. You made the space for it
To be given. Still it is little,
It is calling. It needs to be invented. Now
You take it up. You sing.

Pleasure of a Consonance

At Issy-L'Evêque distinctly
Nesting in pine crests
Chimneypots and pointy turrets
Of a rose château

The Shape

Funny, you keep it to yourself. Not quite:
Scraps of the story escape, take on
A runaway life of their own. Funny
It has to hurt so, hurt so, still.
Draw breath, deep, breathe again, if you can.

Waking in a blinded room, improvising a vision
For her: dawn breaks over a brigantine,
From Patras to Palermo. Listen to the sea.
Mystery Greeks, bottles of ouzo, scent of pine.
This wheeze (it has to be) of an accordion.

Or worshipping one curl, all of a piece with her.
Had anyone noticed it? No, nobody before.
One touch and the cusp unfurls to cling
Close to an ear. It had to mean no less than love,
Perfect in sunlight, more than one half-afternoon.

Now it's nothing, nothing at all, she says.
Drunk as owls the sailors dropped asleep.
What is that faint plume on the horizon,
Not even marking the repeatable sea?
The curl persists, another where the lips

Of her sex meet. But she took off, that was it.
Forest thickens, torn you roll in it alone.
The room, sunken, waits for an oak to grow,
Fresh planks, to house again the shape
That shelters what escapes for it is certain.

Relic

Powdered wood from a beam
And plaster from the ceiling
Sift into dunes among the random
Worm-holes peppering my desk.

Overhead the flying machines
Buzz, on their occasions. I admire
The hood worn by the lime tree;
Scent of its flowers, I breathe it in.

They cluster in threes or fours, like bells;
Bees in the hood and scarabs hum;
The bird with a black mask stops to listen,
Spidery claw on a flagstone.

I am wondering at the fluency of its lines,
And how the tail flits, when all at once,
At the top of the winding stair,
You stand in a torrent of light,

Dressed in silver linen, as you wave,
Hatless, ready to go, your sleeve
Uncaptured, a spray of flower bells
Tilting across the tassel of your parasol.

2

Rilke's Feet

1

Heart bowels hand head and O the breast
So many of the parts fan out
Pressing on speech
Each a shape distinct
At length delivered a message
Classified sensitive

2

Perched in my tree as the light
Tries to unfold over Wilmersdorf

Rilke's feet a phrase
Ran amok in the mass below —

But in the grass
Not a trace left — playing

Woodland god he walked there
Barefoot — before architecture

Boiled the green to stone gray —
1897: I had taken my shoes off . . .

3

Sweetheart, Lou

. . . what is God, Mama?

> "White hinds
> hidden in a thorn thicket"

No compliment to the long
Undulant chevelure of Magdalen

On a billow of mud
          in the Dordogne or Ariège was it
A footmark printed
          lightly
Hard mud in a deep cave

Might last another 15,000 years

But Rilke's feet
          he left them
                    standing
To be invented

4

This hot pursuant of
The Incomparable

A sort of hassock stool
He kept and kneeling on

Upholstered velvet
Worshipped any woman

He had invited no
Not any but this

Was the way he tended
Kneeling on the stool

And gazing up as
She waved an arm or

Cringed and bit her lip
Footless for some quaint

Antiphallocratic reason he
Poised at hers

A projectile
In a catapult

5

Or Rilke had no feet at all
What he had was fins
Up he twiddles into the air

Sycamore seed going the wrong way
Lands in my tree
Owl's eyes large liquid

Blink at me   Contrariwise
He had no body just a head
Thought a little girl

No body in his clean but threadbare
Clothes crossed the room
And took a cake with Mama later

Off again
Somehow bowing
Where can he have put that cake

6

More famous feet
Than these invisible ones
The foot of Philoctet-
Es and Byron's

Hoof with its iambic knock
On the deck of a gondola,
Incidentally — copper,
His horse adored the hot

Weight of it and ladies
Lifted fingers to their eyes,
Thrilling stomachs
Fancy the surprise

Suddenly milord is dead
While muttering Greek
Bandits around his bed
Frenetically seek

To screw the damn thing off,
Here's Philoctetes' foot
Festering in a cave —
His wound minute by minute

Throbs away the years
Four thousand of them spin
Till Troy falls to hexameters
And Rilke's feet begin

7

A Wicked One
When he scraped the Many
Bits together
Must have made some funny faces

Rilke's feet — how
Is this body
To be looked upon: a

Screen or
Not sure a
Scene a recipient interim

And liminally
In and over it creation's
Wavering shapes break open
Yet

Are distorted it is
The dance but done
As if by hangmen

Touch and look
From a footsole run
Tightrope lines to every single organ

8

Voice where are you now
Tree what has become of you
Never a column or pedestal

But a tree of branching blood vessels
A tree trying to speak
Through thunderous pumping of juices
I climb across this voice
In the grip of its twig deletions

9

Hands whose touch is thinking
        How the taste of orange flows
To the beat of a ringdance

Slowly out of its givens
        The automatic body
Builds itself

Might balance feet with
        Strong straight
Articulations but dammit

An orchestra of echoes
        Code of interchanging
Trait and ancestor

All we can see in one photo
    Is Rilke in
Well shone shoes with spats

Its constant monologue
    Broken by torture
Reroutes no signals

And a shoe might hide
    One discord perhaps a hand
Froze an insurgent impulse

And clogs
    In the negative
I am told

Now like an undesired
    Eyeball captive in a pod of skin
For fingers wished it

Footward as a pipesmoker
    Tamps tobacco
Down to the base of the pipe bowl

So blue huggermugger knobs
    When bones obtrude strum on tendons
Fuming toes

Recoil to plot
    Inversion of the message
Train to be fingers and pluck back

Their slice of the power
    Did Rilke then support a claw
Brain-limb feedback

Did it flush his touch of sphinx
    Faintly at the tip
With repression's rose

284

10

Rilke's feet
Wading in a weird
Kettle of fish

        The lobster
Has gone for a walk
With his ghost
The sea
Once
Too often

11

Xenophon Xenophon it were fit to include
Dark as it is again in Wilmersdorf
An echo of your script from Corinth, your
Fictional grammar of the human foot

Anabasis uh I am tired and my secret
Reader wonders where we have got
As did your mob of Greeks thirty years before
Thirty years before you finally wrote

A bit boastfully about the march to the sea
Then how your lines inch by inch
Barrelled along the barbarous coast

But hardly anyone cares now
About the fleetfooted Carduchi
Peltists and bowmen coming up quick

When they shoot they put the left foot
Out and rest the base of the bow on it
Drawing back the string

You must have stopped to see that
And soon backwards the snow
Is opening its white tomb

Illshod columns of infantry
Straggle into Armenian mountains
Was there no shit they could not bite through

Newly flayed oxenskin
Froze that night to the footsoles
Thongs cut into ankle flesh

Many perished
Snowblind thwacking spear on shield
Throat racket body racket made the foe
Feel outnumbered

Small bags later we tied
To the horse hoofs else
In the snow to their bellies they sank

12

Can I speak to you now Rilke
As we sleep
A little for our lives
Though I wonder sometimes what you meant
And my memory is awful
The footless motions you enact or track

In poems where the verbs
Amaze by their precision
Were you pointing
Beyond the combative body which engulfs
All as nothing with its bubble

Pointing to a body more like music
A luminous relator with its warmth
"Transfiguring the earth"
If it was this what have we got
Not evil quite wondrous desires
But injustice

It may be too late
Your invisible
Feet can do nothing but insist
Issue into a space all
Rondure and volume void

Of anything more dense
Than the thrum of air you felt
Around a seagull's wing
As it poured the pearliness in
And fitted feathers

Threadless motion
Through it your truant feet
Sprinkling punctures might
Sustain
Like intervals between them utterly

Determined throngs of stars
Or freely quickening and distinct
These feet it is
That ease
The gasps of joy from children's throats

3

Quasizeros

21 MISCELLANEOUS MICRO-POEMS
FOR HANS VOGT

1

Walking, stopping in
Mid-stride

Leaning on air, word on the tip
Of the tongue

2

In the creases of her finger pointing up
To stress not that, but this, what

Else but

Eloquent minuscule
Horizons of grime

3

Watch the velvet
Black
Big
Birdspider piano
Finger his moonlight
Sonata, eight arpeggios
To cross
Your bed

288

4

All the limbs
But not a stitch

Stretched, then, in their folding, that
Much the more naked

5

Level head, one hundred such,
Hardly to be seen, tilted

Imperceptibly forward, and
If cocked

Not predatory, never a
Mountain top mistily

Bloodying the dreams in it,
Might, no, not even

These might have rectified
The nasty bent

Our species took, ignorant
From desire, gungho with dread

6

Slow wings beating take
Motion from unharmed air

Around children who break at sunrise
Bread and will not grow old

7

    Possum breath
— whiff of the One
     Tongue?
       Imagination —

Heard a mouth
    open
      Looked for unicorn (cornered
mirrors) by

Flashlight a ratlike
    baldish creature
Weaving

    Through fresh bark mulch
Pellets, in distant
    Indigo, still driven

To pick among the
    Crusty spitball
      Subterrene (*Nastürmchen!*)
Nasturtium seeds

8

       Frowned —

       So droopingly
       The roof

       Tiles overhead
       — heavy

       Red beef

9

Hellbent, thunderstruck
Piss-asses, locust men
Grope for popcorn, nip the beercan

Gape at a screen

Face cooked
In a helmet
Stole the show for one

10

    Head thrown back
    Feet skimming the ground, who

    Is this coming so fast she's
    Lost from sight?

11

Scorched wizard
Sloped indoors, heard his babies

— A Squelch of organs — uncorked
A bottle of Ghost,

Ate his Lantern, slept, in his high
Horse head, catastrophic, nought

But song of a katydid:
Darkening a mountain, shaking out

The hair of the world

12

God, pining for whom helps
Keep some slim

Strip from this, pray, tormented
Skeleton the wobbling

Fat rolls that make him speak
Instead of thunder, with a squeak

13

Heavy logistical weapons of muscle mass rush
Up front to fling
A stone

               Hated squirrel
            Gulps another mouth-
                  Ful of bird-

                   Seed frisks

High / lightly   His tail
                   Melts into the trees

14

      Not the eyebrow, its
      Traject, not the gorgon

      Hairmass, lady,
      What is it, this

      Mirrorless me
      Topples them

      Cracking, somehow
      Into your pit?

15

      Cuff tucked
      Back, palms up to

Help you squinny at
Her cuts

16

A gartered swinger in the human tree
Enjoys her husbands to the tune of three

Her flesh still willing when they hit the floor
She signals for a half half dozen more

Those being spent, her art not stopped, she swings
Up, to catch her breath, her heart on other things.

17

Glossy, not from clinging, these
Knuckles predecease her quilt —

Eyelid sliding back peels a white,
Now she called a name, joyfully, it was mine

But in the country she came from
Girls divined their fortunes

In shapes of wax they sprinkled hot,
At random, over water

18

Dry smell, dark yellow
    tugs at heart thongs —
old leatherbound books, bays glow,
    drifting,
when first light stirs up
    the pure fume

19

With cabbage
Leaf ears
Pinned back and young
Stumbling elephant steps I ran
Up to you,
Poetry, but almost
You had forgotten

Me, you
Gave me a lick,
Delicate and
Suspicious, the way
A lion, lowering
His tongue,
Drinks

20

      Hollering into the
    Pool
A wild
  Peony of boys
    Lobs its petals

21

As limestone through smoke
    goes amber
       so goes the world

Through my slit eyes, clenched
    hands, when I
       write these poems

4

A Pinwheel

In his luggage X had stowed a green
Bronze arrowhead. The thing
Came from Armenia, Persian, he said.
Successive satraps in its time
Had all the best Armenian horses herded
South to the Persian king,
Rugs, tubs of turpentine, oil in jars,
Boys tactfully picked —

     On the mantelpiece
Y had a stemmed
Wooden cup from Crete. A convict
Made it. You might think
Fingernails not a knife had oddly
Whittled its
Maze of facets, groping for the tilt
It had to stand at. Piss gold the colour
That man's privation wept
And sorrow sweated into it —

     Since 1940, Z
Has kept a coin, Macedonian. Curly head
Of Zeus on one side. Philip II
Leans forward, if you turn it, on a high
Stepping horse. Silver tunic still
Flutters around his body,
Silver hat brim twisting in the wind —
Years to go before the drink got him
Or bugles blew, at crack of dawn, and Alexander
Floated off, unblinking, in a cloud of archers.

A Different Banquo

FOR ALBERTO DE LACERDA

A ghost speech
I bring you, with my voice.
When you have gone, my voice will be forgotten.

Ghost speech I
Said, friends. But it's not quite
So far along. Here we are, if still we are

Not yet dead,
Nor gaga. True, any
Moment, any, could for ever extinguish,

Think of it,
The wave. So I ask you:
Remember things I said for fun, not insult,

Even when
Your ears, I said — they're big,
Can you wag them? Or: your lisp kissed sawdust. That

Little mole
On the tip of your nose —
A beacon? Could it guide through storm a long ship?

Can you switch
It off? Does it send up
Punctual signals? Intrusive things like that

I said. In
Hope you'd be provoked. In
Fear a soul might then respond, giving me back

Tenfold the
Joy it was to be there,
Humbly, with you, facing you, in natural

Light. The crust
Of this planet under
Us. Or yawning through our reckless candle flames

The abyss,
Unaccountable. To
Your memory admit me and my weird jokes;

The help I
Ever was to you need
Be no further concern. Still, hold against me

Failings, or
Possibly pettiness
I showed at times when talk ran wild, was too grand

— When you die,
I said, Lord, you'll say, back
I come now, but he'd never known you were gone —

For a voice
Can be wrenching, can pluck
Out of a sky the moon, full, mute, properly

Blent with it.
Yet will you raise me up
Again, at your feasts? Also in lonely rooms

Which exist?
Drink whole flasks of me, raw
Red wine, never negligent? Give me a chance.

As for what
I wrote — thumb through it on
Weekdays, and skip, if you will, the rotten bits.

Or else, by
And large, have done with it.
Save your breath to resist contenders, who kill;

Cruel pack
Rats, they are organized
And horror has no end. Acquiescent, I

Cried out, but
The sound in that cry was
Gashed by evil's claw. Heart now full, vacant soon,

At the beck
And call, leastways, of drab
Manipulators, don't we all bide our time?

Little mouse,
With your voice now I shriek,
So small I made myself, hoping to slip through

Power's mesh.
Not good enough. I had
Chosen to be trapped. To be free was far too much

Breath wasted.
So greed abolishes
Good things, and the canny have no place to go:

Thus we loved,
We did, wildly, trusting
One passion. For, divisible, we only

Loved one voice
Soaring, not mine. It comes
From the sky, weeps, laughs, shakes into shape our trees.

Richard Lion Heart

His country, what a place to have lived in:
Farm girls bringing milk for free, taste of berries,
Sunshine all summer long, the salmon leaping,
Snow crisp in winter, smoke from cottage fires.

I'll ride beside my king on horseback,
Rock hard river valleys hear him sing:
His new song in langue d'Oc for the redbreasts
Goes to the tune of silver horsetails flicking.

In time a wise anarchy will be possible.
Bursts of laughter have washed away oppression,
If anyone wants to govern, gracious people do.
He'll cure my wart and I will clean his crown.

No whining nasal voices, no la-di-da,
No craving for empire, no rotting industries;
Village ponds and words and coastlines are unscummed,
No scummy timid souls could haunt that England.

In Byzantium we'll booze it up, feast with friends
In the south of France. Ah, didn't they clap him
Into a dungeon? I'll spring him. Past far timberlines
We'll clatter on mules and ask the way to Japan.

Lento

To be almost unable to wake up
To see the shadow of a spider's web
To be interested in it sleepily

To notice that the shadow is active
To wonder about its reiterated movement
To think its movement varies from time to time

To call it ocean
To feel it living in the room
To lie full length in the golden light the room contains

To hear the clatter of plates in the courtyard
To forget the shadow of the spider's web
To open the door and approach the plates

To feel hunger
To recognize that your hunger is privileged
To raise your arms

To take a knife in one hand
To take in the other hand a fork
To consider the veins in the marble table top

To admire on your plate a grilled ocean
To eat a helping of spider pie
To taste the white infinitive wine

Tadpoles in the Toulourenc

The frog factory is made of brilliant water,
Pools of it propel the great croak on
And weather willing frill
The Ventoux ramps, come August.

Water: but what bubbles from the ground
Higher up and trims the mountain so,
Exactly where its time begins and what
Comes out of it, has to be chance.

What has to be frog? Some visible pulse
Hangs on; down current or up, across,
Commonly with an incipient
Tip of itself. Numbers, anyhow freakish,

Came up luckier less than often. Tough,
Tough as it was, now perfect valves
Swivel your eyes; critical,
They scour the rocky ground, and see:

Up torrent and down, the not
Unpenetrating Magdalenians, footloose,
Knee deep, chest high in what they drank,
Fingering fire, a bone harpoon point,

At home in it. So too these softer types
Take heart from the rondure of
What they cling to. The frog factory
Is made of brilliant water

And they fancy the fact, never once
Doubting it. No itch, no fuss
To follow the pulse up, through
To the holiness of being frog.

First, silence, then the croak. Us eventual
Bonier harmonies hurt. Roofs of reed,
Starlit canopies of thought we spread;
Domes, electric shields, congested masks

Flicker with appetites our fathomless
Inanity compels. But human voices
Vagabond in the creature chorus can't
Hang on, like these blobs do,

To what they've got. Night, for nobody,
Still it blooms.
    Water, talkative today,
Still their Elephant pumps it out,

Amply. Their Elephant, who, seeing
He knows best, goes most ignored. They
Hang so, by nothing at all
But their own weight.

The Mol

There is a mol and in a lake
She said he lives
And how he sleeps
How deep the water is
How cold and dark

Boatmen shiver and the mol
Lifts his mouth like this
She imitated it
Her jaw flew out an inch
She snapped at nothing

There he is and once a rope
Weighted with a stone
They lowered it for miles
Something tugged at it
They pulled it up she said

The rope was bitten off
The stone had gone
They tried a chain
The chain went down and down
The chain was bitten off

She said he doesn't hurt
He only wants to sleep
The mol is gentle yes
He goes like this
A mouth (I thought) we feed

Halicarnassian Ghost Dialogue

What can the old fool have been looking for?
Back there we had the Many in the One.
If he looked back, this is what he saw:
A ridge, a contour, stark, like an eyelid,
Framing a shrub or two. Barefoot
A little girl, where the lane lofts its dust,
Dragging branches back to a hovel.

He never saw her. If he heard
The heaven bird warble in the pines
And the wind foreveraftering, still
On he went,

302

Not anxious that his donkey might break down,
There'd always be another; but he hugged
A secret such a fool knows nothing of.

As in a dream a man's thought swings
Many ways between his times, touching
Past and present, hangs between
Dithering signs that sparkle in the vault
Of his flesh, and others, buoyant, yet
More dim, pained, and these
Exact a meaning from him, they propose
To be restored, whole, put back beyond
His death, their origin, the one thing
He never will have known — so he swung
Out, and capably

The donkey trotted under him, unaware
Of all the torchlit cities, fumes, of horns,
Remote, and ceremonies, deaf to voices
That reeked or howled or sang
Sayso into his cranium.

　　It was the story
Of a girl with a branch, you might say;
Of a hill, stark, contour
Framing sage and oleander. How come,
Everything was changed? He alone
Could sit in the cool and figure, not afraid,
Pen in hand, the monstrous variables,
Plotting their tracks.

　　The air, this
Excited us all. None but a few
Did anything about it. A rose, a white
Pebble, look good; at nightfall, in the mouth
A taste of olive. Nothing was enough
To make much palaver about. Wounds, quivering,
Suck the world into their vacuum, when —
When curiosity like his whets its hook
On the air between impulse and action.

There was no story till he tugged
The atoms together.
      Not only for his own good
Does a man pan from dust a glint
Of original information. Spinnakers

Of oddity, majestic
The ripple of ideas, these, our thread,
Irreducible amalgam of our discourse,
He combed from the gabble of old salts,
Horsemen, crones, bandits.

      Listen, was it
His feeling that any heap
Of rags, palpitating on a roadside,
By a tethered goat, or roping hay
Into a sack, has something to speak of;
That any individual is ringed
By a glowing exoskeleton, the tissue
Of stories and of dreams it craves to tell?

And his eye magnified it into a folly of wands,
Ligatures, with pennons cracking,
Cones, strained pulleys, psyche
Thinging itself into an essential

Funniness, a pupa, something
Like birdsong, or
A ship of resistance, and of wonder
An instrument. No one girl
Who drags her branch down a lane
Matches any other.

      This exciting air, this
Time, this phenomenal
Melting skin,
      chrysalis of inventions, thickened

With sorrow, so he imagined it,
With such zest — no choice, but to display,
He forced it to, colour, with strangeness.
He loved it so, stripped
Or like a woman who walks, walks
As a tree might, or a fountain at daybreak,
Unfathomable.

Was he saying that home, after all,
Depends on the difference you make of it;
Wild, like a sheen; in a heron's eye,
Pigment? Any domain
Warms to delight, hopelessly fragile,
When someone sets a rose,
Fresh, in the middle of a dinner table.

No. He was saying that this little girl
Was born alone, lived alone, dies alone.

Ayasofya

The long bird trails his feet,
Flying over water.
     Not a perch hereabouts
He does not know; but a dome
Mirrored in the water sprays its topaz
     Treasures up, and moans
Beneath his flight's
     Bowstroke.

And another flits into the dome
Through the star of a broken window,
Quicker, the dove;
     A shelf, tilted,
Tops a column, from a stick
     Nest a cry, shrill,
Has magnified its volume, striking
Under the roof angle a mosaic
     Alexander.

Dome, hive, unspeakable the mass,
Honey of power, down
      Age after age it slid
Into and out of you. Still she squats,
Bent, in the black gutter,
      Sightless, turning
Now and again to the sun her flat
      Scabbed face.

An Old Wine Press

An old wine press
With its iron screw
Column down the middle —
Vertical slats doubly hooped
Contain the tub — this instrument
Sepia on account of its being
Not the very thing but a photo, dated
No later than 1910

Higher up, steep slant of a barn roof.
The line of its eave like a lip,
Wavy. A sort of monster
Grin goofily reveals
The stubs of seven teeth, unless
These are beam ends or swallows' nests

And halfway up the slant
Two holes are built, like little eyes, or else
They breathe for the hayloft, handy
Homes of dove, dark lodges
For the grape scented air

All this no more than a glimpse
But the barn behind the wine press caught
And carries onward
A human imprint, rough hewn
A flicker of the torch

Here for once
Doubly precious, considering these
Eight people grouped around the press:

Just a bunch of farm folk, three generations,
The men clothed in stained denims, sweaty caps;

The woman has pinned a flower to her breast
And holds an empty cheese basket;
A little boy had curled his fingers
Around the handle of a hooped
Wooden wine jug

There they stood, tilting
Every which way; splay feet, beefy arms
Dovetailed into a right good
Angular design:

    Three men
Lean against the tub on its platform;
If this beard might crumple into a king's mask,
Still clog and boot crack with mud
And glue these
Dancers to the ground; the boy
Hangs in the middle, perched, dangling
Tiny booted feet —

Any moment
The glass he grips by the stem will spill;
Oddly tender yet, the way
All around him thicker fingers hold
The scarce seen cool substance —
In it gleams the god, red and savage,
Spinning the world for more than money

Yet the money matters. You can plot
Grim pursuit of it in the skew
Cheek folds of the white-haired man.
Hope made the woman's mouth
A thin long line and in her round chin

Totted up
Credits of hair, winnings of eye, decimals
Of nostril

Who knows, it is mostly too late;
The wine that time at least
Had a fair chance;
The footwear might see another ten years out,
As good as a second skin, these denims
Are worn as the sun
Wears its light, or as the god they nourish
Squid-wickedly has thrown
History over his tentacles, a robe
Smoky in colour, a tissue of bloodstains,
Whose, fading, sepia

Mezzomephistophelean Scholion

The place of his birth: some few conjecture
It was Athens. After all, in a letter,
He laid claim to the title 'Attikos'. Others
Find reason to suppose that he was born
In Nicomedia. The chronicle, they say,
Written by Michael Attaliatos might be construed
To identify Michael Psellos with Michael
The Monk of Nicomedia.

    We, on the other hand,
Cannot concede that our Michael (Psellos)
Ever did the sort of thing
The Monk is said to have done.
    Nor can we reconcile
Attaliatos' apologias for Psellos
With his poor opinion of that Monk. More,
Psellos has it in a letter (no suspicion
Of any scribal lapse) that first he saw
The light of day close to the monastery
At Narsos.

There is no cause to doubt
His testimony, either, that he was sixteen
When Romanus Argyrus died, and twenty five
When Constantine Monomachos granted him
A minor secretarial post.
       The date of his birth
Can accordingly be reckoned without error
By persons not unversed
In the history of the Macedonian Renaissance.

       It will be known to all
Who take pleasure in the learning of that time,
The sinuous paintings, luminous artifacts,
And subtle scriptures.

       In so far as the scroll
Of history reforms behind us
Its convolution, but spells
Persistent shadowy figures across
The curve in it we scratch, or tap, and trample on,

       It will be significant
To such as choose to find in that time
A foothold, and from the glow as on great moonlit peaks
Of its regard for the old thinkers
Draw increase of consciousness, courage from its
Unflinching critique of desolate Asian demonologies,
And in its Hellenizing northward drift
See for pity
Among the Slavic peoples and languages
Fortune stripped naked.

Irish

Here as the bamboo
leaf and rod
glisten
in broken moonlight
this harp music

309

I suppose it echoes
the strings of rain, silver
those dark pools
drink up
on streets in Ireland

Say time could have taken
a different shape,
but this, with red eyes that weep
and search the horizon
choose we did

Say a spirit got
knotted
in spilt intestines, a body
of music shattering
the bamboo door

Now leaf and rod,
the fawn I saw stopped
in a clearing, pulsars in moth-
eaten velvet
flash slow beacons

But a perception chosen
digs historic
claws deep down, not
like the bamboo rhizomes
they touch dancing

Pickled
in this whiskey bottle was
a heart, do not listen
the wind sings in its
ventricle, seaward

In Memory of Peter Szondi

He is writing the words
smaller and smaller, no drift
betrays the question, every twist of it
a stitch in the garment, a drop scripted
into the river, still smaller
the drops contract,
so far in fact their intervals absorb
not a trick of the heavenly
changes of light, instead
gunshot is packed, proof,
into a cartridge.

   The original
text still resists, but he
drinking the poison of power out of it
tightens his grip and over
the absent mind of his composite
adversary maps
another compound, gray, sees his automatic
quill soon, horrified sees
bursting from his head

    Gunbarrel blue
searchlight beams raking a beech wood —
old words, once floated breath,
buckle under his gist, their stockade
tangled ugly knuckles,
a scalp shaven, these are skeletons, their
scripture reeks of carbolic.

    Something else
has him by the throat,
something else calling the shots, his
discipline a terror, his protective
passion sapped by the microbe,
intolerable ache
of millions driven living
into the gas, he checks

the clock, walks out unbent
by the weight of his coat, he thinks
the river is that way, full stride
he walks
at last powerless into it.

Cabaret de la Canne, January 1855

Sir, I do not know your name,
Nor do you know mine. So we sit,
Briefly, at neighbouring tables, you
With your bottle, the cat on your knee,
I with my little glass.

In our sunken ship
The third table has been taken
By the fine man of darkness, whom
We do not see. Look, on the furrowed surface
Glittering still, the flake of snow I flicked
From the collar of my coat when I came in.

Each sits watching
The face of his own slowly turning
Universe. Particularly the cat
Has known how the heat
Comes and goes. Important smells
Wrinkle and flex into signatures, you know,
Writ small in snowflakes and the skeletons
Of leaves. Shuddering,
The fingers of a spirit ink into our skins
Mysterious names, numbers, and messages.

Ancient gutters
Accommodate the cat, providing
Fish, spare ribs, a scrap of lamplight;
Spilt milk to lap up, now and then.

There are places where people turn yellow,
Having nothing to eat. Cloacas, attics.
Broken roofs. Through holes the snow sifts.
A Valois song can be issuing, in another street,
From a little girl's lips
For a penny.

Mandolins, a lantern swaying, make it
Difficult to want less than a tree to dance with.

Do we suffer
Most because the bunched worms will hang
In the emptiness you are looking at, this
Dome of mine, bald, this bony cabin?
    What is immortal
If not the injustice?

There was a room I lived in once,
I remember how the early light in it
Fell across two rescued Fragonards.
There was a girl, nearly naked she was,
Tigers ran before her on a leash
And a little donkey woke us, braying,
Or a barge trumpet's echo off the river.

Like a swift in his globe of crisp mud
I hung between sleep and waking
And heard the straw speak in my thin
Mattress. Look, here it is, another face
Of that same
Towering light, again
In this bit of a rainbow, at its peril
Afloat in the eau-de-vie:
I drink it for the dream that spills
Into life.

They tore it down, it was an old house.
They did not tear down
The other room, which, if you follow me,
We put there, suspending it
Outside any space that iron balls
Can shatter.

In that room the last vine still grew,
A veiny green, very ancient.
The last vine, first planted when
The emperor was Julian and Paris Egypt.
From the vine,
Yes from it you might see
A light as from the original stars unfolded

And flew as it pleased, to vary
As it touched the featured walls through
Twelve emotions. With snaky lines
It marbled the stones and old chairs
We had broken by leaning back to laugh.
To eye the stones was to feel a flow
Of female warmths and hear the goddess, —
Moan and shriek of the sistron in her fingers.

What can you be thinking?
No, do not indispose the cat.

The Bow

A little arrangement
The table neat
Napkins folded

An arrangement
Any casual act forefelt
Hums with a thought's movement

314

A plan to get up in the night
For a wild
Bit of dancing

Crazy
Planned the
Unpredictable grace

A cuckoo
Moment we
Plan it and die of it

Two-ply such
A delicate
Tendon

Tautens
You great
Bow of civilization

Conundrum on a Covenant

When did we mean to meet? I never saw you.
Each time I came, you'd gone. Now at my door
You rap, and I'm not there. Write me letters:
Your scrawl divined, how should I open them?

Forest and other calendars you flew through,
Tasting of alcohol, armpit, lotus —
I'm not there. You stand me up, thanks, but
Which of us broke the date, will break the word?

Etymology: it says there has to be, occult
In the abiding nature, before your finer breath
Fathoms the bowl of this bent lily pond,
A place for the likes of us to palaver in.

Or lifting a glass you might have shown,
Surfaced, in a bar. My eyeballs, had they,
Ghastly, swivelling, tipped the whole pipkin,
Brimful as a sundial, upside down?

Ah yes, I saw, smelled, heard. The rosy
Gloss of a thumbnail. Musk, a key change
Spread you. In her believed *feels* and *explores*,
Orphaned Opal d'Orléans, you blessed her.

Muck, too, in a blot of muck I hear, some days,
Mute, goofball, your unstemmed galaxies
Croaking. But where in the world are we to converge on?
Suspense electric — nerves that hummed snap,

Less than a smatter, plot wilts, large characters
Fidget in the wings . . . Who can pretend
Now to picture you? Snarled up, acid,
This air I breathe holds not a trace of you.

Cherries

Cherries, cherries on their cherry trees
Across a snowy slope of architecture
Is this what he has to say and all of it
The pilot with a responsible face
Eyes that grip and penetrate everything

But now the world has come to an end
A squall from the southeast levels
The last buildings
My mother young and candlelit dithers in the church
My father never dead at all runs to the door
Anxious, waving a hand to her

Besides, in albums there are clay replicas of Roman coins
Shelved in this shop with old enigma books
Funny it is stuck in an airport

316

Besides, I have eaten the inside of a bread pie
And now this stickleback still twitching
I gobble it up and wonder at my greed

The world has come to an end
So what is to be said about the cherry trees
The snowy slope
I am climbing the stairs to where I spoke to my toys
Three top rooms are filled with beds
Double doors close over one bed of cherry wood
Fitting the headboard I make it into a tombstone
So what about sheets

And walking behind me in her nakedness
This girl has no place
This girl
Only eighteen tonight she has no place to sleep
A spit curl cannot hide the end of the world
The worry in her face her unknown face

Doussa res we are looking for the warmth I suppose
Should we take the bed with doors
Jump in just as we are and shut the doors on ourselves
But I am stooped like a barometer
A giraffe in this immeasurable Africa my flesh
Has chewed up every sprig of love that ever was in me

The Few Objects

The few objects on a table
Do not read the papers
No sweat breaks out on them
When they work their gentle bells
To tinkle for a pilgrim
They do not startle, nervous
When he lifts a hand
In doubt, in apprehension

Rosenkavalier Express

Sundown in the dining car of the Rosenkavalier Express —
    I am seeing the packed trees and fields of wheat,
Dense greens involved with depths of indigo,
    For the sun — all day it shone like nobody's business,
And I think that a poem should be like these
    Packed trees and wheat, a tuft aglow, an indigo thing;
Then for a split instant I'm happy, a thrill goes through me,
    The dinner of beef and wine, shock of a salty
Taste in the beef, the red ordinary wine,
    Might account for it, but robuster than any reason,
Visceral or not, is the briskness of it, I mean
    The spasm, spliced with a sweet twinge of doubt
Whether I'd ever be up to voicing a poem like that.

And there was the whole day sunlit in Vienna,
Hungover a bit after hours of drink with friends;
    I am still out on a walk at one in the morning,
The big idea was to find, at last, the Mikado,
    But I couldn't, so now I'll never be sure
If a special whore called Josephine hangs out there.
    I am still strolling around at one in the morning
Though it is eight p.m. and as the train swings
    Westward into the night, fields will be warm as beds,
A peace envelops me from eyebrow to anklebone,
    I want to say thank you to someone for letting me
Eat and drink and feel on my flesh, whizzing by,
    These tufts of pine, these depths of indigo,
Rhombs of wheat that surge in the wind;
    Birds and rabbits will be rustling through them,
Smells drift, sprung by sun from June rain,
    Prickly smells of wing and fur, rose and lettuce,
Search in me for the tautest bowstring, holding
    But lightly holding the midpoint of the bow.

318

Ah well, the Mikado stroll was a washout,
    But with coffee there comes a little sugar packet
With "Mikado" printed on it, and a gasp, childish
    Enough — I catch my breath as the large
Rhythm of coincidence wraps me in a fold of fire.

    What is this? Moneyless but sometimes lucky
I have been ways with women that made them powderkegs.
    Wrong, time and again, I have wounded people,
Fallen short of their dreams, risen to them
    Too little or too late; less and less I can tell
What feeling is good for, but have been acquainted
    With animals fierce and beautiful, so to whom,
To what should I give thanks, and thanks for what?

    What have I brought to love, if not catastrophe?
Now ideas flock like moonsheep in my turning head,
    Now I see roof angles, wooden cabins in cabbage plots,
Goalposts and staircases, and so rotund a hill,
    O, distance slips into its blue mist, but point blank
Stalks of wheat and blades of grass freshen again.
    As if through me Imagination wanted, sightless,
To fondle the volumes of objects and read their legends,
    Trim old barns and now the Danube, full stretch,
Open lips that motion to speak, wag their tongues.

    So I think of the tongue of a blackbird,
And that I won't call this moody aria "Mitteleuropa."
    Grateful not to be dead, or frightened, or oppressed,
I think of the call in the song of a blackbird:
    When you patrol the dust of Mitteleuropa
It doesn't perceive that you and history are there;
    It sings with a voice that must be dreaming
It is a petal and so, rosily, all for free,
    In one cool fold of fire the petal wraps you.

Apocrypha Texana

1

Gravity with Popcorn

First comes
The popcorn tree

It is very still
To be seen with blue

Behind it hoping
Gravity so

Simply intended
Marking the time

Construction workers
Dream of popcorn

Most but less
Of mud festoons

And rabbits listening
Less for the clang

Of snow perhaps
Hear the popcorn

Whistling now
To keep me warm

I stretch my plums out
Still somehow

320

And never no more
Need movie-going

Local Roads

These local roads they say
In Texas hug their curves
Or cracks and hollows
Like ancient pain

I looked ahead
I thought a turtle or what else
A flexing clump a shell
Had waddled half across

I ran to find if I was wrong
But there it was
Again the vacant womb
A god imagined human music from

My impulse the reverse
I slipped that hood back on
I shrank into the shell
To shield a scaly head

Whirled into the air I heard
Colossal whistling shoes
And fingers beating time
But vaguely on my back

Caught up with me at last
What century was this
My negligible weight
How balanced in his hand

Scars of ancient lightning
Scollop the vaulted shell
What if they broke open
What frenzy would he feel

Driving Home

Imagine you might forget
The white road
Splitting away from the black road

Not loaded words

Imagine you
Might forget its whiteness and
In the identical moonlight

A different smell of burnt cedar

But it was never white was it
A gray blue gone to violet rumpled
Like denims in a surplus store
White road — pulverized

Limestone bathed in the rays

You might forget the fork imagine
Sound of the owl further down the road
Splitting your time
Between now and the hearing of it

A voice inappositely pink
O whiskered shrimpish owl

But then you never forgot
Pursuing the tubes of light
How it felt

More like a branching tree than a church
Made ghostlier
By the fact of a candle in it

Never so new
It was not to be afraid

Imagine
Talking and happy stripped
Inside not even shutting the door
The forgotten embrace

Now when you came together
It will nourish
All the ways everything moves

A Portrait of J.L.M.

We called him spirit of the place,
But he's more like a good old tree root.
Went off, a year gone, back to Rockport.
It seems, when he'd gone, us not even
Knowing it, everything fell apart.

   Wish I remembered
What he told me. This bit of town I landed in,
These railroad tracks he'd known, secret
Signs chalked on the freight wagon doors,
Hobos bivouacking, and how he'd drift across,
Talk with them. That was far back
In the Thirties, near enough to the yard on Seventh
He got our big old bamboo from, planted it.

   Wanderings, the split rail
Fences he built, him wiry then as now, bird faced,
Out west of Sanantone; any job he could find
He put both hands to. He belonged with
Boilers of big ships, blue clouds
Of working people on the move, tumbleweed;
You do the most you can.

   Far out hereabouts
He'd gone courting, before big money
Rolled the roads in. Remember now,
Hummed the tune once, he did. They walked out

Through live oaks together, rocks, and cedar,
Listening to the trickle of the creek in Spring.
He sat his Mildred down, kissed her,
Same old tune in their heads.

I ate her cakes
She'd later bring at Christmas down the hill,
Stopping to chat a while, propped against
The doorpost, she'd laugh like anything
But sometimes she took ill.

Drains, spigots, carburettors,
The pump, I saw his knuckles whiten
When he fixed them, and later his hand
Shook, breath caught, and as he worked
His mouth helped, with twists and lippings.

Rolled his own cigarettes; told me —
Here's this old song book, found it at the county dump,
You want it? 1865 — Irish songs. Irish
As his Indian scout grandfather had been. He'd
Told him of hilltops hereabouts

Where the Indians hunkered,
Yawning. And how a coach might rumble by,
Gold or guns in it, stuff they could use. And how
Into this cave his grandfather went once, deep,
Now they've blocked it, but it goes underground
All the way from the lake to Tarrytown.
A volcano, too, he said.

I might not believe it,
Not so far off, east, he found obsidian there,
Beyond where the highrise banks and turnpikes
And the military airport are. Trees,
He loved trees and drove miles to see them
At their best, the right time of the year.
Buckeye and catalpa in their first flower,
Chinaberry, dogwood.

All birds had ordinary names,
Like redbird, but once in a while he'd speak
Old words, not from books but from Tennessee,
Like once he said "quietus." Always
Flesh in his words, and bone, and in his doings,
Not absent even from the way he'd knock
A bourbon back, straight, that was the way
He liked it, then roll another cigarette.

For Mildred when her teeth
Fell out he whittled deer horn so she'd have
A biting edge up front. When he came by, dressed
Smart for a visit, he'd be wearing false
Rat teeth up front and give a wicked grin.
There was this park he kept,

He knew all the weeds in it,
All, and told how some weed sent
Cows mad and was taken too much liberty with
By them young folks as went out there
For a high time.

Well, then he'd push off
In his battered pickup, headed for a honkytonk
Some place down the line. Why don't folks look at
That kind of man? Some say insight
Comes when you tell the individual
Get lost. What's all their deep droning talk
To him? He's too smart to think up
Revolutions, what's it, that perspective stuff?
Maybe he's nobody

But he made things work,
Never slaving, nor ginrollizing. Made things
Shift and level with every breath he drew.
Had no grievance, spoke no ill of anyone
Or anything save spindly offshoots
Of tree roots that split drainpipes in the country,
Having ballooned in them, like brains
Got swole, so he'd say, with all the excrement.

Visio Reginae Coeli

A hunchback pulls the last python out of a tank.
Bony women crouch around a pail.
Slithering from the sky these roasted crows
Print their silhouettes on a rock wall.

Not yet: safety in numbers. Casually bricks
Replace forest; valves, windows are fitted.
Not passion but neglect postpones a touch
That finally could lift the roof off.

Induplicable a breath
Lets a lady call to her gardener.
Morning glistens in the fragonard sprays.
Elm roots draw a deep earth liquid up.

Still in rooms the spoons clink against glass,
Objects rustle, delicately moved; the fanged
And happy twiddle their thumbs, now heaven's queen
Swoops across the sky, descending in her robe,

A blue, a crimson. Closer now, unbidden,
Through the ring begun by her motion,
Fathomless music winged with voices
Lifts all her creatures into the air.

Pinyon Incense

Oblong a pellet
In a small
Pueblo bowl

Careful
It could come to bits
A fleck like conscience

326

Burn as you light
One tip
And breathe on it a pang

Possibly a finger
Writing but
A fresh piece

And firm shoots mysterious blue
Scented smoke up
If ever the smoke thins

Look while ash
Blackens the tip it is
Not standing on

Down through the spirals move
Meet
Old man trombone brown

He stands
Where his feet keep him
At a cave opening

Watch the writ of furrows
Groove his dry
Pine bark

Palm he is
Not angry now he simply will not
Let you in

With your sorrow
And your bodyful of pacts
Broken

Let him say
Sorrow let him say
Nothing

Just cup like that his
Palm and cuff
The top of your head off

A Lyric to Stanley Myers's "Cavatina"

(In John Williams' guitar arrangement)

Blue cave, deep stream,
Stream, how you run;
Flow, clear, from the blue cave
For the sun to shine on.

Old sun, clear stream,
Not made for the pain;
Still you receive us,
Now and again.

High, high the falcon calls,
Mocks the world as he flies;
His shadow dips across the stream,
Silver, in the sunrise . . .

What means is not the end
But the movement of such things;
Watch the falcon move to the beat
And yielding of his wings.

Now there is this place, love,
Where we could belong —
A wave means to carry us
In the secret of a song.

Enough, enough that we flow
As often as we fly —
Not counting, old stream,
Time gone by.

A Young Horse

Where can it now have gone
The warm night ruffled
With screech owl feathers
Where can it have gone
When the horse came to a call

The warm night with branches
Haunt of moss web of intelligence
The breath of a young horse
Cooling between fingers
The night vast with bunched stars

Simply blown away it was
The night murderous and milky
The night of old hymns and hot bullets
Blown away by a breath
Curling between fingers

It flew between my ribs
It set a hollow throbbing
Between the ribs and fingers
A sort of pulse had shuttled
Felt as it wove and melting

Melting the shell this mortal
Man nocturnally hides in
His temple void of presence
With a wicket gate of muscle
To shield from shock his hungers

People in Kansas, 1910

1

Now they stand quite still on level doorsteps,
Outside the Drug Store and the Post Office.

A white sky, two buildings underneath it,
Outside the buildings half a dozen people.

Across the dust like dice the buildings rolled,
Stopped under the white sky.

Soon the people prised them open, clambered out.
Here at last. Here, they said, is Dorrance.

2

Stiff, like effigies, almost,
Made of language; speaking
The people came to be real for one another.

A head below the P of the Post Office
Shrinks into a Stetson. A wiry woman
Shoulders the stone Drug Store doorpost.

All six like effigies, wax, mechanical.
Work all day with corn, beans, soda pop.
The letters, few and far between. Senseless.

3

The people insist. But a vague terrain —
How can you fill it. Corn and letters
Stop short. The horizon,

A banker might one day darken it,
Locomotives. This big space frightens. We
Lost here a sense of belonging with the wind,

Now geese and trees that fly with it are no part of us.
Trust your shirt, these oblong blocks of stone.
Trust two dark heaps dropped in the dust by horses.

A chimney pot, back of the Post Office. Plain
Undistressed people, you never dreamed
Of burning letters, one by one, or bodies.

4

That's it. None could know what later crooked
Shapes
History takes when something radiant
All the brain and body cells cry out for
Is suppressed

Behind bars appetites riot; captured
Guards
Sob for mercy; spies are fucked.
These oblong people lived out their free time
On credit,

They could count it wise not to wish
Their soap
Were sweeter, small business not
So methodical, dogs happy to work
Nights for them.

No. Their stark speech I do not understand.
Why
Make of life such a hard nut?
Or did they? Far off, faceless, kin of mine,
Hard living

Salt of the earth, sharply defined, crystal
Flakes,
You were never as oblong
As the buildings that warmed and warped you.
You weren't fooled.

5

Focus again,
So sharp you can smell the cigar,
The string beans taste
Just right. Objects, it
Was not your fault, objects, if
That is what you were, you have to go

Forth, shoulder your signs
In capital letters, onward to a place
I tell you of,
A place of blue and yellow. There
Mountains and people are one indivisible creature,
A grape admits night glow
To become its body,

Absolute, good as the bread
Is dense to the teeth
With death and legend. There, with patience
And the scent of sage,
People other than you ripened once
To a style — some to foreknow
And resist evil. Goodbye

Innocent oblongs, forget nothing
Now it is too late, but
Forget my fist with which if I could
I'd bang this postage stamp through
Into the reversed
World you stand in. It

Would stick in your sky of whiteness,
Perforated, a script of waves,
Muttering to you,
A voice, cancelled:
The sun does not shine for anyone,
The leaf arrives one breath
Only before the wind.

The Mason

came up from Patzcuaro, he said
where the women sell white lake fish,
seventeen women and seventeen fish
all wrapped alike, fish and women, how to choose,
how, in that old market, I ask you,
the right identical
fish

But he came with a chisel
two pieces of wood, one string,
four months flat he worked over these stones,
limestone arches, lintels, coping stones for a well,
hot here, he'd say, not like my
mountains, and he dressed the stone
in a fashion

Nobody hereabouts even wanted to know,
like this, with his chisel and string,
him going on seventy, look
the grooved small diagonals, curved
like fruit, colour of bone the
shouldering, floated into position every face
by touch, he wouldn't so much as
wink at a power tool

One night coming home the house
in total darkness
Could he be there with his homebound Indio
assistant, they'd be
talking Tarascan, found them both
sitting in the dark (that wooden room) and calm,
folded hands, being silent

And of an elevator he said one day
in a city building: Funny,
into that little room you go and other folks wait
outside while you wait inside a bit until
the door slides back open, folks
are still outside, but how come
they're different?

Lines

Never thought but once to walk there, solo;
How the places change — the rage, the spin.
When a death call comes with the sun —
Feel her hair echo soft in your fine hands,
And sweep severally the leaves from the door.

Thermodynamics

Moving in a blanket
About the house,
A blue blanket enveloping most of me
This first cold November night, I meant to ask,
Warming to the blanket,

Just what is the time now,
What century am I living in,
Am I a monk, this hovering floor, tiles,
If I kneel, hard on the bones
Of anyone hit by spirit,

Would it hold, besides,
A moment still, another time silkily
Respond to me? Rich
In the rising wind brocades — am I a samurai? —
Billow, fish head hat gone slap

Through the roof
Hoists me into the sky almost,
Squids, ho-hum,
Vaguely bob, odd, below my junk navy, half
The way to China, medieval weather

Supervenes and soon
Vast carpets of sand coalescing
Fashion the glass
Two fingers and a thumb tilt,
And red Verdillac cools my tongue

Abrupt cut — how come
A blue poilu I'm cloaked in thunder,
Shellshocked, the mud
Is red, but very deep and smelly,
At Verdun

I lost my grip. Higher than cloud
South today, navigating by
The continental backbone,
A V of geese flew on
And on: blanket of sounds, vagabond,

Be damned, honk of geese, a crack
When the timber two-by-fours
Cool or a beam
Contracts — even the wine has hit the spot,
Finding a little sanctuary

To be astounded at, but nevermore the real
Paroles reveal a volume, rasping
After all, distinct
As once a weathervane, old,
Spun a void, or words

Dovetailing, veiled it, in the bowl
A seventh, uneventful peach
Spirits the symmetry
Back, a globe still
Hangs in air over a lake with swans

Minim

White owl over
Surface of a stream
No idea
What supports him

A Road that is One in Many

FOR GEORGE AND MARY OPPEN

This is a little road, this part of it
Like the centre bar of an old hand drill
Runs straight from this bend to the next

Hold tight when you walk along it
Violet orbs revolve under the pebbles,
Daily shadows. These vines have grapes

Shrub vines, bitter grapes, mustang. Hold tight
When this bird spider hauls his thick ass
Over the tarmac, this pothole is his

Hold tight to your straight walk, tiptoe
Certain spots are swept by heat
That is what blows, that is what dries

The inside of your mouth. The signs
Droop or rust, are not adequate
To the events they warn about. Warn

The pecan comes late into leaf, the big
Pecan; that is juniper, a cone, house
Of a singing bird. The signs do not sing

Being, but collisions, they take sometimes
A life or two. Hold tight, don't roll off, all
Sorts of people have walked along this road

This road is old, new, was Indian trail
By water, TU, they said, water; now
Corvettes and subarus, few foot people

This field in summer clings to a thatch
Of slow dragonflies; now nothing lives
In the tin shed, or is it nothing, only

Bugs, but you can moo to the ghosts
Of seven extinct preoccupying cows. Not
A slope in sight. These black

Eyed susans are the prettiest flower,
Later the dayflower marks its own distinct
Fluting off against this sky of skies

And the white rain, the white rain lilies
Really are these fragrant acid fruits
Of rain. Soon it stops. Under the polestar

At night hold tight still, grip this
Ground with your unshackled feet,
Don't scare, these vines or ghosts are

Vines and ghosts. At night the lake
Is good for a swim. Don't mind these bats
That flit crisscross close to the cooling

Surface. Hold tight just once again,
Then let go and be consumed by the cool.
This is in the things and shines in the things.

2

Woden Dog

Wot doth woden dog
Por dog drageth plow

Thing odd dog not
Much good plow drager

But por dog drageth
All same plow

More come jellifish
Sting him woden dog

Jellifish in air now
Other odd thing

A speaking maner come
Round back to trooth

So doth dog plow
Plant seed of tree

Por dog life short
Woden dog long hope

Woden dog keep stung
Jellifish all round back

Dog hope tree grow
Much tree grow soon

Dog want find tree
Find releaf releaf

***

Bus drifer pleez
Make a smoth start
If not woden dog fall over

Bus drifer stop graduel
If not woden
Dog hit deck

Pleez bus drifer
Tern corner sofly
Woden dog cant hold on

You no he cant sit
Propper
You no he cant holtite

Forgoet how to life has he
Lest thing nock him sensles
All you no

Woden dog smoth graduel
Woden dog sofly he scare think
You forgoet how to drife

***

Jakit off jus warin sox like mean you
Woden dog reed times ever doggone day
Nites watchin his toob wow
Haffin the noose hapn

Wow fokes I tel you
Woden dog lap up noose
Woden dog bominate seecrit he reely do
Noose noose he bark runnin down street
Galumfin baknforth to his malebocks

He wannit so bad
He wannit to go
Like choclit maltn ketchup
Hole globe pakitchn pree paredn paid fur
Sitn in his noose baskit

No seecrit make woden dog
Bust out in flour one mawnin
Lookit soaps he buy woden dogfood
Killins toon that po looshn stuf
Brung home in his teeth

Come days wen he skratchn say
Mite try killin sumwun to make noose of me
Paps if I make noose of him
He dont done do it?

Woden dog howcom you loss
Yor own seecrit eye sunshine
Woden dog howsit taist that woden dogfood
Whars thet kemel dog
Ever see canser wok a mile
Smokin up a kemel ever see war stop
Juscos you lookin?

Jeez fokes jus thort
If bad stuf stop no mor noose fur woden dog
Wot then ole flee bit dog
You see nuddin to lookat
You jus sit theren cry

***

Whodat
Striden backnforth in orifice
Who *dat*
Givin ordures

Whodat maken long biznis calls
Eatin long biznis bananas
He look horty
My whodat planifikting plitical fouture

Watchout
Here he come zoom by
Zoom silva jet clatter copta
Weekend in Toekyoe?
Meetin Younited Nayshun?

Whodat now
Widda dame in a yot wearin captin hat
Crakin lobsta
My my

Woden dog thats who
Woden dog how smart you done got

***

Hard inside
Woden dog

Woden dog gon
Sniff aroun for mudder

Mudder soft inside
Woden dog dig

Woden dog swetpant
Nuddin come up

No mudder
Dipressed woden dog

Dog shrink gifm pill
How that now help

Dog body keep movin
But inside he nut

No mudder inside
No soft strong mudder

Nuddin in world
Woden dog size

Howls too purty offen
In his dog house dum

So small he feel
Stinkin wikid woden

                                        ***

Yes derm dawg
Urmpteen snarls
Make nuddin
No bedder

Yew always countin
Countin crazy dawg
You mean
See me through glass

Derm yew lukn so glum
Like eny doods nuddin
Yew like like yew
Say dancein shit

Call yewsell a dawg
I aint buyin
Yew aint no morna
Cardboard ratlsnaik

Yew mean
Snarlin always makin
Fuss yew bossy think
Me mor stoopidn yew

Maybe too
But I countin
The timesnile git yew
Wunofem

342

Woden dog keep stil
So you can feel it
Movin

Rounanroun whirlin world
Why you keep with it
Is that reel

Woden dog
Keep stil so you
Can feel it movin

***

Hey now
Hoo done got hide
Inside you innerlekshuls

Meckin
Yore gin
Roll I say shuns

Hooz
Moovin yoohoo
All ways tokkin

Wokkin long
Rode like you wuz
Uh ginrollized creekin

Rekkernize hoo
He be my my if it aint are
Ole solom fren dubble you dee

***

Woden dog sittin
On the backstares

Sittin in the dark
Breathin a bit

What's this listen
Breathin

Laff
Woden dog

That's it
Laffin on the backstares

Thems wavesnwaves
Them cool backstares

Help dog floatin
Low float high

Not let waves go so
You seem zikazak

Doan it hurt some
Hey woden dog

Not let the laff hole up
In woden dog box

Listen breathin just so
Now no more done hurt

***

Wyso suddn everbody
Rite on walls

FREE WODEN DOG
Anifs time

Like I nevver got
Inclose free

344

Woden
Dog piksher?

Spose no place else
To rite

***

Silva smoak of pine
Burn chill
Woden dog shivver
Owl not heard

Lightslice fix to floor
Think dead
Woden dog like ice
In his box owl not heard

Owl hoot rainbow
Out of owl eyes
Owl hoot rainbow wonder
Dog not see dog bark at ghost

Owl not heard
Dog munch heap white aple
Not feel snow as owl bountie
Not smell snow rainbow

Woden dog eat heap
Aple up
Pip corn all cold aple meat
Not see owl

Not see some owl eyes
Not hear
How pips look sound yum yum
Crunch owl eyes aple up

Dog wine in boxn stay putn scoff
Woden dog alltime scoff
Woden dog shut in wod
Not smell sweet pine

Woden dog not smell wind song
Burn swingin low
Swingin in pine wod
Owl not hoot fur him in pine log

Owl not hear in dog box
He woden dog
Snow owl hoot that rainbow now
Now hootn touch dog heart

3

After A Noise in the Street

It is the small
Distinct image, old as you like,
On a coin, or silvery
In a daguerreotype

Speaks to me:
The trooper Probus,
Two centimetres high, at most,
Helmeted, sloping

A spear
Across a shoulder,
Condenses all
The gas of empire

Into a few
Quick signs. No fuss, either,
Had perplexed her face,
This young and tawny

Woman, but
An anger, fine, makes
Luminous now the eyes
She levelled in Nebraska

At the lens, never
Exhausting it, for the hands
Folded and slender in her lap
Siphon a torrent

Of feeling through the image.
There is anguish
Untrapped, an ardent
Breath sets free to fall

A dew as on a cherry,
To magnify, by sharpening
So far, the resolute
Infinitesimal flesh, this wisp

Of being, only this
A mortal
Tentatively manifests. A
Measure just

One fraction grander could
Put back
Into the spear
Slaughter;

Distend a pleat
In this dress, or blow
A tassel up
Beyond belief — and it lumbers

Back into the flimflam; an
Embossed cuirass,
Probus any bigger, snagged
In power's mesh

Spills, as a blur, or boast,
His contracted time
Into the heaving
Primordial pettiness.

Hot Bamboo

My roots go
sideways
only
they
will
never

grope deep
nohow can
these
hollow
shafts
hold
remembrance
whenever
sounds
trickle
flute
gong
from
the crackpot's
pretend house
I
want you
moonlight
(if you
will)
to waft
them
over a touch
a merest whiff
will
send
me
responding
with a shiver
on my way
down
again
growing
to the hut
impossibly
a lake
is
there
an early
heron

suspended
in a mist
now
drinks
this
open
sky
limbs
of wild plum hide
old scrolled
mountain
so
spread
your
fan
soon
sighed
bamboo

Jerusalem, Jerusalem

White building under pecan tree
Four poles cradle the porch roof

Beyond gap in branches blue sky trackless
Snoozing in roof slope ghost of a pagoda

White wall veined with leaf shadow
Tree unfolds a boom of spray

Homely air, who knows which way moving
Tree pulse drums, cricket whistles tune

Old walls of wood creak when air cools
Tree spoke to folks indoors a rustling lingo

Crisp lettuce on their plates and red meat
Perched in tree same bird sang as now

Pecan tree sole hero still grows
Slowly war and work fetched those folks away

Too bad house now gone to seed
In trashed rooms white devils hang out

Tending itself — a tree in majesty
Glued to gum, soda pop, the white mouth

Look again: no thought can be too high
Of whisper locked in white heart

Tell thought: still harder time ahead
Don't hold against them drift of old song

Coral Snake

I had been planting the sliced seed potatoes
When the snake started up from underfoot
And slithered across the gravel I stood on.

His beauty was not the point.
He was the kind that kills in a minute or two —
Chop off the finger he bit, or else.
But he was beautiful: alternating the black,
Red, and yellow rings more regular far, thick or thin,
Than wedding bands on a jeweller's ringstick.

He had come out of nowhere like evil.
He didn't care about me or want me.
I cared about him enough — it was fear.

Fear, not for me, no, but for him, the snake:
Long-trapped, an old horror breaks loose,
Later you say Alas, the snake was beautiful.
So I wonder what I can kill him with,
And notice in my hand the hoe; he isn't far,
Full stretch in his ringed ripples I see him
Slithering east of the two asparagus ferns.

I whop the hoe down and nail his head in the gravel
Between the chicken wire fence and a vegetable frame.
But he won't let go, I'm wrong, his free head
Rose over the quartz and flint pebbles;
Wild, the taut pure body, to be moving on and on.

Nothing to be done; if I shift the hoe
He'll streak through the chicken wire and I'll be
Cut off. I pressed harder on the hoe blade,
His tough coil resisted and the head
Wove a figure of eight in a pocket of air.

I didn't want it to be done, I didn't.
But how now to stop, considering his pursuits,
Easygoing as he is, pinheaded, slow to bite —

They say his tooth sits so far back
He needs to chew to do you in.

For there was more snake now in me than him.
I pushed the hoe blade harder down
And reached around the gate post for a stone.
That stone I eased
Beneath his tiny weaving head, taunting him,
Then reached around the post for a second stone.

When I looked again
The small black head with its yellow nape band
Was pointing up and the mouth, opening, closing,
Snapped at air to repel the blind force
Which held him down.

I could not do it, not to him, looking so
True to himself, making his wisdom tell,
It shot through me quicker than his poison would:
The glory of his form, delicate organism,
Not small any more, but raw now, and cleaving,
Right there, to the bare bone of creation.

And so I gripped the second stone but steadily
Thumped that telling head down flat
Against the surface of the first stone.
The broken body, I lifted it up and dropped it
Later into a vacant honey jar. The colours
Now have faded; having no pure alcohol,
I pickled the snake in half a pint of gin.

Nostalgia

What metaphor can bring back
What metaphor
Like nothing else can
Bring back the beautiful girls
For all the world
Like nymphs in pools
They spread their limbs
In long convertibles
And shook free their hair
Riding the highways for ever

Wild Flowers

Like voices
They never grew in water;
All began with nobody there to see.
A warmth helped; mud propelled them; early
The seeds rode in animal pelts across immense
Reeling distances, or
Were blown through light by the wind,
Like lovers.

When we were bush mice
They settled, ignored, in the cooling places;
Blood took heat,
Bees ate them, lizards and happily

Spiders liked them. Lodged in the fat of horses
They travelled. Tigers, and us,
Still tree hoppers, hardly felt what colours
Ringed by unearthly
Fragrances without names they had.

Far off the glittering libraries,
Vases of blown glass;
But look,
On roadsides they exist. Songs in our hands
They go along with us. A passion
Means us to pick them, so
Responding to early light we stop; then drive on home
To draw blankets back
And make our love while sensing them,
Their far fields, their darknesses.

Dirge for the Mistress of
Screaming Animals

Woke in the night
Amazing silence
Somewhere moon

Filling my hide-out —
Milk, a truth —
Drank from a mirror

No sound in street
All systems muted
No buzz, no roar

No shout or shooting
Icebox, even
Forgot to hum

354

Ah but I longed
Solo in silence
For breath dream-quickened

A rustle beside me
Flesh on linen
Longed for her

Her scraps of sleep talk
Name she'd murmur
Said she worked

As a lab assistant
Chicks and rats
React to her shots

I see her stand
At the lab door heeding
Quick rat chatter

Her charts record
Behaviour graphs
In sign and figure

Why, mistress of
Screaming animals
Nevermore babble

Of mutable habits
Skills crepuscular
Hiding and seeking

Snap your fingers
Clatter a dish
Play me your heart beat

Give me your long shot
Fathom my sorrow
With your lost love cry

Days of Heaven

Night rain beats down on the roof,
Hearing it
A flesh melts —

Shallow graves, crazy places
And morning comes,
Happiness, we make toast

Bivouac

Among the Polish Chassidim, perhaps among the Chassidim
generally in Eastern Europe, it was prohibited to leave a book
open in the village reading room. A sacred book, that is. Inter-
fering forces might invade it, or escape from it.
A shadow might, otherwise, cross the open pages. The shadow
might distort the features of a divinity which inhabited the
pages, at once hidden and open. Or an expression on those features might run wild in the world, unmediated by any mind, the
reader's, who sat there in his cloak being bothered by his fleas.

The word desired to be dulled. If not by the mind of this or
that reader, with or without fleas, then by the clapping shut of
the book. Otherwise the pneuma might break out and be at
large, tigerishly among the furrowed desks, or hopping mad in
the muddy or sunbaked little village streets.

The book had covers to shield its pages from mud or sunlight.
Not even fingers had any title to cross the track of the word.
The covers also existed to contain the scorching majesty of
the word. At least, a risk was set aside. Who knows, the majesty
might otherwise choose to spill out as idiocy and make havoc,
or too much heaven, among the huts.

It was also an offence to place one open book on top of another open book. The charms of the pneuma were inviolable,
transcendental.

356

The light shoots shadows into this room, across the pages of books and a few squares of Philippino reed carpet. Somehow I love it so. Outside, the trunk of an elm spells out a green shadow across blades of grass, the quiverings of which can only be detected if you take the time to watch, if you truly care, if you quiver a bit yourself. The grass blades tilt at an inexplicable mass of angles. Their tips ought to be points, but actually are bitten off, because every so often I try to mow the shadows down and the mower's cruciform blade rips across them. Underneath the mower's metal casing the momentarily unseen, as grass, suffers this.

No matter. A sheet of paper on the desk surface carries the print of the insect screen, a tight cross-hatching. This keeps the little winged demons out and holds a whiteness in. Nothing written contradicts the self-sufficiency of the word; its complex force, noted only in various proximate oscillations, disdained by the flea, unapparent in action, otherwise in hope, is a fiction so threatening that we devise our most dazzling footwork to pull a little fruit out of the teeth of disaster.

Here, too, on this bitter grass near dusk I saw the cicada come into being. First it had made its long journey up a perpendicular tunnel to the earth surface; the cicada itself had lubricated the tunnel with a juice it exuded through its protective pupa. Now, inside the bronze pupa, which was crisping, a general shiver began to happen. An infinitesimal foot prodded a hole in the pupa, then another foot. Gradually the head was coming out, then the body, forwards, but for twenty minutes it made a lunge, rested, lunged again. Its moment of emergence was so prolonged that it could hardly be seen emerging. The motive and the power behind this effort — barely imaginable — I felt them in my groin as a sensation between craving and fright, then in my throat as a taste, brandy and pepper.

Finally, mute and dull, an oval pellet had shrugged the pupa off. The pellet put a leg out, soon another leg. Its back was turning emerald, then golden emerald, with wings that lay flush with the pellet, exceedingly frail, then larger, unfurling into twin networks of golden emerald filigree tracery. And the

357

head, with eyes, had woken up, was turning this way and that way; now the wings could move and lift. The cicada glowed as if dusted with a pollen out of which, for the sake of argument, the breath of a beyond conjectured the world's first agile anatomies. Pristine forest contracted to the volume of a singing bird's egg. A fiery drop of universe at the other end of a tunnel through time.

So I lay down on the grass and put an ear to it. I was expecting the wings to rustle and give off a melodious twang, faint as the last echo of a Jew's harp in an Egyptian burial chamber.

Then it simply wasn't there. From high up in an elm its first ancient cackle fizzed into the onset of dark.

A Carpenter Verbatim

More or less confident what I see is there
With no place else to go
Call a dog from the stoop anytime
Likely he'll trot across and look at you
You bet a word can be so spoken
It plumbs this thing or that action

Who's to say though what stuff escapes
When you pull up the string
There was this neat house I worked opposite
And people in it
A neat house to warm the new society

Someone shot
Brains and blood I tell you
Stuck in the shag carpet streaked walls
The people went on living there
Never cleaned up

Got the old lady to lower the rent
Two years (because because)
Till the lease ran out
Never took fright his ghost might show
Never shook out the chips of skullbone

Ate their food watching TV
What sort of people I don't know
What can have been biting him
The one
Who shot himself the hick
They near as likely killed

But your spiral staircase now
Looks so pretty
From the top
Hang a mirror from the beam or fit one
In the ceiling sheet rock

Someone going down could look right up and
Never see himself at all
For seeing it

Svatava's Dream

Twice changed, forty years
Different country, different person

There I was, again, you must
Have heard me tell

How when I was eleven, all
The books of this old writer, how

Eagerly I read them, mystic, yet
Only now, back, beyond the river

Was I aware how close I was to him,
And found my way down cobbled

Lanes, twisting
Into his pink museum

Found some friends, a man, a woman
Had made a painting of a house

It was pink and breathing, walls
Went out and in, windows

Pink, the air was flowing out and
In again, I heard the sounds

The city sounds, just as ever
They had been, just as ever

But they said the house was mine
Mine if I wanted the pink museum

Yet the painting was my house
Here, not there, stone, this

House I live in, mine, of stone
It hurt me so to choose, I could not

Tell whose pink house was there or here
To be mine if I wanted

Was it for me, the old museum
The writer's mystical pink

And me eleven, was the picture
Where I am, or in a renovated

Hradshin room, was this a time
When you breathe fast and double

A time in the flush of being
A house you make with breath

Go pink and everything
For you are torn

The Turquoise

Somehow the memories fizzle out on us.
Large black eyes of people starving.
A snatch of music soon
Will be Merida, the mirrored bedroom, not
The pang felt there, but a fountain
Touches palm trees. Pang —

I forgot how perception had to be
Wrenched from its
Regular socket: the speech of folds, eyewhite
And snow the robe a woman wore,
Foreign liquor
The smell of a man at noon in his hammock.

Raw stuff: a crooked
Line of objects. Look, it is put
Straight like hair by distance.
The whole shadow of (our tune) your smile
Oozed first from
Repetition on a jukebox. Careless

Memory cooks
The kind of meal you
Gulp down, because the right place
Had shut, or the old prices are
Out of sight. Compulsion
Turns you still

Back to the same town: the flies
In children's eyes are blue, the drowned
Horse prongs the air still,
Silver hoof; never sensing wrong,
The deadly salesmen frisk again
With girls in the disco.

Swat a fly, scratch the wall
Of an ear with a toothpick: four, suddenly,
The grouped figurines
Loom huge from the desk angle,
And glow, clay Chupicuaro, bronze
Krishna, the wooden African —

As gods. To construct them
Ancestors broke through their skins,
Getting this far at least: the rock
Crystal, coyote, stud him
With turquoise, let the orange fire
Be a tail like a beacon;

For the unseen escapes,
The remembered
Dominion cracks, falsifies
Desire and presence as they fly screaming
Before us, headdress and tail
Bushy, slashing backward in the dark.

A Forge in Darkness

They hadn't forgotten his name
Or whereabouts the forge was,
The brick oven, hot glow
Of charcoal, the hammer floats
Up, held in mid-air now, and
What beer the old man drank.

A heart isn't like that. A heart
Won't wait until the dark
Comes to cool things off a bit.
It works through the blinding
Noon heat, careless of sparks,
Of hoofs clipclopping uphill.

Boys came by. Owls looked on.
A horse tail flicked at bluebottles,
Under the canopy of this pecan.
This hill — part of the night then,
A slope, that's all, crested with a forge,
Like a wave flecked with red foam.

What a letdown for her, hitched
To that limping, fretful man,
The reek of sweat and charcoal on him —
And her arms could take a whole sky in,
Her thumbs govern long ships or fondle lambs,
Yet she slid from her wave and under him.

It was here, right here, where I came
To be living. She's gone, he's gone.
I cook chicken where the forge
Must have been. In the dark I
Pour out more wine to remember
The little old lives of them.

Taking a chance, I think
That's where she must have gone:
Into the artifice of not forgetting
A name and what went on,
When the boys watched and owls
Heard the hammer come down.

THE BALCONY TREE

1

An Ideologist

FOR DAVID EDWARDS

Nebulous, fractured, not too fast,
How come this ring of hair
Falls to the white I doodle on.

If I turn it around by thought
I face unfeatured distance;
It hangs in the moon for luck.

Masts that were trees creak,
With cobalt sky bamboo combines,
And spiteful critics rule the roost:

Spirit is fierce, it contradicts,
Only a presuming, only a wizened
Spirit carps and backbites.

Attend. Soon my bamboo palace
Bathes in the pool that winked
From the fracture of that iron hair.

Unshod I see the earth, old nag,
Shake off its flies and epithets
And run like a cloud with the moon.

Ancient Lace

Sitting silent and a long time gone
Hearing the tower clock strike faraway two
Feeling the sun toil in the skin of your face
Truth to tell waiting ain't so bad he said
Listen to the Carolina wren

Try not to let things ever get you down he said
Carolling like she found a roach to eat
Zucchini zucchini she call in the green bamboo
Tower clock won't ever strike a two the same he said
That's Emmy now knocking on a wood block

Or it's a kitchen pot she could be knocking on
The little changes bring you back to earth he said
No great shakes plain poor old earth he said
But now by heaven that was a woodpecker
Real weird it snickers with a hiccup

Don't always put your life on the line he said
A great shit heap out there and me and you
Leastways we settle up to be a whiff of it
Ten feet up today looking across the town
What speaks to you makes all the difference he said

Might be that little stick of frankincense you lit
Burning in the tree tub and a Carolina wren
And a stroke or two on a bell and a bird's note
It's good when things pierce your heart a moment
Make it pure he said and plenty more than heaven did

It's that warm the sun to melt your mask he said
And did they bring any wine for them to sip
So be it if they did not and enough's enough
Long time since like shooting stars they did set off
Suppose their whispering brocades will pass this way

Anguish

Suppose he stays out in the cold
With towers around him floodlit
And the big birds that shriek around the towers in a trio
And around the birds the sky
Silent as the tomb at two in the morning

This time he can't come back
Often before, he might drift back in, not only for his coat
Paradise was near enough in his belief
He only had to march around himself indoors
To the flick of my eyelids
Making the dreams of men tormented come true

For certain he'll be back, dripping wet
A mess, river weed stuck to his ribs, clammy
And a cold story to tell the children
How he peered up the birds' backsides
Put his arms in the warm sleeves of their wings
Flew first around the towers, then on to paradise

An Angel

Old men who beat their wives
Magyars with feet of mahogany
Mexicans with hearts of gold
They pin me to the wall
And ask for admissions

But young men and women too
Stand sick in a crooked line
Crazies gone to the clinic
Eyeballs falling out
Ask for my admissions

Scholars crouch in a line
Pointing at me rifles
Do I have their secret?
Butchers form a line with cleavers
Lung of pork and sawdust jawbone

— Of my slaughterhouse
The double doors on them I shut
Let them eat some other eyeballs
Let them eat their tripod noses
Altogether somewhere else

Me I frisk
In a fastness of dew
Highly microscopic
I will eat their bullets
Nor drop my positive disguises

Old shop fusty as hawkflight hide me
Implements of domestic torture
Hide me for the wink of a lifetime
Hide me drums that tumbled
When bit by bit a temple exploded

Folks I only ask you hide me
Sickening butchers look for me
And silken scholars think otherwise
Crooked as they come withal
But hoping somewhat

Then from a blackened book
Letters wrought of rock and water
Composing the raven's flight in chipped flint
Quitting my volcano
The devil I skip and frisk for thee

Bird Watching

Old folks with big faces
Get off their big butts
And raise binoculars

Roving for miles and floated so
Open-eyed by their thermals
They come to watch us birds

Finding in fresh air a life style
They are intrigued by blue bunting
To the loon's cry their red hearts caracol

For them we save the day with our tricks
Quaint compulsive ceremonies we perform
Delight back to life in them a long disbanded soul

Rare though they breathe down our necks
We can peck at hickory to suit their book
But when they learn, when they learn to call

Call and be recognized flamingo lakes
Will be for their pink flocks the habitat
They will squat and blink to be owl

Slowly their web of being will float out
Never to hold for long if at all
The thing they never knew how to desire

One day they will know one another
In several ways they once ignored
Nesting in dells and rocks they drove us from

One day ruffling our big butts and faces
We too will ask what secret glory possessed them
We too will watch and want it all

Still Small Voice

When you come to my country, tell me
Why was it, why did you travel so far
What you know of the place you are from, tell me
Fear not the place where you are

Tell me what you heard, many sounds, one by one
Tell me the rain, a dog's howl, out in the dark
Rustle of the dust under a footsole
Tell me a spoon, a dish, a dish, a spoon

The pooled light spread in a vine of colours
Carves through feeling roads to somewhere too
And wild saloons, a dark stream, a field with horses

A garden plot you planted six wild strawberries in, long ago
Rivers of grief that roll through flesh and time
Red holes in the ground where people weep and pray
Tell me those, if you can, I will hear them call
Where you are is half the way

When ghosts rise up, and mists, and silvery presences
You feel a quicker beat of wings in every breath of air
When the hollows open, night begins —
Or sun will spread its peacock fan, moon make hay of
    everything
Baskets prettily woven
People at the doors, talking, tell me
Words they speak or cannot, tunes they sing to, even
How they resist, the people, when times are hard and they
    can take no more

How they ache, heartbreak has to come
And how it is to be not dead, tell me the animal touch
Of a summer dawn, feathery owl's cry
Tell me the wind and walls it clings against
The stones and the water, speechless, and the skin
On everything, cherries and moles and wings
Mountain peak and egg
And what is going on, the reasoned beings being born
The wine glass cool to touch, tang of salt, canvas of a shoe
A broken ship hiding still in a skin of trees —

Braiding the split fibres of time
A shiver of desire to shape a storied music into things
Yes, and the sea to be with you, forsaken sea
Tell me the lost voices of the sea

When you come from your far land, tell me
Tell me what the changes are, their night, their day
And how it is to have believed them, tell me now:
Where you are is half the way

(To the tune of Pat Metheny's 'If I Could', and for
    Doña Brown)

Devil Lyric

Love becomes a heavy cargo
Burst loose from its ropes
In the hold it looked so harmless
Birds in cages, coffee

Now the ship rolls
The belovèd turns her face
Hundredfold as the wind
The cargo gongs around

Not so natural death
Masts rake the deep
Gulls forget the keel
Nothing to drink or nibble

The coffee and the birds
Squirm against the underdeck
Soon a dizzy squid
Has fixed them with its ink

Meanwhile drink your chicken
Carve apart your coffee
Contemplate a third
Source of some disorder

Souls that colonize
This pinball of a planet
Gulfs of glory think you
Sphincters of His Image

Michèle's Rooms

The handle of the willow basket curving
The red tiled unlevel trodden floor
At knee height the clock face but no clock body
Toy clock hands constant at twenty to six

The wooden bowl empty of apples
Balls and hanks of wool in the willow basket
The procession of sea urchin shells on the mantelpiece
The angled needles as they pierce the wool

In coloured sleeves the shelved LPs
Loops of plants I came to water
Pink of the wool and of the towering candle
Snowy bears and rabbits warm for Lola

Rising suns of scallops knitted into a shawl
The way the shawl hangs unoccupied from a hook
A mobile by the window strung with wands and ducks
The tang of wine a moment held behind the teeth

The invisibility of the hook
The absence of electricity
The plant bowl that overflowed on the telephone bill
The tiny bird crouched on the mantelpiece

The lifted latch and the opening window
The breeze that burrows through a shirt for flesh
All these marks to detect her laughter by
The word's very event in a special voice

Curve of the beak of the sacred ibis
Heart of legend locked in a nondescript replica
Spheres that only come to thought as curves completely seen
Two cracks in the wooden beam darkening them

The wooden beam's edges bevelled by an old axe
Absent from the encyclopaedia the surge of the scribe's mind
Flit of the pen's tip crossing two scraps of paper
The ghostly scribe without a name

A Revenant

Now she is here
Again, quick, in a taste
Of lemon, not even so
Much as a bite, she is here
In a whiff

Of lemon peel, no way
Even to tell
Where from, the light
Saffron perhaps, a snowy
Touch of metal

Or, afloat
On a flood of being, me,
I had drawn
A tingle out, indistinct,
A distant signal

Flashing in the hotter rush
Of air tonight, mixed
Into it, funny,
Today, the wiggle
Of a child, head back

Shrimp bodysock, she
Did a glancing
Noonday
Dance across
A crack

In a paving stone, she
Shook
At the sky
Her fist
With a flower in it

Now so long dead
Another
Is here, I remember to be
In the taste
Or touch, or in the child

A wandering
Sensation, mutely
To learn my shape, later to flit
Ghostwise from a being
I will never know

La Morena

My white cow tonight is quite silent
My white cow milking a heart from darkness

What tricks and silks will she tumble into
My white cow with opening parachute lips

My white cow with a shirt of woodsmoke
My white cow with a beehive of desires

Sometimes an abandon seizes her by the horns
Sometimes she is placid and sings in church

My white cow dancing in her field of fire
My white cow walking with dangerous steps

Everywhere she supposes there are cathedrals
Everywhere bells inscribe on air their spiral signs

My white cow with marked ideas of her own
My white cow whose tuft is a tangle of tempers

The baskets of air hang from her solid bones
The jugs of earth lift with her little breasts

My white cow who makes sorrow burn a day away
My white cow who makes sorrow bite like a shark

My white cow who shivers and penetrates men
My white cow who rides men bareback

Often conscious of too many things at one time
Often come times when she knows nothing at all

She has no clock for her timing is internal
No voice but hers alone tells her when and how

She will eat dry bread if there's none better
My white cow who tastes always of oranges

My white cow who goes one better than the snow
Her quim is heaven for whom she pleases

In the nights we stretch with furious argument
My white cow takes every word to its limit

Shortening days we walk together hand in hand
More than once she tore my arm from its socket

I will do my dance one-armed for my white cow
I love her life her ways her difficult nature

We live beneath roofs that stand centuries apart
My white cow in small towns and purple cities

My white cow in a village dances to the guitar
My white cow sipping wine from a cup of clay

When the baskets are hanging bright in the water
They fill with her fish and creak in earthquake

When in my white cow's hair old stories are told
We stop them to start the world afresh redeemed

She is absent in the canyon of her red lust
She is present in the ordinary dishes we eat off

My white cow is a black one to tell the truth
Or else Chinese or else some kind of Arabian

To call her cow at all is a profound mistake
She is a leopard with four cubs in a forest

My white cow in that hotel stripping off her clothes
My white cow who is not mine at all

My white vanishing cow with her dolphin legs
My white cow who wades *toute nue* in the Toulourenc

Her skin mirrors itself and that is it for us
I fall into her skin to oblige Lord Shock

I tongue my white cow in her purity and playfulness
She will never come around to believing I mean it

My white cow imagines me far off running away
Little does she know I run to catch her leaping form

White cow who dances wild in the middle of the world
White cow your sweet dust with the wind blowing over it

Cybele

It is cold outside so she has walked in
Loving my feet for her own good reasons,

Straight in, tail up, scanning the kitchen
She discovers nothing but a desire

So at my feet she winds and unwinds
Her calico skin. When I tap at the blotter

Up she lifts a paw, forgets, listens again,
Looking elsewhere, if elsewhere is anywhere

And curls in a fit of abandon
Around the tongue of my tennis shoe.

Her paw milks the lace, her paw milks the ankle bone,
Amorously unparticular she forgets her milk

Habit, suddenly crouches, licking her tail:
Suddenly I know nothing for her is sudden

For she forgets her forgotten tail, silent
She explores cavity, cavity, for instance

Behind the cutting block propped against
The wall, she has found a fascination

Shadow or moonlight there, scampers off
In a rage of vague desire for shadow

And foot, the raw smell of shadow and foot,
She's stepping over hollows everywhere

And finding what she wants to be hidden there,
Everything new, glistening cushion, clay

Horse, fragile, over it she has to step
A soft way. What invisible spasms of being

Span her heart beat? How come she detects
Here in this room the moon she only knows

From green by the shadows moon-eye makes
Nothing of? Smells are shape, the sharp

Outline of mouse, the cry of yucca white
She evidently smells when tasting my feet.

Not my feet. Them, me she ignores. It is
A very sweet crisis to be constantly cat:

Her senses, precise as Gieseking's fingers,
Track a music, her veins are shivering with it —

Transformation, the furnace of horror
Red in her claw, fact in her leap of fire —

She is arrow, target. The bird, a flit
She hesitates to hear, could prong her

Against a sky that is no sky for her
But promise of open, beak, edible, never

Depressive, it stings, strikes, white glistens.
Bone aches too that way in my meat.

The China Virgins

They tinkle in their glass
Voices more thin than shrill
Coils of mist they penetrate remote hill temples
They are fire tongues capping spires of thought
They inhabit oblongs of ice in orange juice

Often they appear when creation begins
In memory
They rub their fingers and glow when you lose your mule
Hungering footsore in a Tibet of aimlessness
Like an onset of birdsong in heartbreak they capture you

Cool outrush of force
In the construction of a seashell
Meandering prolonged across symmetry breaks
They delineate an evolution
They round the roof of a wren's nest

Pop of champagne cork
Snap of elastic against firm muscle
If not so then slow motioning the convolvulus display
Tremor of a voice when it has caught the drift
Of white bone powder blown across the Gobi

Breath of wind bending the crest of a catalpa
Also the clatter when catalpa bean pods fall
The sputter when wet has called for the surge
Of a body incandescent but then backs off
The china virgins recoil to advance

On the back of matter they pound their bright fists
Flash their eyes in the twice five parabolas of a Leticia's legs

A parchment swept by fingers
Sidereal coin
A nymph spinning struck into the hot silver centre
A song that drinks the scent of a space unborn
Nothing nothing but a phrase no sooner uttered
Than questioned as to its calligraphy
Nothing sooner questioned than the china virgins

Dust with Whisky

Solo the locomotive horn responding
Hollows out the heat of night,

The North American locomotive horn
Responds to the cool, peculiarly

Strained (sausage meat forsooth
Loading a tube of sheep gut)

Contralto warble of Clara Butt.
Dame Clara sings from a *tomba oscura,*

Under mortal pressure Damosel Clara sings,
So profound her breath, dense her tone

They model in air the swept cone of an old
Phonograph horn. Frilling its orifice,

Waves of tin harbour a painted rose,
And fragrant sound, purple enough

With a furor to reverse
The back of time, begins to manifest

(Stranger yet, it honeycombs their hill)
Ephesians tucked by friend or family in.

Seven troughs of stone. So the dead were baked —
El pueblo unido — soon to scowl or grin,

Being vaguely seen, wind-wrinkled shoals.
Quicker spirits hear their call drift up

Whenever those who sing along awake
Drink liquid amber or Saint Paul's bliss.

Far western winds, get this, you cornucopias
Of shooting iron, atom bomb, and Indian bone:

Violent blue above them still balloons
With small mercies, welcome, or a ship.

Then why erase these rough hewn records:
Hope sounds in a voice but not for ever.

Night Wedding in Anamur

Cézanne made men to play bézique
    You look at heavy backs
A hatted peasant head
    Perhaps a pipe gone out
Bonehard still though fathoms deep
    The wily roosters winged by hazard
Shine in the cottage empire of paint

All that was a scene will change
    The table on a shore collects
A foreign gaze a touch far out
    A table clothed in Turkish white
Seven people sitting at it
    Finger rings and tulip heads
Formal around the bowl of salt

Now let the scene unfold their flesh
    Night opens wide its cobalt mouth
Smoke and smells are tucked away
    So black the ovals cane sombreros blow
Across the sand they taste of olive

A fresher wind can levitate them now
    It has them float
The fish mothering sea that never wastes
    A breath when day dawns or doomed
Civilizations cut their bonds to fall apart
    That selfsame sea poises on its crests

Musicians busy thoughtful witnesses
    A heartbeat above
The old as usual unrolling ocean scrolls
    Now mold the air with such sweet force
Again the table lifts and dancers
    Leaping coupled skim the water

Bathed in her moon the bride
    Heavenly arms outspread
Dances to the upbeat
    And she so startled looking like a corpse
Strung with fairylights and coppery balloons
    Still quickening Attis torn and underground

Her table is upheld
    Ghosts around it eating fast
(Softly out of her silken box she rose)
    With lamb and water melon
Froth of beer still ticking in the glasses
    Each a singular shadow out

Circle

They all run around the doorstep
They point at the sky
And for sure the stars are falling
So many it's like the tassles
Of an oldtime dancing dress

But why look
When lost in thought
Inside

Why, if someone you are thinking about
Once in a house long gone without a trace
Might be recalling now
The way rain would start to patter
Across the timbered roof

And in the palm of her hand
How the dog's muzzle felt
The wet nose clean
The tongue warm

Ballad of Charlotte

Before she bought the knife to kill Marat,
Charlotte Corday had bought a fancy hat.

The five-inch knife she bought at a hardware store;
The hat was black with ribbons green galore.

At a hardware store she bought the five-inch knife,
Resolved to take the gutter tyrant's life.

She bought the hat to do the thing in style,
With a sort of Norman Mona Lisa smile.

Consider, when you visualize the scene —
Over his lukewarm bath she had to lean:

What if across her eyes the hat had slipped,
Unsighting her the moment when she gripped

Violently the knife, to push it in?
Or if the hat had fallen past her chin

And plopped, before she pushed, into the water . . .
Marat and Charlotte both dissolved in laughter.

Due to her sense of style it was not so;
She does for history what she had to do.

Out of her dress she takes the knife — one thrust,
Her blade has pierced his body, as it must.

Later the questions. Charlotte acted 'alone'.
Was 'firm' and 'feminine'. Conspirators? None.

Her motive? Folks, I struck the monster dead
To frighten other monsters off, she said.

Marat, mean-spirited, vindictive, shrill
Poseurs like you defraud the hungry still.

Ranting fanatics cast you as a martyr.
If only Charlotte's hat had hit the water.

Charlotte instead is later to be seen
Riding a cart on the way to the guillotine.

Behind the cart, voices sang a song,
Tiny voices heard, but not for long.

The scarlet robe she wore, without her hat,
Showed all her body's curves. Now why was that?

Pelting rain had soaked her to the skin,
No doubt to purify her of her sin.

Whose were the voices? Little girls, they say,
Held hands and sang and danced for that Charlotte Corday.

A Farewell in Old Mexico

Perhaps her husband was the engineer.
Palm up, timing perfect,
She waves to him a hazel wave.
Here is the hand she cups, at the limit

Of an arm's curve, to catch his sooty kiss.
Animal black complex of intestines
Afloat on a thunderhead of steam, to the clank
Of twenty open trucks, you expelled

A hiss. Soon the sunflower field of faces
Lifts as one to swallow cool sierra air.
Wind sang star patterns into the grit.
On the boardwalk begonias inhabit tin cans;

Liquid, they are mirrored, even redder
In the sweat beading her top lip. The caboose
A dot, now she waves, with her comical
Sense of order, to it, not him.

The Balcony Tree

New neighbour say: hope it won't interrupt you
When I walk by your open door?
O no, I say: I'm really not a rat,
At least not so you'd notice. Spring and Fall
Open is the way I like to leave it.

Hung, too, from the balcony tree a bird feeder.
New neighbour say she like it, kinda neat.
Little tree in leaf now. We
Hope this alley cat won't find
Ways to catch a finch, or me, the rat.

We say: before we open doors, we'll watch
For finch or sparrow. If they be there,
We won't step out to do the things we do.
Won't switch on our sensitive ignitions.
Try not to scare the creatures from the tree . . .

Must say, though, I miss
The earlier neighbour, long before
I chained the feeder to a branch.
Miss her mad look, her finger tapping window,
Clothes gone, I miss the skin, the Latin

Nipples in the candlelight,
Miss the swoop and sweat of her sassy back,
Her talk, till she took off, still going on.
Did she find work, make a buck
Where she went, with her perfumes, to look for it?

Or is she fat in San Antonio and fed up?
Who else betrayed her, made her?
Under the tree, with a low hopeless laugh
She coiled her hair up once like a Tarahumara.
Not so my new neighbour:

She tells me there's a gap. Events
To be explained. Touches of understanding
Shunned in fright. Her smile, like a fan
She tries to open but can't find the catch.
What can I tell her?

Jump the gap? Snail has a place to go,
Horse, quick, rumbas over copperhead?
But whole creeds have collapsed into the banks
We borrow lifetimes from, to eat
Frenzy, evacuate abstraction —

New neighbour know it all. So I say:
You made it home, and here is being —
No reverend killers ring this balcony tree,
My door, no bullet whanged it yet, I close
Only when I sleep or hear them march by.

Walking the Puppy

The poet of the abyss
Takes to walking the puppy
While scrolled waves gather shape
To pound the shore
He sees a flowing violet web whisked from the abyss
Furrow the hump of a sea shell

Gentle frenzy puppy digs
Through the salt and oil
She hopes for a smell at least of something
Her quick young claws how like the waves
How like her pelt the shooshoo of the foam

They frolic away to a dry dune
Where gulls glide on down to meet their shadows
Wind lets fly its foibles round the clock
Cooling the backs of nondescript objects

A bottle top, an inch of ocean macaroni
Yield a howling O
Yield an M for the Mothers
How can a puppy interpret such a text
Will she be able to scratch from it a whiff of the real

Soon the night, night will drift over it all
A violet web of swoops and ribbons
And giving tongue to other stars
Breath by breath Delta will begin to expand
Still with beaks to pierce the wind gulls are marking time
Others trot on twilit stilts looking pretty stupid

Even the puppy waits for the poet to catch up
Patting her head he forgets what it means to breathe
He strokes her small throat
In love with every shining grain of sand
He is hungry for her small head and kisses it

She runs in the shining, golden dog, mad with delight
Though at a distance, nervous of course
One small hand brushing the hot heavenly blood away
The other cupping her loneliness
Aphrodite walks from the waves again

The First Move

Looking through window glass at early light
Hearing the moon descend over the temple that was
Combing space I feel a surge of hot day to come
A Mustang glides to the curb and stops
The driver rolls his window down
And in my window's angle a shape so vague
Somehow it might have borrowed an absent limb
Is a man whose bent and only body spills a shadow

His tiny dog a solid sniffling at a bug I think
Still the Mustang driver through his other window
Parting foliage has to see the brick tower beyond

Has the clockwork stopped
Have they stopped their arguments and screams
Now what will the boiling corporals do
And the children too hungry to cry out

Flit of sparrow
Descending on seeds in the feeder east of me
Hand reaching out through the open Mustang window
A whole arm snaking out
The hand has touched the hot or cool car roof
The shadow on tarmac sharp as the dog's *Geruch*
Immobile as this bergamot in a smoky taste of tea
Me immobile feeling through window glass
How absently till now I have clawed at life

Unchanged the light identical the suspense
Whoever moves first will make the first move

The Image

When they finally got around to where they had begun, it wasn't there any more. This was because they'd strung it out behind them. What had been a chariot of fire had become a rickety old wooden wagon. Losing its parts as it bumped along, wheels breaking, then dropping off, the rest of it a carcass of broken axles, bleached boards, rusted prongs and rotted leather cinches, it had eventually, without anyone noticing when it happened, disconnected itself, then vanished into thin air. It would have made not a scrap of difference if someone had been delegated to keep an eye on it, down the years. They never should have hitched it up, to be hauled behind them, in the first place. So now they looked around, checking the latitude. Forgetfully they wondered where it might have gone. Might they have miscalculated their position? Had they drifted or been driven off course? There had been hazards, they could have been driven off course; they could have drifted, there had been spates of negligence. But no, they had arrived at the exact same spot, this was where they'd begun. There were no signs of the four rivers, no views of the mountain. As for the temperate climate some of the old hands had spoken of, now there came over them a blizzard, biting cold, now the withering oven heat of the desert.

Vietnamese Harp

Before first light awake
    At a touch on a button
One taut steel string plucked I heard
    And another, another

Penetrating the dark a music
    Of spine and thighbone
Clear as the contour of a waterlily
    Ghostly as the snow it cups

Floated from its peak
   To ground, a shimmering pagoda
Spreads and folds its wings
   Stands where I lay

Amazingly nowhere, almost
   Too much trance for a body
So soon in the day, cut loose
   From the singing zigzags

I walked outside, by the open window
   Taking the same sounds in
But curious who in spirit
   Now might weep to be listening

Saloon with Birds

If someone barefoot stood in a saloon,
His dromedary might be chomping, outside,
That majestic meal. High olive notes
Plucked from a mandolin. Fumes. Leafgreen.

A dark descends. There, with banana palm,
Consorts forbidden music. Ugly. Ocean.
Delay it. First a clatter, from the birds.
They wax decrepit. Vocal signatures:

Who could ever have so illuminated them
That the letters, cut from stark air,
Assume no solitary monumental pose,
But wavily ache with the boat hulls?

Certain or not, an urgent finger prodded
Epsilons and wagtailed gammas free
From habit, a peculiar glue. No help. No
Waste. In the saloon each dust spake.

In the saloon the spokes of another
Sunlight, still this ocular companion though,
Rolled afternoons around, like meatballs,
Bubbles of corn sizzling in a crystal pan.

Throaty owls also, they could entertain
Quick, tensile teeth. A joy. Pelican moonlit.
Look at a pine nut. It exists, you know.
Little furred insects inhabit vast smells.

For this the saloon is open. A waft.
A waft is all it takes. A venetian blind
Has wrinkled the wash basin. A cool expounds
Blood orange, air in China, appalling beliefs.

Air wraps the mast. Air singing. Air,
The solo invader who timed anew
Our free objects. The saloon twangs,
Dust swims, a gong letting its hum fly.

Closing never. Least of all on syllables.
A split lemon has released from evil
Any soul what's willing. Get that. Now
Never you move like you were shrunk to be.

Or else forgo the little sorrow. Treasure
The big one. Tell, in the saloon,
Nothing of it. Look up. Long enough
The ocean has delayed. You can breathe again.

Roma 1985

Deep underground the sewers must be breathing,
Even abominable temples not yet dug up —

There you might find on stone a wicked scribble,
Or a phrase chiselled from a cantata by Catullus.

Deep down below, the poor and foreigners believe,
A clink of gold coins in a pot can be heard.

All around our hollow now and here, dust thickens;
Pricks harden to the crack of killing gas.

So we stop indoors and eat leaves of artichoke:
Ancient nerves of the city spread such a calm in us.

Or we take short breaths and trot across a street
Winged by grappa, ballasted by chocolate ice cream.

No use. No use at all. Reverse formations dilate
The negative; stress-fed cancers nibble bone and lung.

Yet high on moneyed roofs refreshing trees grow tall,
Hyacinths commit natural acts of resistance.

Earth has to grow one more new skin, people think
Like Rumi: We are alive today with another life.

Another Almost

Almost it might be better
to forget the past than build
ruins out of ruins

Perhaps the ruins are forms
of a response too blocked or timid.
Who can figure a whole house?

Think of the first scavenging Turks,
incurious, they patched their huts
with odds and ends of temples

No, I mean it is tough going
always to remember
so little or too much

Then have it all, or some,
spring unbidden back into place.
The bundle of woe is heavy

Wave to me as I go,
inhabitants of memory,
from your ruins, houses, forests

Continue the story that broke,
somehow, in the middle.
Let me see, let me smell you

Intact to my hearing
perhaps you will open
zones of being I never knew

Mysterious flesh
might blossom, lost hills
tipped with frail churches

Mansions complete
with moats of liquid silver,
misty kitchens, whence

Incredible pastries issue, baked
in ovens I never saw,
wines I never drank

Might redden tables of real oak
in twilight courtyards —
all ordinary as now. So I bend

With an ache for you, child,
and one for you, my only love,
and another for Doyle, Irish pilot

Blown to bits on a rocket range.
More lovely or horrible
things I know

Happen to others,
I write this only to shorten
the time of a music

Which, unless I forget,
will mass ruin on ruin.
The watermill we slept in,

My other love, the rushing
water beneath us,
you had clipped my fingernails

So I forget it, forget, child,
the midnight we were frightened of.
I hoist on my back again

The bundle of woe, but first
I open it, a crack,
to see the bloody rags

And worn-out toothbrushes,
the splinters of bone
and a silver ring from Afghanistan

Which slid into a river;
I sniff the hair beside me,
I touch excited midnight skin

The time of a music
almost now I hear the spell of it
playing backwards

Lampoon

1

The man across the street I thought was mad
Is playing catch this evening with a lad.

I hear the ball he flings plop into the glove
Worn by the lad, who's husky. Is it love?

Can love have cured him for a time? Or God?
The man has dialectically changed. How odd.

2

Push it aside, the surface image. Shove
The husky lad away, the baseball glove —

Recall another scene: J. Edgar Hoover
Drooled over snapshots of his husky lover

Curled up in shorts beside a swimming pool:
O toad-cold passion of 'The Heat' — how cool!

3

My madman, in the winter, scarlet cap
Pulled down around his eyes, I saw him tap-

Dance in the street and scatter in the snow
His brownbag lunch along the wall below

For hungry birds. Once he told me, too,
He used to live right here, where I now do.

4

Then off he crawled. The scarlet cap has gone,
Now shirt tail flaps, his left foot settles on

The broken ground, he lets the baseball fly,
Slow, to be sure, but straight enough. While I

Have scandalous doubts — the lad, is he his son?
Kinsman, or neighbour? Is he his illusion? —

The fact remains that in the USA
It's hard to know, harder still to say.

5

My madman plays the heretic, for once,
If blind Greed is the God of North Americans.

The corpse of instinct spits, when pressed by sport,
A lethal wad into the face of thought:

Yet, healed by sport, not love, that heretic
Can't quench the appetites that make him sick —

Captive of the Social Lie, him too. Down goes
His foot and up the dubious ball he throws.

6

So civilization plays to thwart all dreams:
The depth of life won't surface here, it seems.

He's mad as Hoover still, huffpuffing a sane
Picture of himself, while, yet again

The ball or switch is flicked, the rockets go:
There'll be no scandal. Not a soul will know.

Empty Fifth

> *Des Lebens Überfluß, das Unendliche,*
> *Das um ihn und dämmert, er faßt es nie.*
> Hölderlin, 'Rousseau'

That was in music
        This is not
The empty fifth
        A few folks thought

When flesh was colour
        Poxes death
Soldiers soldiered
        Taxes rose

And queens might rip
    In fat châteaux
Being bored to tears
    Their robes for a song

To be a presence
    Tongue can touch
Or keep from trickling
    Through to nought

Is not your own
    Near-empty fifth
A bottle of Scotch
    In a foul motel

Not medieval
    Sad to say
No meaning wink
    To flash at God

But back it brings
    A mason's pick
Plenitude of stone
    An oak floorboard

Or else in a daze
    Of infant bliss
A fishing pond
    Delays for a bit

By noon becalmed
    The nose of a stag
A vagabond girl
    Who cools her quim

Strategic towns
    Roll off the map
If anything stops
    Remember time

So portals open
     Pilgrims can yawn
Tulips to the wind
     Toss their pollen

And leather smells
     In a barn of stars
To split all reason
     Spin the glass

With one last swig
     Suppress a groan
The best revolution
     Skin and bone

Cool Places

The scene may be water.
Still on some branches,
Radiant with impulse,
An avalanche of almond
Settles in mid-air.

Or smoke may be the scene.
Tugged sideways by wind,
Blue masks, half history for ever,
Spiral off the sensitive
Backbones of horses.

A little love goes far,
Fine words nowhere.
Something unbroken in people —
Spirits murmur round it.
Suddenly ancient an embrace

Speeds intelligence. I broke
Pattern, breathe to attract you:
Speak, if well-being was
Ever by any speech-act
Driven into the script we are.

Or be done with it. See the zebra
Stand its ground, cascades
Happily freshen high beliefs.
Old men want more
Than rumours of women.

Cool places, good cool places
Exist, not far, where
For wasting your life
You are forgiven. What horrors next?
What presences wither in the air?

All It Was

It might be good
To think it did not matter much.
All the way we'd come;
Where had we got to now?

The brisk blue shadows
Nestling in the sheet,
The birthmark on your spine
A forked cloud from a squid,

Still they pointed a way
On and on to an elsewhere
Breath alone, breathing alone
Perhaps could reach.

But into you I leaned
And felt a trembling go
From all my body out
Into your sudden sleep.

Then it was my hand
Moved from your shoulderblade
Up to rest a while
Where your front meets your back

On a ridge where
Like thunder your black
Curls hang and flash —
Not that it matters much.

Next your fingers came;
Proceeding out of your sleep,
They took my hand and held
All of us, warm, in the light.

Tristia ex Provincia

Twenty times in the night a horse ran past
My hidden house. When I looked
I saw a head and back and hoofs;
All the articulations in between
Were solid flesh, the heartbeat of a horse.

It ran between the olive and the broom,
While in Berlin people took to the streets,
Shouted their disbelief at the police
And brought a dismal system crashing down.
Between the olive and the broom it ran

Doing what comes freely to a horse:
Blubbering out through lips an oaty breath,
Or stationary, tossing a mane at the moon.
Whenever I got up I shook with fright,
I pinched myself when I lay down again.

What had called to the horse, what did it want?
Not to be not contained or simply dead;
Thigh to ear the long thrust of a backbone,
And in pitch dark the scent of hay, on hard
Beaten earth, on rock, the ring of hoofs.

A rush of shadow, beat of wings, me shaking still
With fright whenever I got up to see,
All night the horse was drumming back and forth.
It ran between the olive and the broom,
No rush of air, no beat of wings, still shaking me.

The Headland

Beyond the shacks where food is sold
Beyond the booths haunted by carpet men
Beyond the goats and stone lidded broken tombs
Look the headland

How many times have you seen it there
Not knowing if it had a place in time
Thinking you had seen it only in a dream

Beyond any imaginable midpoint of the world
Memory brimmed unbidden with whole colours
Only to end in a choking dust of names

But answering your body which stores light as it can
Answering rhythms that curl but cling to nothing at all
Rhythms given flesh for a measure to feel with

The track goes on up the shoulder of the headland
Saffron earth anchored by rock
Storm torn rock walls to clamber over at the top

How many times did you see from there
Sheltered in a bay the next village
Fishermen stooping at the prow to pull the anchor up
It would have taken a lifetime to get there
How many lifetimes to the city of emerald and snow

How many times hearing a mast creak
Hum of rope drawn taut and dripping
Did you look back to see the headland disappear

Shoe soles worn thin by long walks
Pierced by the long thorns
Then barefoot and kneedeep in the sea
Hardly ever any deeper
In your dented helmet or coonskin cap
There today again and glad but not to be alone
Shading your eyes you will have seen the headland

Stele in Istanbul

The dead man beckons to a water melon
Out of the water melon a big slice was bitten
A cup of clay in his hand he beckons in fact
To the naked wine boy not the water melon
To the naked wine boy he beckons
And wags his beard for he means to speak

However the cup is made of stone
Stone the melon the dead man looks at
Easily it could be the moon at third quarter
A moon to tell what time of night or day
What corner of a lifetime the man died at

Not a corner nor a wrinkle on him the wine boy
Still to make you shiver touches polished his limbs
Any moment now he will dip his jar
Into the big stone wine pot

And erect in her palm a woman holds a corn cob
Back of the man who beckons to the stone water melon moon
Her right hand appeases the stone air above the corn cob
Gently she wishes to protect the thing
Or else the stone caught her in the act of spinning
So the corn cob never was a corn cob but a spool

While blue fish still flourish in this Golden Horn
A greyhound whirls his behind under the dead man's bed
That was how he'd welcome the dead man home

The shades are biting now suppose the man said
But part of me hangs on though the spool stops
Only the dog saw how spent he was from not willing
The known stone thing and the water melon moon

Titian's Venere Giacente

Not a moment too soon: quit of her gowns the lady
Positions herself on the chaise longue
And has crossed her shins; her left hand,
The little finger ringed, cups her sex.
Behind the flower pot with a shrub in it
A curtain of blue is coming down from heaven;
The tree and the glowing Corinthian column
Break a gold horizon. It is nine:
Time for something to happen.

Not a moment too soon the spaniel hopped up
And curled on the crumpled
Yellow sheet that covers the chaise longue.
He is already pretending to sleep and the little girl
Pretends to be praying at the window seat;
Her nurse, rolling a sleeve up, pretends
To be saying 'Honey, come, it's time for your bath,
And what are you doing, pray as you must,
Growing that fine young bottom in your snowy dress?'

Next, as above, not a moment too soon
The smile stole as prescribed
To the lady's lips and turned their corners up.
She is looking at you, in wonder.
Because she is looking at you, lightly her right hand
Toys with a formal bouquet somebody else left;
Hair loose on her well developed shoulder
Falling to cover the armpit somebody else
Knew was unbelievably tender,
Must be soft, cool to the touch; the sun has spread
First light in it for a fawn to step,
Scenting berries, into its coppery glade.

Now she arranges her whole look.
The head tilts, the virginal face finds an angle
To size you up and bring you on
Like a dish so foreign she's hardly curious,
Yet now, not a moment too soon,
At last she is tasting it, then devours it,
Faster and faster, more and more.

What is the snag?
Why hesitate? The black screen blotting out
All but these three quarters of the picture
Is only there to sharpen the lady's outline.
You are only invited to admire,
Surging out of the dark, or actually not so,
Yet it resists the dark, a wave continuous
From shoulder to hip, and a forearm, limp,
There, rested on the hip bone:
A rosy organ, fingered, freed from the very dark,
Which, by the way, also confirms the upturn
Of one breast.
                      Did you expect the screen not to cut
The window in half, not to segregate
Light the window admits like a last whisper,
From the candle blaze that has mysteriously
Clarified the lady's abandon in her undreamed flesh?

Or were you of a mind there should be
A picture in it,
Not this nothing at all that is not even a prop,
A picture of a mirror reflecting a lady
In a mirror reflecting a picture of now you know what?

Go in there. Make friends. She will know when
To shuffle off the dog and pull the black screen
All the way across.

The Clothes Moth

Little as the fingernail of a ten-year-old,
You have the shortest whiskers of a cat.

Up close, easily seen in the slant light,
Two profiles merge, like rivers, across your wings;

And the face of a Chinese emperor is disclosed,
Smiling, moth, on your Mesopotamian back.

Outlined against the pinewood table top
Your shape is less fan, less tulip

Than the Egyptian lotus with tornado lips
They hammered into drachmas on Cyprus once.

So much abstruse cutting of throats then,
Now the history scatters in a golden dust

I catch my breath at, when your whiskers twitch.
A breath lofted you, now gone you are,

Yet I think you might have been there always,
There no less than fingers I will fork to grip

The cigarette, than wine still black in a bottle.
What if now I saw the design on my own back?

What rivers, what profiles, what bloodshed
Might melt into a design to be misread,

As if through valley mist, by a yokel pretending
To an imperfect, imaginary intelligence?

Cloaked in provocative scrawls the globe
Throws to the winds the grids we put around it.

So, in the moment of this furor, you took off:
You wisely muscled in to my thin stock of wool;

Now I hear your soft jaws munch my blanket.
So I became your fleece and you my Argonaut.

2

A Huapango for Junius Avitus

Accedit lacrimis meis quod absens et
impedentis mali nescius, pariter aegrum
pariter decessise cognovi, ne gravissimo
dolori timore consuescerem.
    Pliny the Younger

1

Stepping out from the new Bangkok Café
Digesting the whitest
Meat of spicy chicken

Night hawk heard aloft
Orbiting the ventilators
Of Congress Avenue, this hot hot gulch

His high, strangled cry
A soprano raspberry
Reminding me of Rossini

Whom ice cream polished off
Boom — how come I slow down slightly
Firefly from split concrete winking

Cooks, octets and chickens
How come I slow down at all
All too soon will have had their fill of me

Boomboom boom — unwinding silver ladder
None too soon
Mysterious dame thou penetratest me.

2

Staring at the moon a cat thinks
It is a dish of milk

The cat staring at the moon
Wants to include it somehow

It might be cheese with a mouse
Tremendously creeping up on it

I'll wait and see, the cat declares
The same as I say this about the cat

The urge is there: live without knowing how
Idea is there: for building shrouded systems

Tear off the sheet: what's there is featured
Stone or a royal sport of the unconscious

A point in time — rounded arms reaching out
With heat but no direction, say Come over here

Your aftershave is nice, I'll risk the consequences
Vague, outside, still the traffic roars

At leisure sea shells unwind their echoing forms
Silver in the moonlight fox fur crackles

And crystal fleets whizz oblivious across the bridge
Their juggler, hands behind his back, distracted

A point in time split into infinitely small
Sensitive fibres could tomorrow resume

Existence as a hero, scribbled fish: I exist
Like everybody, waiting for a rhyme or crash

To work the change, a crisis freshening the sun
Yet suppose the sea shell, suppose the idea

Unqualified create only to disregard
Those singular fables which invent the cat

Uncontainable web, trembling with just what?
Whatever frenzy knits bones, whatever tenderness

Desires you to speak, on me your lingo's lost
You might pronounce wrath, or mercy, or both

You might shield me with ignorance
Rage at me for love I want to shake you with —

And how apt, settling under the baobab, the leopard
A dervish hat completes the cook who plays the spoons

3

You turn right
   at the second sign, soon, at the crossways
      of a bridge and a sea shell
         continue left to the cook
and straight ahead to the rhomboid of distraction

You will find a wing there
   and a corkscrew ascent
      to a second bridge. Do not miss the egg,
         clearly marked, you have been there before
and the lights give out, see, just before the dip

There is a field of cows,
   you pass it on the left. Observe
      the pylon, like a picked
         albacore backbone; if you stop
you'll hear the wind bellow in it, likely as not

Later, left at the fork
   and follow the loop. You smell woodsmoke
      if you're on track. Slow down
         at Silken Ladder, circle
Cat Lagoon, then back off and sleep some

There's a tidy walk ahead;
   the path is one you won't miss.
      Cobwebs will catch your shoes and face,
         the first aren't poison, but watch
for the purple ones, the stickiest, they mean forget

The Greater Evil.
   Now all the sounds will keep you
      wide awake: the nosing, quibblous, of the fong,
         click of bullwits, the oom's horn.
You'll soon tune in. Forward to the fork, here,

Or there, for the nth time,
   you have to decide —
      stop till sunup, or fail —
         plod on, dance with your telescope, tongs,
your feathering tool, your grip of loose leaves —

Plod on, soon you'll see the
   gap in the boob trees.
      Then (inaudible words)
         (more inaudible words)
Brisk wind foretold it, boom, the unshrouded sea

Here all things turn
   their backs on you. Nothing
      watches you. Now it is too late
         to save your precious skin, it's
listening the other way, as if to another voice

The load of *la matière*
   and feelings that attach to it,
      the great dusts, groans, the golightly trees
         turn inside out, reform into a hole
and in the hole (involved, turning its back on you —

Or can it be Death Mountain?) moment dwells.
    Let everything go, gaze at it,
        as long as it is there, the moment hole.
            Never think all time is abuzz in it.
Never put your eye so close you could be blown away

By the grace it is giving out, pulse
    never spent, of carnal
        starlight a fountain, supposing earth
            and you, if ever again, eye to eye with a beak-
to-flower hummingbird, can figure time like that

4

Soon is a kind of never in reverse
Save when a phrase's gist is negative
Soon you'll die just when you want to live
A cry from Never posits to disperse

Spun like a top in umpteen kinds of time
Configured as in music or more flat
As lurching on from this dull urge to that
Ugly history leaves a trail of slime

A soon that could be now the future past
Emergent time tormenting in the rose
Skipping an aeon if the ground's too hot

Ah incandescent now again outlast
Soons that never sang a note but froze
To dwindle on the tips of tongues forgot

5

My heron has flown into the blue night wood
My sparrow into the perpendicular dust
My falcon, better than my wrist, loves the sky

What shall I do, mysterious dame, with this thought
It has angles and nodes I know nothing of
I am not very well acquainted yet with the dark

I am not afraid of the night wood, nor of dust
And I love the sky no less than my falcon does
With a pinch of salt I eat food as I need it

Also I hear in corners floorboards creak
As if somebody trod behind the shadows there
But I do not collect my times into a pattern

I do not work things out or drink white milk
Because white things are impersonating me
A white horn in a corner blows for a minute

A white horn in a corner when the creaking stops
Spreads a vista of stone gates and streaming hair
In an ancient city where I met you sometime

And the city to come is a far cry from my thought
The generation of thought a far cry from reason
When I see my falcon's face I am not in doubt

There are skies
There are dusts
There are losses we bear as best we can

There is an old book on the demons I might read
There is a new face to love, which I do not choose
There is a distraction from things and anxieties

It is for instance distracting to know this or that
And how not knowledge hurts but experience
And how you live, mysterious dame, in death

It is distracting never to be disenchanted
To have the spring of joy always bubbling up
To be sad without any thought of sadness

Distracting to be told your sadness was intended
Sadness the snout of a weapon pointed at life
Heron, sparrow, falcon falling from the sky

The tone, of an unfingered string
The fluidity, now, of the flight
The going on of everything at your ancient behest

Come to me again with understanding some other time

Note. Huapango — a Mexican dance-song of Caribbean origin, in which the dance steps of a couple alternate between trampling on one spot and hopping in a low arc to trample on another spot. Junius Avitus — died young, soon after becoming a senator, a protégé of Pliny the Younger, who loved him for his promise, his meticulous hard work, his willingness to learn (*Letters,* VIII, 23).

INTIMATE CHRONICLES

1

Valdrôme Gallo-Roman

By people built as far as may be, in this bowl
Where eagles track the moves of mice, remembered:
The white cubicle, tiles to cowl an eave,
A bluish rose mosaic, in their haunt have lost

Contact with local crops, have little now to do
With wind, all through the night, fingering the pines.
Breathless figures broken from a patera,

Hearthstone cracked in a pocket underground,
Are good ideas: imaginary matter licked
Form into bronze that whangs on bronze no more.

That fatal daybreak passes in a flash,
Perfect, for its makings and unmakings
While you wet a toothbrush in the old stone trough;
So tasting a brioche, you wonder still what's what.

Waxwings on a Workday

Puffed oval by the wind
It rolls across our street:
A single silver bag an aubergine was in.

O visionary ladies, let your crimson frills
Swish about us, flick your fans, off your cheeks
Pick your curls while we are dancing.

It was silvered only by the sun, hollow skin:
The acorn belly of an infant, then miles, imagine
Miles of acorn-bellied infants, rolling, soon

Motionless, in puddles, their thin shit. Lined up
Along a branch the waxwings on a workday sharply
Lift their crests and call while we drive on.

View From Cumbria, 1992

Frost silvering the fells, early light
Has touched a slope, consecrates
Mammoths in the distance, warm inside,
Matted Methusalems, now evidently sheep.

Body awake, felt them close, in a sweat,
For no shells had holed the stone house.
Then a frost spirit flashed out intact,
Through the window, quick:

Unbind the whiskey spell, quit the comfort
Of a land where Norsemen named some places,
And Serbian is not the tongue they curse in.
Frost early, light motion, sheep were lambs,

But who blew, before that, the battle horns?
Plundered hovels, torched the barley —
Who grinned when the shears cut throats?
Who poisoned wells, pissed on corpses?

All the way south, east, winging it
To where the new dead stiffen in ravines,
The selfsame body caught its breath, froze:
I will not starve this winter, or be shot.

The Western Widows

Softly, widows,
You adopt
Euphemisms; the unloved
Contain their howl,
So it reddens,
Running rings around it,
Their skyline,

Haven't you heard
This? — meanwhile
Knock knock, and soldiering on
Poetry digs from
Time and more time
Its cavern, the global,
Echoing,

Lustrous nutshell;
Your horror,
There it slowly trickles in
To gleam with what,
Too long delicate,
You hardly thought you
Had to say.

Upon Saint Crispin's Day

Aha, said he,
      Don't tell me you too
Keep somebody in mind,
      Who, when he squares,
On top of the heap now,
      His shoulders
To uncork
      Another wine bottle,

Holds his breath,
       Listens to the swish
Of arrows darkening
       The sky, and recalls
His forefather, the way
       He drew the longbow
At Agincourt.

Paris

With a name like mine you will imagine
A long monologue to come, ruminative;
Not my style at all, I won't drone on.

It took two subtle moves to undermine
Menelaus, I won't say which. An easy target,
His self-will, strutting around in armor,
The bozo. Then to rip the web of that fine
Family, turds and torments underneath
The behavior they displayed at breakfast.

Imagine me, too, with historico-mythical
Vagueness: the lateral reach of my
Pectorals, articulate biceps, buttocks —
Me and Helen taking off, and the breeze
For once, among the islands, clement,
The flutter of my golden statuary hair.

Actually, folks, I am a stocky half-Hittite,
Dealer in used chariots and standard spears,
Hair continuous from my fringe to my feet,
Thick as garlic. The red of my tongue
When I talked of horses piqued her, somehow.
Made her breathe faster, her health improved,
Poor rabbit. If I knocked her over, so what.
The Greek idiot fell for my fantastic feet.

The pottery she brought along, I threw it out . . .
Hittite or not, she says, still you are number one.
Knit my brows, pretend I can't count so far.
There was a way she walked, true, and her grin,
Not her death-dealing smile, gave her away.

There is a queen for you, I told myself.
Relieved of ceremonial robes and the hoopla
She got into *poshlost* like it was wonderland;
Fawns and thinks small and does *pazarlik*,
Vile (as they say) and spiteful as the best,
So orphans can eat grass and men whack shields.

She took a liking to my feet, wide
As they had got by anchoring my behind
To a bronco. Forget the heartbreak. Wide feet
To walk avenues and kick horse ribs
Are what makes measurable this brute, life.
That was all she ever taught me: measure.
And a fat lot of difference it made,
Her la-di-da, a fat lot of difference.

Ballad of the Putrefaction

The poem of hateful persons hot in his mind
He met the girl whose work was to roll in creosote
Himself he wanted to set fire to the hateful persons
Nobodies governing nations without any sense of what's what
Not victors but victims of their spooks and greeds

Those were to be the subjects of a poem which began
The moment he walked into one of their oblong hotels
He smelled the frowst of power they had left behind
People not born for power but victims of it
Who spray around the scene like tomcats their fear
The poem began but was interrupted by fresh sounds

A tongue moved in a sticky mouth and a snowflake fell
Those were calls from pigeon throats in the courtyard
This was a finger brushing the skin of a tambourine
These were the dawning sounds he heard
When the power of hateful persons first crawls in the dark

Himself had been interrupted by collecting impressions
The kind of work he would have been quarantined for
In a world controlled by the hateful persons
My work is rolling in creosote among carpets
The pools of creosote stick to my hair and skin
And my skin peels off when I wash the creosote away

Himself was interrupted by me when he saw me roll
He called me over asking why I had shaved my hair off
He gave me a fourteen dollar bill for the taxi ride
We should have supper he said at the Kim Kim
A Chinese Turkish restaurant on the lower East Side

So himself was interrupted by a girl with no hair
And the poem of hateful persons came to a stop
But still what made his flesh creep was their peeve
The smell of the "lounge" where they brooded destruction
The carbon script of a menu they ordered fishes from
The pop of a cork as it quit their bottle of Sekt
Fear in their bones fitting them snug in the world's night

Then the blackbird began to sing in the courtyard
For at first light still he did not sleep
Phantoms of hateful persons pushed their faces
Across the twilight between him and me
Again he saw the squat bronze tractor woman
Straighten her headscarf in the hotel garden
Their monuments he murmured their long knives
Hack out the tongues of nightingale persons
Their slug fingers sign contracts for weapons

Typically one who ordered a total change of trees
Resenting the way leaves tore loose from a sycamore
Himself too mumbled how their language formulaic and glib
Formulaic and numb and belittling gave rhetoric a bad name
Mouse gray their claptrap squeaking in machines

But we got along and my lips were clear of creosote
I only interrupted our long kiss to tell him You amaze me
If he forgot me it was the fault of a blackbird
Interrupting the poem of hateful persons at first light
Another moment and I will see him again
Free of his gang of hateful persons and police
He said they live secretly in fortified estates
And don't know beans about the hunchback in the belfry

So the poem will shine through air in the darkest places
So its voices will banish the fug they spread
Sunk in plush chairs or stiff at their tank parades

But again it is me the creosote girl who interrupts
We have escaped across many adjoining rooms
And arrive in a crypt where police wagons park
Waving our fourteen dollar bill we must fly on
Because the shooting will never stop it seems
Up and down streets we zigzag through fields of fire
He has told me he knows where the Kim Kim is
What if I doubt himself more deeply now than he can

Silent Picture

There is a speaking nobody spoke of yet
Measureless an envelope of sleep
And all the speakers in it dreaming picture

We think we speak as anyone who dreams
Thinking he is awake
Speaks as if he were though he is not

Shrunken souls leap up and give a glory tongue
Complying with compulsion so to sleep
Flame perforates a cask or clay breaks wind

A speaker makes believe he is awake
Then horror stronger than the toxin
Speech secretes can desolate Dubrovnik

So the rat counts on the wall of his tunnel
A nightingale on air
Predatory tongues hit on a web of teeth

They may want to wag the web away but they can't
Picture on picture it is too thickly fraught
The tongues connect and weave it more and more

I thought I was awake and am asleep
Should I claw this way out of it
The dream I spoke will keep this picture silent

Missing Frogs

Little frogs
why don't I hear you anymore?

This is your time of the year.
It was your custom to croak.

All through the night, the throb.
Spellbound, repetitive, too,

I was in the house, enslaved,
a frog should croak in deep water.

Your creek was dry, you were frogs,
not princes, I was never a slave.

Where are your needling, primordial
contradictions? I heard them.

Your cry carved the vast sparkling
zero, then, into triangles.

I went into your beaks.
You do not have beaks.

Far back I tasted, bitter,
the green, the prancing, emergence.

The beginning was before us.
There were no developments.

We were qualities of darkness.
I did go into your beaks.

Now I am in the air around the house,
distressed in the coil of your legend.

Later I was driven out; never again
to be sure where the house is.

Still I cling to the cedar roots,
stalls, priedieus

From creek walls they sprang out
and shook with your *a capella*.

My pads crisp for your woodbark.
I am thirsty for the hard mud.

Now your liquid voices call again:
disagree, disagree.

The Cow Heaven

Go trump thy mystic lotterys Elsewhere.
   — John Clare

Where else to hide you, lost domain,
But in an orchard? Oriole and pear
And cherry load contorted trees;
Grass thickens, violet peeps,
Moss is emerald, and lo —

Now bottle green, open to the sky,
A Lancia convertible displays the bride:
As if yon silver peak stepped down among us,
All sheathed in ancient silk her beauty draws
Ooh and aah from honest local folk —

Meats and cakes illuminate unfolded linen; tall
Flasks aplenty warp
Funnily the faces they reflect, and bumblebees,
Numerous, make room for people. Opening wide
Their jaws, how talkative they chomp,

While rosy children monkey round.
Now with a whop the steel band begins,
Delighting in their nests the pettichaps;
Trepidating daisy flocks, it clarifies
And crisps the foam in glasses bubbly fills,

For very nimbly drumsticks tap
Negro keyboards, ocarinas
Usher out of limbs surrendering to the dance
A tender music. Hearing this,
Cows, hoof on hoof, come rushing down the slope —

Breathe again, good cows, the scent of pear,
Moo approval, from your dewlaps lift
Your copper bells, and keeping time,
Do you shake them, loiter, see the people
Drink, frolic. Rifles cocked, the hairy

Partisans who guard this place
Fling their caps up, into nowhere, high;
It is not far, the cows, all their life
In rumination spent, they felt it
Not so far.

Leaning Over

Leaning over this black
Cat of mine, my one and only
Familiar, nabob of the dark,
I gaze, gaze into his wild
Yellow eyes and think

He's part owl, see
The way he squats there, glossy
Gourd of a body anchored
Unblinking to this branch of ground.
Then why does he answer

Not owl, not owl
But a panther. Then why do I
Reprehend him: If so, some day
Mew and faugh, get educated, son,
Will be roar and howl.

Maybe, says he, but that's not
Quite the process. In our glowing
Midst the monster sits, your
Intestine hath many heads,
Ins and outs; insist,

As you will, on the reasonable
Head, you will not raise it
Beyond their magnet; turn its face
From blood's rage, from the ravenous
Intestine fist, and it shrinks,

Shrinks and is prone to forget, care
Not a hoot, toy
With its little time, spoil
Its intractable whereabouts, even
Twist, every which way,

Justice.
                    At this, taken aback,
I touch my familiar, call him:
Fallen star, street wise
Prince of latencies, adept
Of Sphinx, Medusa, Dragon, tell me

Why did you never go
With men, unleashed, on their walks,
Show them the cavern,
Unlit, where the monster
Waits for them, hopes for them?

Quoth now with a wink
The cat: I walk,
Mouse, nap as I please, but who first
Rigged gods, in their dynasties,
Then their catafalque?

Who measured his distance,
Split the rift and wedged
Monster into it? Who
Aims the pointing
Finger at himself?

Thirst Confessed

Face it, you are a little tired
Of the long trek to Troy;
Of other places glimpsed; of the fable
That our throb of time, first felt,
From sixty shrines
Illuminated earth with auras
Now being quenched by sixty lords of change;

Tired of retrieval — a lifetime,
In retrospect, might have clustered,
Detail on detail, round the taste
Of a cedar pencil bitten on a back doorstep
Opposite the great cathedral nave; tired

Of troubling anima for a sensation even
Richer, abrupter, than a madeleine.
All felt, all said and done,
Time is not a thing, nothing holds it
An instant still.
The long trek must go on,

And underneath the layered city, cool,
Below the rock any inscrutable event
Or silly habit warped, below folds in time
Idled away, or made something of,
A treasure hides, a shimmer comes to mind.

What is this mirage if not intent
To lift the shimmer up, give tongue to it
In a tongue its time has thickened
Into an apology for essential say-so;
Face it, or not, a negative will
Has all but bereft it

Of lustre, airy volume, now vague but rapid
Abstraction wizens it, a glance
Over the worn parapets of its features
Dizzies it, no voice responds
To voice voicing action where the action is,

Then to articulate the curve of a gaze
Winging home, as it glistens,
Captured at last
On its wings the shimmer,
For it has passed
Through the other eye of things.

1944

"Our lads have landed in Normandy,"
That's what he shouted. Scouring the pipes
Which propel time, I found them
There, nested in the scum, a figure and a phrase.

Brisk, waxed tips to his moustache,
A little Spartan thorn of a man,
Who in his singlet frogleaped, light
As a flame, across the vaulting horse
And sparred with elfin vim.

Sleep lost sight of, I make him
Shout again. Was it Sam Fox?
Voiced through the loon cry of valves
From pools, inlets, systems linked by tissues
Where hooded phagocytes in cells
Pump their polyphony through the dark,
The words trod out a rhythm, with its own
Weight each marked a notch across a scale:
Crazed Archilocus, now did he feel that way
Fish lines tug from footsole to fingertip?

Tudor oaks, the river Wye, the rosy castle
Reconfigure, out of atoms. Algebras of scripture,
So much gas before, prophesy,
Because a phrase has kept its cadence,
And Sam Fox is a presence, not a name —

Sam Fox who fought once through the slosh
Of corpses on the Somme, ducked through shellbursts,
Sang Tipperary, for the ping
Pong of the powers never was his thing,
And he forgot the Henries, thought Huns, calls out
His phrase again.

                        Barely awake his soldier boys
Attack the last yards to the mansion
From the stable we have slept in. So he stands
At ease, on gravel, at the oaken door, calls
Down crevasses where another tongue
Now takes their echo up,
Certainly, his weighted words. Ebert,

Sergeant Ebert was his name.

Warlords

The blackbird once believed
He cranked the sun up with his song

Likewise but with love
Quite inconspicuous women

Now the warlords crank and crank
Only graves come up

Remuzat: La Combe

Four steps were a staircase
It smiled at me
In candlelight
As I took heart and mounted it

Worn down by years of feet
The stairs you see
I took a second look at
Like lips they lifted

Once the room had housed
A family of folks
Down below not far
On golden hay a flock of goats

Far enough I thought
From economic muck
And stuck with fond beliefs
Those figures on their thrones

Now a truckle bed
Here delights my back
Windowsill and simple desk
To prop my elbows on

Soon gathering in the dark
I heard goat bodies breathe
Long past the witching hour
A whole dead family talk

Across the screen of stars
Iconic jewelled unicorn
You drew their dusty hearse
Who now can know for what

With red wine awash
And a fellow feeling
Here I blow the candle out
Here I goat to sleep

Objects Mistaken in Music

Hearing again the vowels of
That nightingale, darkly
Burbled in *The Pines*
Of Rome, and following them

The large brass starts to blow
From the ends of earth,
Columns of men, rivers proposing
An economics of empire,

First he hears no speech,
No crack of objects, roofbeams,
Only the onward slog of feet
And the wind, shuffling

Through umbrella pines, over tombs
On the Appian Way, and Rome —
Ropes creak hoisting cyclopic stones,
Fresh palaces of echo, a mason

Utters a grunt, captive Gaul
His groan, a Parthian head
Splitting open, ominous
The lull on a border pacified,

Et cetera, to the edge of time —
Hearing it, slightly smelling
African armpits, roast flesh,
Hearing the ultimatums, huge

Trombones herald the moment of truth,
French horns history,
And drums, the drums that mark
Moves of doom, the river's pulse,

He has walked across the kitchen,
Tipped from the old flower
Basket torn sheets of paper
Into the trash box,

The quest is on, for the fullest
Distant object in space without ceremony
Gone, which is here, if only
Only a ghost he circled the room,

Prosaic, took a stand
At his window, loaded
His Waterman, to start over,
Over again, for the first time.

Catacomb

I only want to hear the wind in the sycamore,
To such a height it grew in the garden
Of that hotel, crumbled long ago.
I only want to see under the door the thin
Triangle of light from a lamp that shone
Day and night, in the passage, burnishing the walls;
Cool they were to touch, with an odd slant, inward.

Though I call out your pretty names,
I am afraid you have begun to forget me,
Crooked creatures now, propped against
This other wall.

              And the creak
The window made when the wind blew,
Open window, that I want to hear;

And to think any thought whatsoever;
Time just enough to imagine it was I who said:
All your theologies, all, are fragments
From Aphrodite's shattered mirror.

The Old Tour Guide — His Interpreter

He says there is a Greek house in Mustafapasha,
He says you go down a winding stone staircase
Into a crypt. On more stairs down to a crypt
Beneath it, a secret door opens. Now
There is more to be said, it seems.

I think he is saying that a blue sun
And utter stillness enfold the numen:
He says that in a third crypt under the second
A Christ of Sorrows stands alone, his face
Preserved in the original paint. That the face,
He says, illuminates all memory of the house,
Once you have been there, for your lifetime,
Is not certain.

What was he saying next? He says they found
A lost valley, by chance, two summers gone.
Conical churches there contain sealed tombs,
Full of treasure. Present, for anyone to touch,
A desiccated loaf, on an altar, a curled up
Sandal, each of a substance
Evidently shunned by mice.

Now he says there are many places
Not to be gone to. Memory has no desire
To be disappointed. But, he says, nothing,
Nothing stops you wanting to go there.

He is describing the valley, how across
Its clear stream, from one willow bush
To the next, singing warblers flit: the bird
Called popularly heaven bird can be seen there,
Crested, with blue wings, throat of rose,
Best heard at noontime when it flutes alone.

That is what I think he said. In his thick
Local accent now he is saying this:
You must not cut loose from here and now,
Both hands taking hold have to pull, he says:
Let the crypt call to you, as the long road did,
Let the valley track the turning of your eyes
And always haunt the here and now you see.

That is the gist. Wait, what wild talk is this
Of war striking a far country . . .
                              Stored at home his great bow?
Seven times I heard the suffix
Which in his language indicates hearsay,
The saying a matter of doubt to the sayer,
Critical things might happen to have been
Otherwise.

                    Ah yes, he says,
Ah yes, this is the country of people after midnight;
Few have spelled out into the pleasure of a heartbeat,
Into a knot of mind, once and for all,
The loops of light they see spreading at sunrise,
The braid that snakes down a girl's bare back.
When we go to see what is there to be seen,
The knots and braids easily slip;
We learn to know how little we understand.

But as we go I believe he is saying
May Allah lift the griefs from all of us.

2

The Parrot House on Bruton Street, 1830

This very young man, face all flesh and bone,
Eyeglasses, gold and owlish, perch between
Parrots he peers at and his jungle brain. Those eyes,
So myopic they must blink to capture,

Accurately, screaming parrots, one by one.
In a keeper's grip, wingtip to wingtip,
They measure such and such; he is making moues,
Surely he mimes the volumes of their hornblack beaks.

Then while a thieving pencil sweeps up the crests
And down his own bent backbone strokes the plumage,
Turquoise, into place, people tiptoe in, to watch
Our artist copy the parrot he all but becomes.

Odder far he thinks these wicker bonnets,
Eyeballs which are beads, gnawed snickering lips,
Than they have deemed his amiable psittacids;
And look, now he delineates the people's noses —

Upon my word, how sniffily those humbugs behold
Not a "dirty artist" or "Wog's Robin" now,
But being tweaked, nothing to snicker at,
The organs of their own inquisitivities.

Zagreb 1926

The window swinging open spread a flash
Of light, splendid and warm the sun
Settled on the table cloth, the vase,
Lay on the white bed, singled out the pictures.

Hallo, light, glorious with your rays,
Hallo, linen, fragrant in your wardrobe.
Flowering cherry steeped the orchard in perfume,
Bees occupied our thoughts, honey, the pure things.

Gentleness: back and forth it ticked
And talked, like an affable old man, the pendulum.
Gentleness: the clink of cups and plates,
The smells of cream and stored apples.

And while the slanting rays explored
Crannies where the light and shadow blent,
Our funny faces, caught in the globed vase,
And a snippet of our sky gazed back at us,

In its ample curves we contemplated
Birds that flew in flocks across the town,
The roofs of all the houses turning red,
Right above the bell tower, now, the sun.

(After a Serbo-Croatian poem, 'Reflections,' by Ljubo Wiesner)

Skaters in the Luxembourg Gardens, 1909

Black on white, figures astride a frozen pond,
Long shadows travel, forms unfreeze the distance.
A clock high on the palace façade has stopped.
It is five to one, or else it is eleven.

Suppose there was that year no bombing season,
Though while snow drifts blew into Saint Sulpice
A ghost bicycled through them firing pistol shots:
However it was, here is a lull in a bubble.

Ankles turning as they try to move,
Two of the women wear such ponderous hats.
Shaping her mouth, narrowing her eyes
Another shoots an ecstatic look, at what?

Yes, a mouth can turn lips in like that
When ice absorbs a pond, air blows jawbones cold,
But *le dimanche* has arrived, the Galeries Lafayette
Set free their great bosomed girls.

Knees flexed and gliding from his corner
A waiter makes the scene, white shirt cuff
Circles the end of the longest arm on earth;
And the women giggle, this could be something else.

At the line of bowler hats behind them, not a glance;
Of the grudge fuming into the hat crowns, not a whiff.
Those bowlers heat old soldier headbones knit
In the semblance of a wound, raw, roughly sutured.

No use trying to tunnel back, they say.
Still you try it, drawn to any secret place.
Still the waiter fills his coat, not yet blown away
In a dugout; old fogeys crack a smile.

Webbed with hairlines the wafer of glass
Off which this print slid
Vaguely into the bluebell air of Spring in Texas
Eight decades almost after the event

Is in your lips, image intact;
The scratches hold their accidental ground
And are at home in the picture;
The people smile, humdrum in their hats.

Kin to them, rose Renoirs glow through the shell
Of the palace; air attends Fokine and The Firebird;
Five canvas women rolled under Picasso's bed
Have chosen who shall wear the masks and dance.

Yet unforefelt another ice was catching up on them.
Soon it will split even this mole's backbone.
Where do the long shadows else come from, and the light,
The sweep of light brightening that girl's face?

Monet's 'Weeping Willow'

Involuntarily
    Microbes
In a drop of water
    We see what they cannot

A carrousel
    The unbelievable
Speed of echoed
    Colors wheeling

And reel to seem
    To be seen weeping
Inside a single
    Unimportant tear

Or (duck in gunsight
    Fluting across the Danube
Delta at sunrise)
    A tot of eau-de-vie

Through its liquid
    Walls refracted
The cosmos calls
    Hallo goodbye

Constant Danger

Just now, in June 1994, and in Berlin-
Pankow where *Altstalinisten,* still
In the same old villas, deaf to the same blackbird,
Scowl at big blue TV screens,
I heard tell of a paper maker:
Old sheets from junk boutiques all over Europe,
Old camisoles, old shirts he collects,
Breaks the fibers down in tubs of wood,
Dries the mush, then fixes it, and presto —
Paper for etchings later to be hatched,
Labyrinths by fingertips invented.

Still to be written, fit to be printed
On such paper, in letterpress, by hand,
The poem ruffled and warm as the sheet soon will be,
Folded and finely stitched
With gussets
Like the camisole a moment ago slipped out of
By a factory girl, who unpins in 1910,
Elbows up, her braid, winks to her image
In a fragment of mirror, quick now
She'll hop into her bed
With a frisky, shirtless printer

The Gardener in the Basilica

The gardener in the basilica, he stoops
To cut and lift the grass roots;
Little billhook in his grip he hacks what sprouted
Round the odds and ends at random:
Broken fluted column, writing,
A coffered rose, a marble sun.

While he cuts he whistles.
Same tune, over and over. Headscarf in the wind,
Down his back it flutters. Then he stoops,
As if born bent double. Face down,
He only sees a blur of marble forms;
He smells the wild pig smell of grass,
And smelling it he knows the weight of time.

Headscarf fluttering, hood of flame, fed by resin,
Color of the buried time, round his head,
Hidden in it.
Never to be restored. Timbers creaking,

Low in the water, black on violet, home,
A galley anchors. Fingertips have tooled
In hammered gold an olive leaf. Deer leap
And the dolphin. Likely tales
About a god
Born flesh and bone taunt the peregrine soul,

And him, robed in his dust, perilous
Round his head that long
Gone Ionian autumn, him hacking,
Stooped, whistling, over and over
The same tune.

Fishing Boats at Assos

1

Goodbye bastions Aristotle squinnied at:
Over the hill I have to go, scorched
By a thought for the purposeful
Multitude building you, and down to the cool
Spread shadow of an ilex, phantom, no,
Barbarian to your bronze people.

                    Goodbye
Delight among the drums of stone,
Once temple columns being lifted up
To civilize your mammoth headland —

                  And from her cabin,
Softly speaking, a girl steps, white lace
At her fingertips.

2

As ash flies from the tip of a cigarette
Into the harbor water
Moon on moon has risen and will set —
                      They disappear,
The purposes; we disappear
Among the gunwales, capstans, grunge, lapping;

Lemon crescents on their scarlet,
Flags droop, solitary lights — flicker of a look,
How many smokes ago,

First a shock, then a script
Hook, line, and sinker penetrating you —
Sprint across the water. So does love.

3

Steady now, snowy in arc-light
The loop of a gnat
Did not collapse the model of its whim,
                              A shooting star.

Purpose begins when a blind will takes
A hold on time, toils then to perfect
An image of its matter; aspires in good faith
To provide; persists through loss,
Must keep going till it melts into mind:

Süzül oynak dalga . . .

                    Drifts of time,
Heaving poison cake, layer on layer,
                              Secret in the seen —

Tell me, Lord, to walk to you across the water

4

Canopies flap again, to fresh paint on a prow
The moon tries to pin a medal; the harbor
You could cup in a hand forgets for a minute
How distant, how old it is: everything ripples,

Dazzles, gives. Next, the phenomenal
Winking fabric clicks shut, and, trapped,
A mole thought can mutter only
"Hallo, now here's a thing."

5

                    A surge of joy
Suddenly remembering a blue light,
The shiver of it over the scales of a mackerel,
Warmth of an oar gripped
By fingers far bonier; then curious
Warrens you dug with tooth and claw
In sand; and freshest —

                    The first morn makes pristine
Bastions glisten;
Ovals of air flute one huge
Here-we-are hosanna with a scent
Of bread and woodsmoke,
Pinewood and excrement.

6

                        A silver griffin
Struck into a tetrobol, forepaw raised,
Passes from hand to hand:

Where now, with knapsack and Cannon,
Barbarians crawl, a history disappears,

So a soul's
Random misgivings can
Disappear, detach, for wishing on,

                        A single star.

7

Complete their letter O they cannot,
                    The sheer strakes, though
Hulls float, signs roll, cluster
                    One by one, and point:

Only their being mirrored, mirrored being
                    Can make a little fishing boat
Named Pure Ellipse, complete a melon segment,
                    Say, untoothsome rind,

And find a globe. The mirrored boat, on zero,
                    Surfaces, neither
Boat nor surface, but a canopy spread
                    By the whirl of an *axis mundi*

444

Burnishes deep silence, bids midget words
                    Dance in a last light
Where engines chug and loud all night on a roof
                    There were seven voices,

Storms of laughter, stories, language,
                    Rough-hewn, another bastion
Canopied the mirroring. Notions, move over:
                    Those were the boatmen.

A Landscape by Delacroix

They said shadows unrolled, or more precisely
That trees unrolled their shadows.

Don't believe a word of it: no sky,
No sun at all, but those trees have toppled
Across the slope not even shadows, but savage,
And so intent they have discredited the sky,
A stuff, it might be treeness, a cascade

Of rough bark tearing your fingertips off
In a collapse of earth,
If ever you noticed, in the instant, nerve: plotless
Light inscribes, toiling with its rays,
Protozoic spirit, to stir up

Cool deposits, first a formal blur,
Then this paint you'd like to gallop across
If you were a large French horse, unshod:

Murk, a blot of aquamarine spilling out of it,
Dashed trunks, five, in the foreground —
You missed the squish of the small brush inking them in,

But no matter, the thing speaks, a backbone
Hurting, flayed, the light's body a human sees with love,
Opening a mouth in horror at the moon.

Musa Paradisiaca

(on a painting by Jean Bouchet)

The muse of paradise is a young banana palm;
Nipped by one blizzard, she
Grows back again. Her branches,

Are they bole or leaf? Both: a peacock
Green feather bathes, rippling upward
In shadow, in sharp light —

Shadow from above, light from underneath,
As if anyone remembered now
Which is which. She is Lethe also:

Love as you may her poise, she nods
In a space behind time, and shows,
In a time behind space, how hotly,

Drilling through potent indigo, a never
Agitated rhomb of rose
Burns. At that core her fingery quill

Points, to disclose goal and path. Whereas
Absently she models, in a wave,
Shadow — stepped bars of a moroccan

And apple green, her rose rhomb marks
Peril enough to draw, catching his breath,
Anyone, eagerly, in.

Berlin: Mommsenstrasse 7

— FOR JOACHIM SARTORIUS AND KARIN GRAF

Antiquish tiles in a house on Mommsen Street
Line three walls of a demure retreat:

446

Blue bees seem to ride the backs of butterflies,
Rocks ring a pool, a warbler perches there;

Grouped in fours the figures count as pairs,
Except for threes of sulphur yellow daisies —

Those daisies: All around three walls they sprout
To polarize the green of rushes. While you pee

There's time to look around. One square in three
Reiterates the warbler, swallowtails with blue

Anomalous bees riding them pickaback.
Sore eyes take their delight in such a scene,

Bladders groan with relief, to be releasing
In the round presence of a rustic pool

Their pints or quarts of silvery alcohol.
So folks rejoin, refreshed, the wag of tongues:

While conversation buzzes, wild, in rooms
Vastly more spacious, memory retains

The imprint of this cubicle — a theorem,
Secret, of tiles combining elements in twos,

Except for daisy triads, which are solar sprays,
Except the warbler singing, solo, in the reeds.

All systems finally crush the worlds they shape,
Hydraulic or political they flush our lords

Dionysus and Apollo down the drain;
Some figures out of nature yet remain

And flit, unhopefully, around the pool.
The rising wave, will it be bombers or dragonflies?

Now for a time restored the simple john
Commends what folks complect to keep them going on.

A Picture which Magritte Deferred

    Lookee from the garden
Papa in the window
      Dandles our baby

    Thinks it is a telephone
Nope it is a baby
      Beaming in the window

    Beaming our baby in
Earhead footpiece
      Mighty like a telephone

    Harkee baby sapiens
Billboards in the metro
      Plot your new career

    Solving global problems
Megabuckaroo to be
      Proud homo sapiens

    Working with your body
Welcome this mutation
      Papa points the way

    Internet chromosomes
Acronyms and digits
      Impact his labyrinth

    Telebaby Faustus
Floppydiskiades
      Whelp of the Netherworld

    To your cordless baby
Papa in the window
      Snuggle up and babble

    Lookee in the garden
See us gnomes
      Grinning from the marigolds

On a Photograph of Chekhov

— FOR KATHARINA WAGENBACH

While the rain comes pouring down,
Chekhov, in his white peaked hunting cap,
And prone beside a rick of hay, surveys
The scene behind the camera, narrow-eyed.

While in Berlin the rain comes pouring down
And will refresh the yellowed centenarian
Blossomer in the courtyard, Chekhov has
Anchored his umbrella, gone to earth.

Ivory handle of the slim umbrella shaft atilt
To birch trunks in the background, has a curve;
Eyesight arching clean across the image
Divines, in the cap's white crown, a twin to it.

Chekhov's brother, meanwhile, props his head —
Summer rain, phenomenally somber —
On Chekhov's hip; from his blubber mouth
A howl escapes, the sockets of his eyes

Are black, as if he wore, beneath his bowler,
Smoked eyeglasses; as if he were, perhaps,
A horror Chekhov carried on his back, and still
The rain comes pouring down, and the umbrella,

Hulk become a dome to shelter Chekhovs, both,
Can float across a century, be put to use.
O perishable hayrick! — and its fringe,
Where Chekhov tucks his knees up, will be damp.

Yet Chekhov's massive cap, laundered a day ago —
Intent beneath its peak his eyes are watching
How people make their gestures through the rain,
Set dishes on a table, turn

Vacant faces to the window, wring their hands,
Cling, so predisposed, to their fatal fictions,
Or stroke the living air, to make it hum
With all they mean to talk about today.

The Execution of Maximilian

1890 already, or almost, and not later. This is the room. This
is where . . . Méry Laurent received Mallarmé and Gervex.
This is the room in which they were photographed. (Stooping
hooded behind his tripod stands either a hired professional or
Dr. Evans, Méry's protector, whose diagonal gaze used to rake
the interior of Napoleon III's mouth; or else, having shot a last
glance into Napoleon's mouth twenty years ago, near enough,
Dr. Evans had already quit the scene.) First it is Méry we see,
sitting at her grand piano. Her hair looks blacker, sparser than
it should; by all reports it was a glossy torrent, honey-colored.
We see Mallarmé, his goatee now whitening below his under-
lip. Standing behind Méry he lunges at something, an emotion,
one arm extended low, as if to evoke the buttock absent from all
the bloomers. We see Gervex, who leans forward, arms crossed
on the back of his chair, gazing at Méry, a grizzled profile, short
legs and bony knees in pinstriped trousers. The two big windows are shut. Because there are roses on the piano, it might be
Spring. Do these people, with their aching heads, only feel at
home in sealed and riddlesome rooms? Deep pelmets overhang
mushy drapes of velvet; or is one small window open, after all,
for outside, strangely suspended above and behind the small
head Méry tilts, coquettish, in mid-air . . . Mexican riffraff in
French uniforms are shooting Maximilian point blank. Maximilian stands between two thieves, who are generals and are also
being shot by their riffraff with French rifles and French bullets.
Maximilian is wearing, while the bullets riddle his torso, a tall
sombrero. That is what seems to be going on, that is where the
action is, in the air outside, on this dark artistic evening. Back
inside the room, everything is contained, except the perfume.
In a glass hutch the bric-à-brac is contained; in a heavy dam-

ask cloth the piano; contained in heavy frames the diminutive paintings on the panelled wall, many by Manet. Even the sofa is contained in the skin of a lion, the people in their clothes, the mirror in its ornate gilt; and hung over the mirror, so that she may see her beautiful face, a portrait of Méry slopes, blurred, containing in its invisible back an oblong hardly less negative than the azure zero which still haunts, still excites Mallarmé as he lunges, extending an arm. The oil contained in tall brass lamps is so pure, so still, the wicks it feeds ("humects") do not smoke as the rifles are still doing while Maximilian discovers that the Bank of France has decided to drop him. The tallest picture, at which nobody is looking, can be identified by the lion man. Inhabiting the bottom right hand corner of the only section visible, he scribbles with a white quill an elegy, perhaps for his skin which contains the sofa. Above the disappearance of Maximilian and his thieving generals in puffs of gunpowder smoke floats, or is hooked, a decomposing bird of paradise. Under so many eyelids, the roses on the piano, fresh, presented with a smile by Mallarmé, pretend to be nobody's sleep. They will be trembling when Méry turns back to the keyboard and concludes the evening with a spirited hat dance.

Small Carvings at Arycanda

Not much is left:
Like a bubble with a cleft
At twelve o'clock, a flying heart
Floats from a stem, which stoops
As the stem of a bluebell does.

Somewhere else, an inch or two
Above the ground,
A cluster of grapes, diminutive, hangs
Bursting from its marble slab,
Halfway liquid in your mouth.

All this, equally for the poor:
On several tombstones flying
The bluebell heart, lightly weighted,
And on a sunken slab
Clustering grapes that call

To be caught in the cup of a hand,
To be fondled, every one,
By the flesh of a fingertip,
Till bud can bud no more
And spurts its grapeness out.

Hyperbole, no doubt. How else
To feel the flash and throb afresh
Two hands, a little hammer,
And a blade of bronze
Divined in the dead stone?

How else to breathe again the life
Of carnal imagination working as a hinge:
The door the dead saunter through
And the living rush at, opens:
Here heart and grape mark

The narrow rapids where they meet
And spirit streams, making faces.
Gently now, nervous as the nostrils
Of a unicorn, or, come to that,
Of a gundog, the signs explode

Our electric shellac myths
Of Madonna and all that rot:
For a minute the bilge of our kitsch
Ebbs, heart beats
And the grapes come out on top.

Egyptian in the Tube

The usual rumble of the doors
And at Swiss Cottage in she steps.
I should have seen, there and then, her face
Of golden bird, but it was plain
Until, a picture in my hands,
It flashed upon me, golden bird, at Finchley Road.

Yes, the toes a little splayed
Placed on the border of a Cretan rug —
Rose pyramids at first, but then
Cuneiform wedges, very red;
And up and up to the second foot, there
She put it, on a cushion, sat erect,
Capped in hair which glistens like
The plumage of a predator:

Enormous glance of eyes directed at
A mirror's back, intent, I mean the gaze,
Horus-Eye, it was the apex of
A triangle the fingers of one hand
Had mounted on a base
The other hand, her left, drew taut,

And knotted round her tiny waist she wears
An emerald, ordinary sweater trailing
Down across her danskins at the groin.
As if about to run, the glance, the poised
Seventeen-year-old and lithe
Presence, in a split
Second she'll release the arrow, yet
Spellbound she poses

Housed in a web of triangles crisscrossing
A rhomb that slopes the other way —
An ottoman festooned with rugs of wool,
Pink, to crescendo in the Cretan wedges.

She held the mirror for a cat
To see whatever, perched on fur,
A cat might see in a mirror:
All you saw was the cat's golden eyes,
They shot a horizontal to complete
Another triangle, for her hair is parted
Right above her nose, a line descends
To the spread-toe foot and ricochets
Off one toe's tip,
Past the other foot's contour,
And up to where the cat begins
To hump its back.

When I stood to leave, doors rumbling open
At Finchley Road, I saw no less a marvel:
Opposite, Egyptian in the Tube, my neighbor,
There she was, one shoeless foot
Arched on the nondescript upholstery,
The other on the floor. Golden bird, she looked
Me up and down; I had become
The mirror in her hand; I was her cat.

We closed the book, and it was over.

The picture alluded to in 'Egyptian in the Tube' is Balthus' 'Le Chat au Miroir III,' begun in 1989, finished 1994.

454

More And More

More and more
In this day and age
I crave an old book;

Not one to collect,
More like the book
I saw being fingered
By a village idiot;

That was long ago,
And in Malaucène;
Fingering his book
He would come by;

For what was in it,
For his thought of it,
For the feel of its weight
He would finger it.

And so I wanted
A book like that;
But now the thought

Of the idiot's book
Has fashioned afresh
The actual idiot,
His particular book;

Craving has blent the two
Into one, the figure
Doubles back to a limit.
Still, if I say

I want an old book
Then I am craving it still;
If the craving outwits me
Still I mean it:

I do not forget the book,
But opt to be the idiot.
Could it be, after all,

Only the moment I want,
Unreversible, gone,
At a café in Malaucène,
A wobbly table, and Ann

(Her stars with mine aligned)
Nodding when our Anastase
Moseys past, all smiles,
With his fingering book?

Perhaps. Yet more and more
It is the real book now,
Fundamental enigmas glow
Pictured in it,

Inviolable, an old book,
A pulsing tomb of a book.
My desire has chosen

A book-to-be;
Shooting onward
And curling back
My desire would not stop

Even if I fingered
Its object, I suppose;
Even if it were there,
Now, the book, and solid,

456

My desire would still
Fan wildly out,
A ray of life, penetrating,
Springing every trap.

With all due respect
To the crystal worlds
And companies of concepts
That hem flesh in,

I would put first
This homing of desire
On the old book,

Which never was a book,
Though the book opens
When freely for a heartbeat
Spirit breathes again.

The Owl and the Mare

In some shade those thick wigged
Valley willows throw
A white mare shook out her tail
And showed, with a flick of her mane,
How her volumes of cream unfold.

So she caught the shade and threw it back
More ivory than it had been before;
And for a moment somebody's image of her,
Forming as it flew, contained
Her creek, her mountain crag, her piney smell.

Times also come when the scops owl,
In the onset of night, bends his original
One note in two: it copies
For a blink the curve of a crescent moon.
Born of the owl anew a moon has called to you.

Reality goodbye for now, goodbye moon.
Out of airy metonymies, seeing I am dragged down
By heavier, emptier containments than flesh
Has any mind to bear, I press no consequence.
How else to copy the owl, to ride the mare?

Some Dogs

Hereabouts there was a time of day
When the dogs came out of doors
Content to lie down in a garden.

Autumn's first cool, streets refreshed,
Flesh more than ever willing —
The clouds whiffed across the sky, so pink;

So blue the sky it was a cup of delphinium.
Somewhere else, poplars and olive trees
Were turning into a silver screen, so fast

People walking past them, with a scythe
Or sack across their shoulders, wore
Inexhaustible liquid outlines.

There too the dogs rested from their work.
Wild rabbits breathe again, gazing at space
In his café the old man mutters "fils de pute."

A gap in the bush gives you one more chance
Now, when the dog walks from his house,
To hear the breath expelled as his body meets

The ground, to see him crook a foreleg, fold
A paw to rest the back of it on earth, and tuck
The pad beneath his breastbone. He looks around,

One thought obliterating in that instant
Every single smell or sound in his neighborhood:
My dish was full, now I have licked it clean.

Oaks Near Columbus

Oak I can see
    An enormous, never quite
Tightened knot, implies
    All trees in eyeshot;
Solid they stand their ground,

A pasture, flat, and from
    Such a maze in space
Oval eyes exact
    Hither and anon a whispering;
Every this is evidence of its that,

So the several branching
    Depths of trees recede while they
Stand firm and betray nought,
    And grieve not:
One of their kind, this Columbus

Oak I think, its knot
    Being now
Stilled by their motions,
    Loosened, though never quite
By their grace.

Winter Sun Flower

    Ψυχῆς ἐστι λόγος ἑαυτὸν αὔξων
      —Heraclitus

Beside the old red pepper stalk
I lopped,
Hardly thinking the earth
In its pot
Could bear more fruit,

Stem on a diagonal,
Terribly thin,
Pointed leaves grew from it
In separated steps
You could never tread on,

Bent with growing
Now between the balcony
Bars a yellow
Head opens, the black
Bed of seeds

Reflects and for a time
Slowly rising to it
Still glistens
Without winking at
An unknown sun

Along a Leaf

A leaf on a branch somewhere,
A mountain road, leading off,
Leading off, that's all;

A leaf on a branch anyone could crawl along,
Rounding the leaf, then dropping off,
Dropping off, that's the thing.

Before the great gate of Baghdad creaked open,
At sunrise, Layard had a while to wait.
Shoeless, stripped, what was he thinking of:

I am done up, now bless you, my friends,
Brave bedevilled Bakhtiars,
Worse off than us, fierce in your ways, unorganized;

How many months more will I be on the move,
Smelling alien dusts, the top of my head
Reading the signals of roseblue sky;

Learned alien tongues and smoke; unrolled
Among scorpions my carpet;
Crawled free of the leaf and came to be me;

And recognizing him, while, spellbound,
Gracious, and breathing as usual, English folks
Rode out through the gate, Ross to Layard said:

What happened to you? By Jove, Layard,
Whatever happened to you?
And that was all, and Layard took a bath.

A beak on a bird, all bird, for beyond
Its tip a bird space, conclusive,
Will pocket a scrap of food, a greaseless warble;

Or in Asia, not yet absorbed by the parade,
A hole to vanish through, that's all,
And come out on the other side of the air

In an ordinary place, astonished:
People you wanted to be with, gathering there,
Drink their tea from glasses, talk nonsense;

And here is the ordinary mountain, not mapped,
Here, unknown, saying as usual yes,
Simply a clear blue sea.

Duna Wine

It is red and glass
    It has properties
        To be seized upon

Not by guesswork
    Not by familiarity
        Abstraction saps you

And the thing itself
    Expires into air
        A stupefickle music

Analogy streams from it
    Danubian deviations
        Bend perception's conduit

Any object looked for
    (Even little texts —
        "Product of Hungary")

Has a yen to be distant
    But to be pulverized
        Being waved away? No

To resist or position it
    Let me make sure this time
        A round rim a circular base

A stem going up and down
    A red a glass a pool
        With ellipses intersecting

(Six for counting now)
    Transparently "hand blown"
        Very like an animal head

Sort of tickled along its
    Electric jawbone
        A fingerprinted infinite

Yes red no furious tilting
    But in the glass a breath
        Bubble marks the exception

Here the uncontainable hid
    To know it in fear with wonder
        Then to perceive how I am

462

The Green Lemon

Seen to hang in a lemon tree
A solid emerald lemon

Unremarkable a lemon hanging
In a lemon tree

Pulling at the stalk
The weight of the lemon

One thin brown hand will reach up to pick it
Thin brown hands drop into sacks ten thousand lemons

Inedible as the weight of the lemon
Tough peel of its glossy pod
Hanging by a stalk in the lemon tree

Unremarkable inedible tenacious and primitive
Rondure of one preponderant lemon

Under the gun ten thousand lemon pickers
Will pick from earth's axle of fire
As bread the lemon and as rent in cash

Preponderant and inedible
So many thin children in a ring around it
Primitive but loaded
Unremarkable but coming to be delightful
The hanging in itself of the green lemon

Like other lemons ripening dull
It hangs all alone
Regardless of hanging lemons
The sun and the moon
Object of thin unremarkable hands
All alone it hangs and has gone dull

Bickersteth

Raccoon scuffle in the roof, and music —
Oboe, goldfish, bubbles of a glockenspiel —
Before a fifth sip, silent at first
Memory pays a visit.

                                          No obstacle
The prudent footstep overhead, or you,
Wine glass, while I thumb
Off your rim a residue of olive oil:

For then he would, with snowy lint,
Wipe the rim of the silver chalice
Before we sipped our sacred blood across it;
Barely a sound when his black shining shoes
Are seen to sidestep, on to the next
Opening lips, among the tombstones.

Pearly in the oyster church a swirling nova now
I construe him, though for umpteen years
I never heard the candlewick behind him
Crackle so.

                              If the acidic cells that uncongeal
Oblivion, now and then, had not been matter's long
Laborious design, now I would not see again,
Always brushed so neat, his silver hair. Master,
Never a bugaboo, aeons before Drakul
Took to the screen, he flew, rustling in his gown
Through the long gallery.

                    A man without malice,
His authority, when I was watchful, fought
Another for my wits:

His, of a temperament easily generous, not
Thwarted by craving, therefore easy on power;
But when the other, a peacock, displayed,

The magnet of one shriek pulled from rosebush
And chimneypot a wet fur smell; then mystery
Drenched in bitterness, every Spring,
The east lawn.

                    Privileged by his long,
Symmetrical, Norman jawbone, our master,
Servant when he tilted the chalice to our lips,
He showed, blind as we were, how Latin
Crossed tortuous destinies, gaps dividing us
But not the gods, and could be muttered
Sometimes, in a twilit church,
Recondite as ocean cradled in a grotto,
Sometimes simply etched on air by shepherds' tongues.

He lived on a hill, far off;
You went there, in my anticipation, once,
Equally old, handblown wine glass. To that
Wrinkled mother of his
Who gave me tea and bread,
Now you bring a full flagon:
A salute to his reverence,
And to her discarnate bones.

The Lime Tree

Thank you for giving birth to me in the first place,
Thank you for delivering me from the dark,

You whose round arms I stroked with feeling
Made presence atmosphere and contact known.

And I wanted not that Englishness;
I wanted deliverance from you so soon,

From the sticky stuff you weltered in,
Leaf, branch, and bole in your shade they dispensed

The glue, the fragrant glue, but your blossoms,
Lady, they did provide the pleasure of tea.

You stood in your own glue, fascinated,
Stirring soup, mothering lambs, telling your sex

Hush, don't you bother too much about it;
It, it, the enormous poison tree, once fire,

In your conscience you capped it off, mere fume;
In hope that hurt might never occur, defensive,

You dreamed of hoopoes perching in your crown,
Drenched in your glue for ever their crests of rose:

So the maternal shadow works mischief with men;
Their quarrels rumble first in the glue cocoon.

Now you sleep, sag-jawed, in your wing chair,
Doped, breathing steady, life will not let you go:

You who could see the colors in every back street,
Who told the stories, magnifying into marvels,

Detail on detail, the turns and twists
Of happenings that never were not nice —

Game old chattel who never peeped over the rim,
Who less than once in a blue moon could scream

Uncongealing, suddenly rid of the stuff
Your civilization spurted over you, glue

Twinkly as the round of talk you spread,
Lawn sprinkler, swivelling over shorn

Tips of grass blades, while our wrinkled lips
Sip tea in the bosque it cools.

For sure this line is not easy, but it must out:
Lime tree, your fragrance called me, always

466

Tenderly, back, but on, on I had to go, not
Looking for anything, but at every thing for the sign

That flashes up-down, lightning bolt, a blade
Cleaving the creatures, glued from crisp.

I was for the owls, for hornets, for nomads,
For such fools as never knew they were honest,

Who have wandered far, to come through,
Who have bitten their way through,

Who have learned what it means to be altogether
Alive, unattached. Of nippled hard

Breasts to be sucked, of glue
Twixt lustrous thighs, of moisture

In the mouths of girls I did not speak,
For it is all glue. What now am I on about?

Who? A creature who cares to come by,
A silvery one, brisk, with her own story:

Sixteen, with a child who walks before her,
While in and out through quick disguises

She who shimmers has to slip.
"See this headband?" A motto on it.

"Now you read it," and I could, it said:
"Not one day's help from anyone."

Here she shimmers mercy through my thick sleep,
Gives me her hand, and it is flesh,

Looks at me, leaves me, with what her look can give
She lifts the glue, all of it, out of me.

Resistance

Crow soon, rooster,
Let there be time to remember now
For Mohammad
How in the blaze of day we walked
Up the mountain —

Red earth, white stones —
Walked up and up
To the spring, under the fig tree
And drank
How sweet, how cold

And down again
Admiring the sea haze
Soon he will start to whistle

Through his teeth, and still
Softly whistling
He dances for a minute
And has forgotten
To be walking
So he danced the heat as it moved him

Arms lifted among the pine trees,
Foot lifted, bending a knee, one dusty
Toecap traced

(On white earth, red stones)
To no end, a flickering loop,
For him I can remember
Nothing of his ancient
Ghost of a tune, only

How he let go, gnarled flesh worked thin
Cascaded from his collar bones
And swayed to join the circle
The minute
He felt that way.

468

Naked Truth

What I really wanted to say, I could not:
Animals wear their clothes all the time.

Waking up in the night I find the cat
Has woken up less than a breath before.

So he was waiting to go out into the dark;
He knew the exact moment I would let him.

There are things he knows by his silence.
If he meows it is because he knows

A person expects of him some kind of speech.
Among cats he will only hiss and spit,

And he keeps for himself the purr to relieve
And grasp, one breath at a time, his servitude.

When one front paw lifts, the other three pick up
The tremble of labyrinths alert in other rooms.

What beckons other cats out from behind walls?
It is their sinews hearing those three receivers.

So air in a painting links acrobats or bottles.
So silence walks in the connected fashion of cats.

There are things he knows by his silence;
I would like to speak in his clothes.

A Breeze in Derveni

Avoid time. The topic
    Is all husk. Think of a green
        Window. Imaginary air. The squall

Hit, sand, in seventy three,
    Grains of it blown aloft
        Fondled her face. The indigo
            Gulf a cauldron, hot Greek

Meat, the reek of it, crisping.
    Capillary, but Pliny's,
        An oak was vocal — then a
            Lacework of limbs, never quite
Knotting. The woman of Delphi.

The woman of Delphi crowed:
    My son in the photo . . . No mistake,
        His eyeballs, jaw, collarbones
            Melt into those of the bronze
Charioteer. Times,

Times connect, the hubs clash, a spark shower
    Floodlights ouzo,
        Octopus, a frisbee cleaving
            Twilight in the haberdashery:
Open the window

Wider. Snowy muslin
    Curtain puffed
        Dwindles like a chrysalis; it is cooking up
            A storm; inshore the *méduses*

Float — soon she will shake out,
    Into the breeze, her hair,
        As if by that alone she let all trouble go.

Long Distance in Asia Minor

What if I call her long distance
To ask if her behind, like mine,
Had tingled in the night.

"No," she'd say, "it must be you alone
Sat on the power spot, never washed,
Never combed by the light of the moon.

Yet hear I did, from that secret church
Scooped by monks from a tufa cone
To house their barnacled Greek beliefs,

A grasshopper whistle, unique, unique,
Moon for dear life wallop her tom tom.
Sensing heaven in earth I did behold

The star burst, and was there, all of a piece,
When the wave rose and, cresting,
Compelled the skin you scratch —

For reasons, perhaps, electromagnetic —
To crack under the torture of the mundane . . .
For a syntax of God, turn, turn the fruit of time."

Who'd lark with a person so connected?
Back to its cradle the telephone, once
Hooked, hung loose, swung a little.

A Very Thin Man

Hearing tell one day of the Poseidonians,
He noted a kinship between those people
And the obscure selves that swarmed in his skin.
He felt their fingers poke through the fabric
Isolating him, throats crooned: to his spiritual
The indigo surge below the melody line.

The Poseidonians had been swallowed up
By an alien civilization. Greeks,
They had forgotten Greek, but still spoke
Or sang it, on occasion, when satisfied.
At festivals, or soon after lights went down,
They uttered words their life had sucked all sense from.

The fingers wanted something.
They wanted to go back among the skins
Of leopard, or of mole; back to ores
Still engrossed in rock; out or on to forces
Not yet connected in a form. His tongue
Would follow the fingers, and elide
With the grain dilating mahogany trees,
Conform to laws occult
In flocks of small birds when they turn.

Ridiculous how the man, if so much as a candle flame
Licked with its light the shoulder
Of a full wine bottle, began
To hear flutes and catch notes lower still,
Plucked on a lyre, stooped and ran for the crown
In a contest of one, for now, no longer
Pressed by any other selves, solo,
It was his breath exhaled the finish line.

Sphinx

Whenever a cat happened to die in Egypt,
People close to it shaved their eyebrows off:

What intimate rites of passage were these?
Did the hieroglyph for cat resemble,

Near enough, the eyebrow hieroglyph?
Think of those bushed and sleek

Eyebrows the Egyptians had. Imagine
The compassion, busy with a razor,

Black obsidian deftly worked across
The arched sockets of Egyptian eyes,

The vault of a cat's back collapsing —
Time for an eyebrow to breathe its last.

I see a tabby stroll, supple in his stripes,
Behind a bush, on ordinary grass:

Watch the lines of life ripple on his back,
And call to him with a human mouth.

It hardly matters if the cat is not a fine
Old ancestor, come back again; I only comprehend

How fragile he must be to walk at all,
Vigilant, every nerve elastic as the light.

So if he answers, I, like an Egyptian,
Take no chances, stand to be recognized:

We walk together on the same thread
Spun out and ringed by ignorant meows,

Manifold, for the embroiderer's drum excites
On our horizon scores of liquid pictures,

Taut as a bowstring bitten lips have wetted
In anguish. How else crouches the colossal

Cat, rooted in earth, scanning stars that promise
To spill a fish — and does without. Sacrifice

Is an act can weigh in the scale for a cat:
Sacrifice, to placate, when up it arches,

Torn apart, this flesh, in fury, speaks to spirit,
Loses the thread, and falls to paradise.

Sonnet of the Faint Heart

He loves to be in touch, that above all;
So when his time has come and he must die —
Intimates tiptoe round the bed and sigh —
He says they should put off his burial

A day or two, or three, if possible.
Then the dark visitors — to catch his eye,
Him being set to know what's what and why,
Is hard — they briefly nod and off they haul.

Yet such effusion of respect he takes
To differ not a bit from what he knew.
It's like the palping he's accustomed to:

A glance, bereft of obligation, rakes,
From random spectres squeaking past, the few
Sharp featured icons even he forsakes.

(Variation on a theme by Marin Sorescu)

The Treasure

So this is Iztuzu. The huge blue bay,
Craggy headlands, facing west-south-west.
Turtles bury eggs in the brown sandflats;
For ninety million years *caretta caretta*
Have known the place, have hatched here.

She wept, she said, for the beauty of it.
I take my stand halfway across, on a spit,
And harken to goats nattering among rocks:
Their long jaws bring lips to a meal of leaves.
She had wept for the beauty of it.

And then, then she happened on
A big shut seashell, rattled it, broke the seal
And picked from the dried muck in its hollow
A godsend, from the spirit of the place:
Six old gold Lykean coins.

Exactly where? Organ keyboard waves roll in,
The bay glistens, wind without a bird.
Down again to the beach, through sharp rocks,
I tango and think of the woman weeping,
Red henna hair and not yet stout.

The coins, lost for twenty five centuries,
Found by the woman who wept her heart out;
I will make do with a small white stone,
Shape of a snail on the march, a pocket Arp;
Silk shadow cooling a span of ground,

That there grasshopper will do for a dragon.
Back among beach huts I look to the pines:
Green slope, two flat cabins nesting on it;
Signs of a spring. Was it there she wept?
O turquoise nave of the bay's radiant amethyst!

I will make do with the stone in my pocket.
Ready to go, soon a rough gust, wind rising,
I see a shroud of dusty sand blown off the beach
Toward this bus, and wonder: What if the wind
Has bared a clutch of big shut seashells now?

Cypress at the Window: A Letter to Lotten

A sort of cypress reached
Halfway up the window;
I came to live here, all the same.

Seldom visited by birds,
More often by chameleons,
It fills the window now.

Disheartening any window cleaner,
It filters dust and south light,
A permanent winter dream.

Yet if I go, evenings, to the door
In August, while I cross the room
It's me soaks up the shadow of the tree.

And I remember it was small: on the floor
We sat, if you remember, Lotten,
Watching, flake by flake, the snow

Cascade over, through, and round
The cypress, in a safe place.
The snow was rare and fell thick,

Whitest on the ground, for interposed
Green, like a whisper in the dark, is buoyant.
Now in the wind it sways, dusky thing,

And if hot light still floods the south,
The shadow of it whisks across the wall
Where camels loiter, silhouetted, in a desert.

Camel humps with saddle bows ink the dunes,
Alongside the shadows of their drivers.
The shadow of the cypress, waving, also

Includes my skin, now a sort of cloak;
I feel it in the desert for the first time
Lightly rustle round the shadow's tree.

Supposing, Lotten, you can catch
In Stockholm shadows that prolong,
Northward, articulating it, the violet

South, to swivel east
As fold on fold, reversed,
The desert veers away

And forges west, through snow, remember
How lightly for an hour you felt
The shadow rise, the growing tree.

THE WORD PAVILION

1

Children's Corner

This music disappears into itself
— before you look, listen,
hear it sweep the sky
clean of soot, clean of stars, even.

Still, there it is, now domestic:
humming in her room below the roof
she services herself — a cake of soap,
a china jug, a bowl of water;

And scrub she must her skin —
a breast, a shoulder, carry, shaken forward,
chords of hair, coppery, unfolding.

She opens up the skylight — dare you look?
Circling now her mountaintop the witch, hallo,
star after star she taps back in, like new.

Lines for Jennifer

Ballerina oracle on a barstool,
You told me tonight of the foxes,
They are not extinct, but audible,
So your mother opens at nightfall
Her window and hears them bark,
And listens in late Spring to the chat,
Yellow-breasted, warbling, to the tiptoe
Scuffle of a coon, to the chirrup of her young —
A fine tale you told me, innocent,
Your country spangled with rivers
Pales in comparison, ballerina, even then,
With a daydream of yours, there on the barstool —

All your people, come through the hoop,
Reconvene, inexplicably remembered
In the bubble of time you sit bewitched in,
Now they tell how it was, ask if at all
In thought, in gesture, you resemble them,
Tell how memory smoke smells of apricot,
Colours of an old quilt, a lake in a wooded coomb
Perk up and shimmer in company with a mind,
And prompt as bell chimes constellating their days
They mimic ancient rages and Who Fought Whom,
Who starved, who wandered away for ever,
Show how strings of coincidence bring us here
With all our trouble, growing, to be alive,
Them, too, whispering of evils they resisted,
How to shine as long as you are alive,
Them, sharing your features, our secret
Transparent in their round, slow dance —
So they drink up the outline, liquid, of our exile.

Aladagh Mountain Sketches

1

The old Turk joined his two sheep near sundown,
Sat on a tree root, spoke now and then:
Tukurruk tukurruk. The sheep spoke back,
Not as sheep to sheep but *tukurruk tukurruk,*
The right way for a sheep to speak to a man.

2

All day since dawn in the blazing sun
And hauling what he has to haul,
Logs and apricots, hay and men,
Serene when he drinks, happy trotting,
The donkey brays a bit near nightfall.
When he brays, hold on to your hat,
His heaven is near, might sweep you in.

3

There was this bird suddenly with a trill
Delineating all the apple trees,
A trill like a whisker, the whisker bird;
And after this, the high call of the muezzin,
More whisker; the tractor, whisker; the apples,
Orchard whiskers, globular and green.

4

The wrinkled cloven features of the rock
Outcrops hereabouts, and this granny's:
Tenderly she gestured beside her —
On the road shoulder, at last gasp, her sheep.
But it can't die in the trunk like a hostage,
Can it? So we drove on, but granny
Who tutored sheep through misty generations,
From lamb's first leap to milking, to wool,
Each a silken pocket, full of foibles,
We left her looking back down the empty road.

5

"Life is hard, still harder when you're dumb"—
But they aren't, in the one-room stone and plaster
Huts, the graceful girls, headscarf knotted right,
In clean clothes, the mother with a scalded foot,
Taking the pain. They all sweat it out, him too,
Dawn to dusk, among the white beans, baba,
Granite face, who talks a streak.

6

Where from, the slender fingers?
With a carving knife she hacks
The block of snow somebody carried
Down the mountain. Just look,
How the slender fingers dip a piece
In the mound of sugar and establish it

Between tongue and teeth. In the town,
Wintertime . . . but it's far off.
Up here, we make do with snow cream.

7

Stone on stone, four walls rose
And a cupola was rounded;
A low portal pierced one wall,
So you stoop to go on in. The spring,
Five outlets in a wide
Arc (cold star), whence gushes
Crystal water still,
They housed it in a shrine, you see

Here the huge root spread:
A willow hit by lightning, long
Before we came. Before the roof caved in,
Trees all around,

Their graves in the rock, under a green hood
They heard willow speak to water,
And housed the spring, so it could dwell
In itself, as such a place might wish to.
Yes, dwell in itself.
                    Yes, them, not us.

Dead Button: China Command Aircrew

Now the dead button does not stick,
Where should we put it? The rock face
We hit, propellers feathering, off the map,
Provided our skeletons, but first
Sorrow, deep, no news, a lacuna cut out

In the air. Twenty-six I was, ships below.
Our bombs away we headed for home.
No home. Told it was under attack, we
Deviated, where to, beneath us brown
Rice-paddies, we supposed, then up

Soaring toward those mountain temples
Ancient painters faintly inked in.
Off the map. Again we deviated, where
Nothing spoke, the radio spat and crackled,
Rock was it, or sea? A bad situation.

So you take hold on the controls and hope;
It is a ghostly moment when the engines quit;
And everywhere there was a whispering,
Which explains the blank looks on our faces.
The first thought, of *mom* and *dad*

Or *little sister,* soon forgot. No whiff
Of pinewood. No warmth of Dairy Queen. We
Feathered another minute, numb, then the impact.
Our different fuses blew all pictures out.
And fifty years it took for an old man

To crawl up close to the ice, with his sack,
Hunting for rare herbs, a Chinaman,
Real old, in a straw hat, raggety pants,
A bit puffed, he cursed between his teeth —
If we'd lived, how fiercely our skeletons

Would have jumped from the wreck, waving,
Taken him into their arms, felt him solid.
As it was, the dead button still stuck.
They dragged us down, there being in us
Money. Then the ceremony of bones. A story,

Heaven sent for commerce between their systems,
Those peevish faces, those bugles, flags,
High beliefs in freedom emptied our air.
So the merchants' fingers hit the buttons,
They counted advantages to be got, pronto.

We'd have liked it otherwise, kindlier,
Tunnels of glaze, Peruvian sigils mounted
On silk, beer, female fur, vaginas.
A ukelele melody fluttering, a blue jay call.
Harvey always wanted to visit Leningrad.

The Glummonging

Ah, Thomas Chatterton, I hear
They cut you short,
Those tittering, merry English,
Their phrasing sold, imagination bought.

Your archaisms, real thing or no —
The *peede chelandri, faitour, autremete* —
Ne buttoned up in golde your tommy rot,
You laid it at their flat field marshal feet.

Those eighteenth century smooth gentlemen
Booted your writ away;
Your syntax made a lattice for the tongue,
A *welken* game their tut-tut could not play.

Pundits looking down ignoble noses,
Comfortable in their camphor privy Lent,
Poohpoohed the new life singing in decay,
Smelled in your Carnival only excrement.

You had divined the slithy worst in their
Relaxed iambics, unction, politesse;
Your diction was too crannied for the toffs —
Crystal resistance, not a *clymmynge* mess.

Easily said: imagination, phrasing,
Bought and sold — so what of me?
Unhailie vagabond, am I your abbot,
Riding easy, you *binethe* your tree?

Your aim was high, your elbow only
Swung at an angle too far out:
Still the tubs of grease they trade in
Glummong the rebel shout.

Gentle Reader

In Salieri's Concerto for flute, oboe, and strings
The second movement brings to life a landscape:

Of poplars by a silver river, slender trees
Shimmering in the river, in the air. At noon

The music and the landscape are reciprocal:
Fields, a horseman trots across, and stops,

Soon he is hiding, just an elbow and a hat,
Beneath a tree; his back is propped against it.

The horse, its bridle dangling, crops the grass,
Enjoys the cool, the chirrup of a wren, perhaps.

Oboe, flute, and strings deliver from the air
Just such a picture, like a Claude Lorraine.

Another fifty years — with different trees
The picture will be mistier, Corot.

Greedy for images, gentle reader,
On the web you surf, or on a tattered page

Rescued from a dust heap, what you read —
You need not think its product in your mind

Resembles in the least what's being written here.
Salieri knew the worst but never saw

In 1942 the Lithuanian women,
Their hard-worked hands given so little time.

To shield their breasts, cover their genitals,
The looks upon their faces blank,

Stripped to be shot into a pit
Not yet quite filled with other naked corpses,

Nor did he hear the shouts of thugs
Clubbing to death with crowbars people

Rather shocked to find that this was happening
A few doors only from home, for no good reason,

And happening to them, in their marketplace.

Another fifty years, imagine, gentle reader,
And other women, other men . . .

The Swallow Diver

The swallow diver, but of course, when the owl
    Is calling, not Minerva's, late in the day,
And slowly the swallow diver comes to mind

For the owl in a way tells they still exist,
    These oaks, in an ordinary neighbourhood
Yet rooted in earth by systems intricate

As the acorn interior to a grievance —
    Ancient grudge — and the dead are unappeased,
For it is tough, the human fabric, said the owl,

486

The owl that tells of hurt still to be done,
    Of the damned, of slaves, of the decomposed
Who haunt this tract of earth, at this little

Window asking to be named. Did they belong then
    To nobody, the swallow diver's antics? The moment
When foot lifted, wheel stopped spinning

And there it stood, the Chinese jar, for nobody
    In that moment, furnace cool as yet, before
Twigs took and the fire began to roar,

Then the swallow diver breaks the pool surface,
    Hollows the pool but fits snug in the hollow.
The moment of his descent through water,

How long anticipated? How to judge its emphasis,
    Until his body turns, arching, and spirals
Back to the air, to air in an interval, one only,

The interval between the crematory rages
    Escapes in the spring of the swallow diver,
The board booms and in mid-air he jackknives

To meet in a moment, head-on, the water, so
    To spear it, through, and has arched
His backbone, soaring up, once to whisk his head

And breathe again, as in all likelihood
    An acrobat feels the plummeting trapeze
Bar slot into his palm, and breathes again.

For so it was. The interval is over.
    It was a verb that sounded and was foreign,
Kin to a tongue the sun dries a stone with;

If the swallow diver has altered the water
    Into a sole blue star for a moment,
By name Anemone, no pool remembers it.

A Saint in Japan

Is it shock or boredom or disgust
Appearing in his face? The lips
Are shut, with corners turning down,
But only as if they might turn up
If a duck or blue heron under his gaze
Simply behaved in the mirror of its pond.

Look again: not shock or boredom or disgust,
But sorrow. Horrible
Occasions have not passed him by. Nothing,
Nothing has been lost on him. The tilt
Of his oval head, eyes untypically open
Forage into the thick of things —
What can that tilt, this look, happen to mean?

That with compassion tearing at him a man
Can still be all of a piece? That a joke
Might be told well enough in his presence
And he would chuckle at it.
And that the "peace" would not be "disturbed,"
Carnage in the street, a blood slick
In which he might slip, if, serenity itself,
He found his way there.

                          Was he actually
So, or did the artist, here,
To placate a tyrant or to please himself,
Project the head, the folds of a robe,
The fingers joining, thumb tips in touch,
Project this tough nut with human features
To contain in clay the hollow not to be seen?

And for how long had the rebel disappeared,
Huge boles of bamboo sprouted
Where a bewildered old man often sat
Finding not a thing more sensible to do
Than fathom crow flight, brainwork of the ant?

That he might not, when all in a flash
The foul and hurt out-there evaporated,
Be quit of fellow-feeling, naked thought,
The breathless saint exhales
Imagination on a mahogany chair
And with beauty ripples his clinging
Terracotta robes — what a wish, not hollow.

Can this codger be taunting all the world
To wiggle free of its pupa, violence?
When the lights go out, still the figure is there.
When frogs call, he is listening still.
Some ceremony he expects, but not such
As might turn the tea sour or the gods off.

That look is the look of a man who knows
He does not know it all, has only choices,
Not answers; and forgot that we might look
At an image of him, look back, having questions.
Yet he knew that a potter with a skill
Might one day hear of him —
Old crosspatch who haunted one or two
Faulty memories and spoke little —
And pound some clay to fit him into,
Lift him up for show: "Look hard now,
Partake of this."

A Square Look in Slant Light

La couleur est une mesure
    — Claude Royet-Journoud

The colour
a measure

She flies
in pursuit

of objects we
(knowing her)

know next
to nothing of —

*

Which was which?
Human time

techno-
philiac

faster
than ever —

willing yet
seeming bereft

of a will
to be distinct

I might shuck
chimeras off

only to drift twixt
clashing rocks.

*

Maybe blue
is dust, good

wicked.
Appended

icons burn up
senseless

sooner
than you may think —

Holy Vomit!
Such a flux —

*

Such bravura
yet again

nothing settles,
later, elsewhere

in the nick
of time you'll sift

grey from pink,
short from long,

devote yourself
to a dark task,

rise for once
fortunate

to walk on air
as they foretold,

grains in your cup
sedimented.

*

Nomads of old,
luckier far

than us, how come
it felt right,

one pair of feet,
one pony's back

— but milk, Omar —
did it for now

and that blood
is fire, bone

wilderness, towns
powder, you

could not believe.
A variant

bird call, changes
of the light,

temperatures
and waterways

were homing signs:

*

earth not yet new

is earthier,
gunshot or

ocatillo,
that scorpion flower,

the deadlier,
redder,

simply
for being so.

An Open Door

The atmospherical metaphors
    And visions on a mountain top
Never did placate the vague
    Tormentor. Willing to play

Agent of our deeds, in her
    Breasted body bag, or his
Goat with a clatter disappearing
    Into the mist on a scree,

Both, for sure, having needs,
    Stank and were pure,
And they gave rise, they did,
    To a torrent of artifice:

Everlasting debate, balding heads
    Busy with orbs and wars,
Triangles, nutrients, the fashion
    For ceremony and pierced feet,

Columns that strode erect with fans
    And roofbeams to regularize
The maze of space, not to mention
    Time, to each a measure of it,

Still contained the breath
    From a grasshopper's wing
Or a crack regiment. Now arcanely
    The black stray cat slinks in,

And here it is, a silence, again
    Isolable, coated in fluff,
For humility becomes the cat
    Reminding me of them.

Yet artifice only diminishes,
    Language airily displaces,
Any sense of an *It*. Catching
    Like flesh on a thorn,

Truly thought is ripped
    And settles for less than a bison
In rock, a fish in a sliver
    Of limestone, flat;

The hand, its negative imprint
    Lifting all heaven to beckon out
Responsible kin, presses the glory
    Back, and the horror, of *Them*.

Septuagenarian Goethe Musing

Day or night they sweep
A darkness from the sky,

Carrying eyes and thrones,
Our continents and foaming

Vats of liquor, faces
Of people we have fought,

People we have loved. Ancient
Nobles populate our clouds,

Even the spawn of squatting frogs
Helps to condense the drama.

Forget the clouds, murky monsters
Flying to the north tonight:

Was that not a friend came by?
Did not need to be persuaded?

So you ate, so you drank.
When the ginger cat strode in,

Happening on you, just like that,
It gobbled up a chicken skin.

494

Such a clean and rosy mouth.
What music haunted then your head?

And when they gripped the fork,
How solid your friend's fingers,

When he swallowed wine,
How huge his gullet. How

Nice you were not . . . . .
Badgered by police, or blown

Skyhigh for nothing by a bomb.
How ungraspingly tonight,

Phantoms of thrones, tonight benign,
They cruise across the sky, our clouds.

2

With a Flute in Provence

Sackbut and viol, the wind and the cords
Lick around this room with a white
Beamed ceiling, skyblue walls;
And this medievally quick

Strangled music, why hear it happily
So, on a sofa? Better from elsewhere,
Better to hear it, ghostly, from the street,
Better to want to be in there, and alone.

Who hears it inside these blue walls
Imagines a cave. Caskets of treasure
Flip their creaking lids, one by one,
Wide open. And the air, the air

Is cool, cool with musk and lavender.
A cave, how lit? Do the golden tissues,
Ruby-crusted diadems and whatnot,
Flood with a glow that secret place?

God knows, it was a sublimate, the music.
Terror, greed, butchery, and plague
At every turn — composers knew
How shit-kickers clung to the mud in those days.

But how the room justifies sorcery, explain that.
Throw the shutters open: on the paving
Down below, snails have made with slime
Silver tracks, for early sun to swallow.

Go figure. Now a housewife takes to song,
Crawl back along the street, listen,
Listen for it. Peer into the young cupped
Palms and into old ones, cratered, these

That have no home to hurry to, and nothing,
Nothing to hold: hear it dwindle there.
Or else with a flute
Whose keys a lightning touch triggers

Tell of the begging on every level,
For food, for work, for a piece
Of the beauty, a lick of the calm,
For a nip, no more, of the holy one.

Between Two Owl Hoots

A foot or two
Yet far away
The mouth wide open
And a thousand
Glittering needle teeth
The mouth — no lips —
Bared fangs more like
Or is it scooped

Out of the mountain
A cavern crammed
With shining dancers
Transfixed as if
All motion slipped
Between two owl hoots
Off their swarming
Selfless flesh

  — But do not blink
When palaeophobias
Froth up again
Or stay too long
Or smiling soon submit
Again to the norm
Stand on the rim
An instant outside in

That was a pine
That was your piddle
A flashlight moon
Cleaving the scope
Of lonely branches
Made them glitter
Stand on the rim
Vertical vertical

The mother of worries
This was her jawbone
The uncle of actions
This was his snout
Go undeceived
By owl or raven
The painted show
The bust of Pallas

But touch the tree
In time the roots
With stars conspiring
Clasp and lift you
One hoot for death
So they did say
Two for the stories
You can question

The Red Restaurant

Beautiful not, but positively
One neat woman — her slant eyes
        Remind him of someone, back home:
The spatulate nose, retroussé, but long,
Hair drawn back in a blonde wave,
        Her nape in its bush. Now she tilts her head,
Downcast for a second sip, for emphasis
Spreads her fingers, but brightening; even
        The whosit she smiles for, might he be Tim?

And what kind of poem is this? Back home,
Sooner or later, sighting again the original,
    He'll wonder who she reminds him of.
What kind of a poem, if it's her he finds
Reminding him of a woman to be counted on
    In another place, a heartthrob
He cannot identify, let alone the haunting
Red restaurant she chose
    Twice to appear in?

Karin's Parakeet

No face to speak of, eyes
Inconspicuous, the beak vestigial
But a glossy torso, streamlined,
And tail feathers erigible, echoing
A razor shell. Let him hop,

She said, and from her finger to mine
The parakeet (each wingtip twice
Trimmed with a pelmet of driven snow)
Did hop, only to ratchet crabwise,
Yet elastically, up and up,

As if drawn by some force or friction,
Past the elbow to my cotton shoulder
And perched, out of sight, looking back,
Out of mind, into whatever it saw
Back of my back, so light this bird,

Having scaled my arm as a reptile might,
Could be forgotten. They had placed
Before me a glass of wine and a square meal.
The parakeet, no cat, wanted no part of it,
But I made a hopeful bird sound,

Letting my tongue's tip click liquidly
Against the palate, and then to the fore
That white, weightless bird swivelled.
So for a time we talked, the clicks
Alternating with tail flip and whistle.

It was not long before the parakeet
Discovered I had nothing at all to say . . .
Then he was picking at my ear, the ridges
And craters, arroyos of rose and tone,
For all I knew; significant hairs
Or particles of dried sweat drew the bird
As facts of life, to be enjoyed, for now,

Now he really got going into it
Ardent as an archaeologist who, having sighted
Chips of flint near sundown shining
On top of earth fresh turned by the plough,
Will map their densities, keys to culture.

But if ever I backed off, he'd whistle,
Only to be consoled by another triple click
Which drew him out of a fugitive chagrin
And on again, to deepen his inspection:
My ear, I felt him (breath inaudible) shyly

Circle it, deep inside, something
He did not need to know spelled
Dabu kadar kalehra, though he chose
Not to peck at it. Any moment,
I was thinking, he will penetrate — what then?

He did not. My clicks kept him
Comfortable with me. We had an African
Relationship. He understood, beyond a doubt,
How stealthily I'd focus my binoculars
Whenever a crow or kestrel

Alights on the tip of the telephone pole
Between my door and sky to the south-east.
Something in his body was one with that.
But what that is, a plenum
Of air which changes the hollow

Dome into a bond complecting,
Articulate, our actual
And imaginary gestures, only the parakeet
Might then have known,
In its diminutive and vulnerable song fluff

Known a vast
Congenial aurora — the ear
Of a creation we so insistently desire
Might catch whatever
It is we were meaning to say.

Feuilleton 3: Alchemy of the Word

Manuel Bey, born about 1935, in Istanbul,
Sephardic Turk, fluent in Portuguese,
Spanish, Italian, competent in French,
Bears the head and features of Gustave Flaubert.

And Flaubert, that November, on his Oriental Journey,
"Limbic" Flaubert, who fancied women small,
Dark, and fiery, did he plunge into
Une existence gorge-de-pigeon, having dined
In Pera with the French Ambassador?

Manuel Bey (his line is global business)
Claims there is nothing he can't buy and sell.
Robust, athletic, shirt of denim, blue jeans,
Underneath the Cappadocian stars
Philosophizing with a metallurgist,
Never at a loss for words.

Nietzsche's Hands

Celebrated, the moustache,
And near enough ignored
His "beautiful hands".

Capable on a keyboard, improvised
A polonaise, his own artistic
Compositions "dull and decent".

He could see, some, but much swam, out there:
Knives and forks, print, street signs.
Then, his mind made up, he laid about,

Sank immense nets into the cultural acid.
When he winched them back in, on fingertips,
They rippled with rainbows — herring and sprat

He could fling, raw, in the teeth
Of the *Bürgertum*, God rot it. Ah, no God:
So to invoke the impact of quanta on quanta

And extirpate for keeps the German cabbage,
His fingers, subject to whim, and rounded
Like objects in a metaphor, made good the feeble

Peering eyes. Each tip housed a labyrinth,
Circling in or out, from ivories an octopod
Pressed the torrent of a tune. From Cretan pots

Their gestures, snaking out, apprehended,
Turn on turn, a tumbril in the stars.
Those fingers must have held, no less, the comb

To bush his hairy icon out, to primp.
On long mountain walks they jotted Gothic
Letters on a page, deleted angrily

Brainwaves, on a page one trouser leg
Segregated from his knee. What a joy,
At long last, to know the knower not deceived

But disobedient, at his word. Underneath
The creams of language here's a tongue can taste
A universe, cyclopic, but propulsive, alien

To a species blocked by self-torment,
To shopping, authority — all the cockahoop
Engines of flesh not fuelled by despair.

When Nietzsche, squinting, trimmed his fingernails,
Did he care for suchlike slighter things?
To a turning pot a potter's fingers do not cling.

Is there No Name for What We are Losing?

Finally we found it: a square of dust.
Ancient walls festooned with moss and flowers;
Not far the hoot, again, of a little owl,
Drop by drop in water. And laundry hung
High on the walls, bedsheets, shirts, pantaloons
Danced in sunlight, taking the good air in,
While a boy on a bicycle rode around
And small shops invited our attention.

Yet this, after all, was not the place.
You know its touch: a cold oblivion.
How does a real thing come to haunt a picture?
Distance is not contracted on a road map,
Monsters on impulse crave to be included.
Postcards, anyway, gave the place a name
Not the one stuck in our craw that morning.

They told us: Up the hill your other place,
See? Turn south, but why? Nothing there.
Still, if you wish it. So uphill we went,
Found the dirt road and cruised along it;
Treeless fields, weeping meadowlarks flew past
And the day's journey advanced longer and longer.

Then we saw it: west, the lake, the twin hills,
Vaulted, steep as if constructed. One
With a house on top, bald as an egg the other.
Shorn hills and the lake stagnant, dwellings next,
Of pink stone, or darker, coral, derelict,
But several held up as best they could,
And the track snaked up among the cottages,
Broken cobbles, difficult now to walk on.

And rising south a slope came into sight,
The slope we had so long been drawn to,
Conical mountain peak beyond it, ways off.
It levelled out and over that plateau,
Featureless in a vast and glowing atmosphere,
Thousands of heaped stones absorbed the twilight.

Their presence hit us first, a shock,
Then all at once our own, striking downward,
Through lung and heart, as heron strikes a fish:
Our own Byzantine barracks, shook to the ground
By centuries or earthquake. — Soon tinkling through
Came a straggle of sheep, headed for home.
Dogs. Children. Touching his knitted cap
An old man on a donkey nodded his selam,
For things had gone wrong, plenty, in his lifetime.

Armies from the south, scattered to roost.
Armies from the east shrank back to Diyarbakir.
Now not so sinister, marked on one map in ten,
The citadel, untrumpeted, the squalid lake:
Vigilant hilltops haven't a thing to do;
Even the ablutions you would not understand.

But can it be kept, the secret of a place?
Diggers will be hired, analysts of earth,
Scholars to sift and measure, lift up skulls,
Masons to dress archways afresh and set them
Foursquare, historic and substantial.
Will a stone shatter, crying out for sheep?
No children sprout from crevices of dew?

504

Busloads of people soon will be dragooned
Around the bakery, through the necropolis,
And afterward settle, yawning, in the tea house.

Strange, those we thought we had forever killed,
When they come, it will not be to kill us.
They will confer, point, be interested.
What if one, alone, go so deep into the marvel
He comes back flighted, whole, the more for love?
No. Soon guides will shout in a host of tongues
Invertible facts, figures that strike no chord —

Just who are they, those people? Surely not
Of other stuff than torturers they hatch.
Yet they will pose to be photographed,
All smiles, among the artfully
Reconstituted quarters of our men, and scoff.

Rodrigo, his Adagio

In a freezing attic,
No room to swing a cat,
Blind Rodrigo his adagio writes.
Blind, he explores the ivory
Piano keyboard and conceives,
Note by note,
In braille a counterpoint.

On the far side of town a hospital,
And sick to death in it his wife:
Horrific grief in his gut, and now
Composing itself in his adagio
A music, think of that.

His frozen fingers travel on the keys,
Note by note their thrusts compose,
Lowly and magical,
A music mapped across the storm
In his amygdala, think of that.

Is it for her, the guitar, to bring her back,
Solo, a plaint, soft notes that surge
Across the scope of hearing you
Now hold out to it; no, it is
For them, the gods, to them

He is showing visions of a hearse
Never seen, though some such
Rushing through dark air and the strain
Of springs that wheels depend on —
He was balancing it between

Eardrum and fingertip:
The flashing rush, the opal glide
Of a certain cadence.

Note by note he shields
From them her breath,
Guarding from them, in their own creole,
The hollows of her body.

Altogether yes, frozen fingertips
Tap out on keys most probably
Out of tune the secret
Parts of those placed instruments,
To shroud the tender notes of one guitar.

Finally in the middle air
He leaves just two or three, to float,
Hesitating,
In hope they may be pleased, and relent,
Those gods, whoever might be there,
And bring her through, home.

Gelibolu

FOR MARIUS AND BOBBIE KOCIEJOWSKI

I

For the seven minutes it will take, at most,
To slant these figures over their borderlines,
Surprise yourself: Be the lanky waiter
Waving his tray in Çanakkale.
                              Along the Promenade
People dawdle, arm in arm. He feels a cooling,
Feels in the air a cooling, and he knows —
A multitude of Greeks, Armenians, and Jews,
How they felt it ninety years ago.

II

Soon after eight, at last the sun hangs low.
Somebody signs to him: collapse the parasols.
Under each canopy he takes a stand, reaches up
And puts a thumb against the latch.
A cascade of soft materials is whispering
All around him. Afro song
                              Stopped in its track, he flexes
To the jangle of an oud,
                              Squeal from a clarinet . . .

III

Who knows how it happened in those old days?
Will the lady have taken everything off?
                              A snap, a shrug,
In a torrent of frills and folds
You catch your breath, she catches hers . . .
                              Nevertheless

507

IV

With octopus arms he plucks the iron stalk
Of each dismantled flower from a socket; slashed
White on red, or red on white, the shrivelled calyx
Blooms again as a barber's pole,
Or hardens as a peppermint stick.
Now he clasps them, one by one, lopes
Sighing across the broken paving stones,
And has dropped his trophies in the shadows, flat.

V

Nonchalant now he stands and sweats,
                              Sinister hero,
Hearing the gulls cry, a little dazed
                              By so much clarity.
The last moment, sweetest when it comes —
Over the thud of ferryboat engines, a whiff
Of grilling fish delights his nose,
                              And here she rides,
The schoolgirl, on her bicycle. She brings
For him her smile. And from one handlebar
She has unhooked her twitching fish bag.

VI

I wonder: do I turn my gaze to the hills?
Does he acknowledge those huge burned hills?
The soldiers flit there, Anzac and Turk;
Ghost mouths agape, asking for water, water,
They bumble toward the doorway by starlight.
I have heard tell old villagers oblige them.

VII

Can I lift, now the waiter downs his tray,
A last glance, even, to the hills?
                              Convex craters,
Ivory on dusk, the honeycombed efficiencies for him

Have no possible interest, constructed there
Some distance from the graves,
A more or less decent distance from the graves.

Tin Flag and Magpie

A tin flag and a magpie face
Each other over roofs I know;
A stiff tin flag turns in the wind,
A magpie perches close behind.
The world is an entangled place
Whichever way the wind may blow.

The stiff tin flag is black, the bird
Likewise, but port and starboard wings,
Paunch no less, the snows ignite:
Analogy intercepts all things
That pour their forms through curves of light,
So ghostly harmonies can be heard.

The flag a wing, the magpie's voice
Creaks, as if it were hoisted high
On a mast atop an old clocktower;
By chance a chord was struck, but our
Flagbird, on an urge to fly,
Quit the picture then by choice.

Those things go, disentangled, free,
Whichever way the wind had blown;
Shattering schemes of you or me
A flag revolves, a bird has flown —
Our objects, humble, they aspire;
Learn we our ashes by their fire.

[Malaucène, Vaucluse]

Feuilleton 5: The Buskers

Four buskers almost balkanized, tonight,
August 4th, the Place de la Contrescarpe.

Every one of them in wind and limb complete,
The accordionist all but a hunchback —

After the first melodious flourishes were done,
The clarinet began to take his instrument apart,

Blowing shorter tunes, to show the way it worked;
But on a keyboard hanging from his neck

The carpenter pianist banged out routine chords
And the violin a beanpole man was fingering

Sliced through the edges of catalpa leaves
With long shrieks, rat trills, and all in fun.

Cars now orbiting the quadrangle of trees
Turned into tubes filled with human meat,

Noses took the scent of carnage from their lager
(Even so, the buzz of talk, no way to stop it)

And cherry red the sanitation mobilette,
Cherry red the track suit of its rider,

The sliced leaves, iron chains that link
Old mooring posts around the beds of flowers,

Fogged the eye with fright, and meaning trouble
Identical white camper caravans

Rolled into view, the one behind the other,
For thugs to jump from, us to be flung into.

Rohmahniyah! he shouts, shaking his money pot,
The clarinettist, *Ceausescu, fini!* Whereupon,

Classic features, stepping light and fresh
From reeds that told secrets of a beauty parlour,

A nice Missouri girl, in green, with pearls
To plug each earlobe, pushed her wicker chair aside;

Showing a dainty midriff, on steady legs
She strolled across the street, as if to depollute

With every breath, every stride, the air
Our music for a moment had inhabited.

Then the white, lost caravans came back again,
Carnation milk inside, stringbags of potatoes,

Family snug inside, in each a Belgian grandpa,
Peering every which way, at the wheel.

Loom is Being Granular

This room, too thin, nothing hot in it,
A thousand books, carpets nomad women wove

And daybreak when, splendid on a piece of ham,
Enormous light diagonally slices in —

Still I make my exit, eyesight eases up
And down the book spines, nose takes comfort,

Off I careen, down the steps, a tumult
For scattering cats, how graceful, them,

Though it happens I am long gone to Berlin,
Haunting whose saloons, destination Belgrade,

Pretend dead, play possum beneath bullets
If only I could burrow through the flagstones

For Istanbul is next and means choosing
Free speech in a certain torture chamber,

Only in Antioch, more precisely Daphne,
Am I released, for dumping in the sea

Still at the foot of my steps, still here,
Not along the continuum, O no, the elastic

Broke, groove split, creamy voice knocked it off,
And reconsider the room and me, liar, in it

And the sea crashing through it, thoughts
Loom, purple, and tastes fade into cheese,

Sensation as on a quivering ship of wood
When it turns about, into the wave's whack,

And if it crests, hot slit, matters not one bit
To the moon. So my orbit, back up and home,

Draws out threads and rams them forward in,
The while, archaic, cloud cools my head:

What's to do out there, this music lacking?
I marvel then that shipwrights, long ago,

Fitted their pine planks and braced them
With mortice orthogonal and tenon, tight;

As masons might pitch a temple roof
Foursquare on tenuous illusions of oval,

Dancers danced to it, in a ring their muscle
Wove to contain, 'confusedly regular,

The moving maze' or to transform the season
Their twin rows with a shriek of flutes meet

Spinning, in, out, for their pomegranate housed
A thousand pips, soon apart, soon again together.

3

The Redbird Hexagon

1

Redbird

It waylaid my eye
On the loose,
As it obscurely scaled
The staff of a Venetian blind.

Now behind the open slats,
Beyond the windowpane,
Busy among the cedar forks
A figure was distinct:

Beyond the books, their spines,
Outside, and south,
A throat, a thorax. —
To judge

By the silhouette,
It should be red. It could be.
Then how is presence felt?
Can time undo deformity?

Southern twilight now descending,
Dull cedar green devoured
The colour hot — and solo
A profile agitated

The retina. A saucy crest,
A tail that flipped,
Perfect balance
Lost in a wink, in a wink recovered.

No fanfare whatsoever,
Volume, until dauntless
Off your twig
You quit the signature:

Then, songbird, I assumed
Your absolute disguise,
As from his eyes
A horned toad spits red liquor.

2

Of the Nautilus

Late, into the night,
Touch the nautilus, unwinding,
Winding. Its mathematical,
Its oceanic equations, which
Aspect is then
Your finger to rest on?

                Curving,
The shell gets warmer
In your palm, vacant sleeper;
Along with it you meant to have
Some kind of dream,

Secret at the far
End of the tunnel: but another
Day broke. So was the dream
The void itself of all those
Images that return, return

To be shot, forgotten
At the first whistle
Of a little wren?

Otherwise, first thing,
In a taste of bergamot, or else
Later, on the treadmill, dare you
Say, during an interval,
Through the smoke of a cigarette,
Out of nowhere comes back the dream,
Full flush, already disappearing:
. . . and words drove them, these —

"Sacred rage," a multitude of peoples:
On horseback; building forts; adrift;
Some to throng the air, where
Faint harp chords sounded very deep;
Some few who smile and huddle
In a dry cave, the boy carving the flute —

Borders thrust up gradually to subdivide
The fluid. So thickly
Crystallizing steel and glass cones
Circle the cubic hollows, the explosives,
Anaxagoras.

Any moment now,
And real sacred rage, for the multitudes
Invert, convex, driven by new words
Headmen enact afresh ancient evils,
Calamitous compulsions.

Whatever they were aiming at
Extinguished every flicker of it.
A token incised in a tablet of clay,
A hovel, storage for a minotaur,
A myth of maybe, infinite, consoling,
Gratified one savage heart, another not.

Fast as they built, slow as they drifted,
There is a power streams to lift up back
To the light their luminous faces.
                            A fear of it
Dimmed their faces. To touch them only,

Recognize, love a lunar distance
In the parabola of a cheekbone,
Almost home — of that light in feeling
Has a history been told yet?

                        Vomit and blood
Spangle the traces of these persecutors
Who are hooded;
Having no passion for that,
Hoppity in their traces, hoppity whistles
The little wren.

3

Prima Materia

In this knothole I can hear them clearest.
I prop my head in my hands and listen.
These are human voices you might wish to hear.
Voices in the night from a balcony across the way.
Voices in the night have brushed other sounds aside.

*

From this knothole you can peer through the juniper.
Peer over the narrow potholed street.
Peer through the branches of ornamental pomegranate.
Then you pick out the distant fairy lights.

*

What they say on the balcony cannot be understood.
What I like is hearing voices only in the Spring night.
Voice, in the invisible hand a complicated plaything.

*

Sudden gusts of laughter breach the murmur.
Under gunfire they will remember this conversation.

*

Go by all means where none has gone before.
Still the silence around the voices concedes no evil.
Old as the hills they make not a noise but a sound.
No need to hold onto it, let the voices go.

*

Listen, listen, and let the voices go.
A bit of a mystery, this.
The rim of a mystery spinning very fast.
Any least touch burns away your hand.

4

Triple Coda

Through the glass flesh shone essential light,
    And that was the Always Other, who has come
        To winch our cracked old pitchers up
Out of a clogged well. What if they shine again?

A thought, gentle Zeno, so fragile. Give me time
    To think it when the bullet stands half its way
        To the back of my skull, or still distant
It sizzles from the infinite pinpoint.

*

    This widow on a mountain may not enter Macedonia.
    Her child died of hypothermia in the night.
    Holding the child she has cried her heart out.

    The dew shaken from a tree by the wind
    Still looks for kindness from the dust.

*

We have buried
The treasure under our tackle:
     Resplendence;
And community we have ranked
     In the order of things
Far behind commodity; to everything superior,
     Ravenous ego.
There is a surge
     Crusted by existence,
The crust thickening
     The surge is dispersed.
On the march
     In progressive reverse
Who'll dance for the dance, the dancer,
     For the flavour of it?

With stuff and more stuff
     Blindfolded,
How should the limpid souls look on
     And indicate what is what,
The great souls, among asphodel?

     Over the heads of crooks,
Scorpions attired in tinsel,
     A sack splits, the downpour
Is fetid, delirium.

     So climbing, still a tremor,
Stair on stair, to the throne,

The surge that shook the Spring night murmured,
To make it sing, clear, six notes, the redbird.

[Note: Lines 4-5 in the second coda come from Ts'ui's letter to Chang
in "The Story of Ts'ui Ying-Ying" by Yüan Chen (788–831 A.D). See
Arthur Waley, *More Translations from the Chinese*. New York, Alfred A.
Knopf, 1937, p.114.]

4

To the Ghost of my Grandmother, Anne Shepherd

My garden too, I cultivated it —
Some of the bulbs were not molested
By these raccoons, these armadillos; others
Were gnawed by a spectre, aching love.
It was a garden of artemisias,
Reliefs, anxieties, moss from Kolyma.

A fringe garden, *locus amoenus,* a park,
A point of light, a pinpoint on a globe,
The globe of English that encompassed it;
Large, ancient, fathomless, in my time
That globe pupped for Caesar
A pingpong ball, for Cassius a shuttlecock.

My schoolgirl garden — I wanted
To shelter you, not in a crypt but openly
To prove your bright whirling in the teeth
Of atrophy: in nameless pods new plagues
Beamed down to earth by avarice
Torture the poor, set fire to the forest.

I was putting around my schoolgirl
A picket fence, good sound for whitewash,
Twisting jokes and ironies to wire
Any solemn aha not worth a cuss.
A wobbly fence; yet halfways it admitted
Colour and scent into the bells of hyacinth.

What if I'd had the buried stream
Rushing clear, entire, articulate
Through my bones? I had a trickle only,
And diverted it. Other languages,
In them a purity might exist.
A foreigner I felt them to be pure.

Wrong. Still, if one unbeaten track
Shone with mutant myth, it held a promise,
Half holy to the foreigner, at least
Seeming so, because his mother, on the floor,
Was being poked in every orifice at random,
By each gross faction claimed, by all abused.

O schoolgirl garden, I do not forsake you.
I'm here. See me flourish my trowel,
Shoulder my sack of propitious horse dung.
Yet I do wish I'd felt, filling imagination,
The sympathetic breath that still compounds,
Ins and outs, the thin red line of English.

Generosity, flexion, tautness, lift —
Call it *give* — how sunlight
Scuds across our hills, how it spawns the talk
Even in Cornish villages. How blue
And silver flashes turn our spires, spokes
Of an old cartwheel grinding through wine bars.

The bittern booming from his rushes . . .

And a twitter of linnets riding the breeze.
Almost Ovid. No. I echo oblivion,
Thinking. A migrant on the loose
Cares for his country still, but his tongue —
That he would rather eat than claim
A sentimental home he chose to quit.

Grandmother, I have not gone far enough.
Anne Shepherd, milkmaid, when you sang
Ditties to the cows, how cold was it?
How did you keep them soft, your fingertips?
Your children, how did they come to music
If not through your gift? You went in, I out.

Be with me now. Open the English book.

Antiquity with Epithets

etiam recente terrae sola sanguine maculans
niveis citata cepit manibus leve tympanum
  — Catullus LXIII

Evening stroll along the wharf,
Fishing boats, Halo, Sunbeam:
Sacred to Cybele, gouged in the rock
A vacant shrine, prows angled at it
Risk a smile.

                    Near sundown
A steely blue invades the harbour,
And on a box, for sale, trinkets glitter.
Little rabbits huddle on the box;
Round their throats the whiskered
Trinket man, all thumb and finger,
Hooked ribbons — blood and silky
Red, to trap the eye;

                    hot red
To slit the bag of memory open:
For instance, Agamemnon;
Also splashed against her bathroom tiles
Unhappy Mrs Herington.
Sometimes you only see
Oyster people walking past. Sometimes,
Pouring out of every head,
A red webbing very like a parachute.

What's in a man to choose what he remembers?
One voice only tells him:
                              Don't forget the rabbits —
They huddle on the box, the fingers of
The trinket man force down their heads: a slip
Of paper that they bite will tell your fortune.

Those rabbits, how they sniffed the fishy air
And held it in
Their pussywillow bodies — not for long.

[Eski Foça, 1995]

Tussock Moth

However stiff, having eaten
Of several trees,
The solo cadaver,
Nobody comes to touch it. Joy
Has taken the night off. The object, even so,

What now, a coupling occurs,
Here, a moth, to be identified, by name,
Waits for it. The feelers erectile,
Forelegs cradle an ellipse. Those wings

Are folded copper. Stir as it may,
When you stroke it,
Soft Sphinx in a tobacco sheath,
We face it,
A death, I mean, and hear the beams
Of a hollow ship —

Friction of woof against
My warp and the whole creaking fabric
Woven through starlit
Shores I do not forget, if only
Echo, my nymph, in the deep flow
Parades her limbs — begin to break apart.

So there, in anger or else disgust,
One of us has to stand up and smartly
Flit into the kitchen, do the dishes.

A palace in your body, bright moth,
Contracts. The candelabra go dim,
Yawning patrons
Quit you, downstairs the people
Wash their hands, brush their outfits,
And descend on the village to dance.

Adagio in the Shipyard

Traits there are,
Traits you happen to follow, in earth
Ravines cloven by the ploughshare,
Wet, and wedged in the earth
Pressure-flaked a flint tool,
A skin scraper.

A smell of coal, how it curdled
In that back yard the air around you.
And Hector Llewellyn, scrum half,
Plucked out and flung the ball, his body
Flew full-stretch and still, as he did so,
Is suspended in the middle air.

The traces, which way do they go
Back or on? Up, too. Never quite
Levitating, the dancers. Not knowing why,
You took to the darkening theatre. Distant
Arms, all at once they cleft the air
And with light feet that made no sound
How come their flesh folds into a rose?

Around the disc of bronze, magic letters:
Rare, the sestertius of Pertinax,
Rarer the silver horses galloping right
And Syracusan Arethusa, her
Streaming hair and ghost of a dimple.

None of this had to lead anywhere. Each
Instant of uplift
Secretes (does it?) a church bell. Recalled
Or prospective time, incised in it
Every trace of there and then, here and now
Might have pronounced the note,
Conspired the sign from another world.

But no melody selects itself.
Even your dead do not lie still.
Everything sickens the heart,
For it has chosen not to stop beating;
Back and forth its bellnotes
Swing, take their toll, so modulate,
But the swirl of the world, its offing,
They do map it.

A haze constellates, the new ships
Hoist orange sails, happening to loom
Through: sharper prows, lighter poops, masts,
Look, they balance broadening day,
Dancers need no decks,
Their arms reach out, embrace, as if
It were nothing, the wind.

Recovering Dream

A feathery tip of something traced from under
The prospect, not the action, of a dream
A feathery sensation; a contour, but relieved
Of any object, grief, or ghoul,
Sprang from a source in me apart from the me
It hardly meant to be remembered by:
A windgust rumples for a wink, like that,
A furlong of the sea.

Asleep again I open an old folio:
On buckled sheets of rag paper
A sepia script, the pointy hand of John
Donne moves composing his lost inventions;
Word by word whispered across the page
Squibs to wrench the heart, tumultuous deletions,
Luminous arcades they spanned his globe,
Building up to puzzles, agonies, paradox.

The Dundaries, a light voice fluted soon, in splendour
Outshine the Quandaries; they echo
Stories of strolls in a free city,
Forty-eight fountains, holy sounds, inhabited
Houses in the air, their gardens, all
Of a spiral substance, unpoisoned,
And not satisfactorily explained so far.

Feuilleton 4: A Goldsmith in Cappadocia

That chiselled knob of stone a goldsmith showed me,
I turned it in my fingers — Aphrodite.

Hairdo ruined, chin chipped, nose all but gone:
I told him — *Aphrodit,* look, her expression.

Across afterthoughts I hear him wheeze:
Lonesome infidel, *galiba* he sees

Aphrodit in everything? Suchlike stones
Turn up among clay birds, tiny cows in bronze,

Time and again, when we dig our orchards.
Not so special. Twenty-thirty dollars —

Turned away from the wedding feast . . .
Lips opening to speak to me . . .

Little Red Matchbox

A grey X and a yellow X on a red ground.
A black frame, funeral envelope. Each X
A waiter with a tray on his fingertips.

Oblong on the grey speckled shingles,
Grey shingles of a shining bar counter,
The little red matchbox spilled a green.

A powdery green spilt from the matchbox,
A green — the wings of that enormous moth
Which clung all night to the insect screen,

Green of the emerald moth, like its name,
Mitigated night, black, a throbbing cave,
Insects enough alive in it to melt rock

Gave out their uninterruptible scream.
How come now this green got to be there,
Spilt from the little red matchbox?

Look around. The strings go out from eyes
And trap a silver cocktail shaker, settle
On a red bead in the glass ellipse, your wine.

Or tighten: glimpse the pink profile,
Leaning on her elbow, her legal man
Stiff in a suit, the vanilla sheath

A supple torso, Jessica, pouring gin.
No green, no moth. The matchbox only,
Oblong on the shingle, definitely redder.

Enoptic colours happen. One glance
And all the hues of heaven bounce off
Their complementaries into impish objects

Seen and waiting, waiting to be seen.
Then they perform, concave has swallowed
Convex, yes no, catastrophe elation, starlight

Abysmal time. So now, how to capture
Again that active, uninvited aura,
Green? Let the strings go loose,

Vaguely wandering. A silver cocktail shaker,
A stiff suit, still, a warren of a hairdo —
Not them. See, the strings can swing, softly

Focus revels, later back to the matchbox,
And there the wild intruder is, no question:
The mouse a moment on the threshold, green.

This, exquisite. And you don't notice,
A moon of many watts, hanging steady,
Bathes in the liquors, burns at your elbow,

But the place, this envelope, illuminated,
Rushes on, not knowing any numbers, yet
Multiplying in a flash the shape a tree, say,

Consolidates by pushing through slow centuries:
The space is branching out, blown back or on,
Not knowing which, it fills and spreads

Itself in heads, unforeseen environments,
Hands, little, big, throats drier for the liquid
Speed the place contains turns into spray

As on or back it hurtles. This is what
Not you should see, because, because you ride,
Giving no offence, a lion, ferocious:

This is what spilled from the exploding
Envelope, you and your fugitive smudge
Of green are riding bareback on a dragon.

Party Night at the Yellow Rose

Oftentimes old snouted ladies swarm
To talk their hearts out at the bar;
And their hog men, with skins of whiskey,
Huddle among them, then cut loose
To shoot the breeze about the law.

So they trumpet, so they snort. Vociferous,
They plant on vanishing horizons
All the orange dust their throats
Harbour as paradise, consume as beer.
Flesh squeals under the knife,
Still grunting out the football scores.

Then on their breath you catch a trace
Of something else; and sparse grass tufts
Whisper to contended ground
Grandpa and grandma carpentered a porch upon;
A pang of hunger hits, a whiff of cordite.

Coyotes howl in the pig voice. Apollo
Incinerated all the corn; pier and beam,
To cool the nether air, took in the poison
Fangs of the copperhead. Projectiles
Momentarily suspended in the bar,

Those old buckaroos and ladies hoot
Aromas of a shrivelling religion
Into their food; potted by a child a marigold,
A Mexican shot dead, wounds of their own
By some dimly recalled, load their table too.

An Idle Day in the Dardanelles

1

Flame, there it is, far off
                on the enamel
back of the ocean — sprouting

azalea, a little yacht emits
a volute folded in its flame —

a snowy scoop
or pocket for the wind, waiting for it,
azalea
                  who said "on the glistening . . ."?
toil of the sea, hard, lustrous

8 a.m.

2

a powdery dark
                mass bore now down on it

and down on it bore a dark
possible Leviathan

3

Still no wind, the scoop
    ineffectual, points north
        of Lesbos

ah, only a tanker   and hm, the spires
                (Marcel in his pony wagon —)
which do not change position
however you may move, connecting, dis-
connecting them:

so
(*loquitur Demokritos*)
      "shape, position, configuration"

             a powdery tanker
still bore down on it.

4

azalea infolded delicate flame
    so snowy white,
a fabric of Byssos being airily thrown
          around a naked woman

but stuck —
   a position, under the

whatever? a position, as if
         in this blue colossal
heat, this
        asthma of an early morning . . .

5

Tenuous the sight lines fix
    variable objects all askew
not wrong, but now heave, so hot it is

        your clutter of bones
half a mile, the shift of a lifetime
    and so have split what looked

coagulant or set to crash — a
    bursting pomegranate fills
with shot the pale
    stiffening village children,

spherical
    geometry of a yacht hull

530

6

and a day is said to have a middle
          nothing, but a dip
was that a pontoon? was this a dock?

Slide down the iron rungs into the icy
liquid salt, try
                    striking south.   Void

"nothing is more real than nothing"

still it was something
                    cool, salt, molecular
surround, sheathing live flesh,
surrounding
          a blind spot
     .   a funk hole

7

and remember under green oaks a table spread
lampions on the patio illuminating it

purple aubergine, emerald of cucumber
and several reds, tomato, then peppers

sliced in figures of eight, when from on high
a single acorn plopped into my lion's milk

whereupon a black dragonfly spiralled out
and whipped across gunpowder dusk

first one but soon in a frenzy zigzag
splitting the dark air with wings another hovered

and more and more, a hood of dragonflies
capping the oaks, all acorn life let loose

a host of holes and wings and pressures, random
joy held the swarm in place till a south wind,

as the thud of guns, it was Gallipoli
and the crash of armour where they fell at Troy

blew cool that crystal hood of dragonflies
north, we looked again at aubergines

crisp sprats had snowed upon our plates
while Güney sang the song for acorns and the moon.

8

Poem —

Cultivate your secret
or else
when it leaks out
it will be ugly

Placate what is in store,
the pristine, the mayhem, unhatched,
or it will destroy you.
    No good ever came
of grovelling to ghosts.
    Answer them kindly.

With feeling clarify

    latency.

[Note: *An Idle Day in the Dardanelles* is dedicated to the memory of the
"wonderful Snail People." Their myth is recounted in Frank Hamil-
ton Cushing's Zuni Fetishes (Flagstaff, 1966), e.g., "Then the earth
and winds were filled with rumbling from the feet of the departed animals, and the Snail People saw that their game was escaping, hence
the world was filled with the wars of the Kâ'kâ, the Snail People, and
the children of men."]

Feuilleton 6: A Sculptor out of Britain

1

There is a green hill far away
Without the wall of Blanco, but, exactly,
Blanco, Texas, has no wall, the hill,
Besides, is not so green, caliche breeds
An archipelago of grey tufts, mid which
(And whistling flowers, bits of rock)
There stands a pole and round it slung,
Warped in a furnace, wrenched, archaic,
Writhes the scrap cadaver of a man.

He who walks upon that hill
About it and about must go:
Oftentimes against the flow,
Like that truth seeker in the verse of Donne.
So Philip John Evett, at seventy four,
Selects from a rack of them one walking stick,
Then steadily up and round about
His knoll a daily stroll he takes.

2

You look into his sculptures later
From underneath, head-on, at eye-level,
And think the wood, every inch, belongs
To the tree he looked up into, or from its core

Outward. Sound wood he can smell right
And work on, slice, round out, make to tower,
Do a laminated loop, or horned
Cascades conduct your peepers simply
Through a circuit as it flies.

Was it Sunderlands or Ansons, neither,
But Hampdens, in them he flew,
An air gunner, penned
In an egg partly expelled,
There in a pendent bubble Philip squatted,
Thumbs on the triggers, just in case.

He'll say the advantage was that bandits
Rarely hit Coastal Command patrols.
Yet the gun turret under the fuselage
Cramped a man. That landmark on his hill —
It is a monument, believe it, to the full
Stretch of compassion reaching into pain.

3

He had been a boy, ignorant then
Of the woodworkers in Cambrai, of Zennor,
Of Auch, Winchester, of High Garonne.
A dream had perched him high
On a Suffolk Punch, a stallion,
And slid him off the broad back of it;
Rounding the belly, there, in that dream,
A new Columbus, looking up

He saw the splendour, ALL IN PLACE,
Saw the heavy hanging equine genitals.

Always looking up!

Into the star branches of mahogany.
Into the maple.
Into the anatomical twigs of bird on bird.
Into the stretch marks that streak

Pregnant wood with beak and talon,
Feather bowers of our aspirant skeletons —
Cradles of verdure our evolving nerves
Pirouette around but seldom glory in —
Not always on the bright side, looking up —

4

So comes the ringtail cat
When Philip walks his usual track one day:
Big as this, he gestures, his arms
Holding out, full stretch (and him
No giant of a man) a make-believe accordion,
And the banded tail, he whispers,
Huge as in the stories that are ancient.

Now you know, he says, with an animal,
An animal, mind you, you must look down,
Come to a halt. The animal
Appreciates that. The animal also looks
Courteously down. So we faced each other off.

And I murmured something to him.
The sound, they want to hear it.
Gently you breathe it out, but loud enough.

5

His hands now poised over the table cloth,
Not as in prayer, but cupping still the grain
And cool and scent and weight of trees;
Then folded they were, for to negociate
A deal with the cat. So he murmured it:

Hallo there, old chap. I'm glad
You came back, hope you plan to stay.
My place, your place. And if
It's out of the Chihuahua you done wander,
We've rats galore for you to relish,
And plenty of water, so tuck in.
But now, if you don't mind,

I'll hie me back to my barn down there
And see what more I just might try to do,
With my chisel, for that mantis
Girl bird with a hat of antlers,
Who has moved into my imagination
Out of the stored centuries of an elm.

Of Primo Levi's Death

While I am hearing tell
Of Primo Levi's death
I see two doves, first one
And then the other fell

Buoyed up by air alone
Filling their wingspread:
Four floors down a stairwell
He threw himself, they said.

Still the coincidence grew:
Those were mourning doves,
And as the story ended —
"Nightmares hounding him . . .

Graceful imagination
By evil still tormented . . ."
Hardly having touched the ground
Back up again they flew.

5

Adagio for Diogenes

Little maple, in your tub,
Teach me (I want to say) how to resist
A sleep that stretches into me,
The careful sleep of strangers in a cabin.
First your top twigs will sprout,
No effort, a vestigial red:
Show me how to think of that.

Look at you now, with your limited
Root spread, your vermilion
Twiggery flutters. Cold sleep,
Look at you resisting it, the grip
Of a negative I feared you just might
Come to be. Look at you: thin bark
Sheathes new stems you lifted up.

As I hoist this apostrophe, no sweat,
Out of archaic dirt, you from your ballast
Draw nutrient sap for me to excogitate.
Deeper into my tub I ram it, look at you,
Airing it now, all winter wide awake.

Look at you, impavid and full
Of sparrows that seem, if I give up,
Blobs chirping, automatic, and basta.
I wish to hear the sense of those songs.
Of knot and loop a twittering thread
Thrills the web of being, does it? Their
Solos are so short, and you their perch.
Faintly those trebles delineate a fact:
"It's me today," the sparrow said.

But to resist, to let fly at bleaker
Matters, admit the Inexorable, with a mind
To joy more harsh as volume shatters
This tub in which my roots are buried —
What of that? Your contorted trunk,
Crooked growth you could not help,
Tells me not to panic when desire
Smokes me out, me, not a moment whole,
Hospitable only in small ways.

Across grime sunflowers will explode.
Sky splits with the racket of Neptune.
Hereabouts, rhythm lost, lives are shook up,
Signposts churn the blue like weathervanes,
Arteries clog, power stupefies.
Over there, little maple, what gives?
Steady in the design, a hand, are you that?
Immobile, but a fountain, mapping sky,
Flush with air, a liquid wink?

The Prostration of William Cowper

O Muse, make little of my gratitude,
It's real but only when I read your dreams.
Your intermittent whisper is my food,
But speaking for myself I starve, it seems.

Appear to me, if need be, upside down.
At least rebuke me, if I set you straight.
If on my fragmentary work you frown,
Frown only little and too late.

Me, born cracked, they say, upon this midden —
No, but ill-mixed, part ant, part dog, no shell,
I've glimpsed and sniffed in words the seed of Eden
And woofed and laboured, empty thrice, through hell.

Please do not let them kill me in the street.
Suffice it that I stumble where such people are
As make their lives, how should I say, complete
Nor ever quaked at the magnitude of a star;

For terrible motions do afflict a man;
He babbles on, no wonder, putrid enough —
I mean a mute rage rakes the also-ran
And strikes a has-been from the script of love.

Bare bones on my plate, this baked potato skin.
Take me or leave me, I will stuff them in.

Elegy for Our Wilted Tigers

One beside the other, each with her other feeling
Sister to the one, their brains blended,

Two cats, one cloudy grey, the other
Gold and chocolate, scantly fed

Long years they clung to one another
"Sitting in the sun under the dove house wall."

There was no dove house. Only the hot
Underground water pipe to warm them,

Through any hard winter freeze they crouched,
Snuck up under the wall, and stole their sleep

On a bed of concrete. The chocolate one,
It pulled at the other's dug: Juliet's

Nurse in Verona, her infant Susan dead,
Would have told herself it was practical —

Sucking, and giving suck, so to stay alive.
Curious. These cats were not assimilated,

Or interesting like the cats of Possum.
They were eccentric, but from hunger dull.

What was indoors they did not care to ask —
Great bags of biscuit? In their scope

Only the crumbs mattered, strewn on the carpet,
Threadbare, muffling heeltaps in the portico.

In their hearts, horn never called to the chase:
No chase in them, no picture of plump young rat.

So they hung out, in suspense, flies with feet
Trapped in glue, still hoisting wings, their analogue,

Or people with tattoos who nurse a grievance,
Or Pompey in the ship where they hacked off his head.

Now that the grey cat has been four days gone
Into the vague terrain, or curling up to die

In the bamboo thicket, weary of it all,
I can only wonder if, or how, or when

She might have said goodbye to her friend.
Now into the steel thrusting oil

And captive air with red rear lights ahead
Need grinds me, me also adrift

Empty across limbo, I sniff out a reason
Why her scowl hurt you like a bite,

Why she never let you touch her pelt,
Why, half-shut eyelids narrowing her gaze,

She took off, quick, if you so much
As asked her tenderly for her name.

Feuilleton 8: The Solitary Welcomes

1. *Italianas in Berlin*

How very welcome, now and then,
The laughter of those ladies in the sun;
How very welcome, always, every rush
Of laughter, theirs, from the courtyard
When sunlight folded into it
Lightens the green, stealthily picks out
The tunes of ivory and rose those Maytime
Candelabras flourish, pinning flounces
Around the huge rooted chestnut tree.

For when you hear the ladies laughing
You see a laughter, welcome, lift,
Parallel, from pink and white and green;
It whirs with the electric mixer,
Plucks the cords of a double bass booming far
Behind it all; it tastes of the cream
Those ladies have been whisking up
With strawberries chopped fine
For their holiday tea time.

2. *A Hotel Foyer*

To the dog in the diagonal mirror,
The dog at the top of ten steep stairs,
Who with his long motley hair terrifies
Wolves at the foot of the stairs

And wrongly branded sheep,
Sheep wanting a fold for a night,
To the dog who looms in the flesh with gravity
When you are mounting the ninth stair,
Woof a welcome.

3. *A Benin Woman*

Should it be you she welcomes with memory
Of bronze, the Benin woman in the Metro
— Her chin so round, her jawbone swept
Back as once the blade of a ploughshare,
Now her nose with nostril grottoes,
Slanting hazel eyes —

                      Welcome in return herself,
Welcome her spindly braids
                Siphoned up into a topknot
So tight the roots of hair showed their furrows
For glistening skin
To make her nutmeg skull a helmet —

Her buttoned coat, glossy pantaloons,
Eventually shoes of jet have housed
                  An earthlight still in bud:

So she slaves on, her body magic
Not to be touched by these razors
Of numerals and smells and pictures —
An Africa deep underground, welcome
                As a pool in Yucatan.

4. *Historiette*

Welcome for once to the tune
Secret in Czerny's tripping drills:
Here she goes, the child —
Grasshopper
Fingertips touch
Notes in a flow of
G, for soon the sharp —
Angled sunlight prompts
Our rooftop songbird too,
And here again is France.

Welcome back, the *historiette*
And easily requisite
Opening bars of Gretchaninoff.
Sixty years on and a touch
Light as mint on her tongue
Can welcome one day back to her
The whole tune magnified
By an atmosphere, all gist —

Will her drinking cup outlive her?

Then those notes for wicked Pépé,
Haunting presence, ran huge
Down their channel, like a blade:
The act, welcome again; in a phrase
She stumbles over
Echo happens, dark nymph, with a click.
Still they knit, the skinny women.

So in her knots of pain augmented
France diversifies; as high comic

Her shriek of rage
As dry his covered well.

5. *Palmetto*

Sun gone almost down
Cloud hoods the ring of hills,
And a gentle rain — there
Troughs that groove palmetto spears
Decant small whispering worlds

Down into the knotted
Cactus heart. Welcome,
Housed in the coffee maker,
White cups, a brace of them;
Bitter drink for one alone.

Still, in the minikitchen, welcome
At the top of the stone
Curved stair, for you,
Renegade ghost, longest love,
Brimful of grit, the other cup.

Welcome, on that score, such peaks
In the heart, and coiling
Valley roads, the slopes
Regular with vines; here the *tilleul,*
Greener for dusk, growing rotund,

Welcomes a bee throng throat-singing
Halfway to honey. No gradual
Landmass, no sentiment
Stony in denial, in lungs
Puffed by mundane toil,

Can escape, again and now tomorrow
Sighs to set the unfarmed
Hill crests pulsing.
                    Welcome, shadow, sweep on:
Defang with your calm
The brute, Vacancy.
Bolt against grievance the door.

Black Saturn

From time to time
The table shook
The grandpa drummed
His fingers on it

Summer nights
Swelling pods
Heavier heavier
Older and older

The tomcat too
Him snowy ginger
Beside the grandpa
Sat and blinked

See grandpa closer
Skyblue cotton
Shirt and pants
He look so sharp

Two glittery eyes
For fighting war
And shimmery shoes
He trod so light

He peers around
Then straight ahead
Not rapt in thought
Not feeling bad

The hoary tom
With a butcher board
For furrowed forehead
Listening flicking

Ears the grandpa
Seeming equally
So-so heaves
(Forgotten why)

A sigh the table
Shook from time
To time but not
So you might notice

Whining gnats
Belabour grandpa
Spooks of ice
In a crystal ring

Some time long gone
They made a moon
What a bang that was
When it exploded

Says the grandpa
How do crystal sing
So a gnat be ice
To Tom she mew

The Counter-Missionary

Somewhere along the trail he took
A wrong fork. Front and rear,
Vegetation thickened. No machete.
No knowledge of the creole spoken
By indigenous people.

Still he could cajole them, not with talk,
But action, till he died at eighty,
Into fine cooking. How not to fear
But love their gods. In token
Whereof no peculiar church with steeple

Did he construct. He bequeathed,
Before he breathed
His last, only a tall tin stove.
No wick, no paraffin, no flame.
They loved it all the same.

The Word Pavilion

A very tiny European dog, it says
In the book of roots, a dog, that's all,
Derived from *papillon,* butterfly in French.

And the pavilions are disappearing:
A dark interior where the amber glows;
A hogan housing streaky smells, body-musk
And pinyon incense; a home of goatskin,
Bakhtiars on thrones of scarlet wool,
Planning peace or revenge; even a pavilion
Odorous with linseed oil, where the spin bowler
Fits his fingertips along the stitching
Of a scuffed red ball; an airy marble hall,
Uproarious with banquets, laws, armour,
Harps and the rest of it, is disappearing too.

One pavilion stayed put, it was a tent,
A tent with a flap to keep insects out,
Impenetrable to the moth or butterfly,
Even perhaps to the tiny European dog.

They seem to disappear, nevertheless.
The road is not lost, only the real pavilions,
They vanish, one by one, the frontier forts,
Assumed attitudes, defensible positions, absolutes,
With their poles, canvas, and safety flaps,
And stones to anchor them against the wind.

Then they will be coming after you, the Prosops,
Slime-blue, some torpid, some in a frenzy
Squeaking, bubble faces eating in blank time
The air around you, Prosops, mutant faces

Of apathy once vigilance,
Of acrimony once a sweetest fellow feeling,
The pad of their paws now a duller heartbeat.

So with his music the god
Abandoned Antony. But remember
The musical children trotting along the sewer,
Beneath the road south, out of Alexandria,
They played the flute, the lute, the hand harp.

All merrily trooping through the slosh,
Their music heard above ground as the awful truth:
So the myth disappeared, the myth
Put about for the benefit of Antony,
It vanished.

                    Vulnerable Antony,
Then with his wound
Haul him up, she did, into her monument.

Let them be, the vanishing pavilions.
Others may make more of their fabric,
More of their finery than you could.
There will be remnants, surely, for someone.

And the road, even if you lost it,
The road does not lose itself in such a darkness,
The dark beginning to glow, all air
A sparkling darkness to be created
For more than horrors to inhabit,
For the old hardness that means to dance
In those bare bones.

Old Milwaukee Man's Wonders

FOR DONALD WEISMANN

Not any more that lake with its cataract,
A crescent moon, afloat on it;
Not any more the brush, free of its fidget,
So an image flowers, lightly, under it.

Not that any more, nor new metal objects,
Not any intergalactic whatnot;
Nor confusion of loves, you catch your breath,
But ride on over it. Not any more,
Even, grief at the death of friends.

It is, he says, a pebble standing out in the grit.
A shadow it throws on the road. It is an ant
In the shadow, *in* it. This dear dog now
Likes to hear the cars go past, leaps up
And lies on the stone wall, listening.

                    No regrets
When they pass out of earshot,
And I am looking at this ant, how it shifts,
At this pebble, no part of me,
Going no place.

Language Learning

Never mind the early
Imitative stages: each
Blessed thought
Absorbing words as

Supplied, words
Macerated in
Emotion vaporous
With age, and thought

On "warm," mechanically
Roasting, itself soon
"A memory," garden
Speckled with monuments.

At three score plus,
Your word-world splits:
Things persist, the matching
Words are not quite yours.

You forget names,
Mango and Morandi;
You recite the alphabet,
Hoping memory will snag

On a splinter, but if
A name comes back it seems
To tiptoe out of nowhere,
Voiceless, random,

A reason to wonder,
Wonder if all things, all
Words together intend
An image of something else.

Then beware: catch
The fugitive, arrest
Memory by the moment,
To that slack muscle

Tone returns with art
And exercise, you can thwart
Memory's monkey tricks,
The words team up again.

But the things, have they
Forgotten where on earth
They put their words? Words
Now do not constitute them;

Or things retract their
Public names, and you,
You still profane
Their secret ones.

How then to hear them? Though
"Dialogue with a person who
Forgot the words"
May delight the sage,

Still they rattle
Ghostly chains,
Scare not the things
But you away, perhaps.

For the things at least
Look distinct,
Are done, happening, still
They float, they hurt

Something cruel: not certain
If they want back
Into their words
Or out —

The fresh adventure,
The brighter air.

Hotel Asia Minor

A sickly smell pervades at five
The tiny shower. Pull the plug
And from the unstable toilet stool
Bright water spilling on the floor
Might cause a gentleman to slip,
Grabbing the basin, which comes loose;
But now and then the water's hot,
So praise the bathroom you have got.

The little room for sleep, oblong;
And many splotches on the walls
Betoken battles; bladdered gnats
Exploded there, attacked by towels.
But it is snug, in summer too
A nook suspended in the air;
Two windows in thick walls are square
And under one a table fits,

Place for an ashtray and a book
And elbows propping up your head;
Its shadow falls — from forty watts
A golden light licks every page.
A patio, outside, festooned

With trumpet vines that wind around
A pinewood column, fretted screen —
Ottoman origin, I suppose —

Contains, beneath a roof of slats,
A second little table. On
The tombstone chipping floor its legs
Might well be steadied by four pegs,
But it will do to scribble at. —
Innocent reader, persevere,
There is no spiritual crisis here,
No opera of the intellect.

The tufa cliff behind the house
Is pierced by cavities: old graves,
Where nothing sprouts but silver doves
And tufts of green for dragonflies.
One cavity is overhung
By a rock lip, and snuck well in —
A dovecote: he who scoops the dung
Has a royal crop of aubergines.

Two benches on the patio,
Each like a long sarcophagus,
Adjoin to form the letter L;
Not marble, not upholstered, no,
What buoys them up? So hard to tell.
Yet there I lie, to catch some zees,
On stucco, prone; a groaning bus
I hearken to, the gasp of a truck

Hellbent on something, then the knock
Of donkey hoofs on cobblestones.
A magpie's chatter in the trees,
The flit of sparrows through the vines,
Desist at night, and nights are cool:
As slow plops in the water tank
Echo a starlit owlet's call —

I fold my hands with her to thank.

Envoi: An Apple Tree in Normandy

FOR JOHN AND ANNE WILLETT

Did the apple tree fall down
Or was it pushed?
Boreas hopping the Channel?
Someone heavy and drunk?

Four thick fallen branches turn
A static cartwheel. At the broken
Base the buried fibres, even then,
Conduct the good. Leaves evolve

And apples in due season.
A crooked scheme of shadows
Brightens the lawn. On a fine day,
Dawn to dusk, it swivels, ah —

Hissing, two characters at loggerheads
In a sketch by Guys or Cruikshank.
The trunk, a mat of moss to perch on,
When a lookalike, yours truly, quits it,

A flycatcher flits in, the early bird,
Occupies a nook, and unimportantly
Targets, minute after minute,
Something in the air.

OF THE MORTAL FIRE

Memory of the Vaucluse

In this French September light
Picking out profuse

Corals that invade the vine,
Yellows in the hayrick

And pools of blue somehow
Round the rooster's comb,

To die—undiseased,
Tending a lavender field,

A naked eye
Braving the angel, who descends

As angels on the loose
Holycards in a junkshop do,

Still with time enough—
Fear forgone, bondage to speech

Waved away—to sense the feathers
Rush and whisk,

Then giving up on it
To stand, the more to live.

A Report from the Euphrates

Only to see what was up
At Deir-ez-Zor
I rode downriver on horseback.

A blank on the map, and people,
Swarms of them, shrunken, their dead
With no way to be buried.

I hear the shrouds they lug
Wherever they have to go
Are nowhere now to be had.

Then this widow hanging about—
Carefully she isolates her brat
From the scab on her forearm,

And picks from the apples
Dropped by my horse
Three seeds, undigested.

I must have stopped walking.
Smack went her lips:
So she could swallow her find.

They are no riffraff. These
Are clean people. In our own
Innermost filth we bury them.

Might she have seen me?
A wisp of straw the image
Of me, debaser, debased

Blew across and away.
I was hard put to recall
A sura that speaks of this,

Of a glint through the fog,
In the horse's apple dejected
A glint of inexplicable glory.

None of that. Not so much
As a goat-track leads out. Dis-
Membered—the bemedalled, who strut,

The good who hum at their work
And look in the other direction—
Here we all squat in the trap.

Pass by, pass by. No question
Of disobeying instructions.
No fond idea of reversing

The irreversible. My report,
If ever it went to the top,
Fresh nerve to the evil,

Design and detail, every word
Would occasion only a nod.
With the instigators of these

Expulsions of 1915
There can be no intercession.
There will be more to come.

How like a streak it took me,
That horse, all of a shiver,
The first mile home.

The Cappadocian Chandelier

With a bed for two and on the floor of pine
Oblong cushions, red and black
And white with stars and lozenge shapes,

With walls of rock, since all the room
Was hewn from a cliff and a barrel-vaulted
Ceiling belted thrice with rock

Mimics a fountain's rise and fall—
With closets burrowed in each wall,
Latched their wooden doors invite

A thumb to trace carvings that counterpoint
The vertical grain, while tiny pots
Peer from orifices, emit

At certain times of day their gleams,
The room is lit, from the southern side
Two windows funnel purest light,

But flaxen drapes dowse the August beam
Till late in the day seven goddam flies
Bother no more, quit carnal pursuit

And round the chandelier they go,
The chandelier suspended from
That central belt of chiselled stone,

The chandelier, muscat grapes in glass
Or a cascade of tears blown by steady breath
From such raw stuff, you might look up:

Watch nimbly from his tube the workman tweak,
Fashioning it with tongs and knife,
A moon for the flies to marvel at.

An Image in the Hatch

Now you wonder what they really looked like,
The two who for a moment only in the hatch—

And a bottle of sauce, asters, yellow,
Crowning the white vases, clustered beside

A sweating shiny metal jug of water
Between you and the profiles in the hatch—

Lingered for a moment, one who paid the bill,
Broad in the beam she spoke a word of Spanish,

The other who was dark, whose little dog tooth
Shone in the light of a single candle flame,

Waiting to take the money and be gone.
A dozen paces, at the most, between

The bar you sat at, and the dining room,
What were they like, those paces? Who

Took them? Who did not, but stayed to see,
Framed in the hatch, the profiles and the candle,

The candle flame that lit the inexhaustible
Features of Madeleine in a canvas by Latour,

Lit the blonde who paid and little Laura,
Their semi-faces lit behind the water jug,

Behind the vases and the yellow asters,
Behind the slim sauce bottle on the hatch shelf.

The objects, then the faces, so triangulated
With a memory of paintings, Dutch not only,

Opened penetrable space hither and yon;
Idea could construct, even before the objects

Assumed intelligence freely and appeared.
Idea could dance a thing alive into its orbit.

This differs from the peaches in Russia tearing
Two selves apart in the anxiety of an exile.

It differs from the music which is not a thing
But covers ground before the thing enters the hatch.

It is the old, in a light that is half-hidden
As the faces were, a shadow of the potential

Consuming a cheek or a loose hank of hair;
It is the new intact, now coming into leaf.

It is not who, it is how such minimalia accord,
Accord when nobody need be there, but being there

You will have tasted flesh the courage comes from,
Agile, dispassionate, for the taking, yours.

Pushkin and the Cat

No rhyme tonight but a large man pictured
Foursquare on a headland, saying No to a rock.

Then this cat, after the wine and conversation,
Under the streetlight, black basalt,

Sat there, for all the world an old Egyptian
Until she hopped down from the car hood

And coiled and uncoiled at my steady feet.
Our exchange of whispers then she interrupted

Striding suddenly off into the velvet;
But hesitating, tail up, back she looked.

A dark animal about to cross the street
I stopped, in a daze the conversation

Had wrought, fur behind my ears gave off
Not a single spark but a rapid firework

Splutter: this cryptic naked phenomenon,
Tail up, with knowledge of where to go,

Of what to find there. Come see, she said,
You too can play with this lonely, leftover toad

Who slithers between slabs of concrete,
Cracked foundations in the vacant lot.

Listen at least to the cataract of its slippage.
Give it a scare, so make its day, tonight.

I climbed the stairs. The smell of candlewick
And orange filled my little room. Here, on the white

I place a hand, and stroke this fruit of cotton.
Strange, how those fingernails have grown,

562

Are visibly growing longer, sprouting sharply
Pointed curves, longer even than Pushkin's.

Almost they are ready to share her toad, ready
For any time she might command me: Now.

Figurine of a Chinese Drummer

An agitator, to the life, so he has survived
Some sixteen centuries, none the worse for wear:

Gouged, all of a glug, out of the yellow muck,
Now he skips on a disk and beats his bongo.

Still his grin invites us into his tongue-hovel;
What's here but a thin chicken, a battered child,

Yet he spoke the language of the Emperors,
Probably a mandarin fashioned him and the scripts

Of all his stories, all his fancy stories
Which gave us windows, took the good air in.

That kind of rhetoric, his, the top dogs welcome:
Whiskered statistics, plus a plug of grievance,

Promise that power stoops: it did, but sprang back
Offended by the stench, that much bulkier.

So we slope hoes, the bongo makes us hotter,
We stone our butchers, he holes up for years

And sharply, round the corner, reappears
Stumping along, legs all of a dither,

To make his village hum like a shut hive
With the wrongs of his clay, the rhubarb of his bongo.

Antigone's Drift

The huge mint or pistache
Pecan foams from its cornet—

To be populated by nuts
When song begins to fade

From the appetite of katydids:
A high dome, in such perspective

Soon to match, high above it,
A lobed vanilla thunderhead—

So up and up in a pair they go,
The nut tree, the polar cloud,

Embrasures of a million tongues,
Twin bays aglow with goldfish.

Ha, the cool of evening comes
Now light toasts an urban sector,

No noise from the boulevard
But a frying of doughnuts, a hiss—

How timely it would be withal
To dowse the fire below the brainpan

And listen simply: a misfit
Redbird scours away the scum,

June already and he mistakes
A rodomontade of clucks for song,

Hiccups, hiccups properly meant
To boomerang and twirl

In grace notes, melismatic.
Imagine, next, how on her roof

In Tokat absently the beldame pits
And sets in the sun her apricots—

She points a crooked index up
And down to regulate his rays.

Twitching your backbone, burro, too,
Baring your teeth for no-one,

You turn your dependable tail
On the mystery of the mountain,

Shit on the beanfield track—
And bray unprepossessed withal.

See how easy they have made it
As never before to love, but love them.

A Gallic Cat

This is to be a mortal
And seek the things beyond mortality.
   —Manfred, *II, 4*

In this twilight crossing freshly
Fallen snow
The tomcat raises his meow,
A white and ginger tomcat;
Hereabouts, halfway to the equator, rare,
Ruthless and imperial the snow
When there, on sentry-go,
The tomcat yowls:
Mon rêve! Mon rêve!

Or did I miss the gist, milord,
Of what you had to say in Arquà,
Seeing Petrarch's cat, embalmed,
Still in its niche above a door:

That the affection constant in a cat
Put to shame the cold
Heart of a Laura? Before passion bites,
It must range and swivel?

Arquà, still in Italy; September
1819, that would be long ago.
This Gallic cat is doing fine, so far,
In a Texan city. No, they are disposed,
The cat countries, otherwise.
Cat language brims
Nocturnally across the borders.

Then out you went, arm in arm again,
First to the tomb, soon to the fountain;
Children were chasing butterflies;
Downhill to her coach
And yours, you heard the shouts
Of rage, milord; postillions
And footmen actually fighting.

Anecdote of 1917

Drop the Austrian, I say.
He will not. Drop the Austrian
Or I shoot. No, he will not.
In Italian I speak.
Did he understand? A medic,
Yes, but a big Americano.

Shelling on the mountain, smoke;
Soldiers, many thousand, dead.
Guess how frighten, noises, dying.
Then he stop, I take my aim.
At him, not at the Austrian,
Feet in socks, across his shoulder.

Orders are to shoot, paff,
Unless the wounded is Italian.
Me with rifle lifted, aim.
Boys of twenty, both. We look.
Did he understand? Next moment
Both of us we burst out laughing.

Up from under, *zampillante*,
Comes the laugh and through our bodies.
So we laugh. Not long. And down
Down the winter mountain goes,
Picking his way, Americano.
I watch for him, he wish me lucky.

I tell my story only once,
Once before, much intimate.
My really not important story,
Why, hopkin sonnet, lady say,
Just like that. Lady speak—
Racing lambs have fair their fling,

On a pear tree, yesterday
All of glass, above the lambs,
First bloom, now leaf, little faces
Brush the blue . . . For pity's sake,
An old man from a sweeter tree
Such laugh as then might never shake.

A Water Insect

Those who have the right view call it daimon
and know it is outside them.
—Plutarch

Admittedly the water boatman,
On his way upstream, sheds a shadow,

Cinque-spotted, on the sunny bottom,
A shadow fringed with colours, as if spilt

Briskly from a prism. So he ploughs,
Adverse to the stream, a lonely furrow.

The water boatman, head-on, up the stream,
His element, has to concede, then taking

A chance, full stretch he slashes through
The counterpushing surge, right as rain.

He feels no water, does not see his pretty
Stygian shadow figured on the rock or sand.

Or flit across the mud. He does not
Ache to have been so driven back awhile

Or sense a place he should be heading for:
Success, pleasure, the cottage under oaks,

Cream puffs every afternoon for tea.
Nor does a water boatman heed

History in a stream of bullets; no feet
Are torn away by mines; no shredded

Wits result from his pursuit, for he
Has no profession to mistake himself in.

And even then—imagine this picture postcard,
And coming round a corner by the old café

A figure in a straw hat: sinew stretches
The figure out, a lunch hour

Engulfing Alexandria, and there perhaps
Groggily beneath the hat Cavafy strolls,

Between ocean and desert, folded in his clothes,
Wading through the temperature, as then it was,

Acid noon, a summer day in Alexandria,
For beads of sweat roll down his back.

And Lehnert, the photographer, travelled too,
Out of Bohemia to Sfax, delayed in Constantine,

Explored the souks, portrayed the North Sahara,
Snapping long camel shadows on the sand,

Warrior profiles, filigree tattoos
On chins and cheeks of the bordello girls,

To end in Egypt after twenty years,
And never knew just who it was, just who

Selected from Greek ghosts and adolescent
Flesh he dreamed of touching quite a myth

And trotted now, haggard, from the shadow,
The Mariner, actual, ever on the look-out.

A Static Raft

On a raft of débris, somehow static,
Squats the cormorant. Round his raft

Slowly it slides along, the river,
Flanked by bare trees, by hills receding.

Now the cormorant has to lift and spread
For a while his wings. His intellect

Coils back on itself. While he desires,
Desires the air to dry the delicate fabric

His wings compose, feather by feather, I
Discern in him the midpoint of a labyrinth.

While the double axe in the deep lifts with his vertical,
Doubtless he is hearing the waltz of the water;

Where he feels a webbed but sinuous temperature,
I see a semblance of the Christ crucified.

Even then, what subaquatic secrets occur to the cormorant?
The cool out-there I mark as a holy tomb,

Substances pumping, too, through aged, slant elms,
This grass underfoot, seething behind me

While the girls and boys in a dance perform
Outer loops of the labyrinth, and invite

At last a stranger into that recondite hollow
Where the cormorant still holds his pose,

Mean not a thing to him, cannot fit
Into such time as he has an inkling of.

Here precisely time does not take him in.
He is modern, where my spiral fizzles out.

So he is filled to the brim with pleasure
By the wind that licks his tendons lightly;

Music for him the measure of his feathers
Whispering as they are ventilated, one by one;

And he will love the more to be skimming
The river in flight, when his rite is done.

Ground Zero

1

Across fresh-cut slabs of local rock,
Myself stalking it, primrose the light,
My shadow moved. Deadly silence fell from it.
Freeze, husky women, preening in your shrouds.
Hush, till I heard the old tongues wag again.

Persist, percussions a cosmic loom emits:
Simple donkey hoofs, clip, clop,
And only intermittent, fainter,
A drone of motor traffic—

2

Breath spins a thin belt round the nightfall;
A song, solo, from the clarinet, intangible,
Then, all along,
Suddenly shouts,
Sibilant whispers from children in a huddle:

It was a world unbroken by the two-stroke
Clack of an archaic motorbike.

3

Fluid as in springtime
The anthem of a mockingbird,
Twilight is hot and craves;
From accidental sounds
A texture, inch by inch a shell evolving

With a sheen to twit
Sparrows busy stitching pleat by pleat,
Craves to gather volume into itself.

So fold, if you will, the tune again,
With due reverence, into the tango
This old bandoleon inherited—

4

All the calls, fading. Pillars in the storm,
Powder. Still some part of it
May, like a mute volcano, wheeze.

All is turning slowly into its Other:
Reach into this memory, deep. Extend
The hand that clung to little touches,
Caliban to the sexual,
Once in a while, only, got it right—

How to flow, to colour all, combine,
Temper, and crystallize
Wild perspirations of the absolute.

Your coarse expiring cry, pigeon,
Was copied from the ricochet of a musket ball;
But in mid-flight how cannily
You disappear into the darkening vine.

5

Now with long claws nicking cobbles at the gate
The dog is on his way to the dilapidated palace;

Long before the first stars fade his barks will tell us
The truth about a solitude he has discovered.

(*Ürgüp, Cappadocia, July 2000*)

Domicile

Open the door, the wind blows in,
Tries to roll it, blows and rolls
Half my carpet up again.

Not a carpet, it's a runner;
Not a runner, it's the girl,
Konya girl with a red dress on.

Girl in a red dress, lifetimes gone;
Now lightning tipped by stars in cups,
She milks a flock of pollen, tinkling.

So she wove. Her holy lamps
Illuminate (and still they die)
Armenian children, women, men:

Carpets of them clog the trails,
An airman sights the convoys plodding
South and east, across the room

To Golgotha. All but for them,
Konya girl with a red dress on,
I take a hint from the wind, and run.

A Brightness

(from the Turkish of Sait Faik, 1954)

There was a brightness rising.
It warmed the deep
Waters, the city, all the people.

This brightness, it began
Inside the ground, like grass,
Like trees. I asked myself:
What can it be? Stones and trees,
Buildings, people, everything
Was asking: What can it be?

The brightness gradually rose.
Then it stopped, halfway up.
With fear we looked and saw
Halfway up ourselves.

Brightened from below on holidays,
Once we took a look at one another,
There we stood, like statues, in the street;
One and all we looked with fear
Halfway up, but then with pleasure
Saw more things and more in things.

Later, having looked at one another
Down from halfway up to see what else
Might be brightening, we could not see,
At first, the brightness rising
All the way to reach our eyes.

Now it reached our eyes,
We looked to see what was above
Halfway up: crazy, but
There was nothing to be seen.
The halfway up had no above.

The Invisible

With a flutter and a pitterpat
The pigeon settles on the parapet.

Draw down from your palate then
A tightening tongue, and cluck.

The pigeon turns his iridescent head,
But how he hears is anybody's guess.

By what other channel than an ear,
When he has none, can any pigeon hear?

Along the parapet he waddles, next,
Not closer, but away, and eyeing still

The middle of a nowhere (Schumann said),
Root of a distress my tongue alerts him to.

Could this be it—one godly cluck provoked
For ever and a day the waddling off, evasion?

Does this body in motion put to work
Reciprent membranes in each half of his head

Telling him with such a grace to tilt it?
While his vermilion eyes have side ways to wink

And mine arrange for contact on the level,
Whatever should be there for him to look at?

Air, for sure, will have stormed across the membranes
As in a band, scraping a drum, the snare;

Yet my cluck, travelling light, planted itself
In the nerve cell where an alarm goes off.

A second triple claw touches the parapet,
And fear is a force, molding the invisible.

No big deal, pigeon. You are wise to scare;
Wiser than me to see nobody there.

Hunting in the Old South

Like anyone would
        I went out with them.
The invitation interested me,
To hunt, with a gun, in the South.
        And I thought, by the way,
Never pass up a chance to look on.

We got there. Pretty well drunk,
        All the people were rich folk,
My son was with me, taking it in:
Cartridge pockets, pants, boots
        Are antique finery for such
As him, I thought. Then the gallon
        Tanks of blood
From the kill of the year before.

Those we unloaded and opened.
          Smeared the deer blood on:
Face and hands, all red,
And a hard smell to it. The rich
          Enjoy any ritual, strict, and waste
Never a moment before
Glugging the liquor down, scooping
          Blood from the tank, soon
Nothing is white but the eyeballs.

Into the woodland then we strut;
          Me, I observe bird calls
As well as the angle rifles are at—
Best when the barrel is up.
          Some of the plumper folks
Puffed in the undergrowth,
          Oh, and sonny along with us,

Most of us felt pretty spry
          And I saw the deer suddenly,
Mine, arched in the air,
Aimed and shot, the bloody
          Faces were beaming around me:
Dead as a doornail the deer.
          My bullet had gone slap
Clean between the eyes. Luck,
          I think. The pelt, velvet,
No, but its throat was, and ears.

All day out there, on we went,
          Shooting a lot, and sipping.
Blood on our skin dried up.
Men's bodies, I note, smell sour
          At lunch, in their togs;
Squirming through thickets, what
          Dummies we are, I thought, and
A whisker away from running
          This hell of an organized country?

Just a whiff of gladness then,
            And it got to me: the difference.
God knows, we could be hunting me.
These painted heads popping out
            From somewhere in the deep
And crawling wilderness of mind,
They did as the unshriven
Spirits do: to hog the power
We living wield, first they mimic us . . .
            Soon they'll feast.

            Stashed in the truck
My animal. The boy had joined it.
      I gave those church-goers a half-
Hearted salute, called it a day.

Late that night I looked in on him,
            In his bed, my son.
All evening he'd sat and sulked.
Asked how he'd liked his first
            Real hunt with grown men.
All he could say was: Well, dad,
That deer, in the air, did you
            Happen to see it was beautiful?
He did not want to touch my hand
            When I tried to take his in it.
Now I see your face, says he,
            I want the blood off it.

At the Hearthstone

This Infinit Space is a Thing so intimately known
to the Soul, that tis Impossible to remove it.
    —*Thomas Traherne*

        It must be worked
The way a potter works
        His clay. It must be pounded
As the baker still,
        Or home provider,
Pounds the dough.

        Not one sign of this
Will you allow to mar
        The pot or loaf;
For those fired objects, both,
        The oven's heat also
Will predispose a fate.

        Make no mistake:
The matter of language is endless.
        A poem born not made
Irradiating scraps of chaos
        For a wink proceeds
To father on its substance
        Cosmos beyond dispute.

        For model take a throne, perhaps,
A breathing throne? And there
        (Since nothing real sits)
Some great spirit who defines your days
        And is lowly as a vowel
Imaginably levitates.

        A pattern, should it cut
Loose from silence, mindful of it
        Will set for spoken love
Another silence free. Dotage
        Approaching, nevermore
Harangue, or ply the air with precept.

Focus: in full bloom suffering
The mundane shatters:
        Bring them together, singly,
The abstruse fractions.
        Jettison shabby epithets:
Nothing is one and the same.

        So hear them sigh, loaf and pot,
Those comprehensive heavens
        Of Traherne, of Kant, of Hawking;
Hear a ticking in the furnace,
        Languid time is not done yet,
And I forget what I am saying.

The Three Cottages

The dirt road could be drying out now—
The trunk of the tree collects its volume
From a patch of sunlight; stricken too,
The forks of branches near the top . . .
And under inky foliage the thatch
Of this first cottage brightens a little,
Less then the second thatch of three
Etched by Rembrandt in 1650.

What do they say, the vertical
Poles that jut from the apex
Of triangles above each little door?
Welcome, storks? Or (you can be certain)—
We be poor but flourish an ornament:
We make, into the air, a thing
Which holds its head above the mud.

What industry, in cross-hatching,
In curlicues to suggest
Throngs of leaves, a million straws;
And past the three cool cottages
The road crawls, perishing in distance;
Still smaller trees, ponds, cottages.

These white, hooded figures, who
Or what? Can they be
Remotely people? And indoors,
What can there be to write with,
Write on? But hereabouts people
Huddled over embers and spoke;
They froze, they bit their lips,
Not altogether unaware of trade
Overseas, of their compatriot navigators.

From dirt they also sweated out
Fidelities, betrayals, bargains:
The nub of indigence only Rembrandt knew,
Rembrandt in his turban—that an empire
Depends on all its worms; that the road
Can lead to nowhere, but the edge
Of so much mud is brighter, sometimes,
And opener, always, in the expanse of art?

Not at all. Potato face, with a wink
He shut his picture at the skyline.
True, to Italia with a turquoise
Sky the road of dirt could take you,
But here distance unwinds in fast reverse,
Colourless, at most a quote. Likewise,
One inch under it his name he wrote.

This Is Not a Painting

Real space a sheath,
Not for a knife—
And in it, this:
What time it was drawn out,
Colours and their shifts
In transit clean
Across the spectrum stuck to it;
So their objects, first
Oddly breathing in, detached,
Now blow away the sheath.

Who can fathom it?
To feel the tremor of its echo
Colouring thought is easy;
Crushed out of disgust
Primary tones, vigorous hues
Blow too a lightest breath
Of fountains
Through a curdled
Horror that, any time at all,
Might deject the world.

So you will have seen,
Flying, the tree roach,
And caught it quick
In one hand. With fingers,
Crushed it: a sulphurous
Pool of spew, not hot,
Irradiated by
A twilight then,
Its abdomen spawned,
Exceptional, bitter,
A family of fragrances
Out of a time before
Anything grew
Stately, harmonious, small.

Silverpoint on Parchment

What wholesome tension
Must be haunting
The Big Bang
To have come to this
Tilted sun hat
Saskia wore, a bride,
And this countertilt, under it,
To history no stranger,
Her own inviting smile.

Carracci: A River Landscape, 1600

It is the depth, with blue
Volcanoes, both extinct, limiting it,
And cirrus delicately
Stratified that make off with your eye
At first, beyond the bridge, beyond
The watch-tower.

    Then, left and right,
Margins figuring trees in goldleaf
Retrieve it; all the eye again
Is funnelled back; re-concentrated
(No witch or heretic on fire
To interfere)

    Forward it will float,
Navigate with little ships, for boatmen
Pushing punt-poles through
The painted river, to the ground,
Soon will pass,

    And (ripples licking
Wooden hulls) one of the oarsmen
Eyes the heavy cargo as he leans
Strenuously back, as if to lug with muscle
Not his little ship alone
Laterally toward the arches, but
Also red and central masonry, the tower,
Up to touch a blue-capped cumulus.

    (Perhaps a drop
Of Borgia spikes
His drink, unseen underneath

So many bricks, the local prince?)
Meanwhile it is early evening,
A conversation had been opened in a shadow
Shared by two figures, underneath twin trees,
And leaves that blur above them, gold and umber,

Echo their tinted aprons, in miniature
A lutenist, a girl with her guitar,

          At last redeemed, their speech?
Or no: their perfect song is pastoral. Turning
Brightly hatted heads a moment since, now each
Picks at invisible strings
          And peers undizzied
Into the other's eyes (which brim
Probably with other pictures). Labour
Is not the object of their music. Still,
Their diddling will have filled

Fragrant air with glides in descant.

Those disappeared, like all
Four little ships. On flesh at fingertips
The print of strings also dies.
          Yet quick or heavy-going,
To this, every anguish in transition, this
Image of many thresholds, must have tended;
Imponderables of downpull, uplift,
Flux and stone, sprinkled

          Here, for once
Igniting in Carracci's memory
From a source of light in time
Yellowing one stretch of the horizon,
These daily, solid, gradual goings-on.

          The watch-tower, even,
Threatens no-one. Distance—and still
No sign of us. In one volcano sunk
Perhaps a murmur was left by their principal,
Vast pooper of parties, at large in the cosmos,
Exploder of stars. But not yet,
Hooked by death wish, gnawed by his worm,
The howling factions, jittery cultures
Herebelow fogged by electric palaver,
Magma of biophobes, thanatophores,
Garblers of the Name . . .

Articulate as a dandelion,
Up through a crack, here
Between slabs, tombs, paving stones,
What a world sprang up to defend itself,
And has become, this too,
An uttermost of worlds, a breather;

Or else Carracci, catching his breath,
Simply had to tell the duo and the boatmen
Why he made rectangular, to catch the oval
Undulant eye's attention, this rift in time
Their beauty issues in and out of—

Content anon to dwell
On earth as refuge, while, as may be,
Other planets rising will subside.

At High Noon Mourning Dove

Your good medicine, Catullus,
Nowhere near it, most of us:

Is our retort shot through with holes?
There is much air escapes from it.

When elements, from their positions,
Are jumping in and out of line,

Air escapes, demons by the dram
No busy parson quelled, or saint,

And, breaking through, in consequence,
Each lusty construct still foams up,

Away the balanced animal flits,
Your tart repairs again her make-up.

584

Or might you not have been so much
Of a Daedalus in the first place?

Just lungs, pumping faster, faster,
In and out, the smoke of politics?

Yet your hood was off, daily the falconer
Launches into the blue your scribbles.

Monks and militias, both beholden,
Their flesh crept to your flutter.

Nostrils flared in Irish coombs,
On docksides in Marsilia, sensing

How you could fuse anguish with contempt,
How low and high cadenzas flip

In the risk of a heartbeat. Your
Measures in the mouth, they rose

To tiptoe over summer snows on Tauros,
Then dropped to the bogs, to slime

That swallowed whole a flimsy sandal.
To this day the crunch and squelch

Invite, while knives are honed,
At high noon mourning dove has much to do,

In stinking alleys people fall down dead,
A nod in the direction of the air,

Another, giving thanks—
To whom?—for time.

A Bagatelle

Who captures the wind
And its actual rages
A gale sweeping the heath
Cleaning the peaks
So they brighten at nightfall

Aeolus in violins
Zephyr in the reeds
The cello squalls, too, and sighs in measure
When an emerald empire heaves
Itself apart into whistling
Branches of colour

Flake of clear woodwind, tall
Tornado corked in the trombone
The dust of galleons beached
Rules adrift however an eager tune—

O great herald, legate of an era
When real estate was large,
Rage rare, an age
When ladies after lunch
On lawns unravaged played croquet,
Legal and gloved
Floating at the first gong
Down long escaliers in oriental regalia—
Is now, as then, a world to be made of the wind?

Chopping, the regal bows, air
Arguing with an eagle up there
Strings are hauled into tune
Across fragile frets
Top gallants tremble for an east wind
Afresh, an elegant

Caravel argosy swoops across
Ocean, deep
And gone
          A bagatelle
And all for Elgar.

Bove's Move Recomposed

It was always a dump, this district of the town.
A woman asleep in her lover's arms,
A boy stamp collector magnifying a foreign stamp,
Near enough unimaginable here.

Unimaginable, a girl dressing up for a party,
A housewife dusting a windowsill without contempt,
Or a poor man who opens his mail, first thing,
Only to learn that he has made a fortune.

It all came true—except the happy moments of life.
No memorials, not a stone with names incised
By which to communicate with the victims, one by one.
Nowhere a token that the perpetrators felt remorse.

I think of the many people I have known here,
And today I am to leave it all.
Perhaps the place will die in a month or two,
For it is fragile, fragile as a human being is.

One morning when I have missed the newspaper,
It might die but nobody will have told me.
Thinking of all the people I knew there,
I will go on believing that it still exists.

I might, till suddenly later I learn
That for years it has been gone, for years,
And there instead the Emperor, peeping from his robes,
Consecrates his latest Bicycle Racing Stadium.

(after prose by Emmanuel Bove)

On the Latency of War in Things

It is in the field that man takes heart again.
    —*Schiller,* Wallenstein

Bad, bad dog, gnaw on your knuckle now;
Believe it a marrow bone.

         Slope away, rippling and Roman
Tiled roofs. Walls, indefensible, ours
Are painted ochre, painted pink.
So our windows fix, oblong or square,
Sensible qualities. In jaws of frogs at work
From grot to grot arcane geometry carols.

            *
          * *

Who did so love, all of it, a world,
Fashions for our town his morning still
Into the curly road that warps,
Never yet buried in magma, a lavender plot,

And has brought the cultivator's labour
To ravines packed with cherry, to high terraces
Where olive trees twist silver in the wind.

            *
          * *

         Shrapnel, a twisted inch,
Stuck fast in the track, flush with it—
What from, the strutting, the swarming, and swollen
The industries of destruction?
What for, the hallowing
Of raw torment? In our town
         Even good men forget—

The right songs do not.
Old frogs with vowels also trawl the air.
From grot to grot in our town

Their throb incites an antiphon. Oblong
Or square, windows in our twilight
Flicker when a roar goes up
From the battlefield of international football:
Level, one with another,
Punctuating cypress, ilex, and poplar,

Eastward they seldom search, for the angel,
On his toes, the colourist
   Who fills the screaming loops of swallows,
   Who sank his measure
Deep in the grit of an antique tommy.

     *
    * *

We wake to pain, but Igor's instep
Grips the golden stirrup; tread
Spirits down, they only rage
The more to be proven.

     *
    * *

Rollers in the mill press, none too soon,
Newsprint from water; now to its pool
Water talks, enshrining aeons;
Galleries in the mountain, spillways brighten.

Blood never shone so
Spouting from lamb's throat, groin of a fusilier,

     *
    * *

Gnaw the bone, bad dog: back to your niche.
Expect no condescending hand to stroke,
Should it grope down among the massive
Mottled trunks of these platanes,
In our town, your pelt.

(*Malaucène, June 2001*)

The Curlew

Curlew's cry, sweet as air,
Delicate as bone
Speeding the wingbeat
Many mothers breathe,
And a boy must
Wonder how
If that cry was born
Over ancient land at peace
Without palaces, it came
To be modified, carolling
Glottally, tongue torn out,
Aslant some Roman,
Then Saxon killing fields
A buzzard alone
Might mind to see.

How now to say it was
Not always so:
Of wet earth fresh ploughed
I have with a thumb,
Hearing its folded note
In Norfolk, cleaned the deftly
Flaked but cold flint
Scraper I had found;
Not much less long ago
The cry unfolded,
Quite at home in me,
When first, mindless
Of me, I cupped
Firm in my palm
The breast of a girl.

Well, he has done rinsing the sky
Clear of ghosts now.
And the true, still it fools
All the hectic sectarians.
Only the hermits hear

But obey the cry's lash. Heavily
Clouded vistas they spread into
Seldom welcome
Such questioners, each in his arms
Or hers, as they patrol
Targeted streets, cradling
An old cave, snatched up
At the last possible moment,
A crystal hollow torn
From its crag, now distant, each
Coolly questing equipoise.

Little William

Mud, frozen, but the puddles,
On a closer look, also hatch
Tiny fans, as from a stone
Church the many voices press
Salve Regina to the winter air.

People are cheered, hearing them,
Rags on their flesh distribute
Suddenly finer smells, the herb,
While lavender in its bed
Beside a cottage, with a chime

Exults in the ice-providing wind:
Flageolets, and tinkling tongues,
The forest heaved, and snuggled
Foxes heat their burrows in it.
Here's little William now

Awake, winking to the flames,
Hugging himself, a red nose
Reading their Greek and islanding
Vocables a golden log gives off.
If all must speak, who may speak best?

Through all the cracks it comes,
Air, the invisible, warming only
When it honeycombs his crepuscule.
For with it, biting air, that is,
The *Salve Regina* sails indoors:

Music, silken, the vocal damask
And opaline, frozen yet liquescent
Fabric from heaven! Little William
Lifts a finger, hums along with it;
All its purpose fills his pleasure.

The Pigeons and the Girls

Quite early in the day I saw them,
Side by side; perched on a twig
Above the traffic, those two pigeons,
They raised with a single motion
Their heads toward the light.

I must have raised mine also
To have so rapidly glimpsed
The beaks they lifted, in unison,
Up to the light that made such gleams
Glide across the troubled cars.

Two girls came to the vacant pool,
Stepping tentatively down the stair,
And one dipped a foot into the water;
Still she held the other by the hand,
For the other was thin, she limped,

A thigh or hip bone was not working right.
The girl who led this other one along—
A perfect saint, at such a distance:
Firm breasts, the fair hair swept up,
A white towel knotted round her waist.

Quite ordinary motions, daily gestures,
Apparently disturb the sheet of time.
Becoming very ancient, birds and people
Fold back the sheet; locked in traffic,
Or waterborne, you hardly notice.

But watch too long, prone among junipers,
The formal cloud, while dragonflies
Briskly penetrate, to no purpose, air—
Girl and pigeon, stripping the sheet off,
Wake up to immortality's aroma.

Then hear Spirit settle in its woodland,
In its throat a growl, a heavy breathing;
See sprayed from great eager eyes the sparkle,
Bushes whisked apart. That was Dios
Vanished into the open, with a spurting wand.

The Images in the Window

Now she is blue, the circus rider,
Blue the high reliefs
In marble from Aphrodisias.
Seurat would not have liked it so;
There should be motley dots to etiolate
Muscle mass, the stubborn
Clog of matter, galaxies to house
Firmly the luminous at last.

All five picture cards, even Morandi,
A Babylon of bottles, tacked
To those twin sides of wine crates
Where biographies expose their spines,
Have swallowed what you miss.
The blue flood was gliding in,
Opaline, a sigh; and all is granted,
Day after day, hear it or not,
A breath when Mary lifts her gown.

Absently so, lifting my snout, I might be
The little dog who grew under Carpaccio's pencil,
Startled no less than Augustine
By Jerome's voice when it spelled out
In a blink
The mystery tremendous at the window:
Fourfold now the three-in-one,
Other the light lucking in at the door.

Cairns

On ridges inshore from Sligo
You might notice the cairns:

Of old stone and umpteen
Shadowy hues compounded,

Here a heap, there a heap.
Spared by a narrow squeak

From an avalanche in the Pamirs,
In the Pyrenees at milking time

Solid alongside a fickle flock—
Of old stone, of zest, of shadow

Those cairns. You might suppose
Their heaping a work of reverence;

Or harmony even compounded
The hoot of the wind in a cairn.

Something Like a Pendulum

On all sides nose to nose
With the incalculable,
We feed our faces in a daze.
Disorder is our dope. Our frames
Have broken free from measure.

But wherever a measure ruled,
What constraint, what a crushing
Load encumbered the brainpan.
Better the higgledy-piggledy, raw,
Than portions we cut up to cook.

What if I see, all of a sudden,
Our names cut on tombstones,
Silent across a tombstone
This light in Scorpio pencil
The lynx who hides in a birch tree;

What if I suppose our griefs uneasily
Conjugate an inkling of right measure—
Those names excite each other then
To tell the heart fly open wide,
Ceremonies of tooth and claw forgot,

Go live by grace, not spilling over.

A Postscript to the Great Poem of Time

The poem is about itself, as life is properly concerned to produce, diversify, and maintain, at all costs, life. Of course it is not
like music, for it impregnates its subjects, currently, with the illusion that, though massive, it is linear and moves from one point
to the next. The poem has a back which it hides; so does a huge
snowball. It is no more linear than earth is flat, and it envelops
its solar system, in which, unlike a snowball, for its extinction
would not be rapid, it has built a nest.

Some of its rambling mutations last longer than others; as in nature, so in the depths of history. Uniquely self-interested subjects having no part in either, browse as they may in such pastures, turn sickened from its crimson blizzards, dazzling chasms.

On its back, then, it carries innumerable spores, which are flung far and wide by its motion, that is to say, by how and where the motion was, before subjects became involved in its rolling. The spores, which include bacteria, have sprung from what was and from what might have been but, inexplicably, failed to be what it had barely begun to be. Atavisms, some mothering splendour, most fathering horror or filially abetting it, erupt among the spores, are conceived and hatched by spores that seem—so swift is eyesight in a mortal span—to have vanished.

Some larger spores resemble globules, multicellular bubbles. These are the "kingdoms" of animals, plants, of any organism among the natural orders. The globules that house living humans are not mistakeable for those that house dead ones. Here prosody itself provides markers. Occasionally globules collide, but the living group is articulated in a rotatory syntax (sestinas come into play), the other as anagrams, the rigid anagram substituting for the inevitably garbled but apparently real (and repetitive) speech of the dead.

The poem bounces, at times it breaks off, floats, executes spiralling parabolas. Its leech-like bacterial spores may be ineradicable, though they might come loose. The climates of its feeling, crystallized not only as cases of divorce or mutual rage between nations, are seldom to be predicted, because their variety has no limit. Are there, even then, seasonal promises, glacial Springs, Autumns of fruitlessness?

Certainly the poem smells: of coffee roasting, of a witch's crotch, the reek of ill-nourished galley slaves, of martyrs burning, whiskey-soaked saloons, broken drains (the heady fumes transport teams of spores in track suits by air to stadia in the Caucasus), and pinewoods, the iodine sea-coasts, cordite, and many smells that exist, like ghosts, only in the memory.

The voice of the poem of time is polyglot but no trumpet. It comes, this voice, and it goes. Irregular waves of gravitational force brush it away, storm it out of earshot, return it singing in the bright contralto of a wren. Yet even the apodosis of the sentence it was about to revoke trails off, a snippet.

Into each snippet, however, are built the outlines, now marked, now fading, now gone again, of a waiting room. Over the heads of the multitude inside, stiff in sedimentations or moving about as the travellers strike their antiquated attitudes, the roof lifts majestically and on every side the walls expand, roof and walls perform an immense and constant inhalation, constantly (in the illusion of this idiom, rotatory or anagrammic) the space expands, the furniture dwindles, and it is less and less likely that any transport will ever arrive, for the waiting room is coming to encompass, inescapably, whatever journey might have imagined itself into these multitudinous heads.

So to have read the poem at all is to have read it only at random; but when there is time you can pass it by reading again.

TWENTY TROPES FOR DOCTOR DARK

'Dite costinci, che volete voi?'
cominció egli a dire: 'ov' è la scorta?
guardate che il venir su non vi noi!'
—*Dante, Purgatorio, ix.*

Heavy Dog Sees Fish

Calm harbour water
And in a hunting pose
The heavy dog sees fish

Heart skipping a beat
Calm under the wood
Hulls that only surge

Forward to retreat
These darker reflections
Contiguous calligrams

Heart skipping a beat
And in a hunting pose
The heavy dog to those

Not biscuit in his dish
Nocturnally he sings

The Diving Apprentices

Sometimes you watch them going out to sea
On such a day as this, in the worst of weathers,
Their boat holding ten or a dozen of them,
In black rubber suits crouched around the engine housing,
Tanks of air, straps and hoses, and for their feet
Enormous flippers.

        The bow, with such a load on board,
Hammers through the whitecaps, while they talk;
Junonian girls, Praxitelean boys, pelted on
By bursting clouds, by spray, eventually heave
The tanks upon their backs, the boat drifts at anchor,

And down they go to the sea floor, by the foggy headland.
At least, you can presume they kick the flippers
And plunge to where the water is more calm. The cool
Instructors must keep eyes and ears
Open. Accidents out there, they happen.

        You might imagine scraps
Of cultural débris, a broken pot, a ring, a cogwheel
Come up, clutched in a palm, and interesting,
A wave pattern in it, the blade of a sword,
When a lucky diver breaks again the surface. Time,
Time and again frigate and schooner cracked
Blown against the rocks, holed below the water line.

        Even an inscription
Might now be coming up from those green deeps.
Yet the divers do their silent thing. On the sea floor
Expect only the sea, a multitude of sand without an hourglass.
Round somebody's ankle idly it swarms. A diver
Hangs by a thread of breath in solitude there. Some go down
In all simplicity curious; to have tales to tell;
And who knows, what they learn
Just might, long after this, be usable.

Something Vesperal

Spectres, vast, remote,
Uneasily wagging their heads
In shrouds of crushed amethyst:

Tomorrow I will confirm
That they are hill crests.
And slopes parade the green oak, olive,

Serried cherry.
           On sunken pots of Rome
An iridescence, thick
Or light, signifies the human:

Should the moment return
At sundown's onset
I will ask what is this colour,

Again a few score of breaths,
And scaling the underside
Of pine branches

An aqueous rose, diffused.
Neither quality, nor adjunct.
How long so old.

Lucile / MA 632883

What power goes for a walk on the water,
Opening skin, aromatic and musical,
Feeling a way through ears and nose.

Boats full of people heeding the bullhorn
Head for the sea, first slow, soon faster,
A white wave smiling at the bow.

An island to eyeball, coves of granite,
Happier people, the feel of the sea,
The way it pulls at womb and scrotum.

Their faith in the captain; cry of a gull
Afloat in the wind; whatever it is
Crying and crying for, try to imagine . . .

A little blue boat going putt-putt-putt
Is my desire; it turns away
And eludes the cordial hug of the coastline.

A fresh paint smell, beat of the engine
Regular, dependable, fins at work—
Once I was part of a Cornish mackerel:

Lifted, mute, from a colony of heaven,
By stars and elements taken hostage,
Helpless I squirmed in the cannibal air,

Underbelly silver, muscling the backbone
A mottled azure; the look in its eye
When I slid from its lip the barb of the hook.

Turf

What was it made of, that barrack,
Pinewood? Filing cabinets
And offices, how many in it,
Five or three? I dithered there,
Writing reports, for months, how many,
Nine, or twenty. Acting Sergeant M.,

Signing permits. Was it me
Signed, for turf to be dug, *Torf,*
Or was it Sepp? His cursive longhand
Admitted trespassers, a few, but still
Dozens did work, hacking it out,
Torf, a. kind of fuel, was it?

By the gnarling of their fingers you could tell
True workers had no gloves. The fingers,
Them, and ploughboy Opa, eighty,
Aus Ostpreussen, D.P., him I remember
Accepting a cigarette: 'I smoke
Later, else the wind will smoke.'

Gently into his tin he laid it
And never burned the kilo
Of potatoes it was valued at.
Later snapping at each other, jealous
Of 'turf', those professors, gloves
They must have had, so to take them off.

And in *The Inferno,* of the least tormented,
Writhing in filth, thick gloom, the tornado,
None could slither naked from one chosen
Circle into another. Territory held.
No trespassing there. Heaven disposes,
No massacres, no refugees.

Buffoon Voice in a Small Port

Here is a choir. Think of the voices.
Poulenc, from his *Tenebrae.* The granite,
Hard and white granite comes to mind. So,
Sorrow floats a silver-threaded fabric,
Yet, toward the sea, through the glass
Open door. Door. A sensible name for it.

Dizzy sea-haze. Sunlight whirling. And sad
Sopranos celebrate granite. From this position
You can watch the wakes of wooden fishing boats.
There are nets to be sunk in the haze.
Today a glossy, bluegreen, flat furnace
In which worlds melt, moons are eaten up,

The sea is not by any stretch receptive
To sorrows being carolled now, at Tenebrae.
Nets it absorbs, nicely, also hulls. This mango,
Should I pick it up and fling it, ho,
Pick it off the balcony table, hurl it high
Out into the furnace? That is how the saint

Hurls his will at the invisible, blends it
By faith into an infinite desiring. Sacrifice
To the imaginary, that is what the mango,
Mango flesh, the tint of sunrise in October,
At a wild guess, might tell the saint,
Not you, to do. In this selfsame house,

Booted German captains in a squad obeyed
Exactly the instructions of a high command.
We are not, on that score, so malleable, or so stern.
Into fraud we see murder locked, and venom into visions.
To the tongue of music lolling out of a radio
Angels play tennis on a streaked court of clouds.

Out of your town, a steady trickle of painters,
Did they export the light?
It was never diminished. Squeezed into colour,
Extracted light, they squirrelled it away.
The images dispersed, we hope, will be seen
By the littlest children, bony in Bangladesh.

Sailors who spoke Phoenician, somewhat Greek,
Ran their keels up the sandy crescent
Below the medieval fort. Now Michelins
Keep the Moorish house and crumble brioche
At breakfast there. Oh my, what a difference
Quick changes in the goods they market make

For such folks as live for their dogs, but die.
Children, here is a puzzle for your pleasure;
It may go nowhere. Yet look at us
At 3 p.m. on yonder tongue of concrete,
Where the lighthouse briefly casts a slender
Futile shadow: people screaming,

Drenched, delighted, when a colossal whitecap
Thuds against the wall, shrouds with foam the green
Beam housing. Salt flecks
Sizzle on clothes, make luminous human skin.
They signify the rampage we dawdle in
To dream a bit, between bouts of toil.

Really, in the upper world, a cherished terror is
No small thing to be here for. To the edge
Loosely we conduct ceremonies of sweat
To avert the grim. Abstraction, pure, can make
The mechanism switch to kill, all action, senseless,
Bite to the bone or slowly, gently, chew.

606

'Abstraction', 'pure', who can mean them now
And not in irony deplore their barbaric abuse?
Nothing out there pretends. In vague words fatality nests.
Sharpen the angle, still we impose
On phenomena nicknames, Mothball, Beaky, as if
Mirrors might coax, trembling, into our tutelage, the real.

Here is a 'choir'. Patience, before 'voices'.
Poulenc; Tenebrae. Somehow 'granite',
Again it comes to mind. And sorrow, pause,
Toward the sea it floats a, floats
A 'fabric' through the glass open door.
Door. How heavy it was, now how light.

A Bat, Less Familiar

Twilight here, a matter of minutes.
On his rock, the fisherman
Sits, a bat, less familiar
Whizzed in a spiral
At my window.

Drum taps
And a company of strings
Expose the deep.
A foreigner must be shaking the sea,
Far off, to make these billows
Roll slowly like a sheet.

Next thing he'll fold it up.

Now what's the trouble?
              The fisherman
Scrambles to his feet.
Not to go home. Only
              To make a wider cast.
Does he feel his sea?
Does he only peer
              At his permanent float?

And how should he know
The house-plan,
Whereabouts the enormous closet is
For the folded sea to be put
In among the sachets
Of lavender, like grandmother had?

Charles Meryon

1

Meryon saw it coming (who was he?):
No people, so no noise. As it should be.
The Bridge. The Morgue. Ghostly round his bed
Antipodean atolls and tattoos had fluted,

Volcanoes puffed. Then borborygmic sea
Forked, at its last gasp, into a V:
Down that black gallery and backward slid
A syrup, foul, ovum and sperm concocted,
The foggy groan of Antichrist. 1863:
People mattered nothing, live or dead.

Paris by his impeccable etchings emptied:
Pointy turrets, windows, not a single head
Poking out—and there across the sky,
Tortuous, the skeleton birds creak by.

2

As if all that steps had stopped
As if all that takes had token
As if all that creaks had croaken
As if all that weeps had wopped

As if all that flips had flopped
As if all that mocks had moaken
As if all that speaks had spoken
As if all that drips had dropped

As if all that hopes had hopped
As if all that leaps had lopped
As if all that aches had oaken
As if all that peaks had poken
As if all that creeps had cropped
As if all that peeps had popped

3

The old aquaforte art is back, thought Baudelaire.
Multiple majesty of stone piled on stone;
Obelisks of industry discharge into the air
Their coalescent smoke. Almost airborne
Scaffoldings roped to monuments under repair—
Very poetic, beauty so paradoxical
I never saw the like;

            and the sky over it all—
Eagles. Tumult. Perspective deepens there
With all the dramas that have come and gone.

The artist: Once a sailor, now he'll seek
In nooks of masonry a sphinx.

            I think you'd get a scare
To hear him talk: 'Poe did not exist, aha!
Poe was a syndicate!'

        To Madame Aupick:
Au fait tu as peut-être oublié tout ça.

4

How should people promenade on maps?
My map—I image what goes up, like steeple . . .
On map there is no space, no time, for people . . .
With window slot I thicken this façade, perhaps?

I map the time. These arches, tenements—
Voice the design of fate, exact. Why folks?
They are confusion. Burin cannot coax
Their hollow little solids to make sense.

The earth, a globe. On it Paree, immense
Phantom, or ulcer. So I map excrescence.
I probe its twisted fibres till I find
The core of its cabala, in my mind.

Ah, you are being faraway too kind.
Dark, beautiful cabala!
                    Goodbye, gentlemens.

The Moon from a Box of Lokum

In a country garden outside Rome
A Doctor Dark, Madame Smirnova's guest,
One summer evening took a box of lokum

—Children all around him breathing fast,
His Russian fingers taking lokum out, so lean—
And made a moon of it. The closest

To something in the sky we'd ever been,
The empty box, a moon at full—we passed it
From hand to hand, wondering just why

The lining he had smeared with olive oil and spit
Shone so sombrely in the dusk. And gasping,
All of a sudden not depressed, the doctor

Skips around with it, finds a candle stub,
Melts the wax, plants it on the nether rim,
So now the paper lining glistens, silver.

We children were allowed to touch the moon
And with some ceremony hang it in a tree.
We said: Here's our theatre—as of now

For all our future dramas this confection,
This moon, transfiguring desire, will glow,
Our bodies measure heavenly perfection . . .

The doctor struck an operatic pose,
And funnily twirling a finger up: Beware, he boomed,
Celestial equations tip the scale with zeroes—

Our rhymes, they tumble past us, unredeemed,
The only total herebelow is night.
You see a rising moon, I see a Cyclops:

This garden incubates our grand collapse.
Industrial wars will torch these fantastic empires;
The children of your children will be cindered

Like that, he snapped his fingers, by the Cyclops.
See them extinct in the bowels of the Cyclops,
And soot our candlewick.—

Oh yes! We cheered for more. But like a dancer
Now the doctor turned, with swift wide soubresauts
Bounded across the lawn, and disappeared indoors.

A Far Cry from Fear Island

1

The small square house among the trunks
Of pine and cypress

The pink house with red tiles modulating
'Monk and nun'

And the sea calm, today, a turquoise,
But black skin glistens like that
By rushlight, drawn taut
It is the roofing of the hidden fish house

Of the sea—somebody threw,
To let its whisper in, those windows open:
Pistache shutters folded back,

More secret still
The piano notes; tentative, proceeding
And never wrong, twirling up
Or in a leisurely cascade, fingertips

Not for once, never quite
Settling, loft them into this October air.

2

For in the house, there, Carlos,
Your child is practising
Mother Goose, I think, and far off
In the fish house

Mullet are lofting minims with their lips.
How steady, her concentration.

Her timing hesitant, perfect.
Almost a spirit might be sounding through
All three of us.

3

She does not hear
The wind gusting in the pines, raking with open fans
Deep water;

From Kalashnikovs the bursts of shot,
The chop when the machete hacks
A head away, the next, then the next . . .
Even the reek of thatch
Burning does not crook her thumbs.

4

Judas tree, periwinkle: incognito.
So who is this to stumble after names, to load
With cacophones and rage, her arrow?

Square pink house, the spiral notes
With chords that open, flighted, into trills,
Progress in it, and live, as in a shell
The pivot, the torsion, and the ripple.

The Digging

I had the coloured tombs in mind,
The elegant parlours, barrel vaulted;
You did not have to dig so deep;
By mid-morning the spade had opened
A sunlit vault where the dead lay, smiling.

Not even a king and his consort. A Captain
At most, then a Baker by the name
Of Smart-Ass; it was written
Bold in sepia on the wall of the vault.
Nameless lovers, they captured interest,

Because the artist had painted a musical
Instrument only. For animals a dish
Of water and a rib with meat on it
Were sufficient; children had their names
And dolls, quaint, with amiable features.

      *

Now it is difficult. The graves go down
Deeper. The dead are tangled in a heap,
Scooped up and in and left to rot.
Waves of them come up with a stink,
Agony in the gaping rhomboid mouths,

Some with bedroom slippers on their feet.
So many, how to identify them? How
Insert into such a moist dissolution
The fizz of feeling what they felt?
How hard the spade treats their pit,

For the antique mass graves were no prettier;
Below bright multitudes there was only earth.
Herded by radio signals, decrepit codes,
And closing now the hoop, above the business,
Killers converge, dull as the dirt itself.

       *

I dig and dig; still no rockbottom. Up
Through layers goes the life: the damned (select,
Graded along the lines of a belief system);
The purged; then the beautiful, sublime—?
A breath rotates the stars? Up my street

The ordinary, the losers, and police patrols
Pull back, then squinny as through chinks
In a forest: there still might be a glade,
Filthy with condoms and broken bottles,
Where someone hangs out, punctured, with a cry

Claiming he's been abandoned. Who,
Who but a fool would lend him a hand?
He's a statistic, we have jiggered our symbols,
And blink unawed at the galaxy. The one wand
Deploys vacantly its many magic darts.

       *

Love one another, they said, as if a say-so
On Dover Beach, or in Manhattan, shamed the cruel,
As if it purged away the myth of purging.

Words that taunt waken only the bad blood.

I should return with my spade to simple tombs.

Trawling

There were to have been traders, bronze, manioc.
Then the people, in particular the women,
Wanted none of it. Earthen ware, hempen tissue,
Fresh local roots—nothing to barter. That,
In parvo, was the initial picture.

                    On it went, unfolding
Not like lava, not like pine or oak shadow
Swivelling as it prolongs a cool across
Earth, lake, stone, irrevocable substance,
But dithering into a blank my whole supply

Of commerce dwindled. The oppidum wandered away.
Ash on the oilcloth. A red winedrop.

                    I had been imagining
The slow increase of trade, the rupture
Of barriers between tongues, slumps punctuated
Spates of war, famine called
For conduits, and for crops
Conquered terrain circled bulging cities, till
Nineveh collapsed.

                    I had forgotten
Complications, women hoeing vines to break their backs,
Men taking deep delight in fields and animals,
And the old still willing to drudge
Till they dropped dead. Lifting mutilated hands
The boys and girls who slaved at jennies
Implored this to stop. Others whispered—

When did you last push a corve in a coalpit?
You know nothing of us.—And still
The traders kept pouring out of the dark;
On camelback, by international truck,
They hauled the stuff. Civilization's ballast.

Turn to the wall, I said,
All the inscriptions on those packaged goods,
Extra from Kellogg, Sony, Lindt, Arabica, Ricard.
Insidious lettering. But leave the solvents
Vacqueyras, Clos du Bois des Dames, Ventoux,

At least until I have detected why no fish;
The mackerel, the prawn, the mullet, spill no more
On beaches, from abundance; why no more living fish?

Back the traders come,
Predatory, steel nets lowered into the Pacific,
Pulled up into the squall by electrical winches:
The turtle's cry, hear it, squeak of tiny outraged
Creatures who dwell in seawrack.

So, and so it is when the net
Of a phrase has sunk into the synapses.
It is too late for them to turn about and flee.
The system locks, the phrase, too fat, gasps
Under the strain, it cannot loosen it. Foul matter
And confused, if edible, swarms to the surface.
How caring can he be, the cook who mixes such a soup?

Presumably this gives pause
To the prongs a Neptune flourishes
Over his dinner. It is real stuff that dumb
And shrewd rave on about. But of resistance
To the clamp of the net

Something still is capable,
Something not diversionary, to be noticed when
Gulls flock before sunrise over the small
Blue fishing boat, and the fingers
Of a fisherman fling out for them,
Clawed from the toils of the trawl,
A shred of starfish, icy,
The tentacle of a squid.

Cassis, October 23, 1999

(IN MEMORY OF NATHALIE SARRAUTE)

There are incidents that still give one pause
(As they do say), and, not evident or dramatic,
They call to mind something you can't put a finger on.

Storm, for three days, now the calm, brighter people,
Children skip with small pert dogs along the wharf,
Kisses exchanged, patrons embrace again cafes.

A table with a circular top like all the rest
Was parked in the street; inside the circumference
A replica, blown up, of an old local photograph.

A septuagenarian with a dragoon's moustache
Hesitates, glimpsing it, and he resolves to look:
Everything he sees, grey, white, is upside down.

For twenty seconds at the most he stoops
Toward that huge cotton reel hanging in mid-air,
That enfilade of pointy-bottomed boxes on the ground.

You best would have known, dear Nathalie, at ninety nine
Newly dead, what the gentleman was murmuring,
Not to himself, not to anyone, no, out of the image

A murmur slid, filled a moment, and he received it
As an animal picks up fore-shocks of an earthquake,
As gulls hope for fish tomorrow's tempest will dispense.

A murmur, for a moment. Nobody else attentive,
Hardly even him. In the commotion of morning
Then, he looked around, fingered his dragoon moustache:

Upright, slim, as he walked inside, to the zinc,
He stood alone, a touch, among others who were talking,
Among the iron capstans, rows of houses, freshly painted.

Of Paradise

Many different people have to have been there.
All sorts have been going to go there.
And legends have relayed abundant information.

        *

Those legends might be something to start with,
And to end at. Why can't anyone be there?
Is that the secret? Without paradise
There would be nothing at all to think of.

        *

Legends led you on: there was a Nowhere,
A World Reversed made sure the thinkable could happen;
Moreover it could happen to Anyone.

Well, for a moment fortune dispensed with torment.
For everyone a garden to cultivate at leisure
Floated from heaven; there would be leisure
In which to touch up the shrubbery, leisure
To scythe the lawn, so amiable ruminants

Might also have holistic fruits to chew.

        *

The simultaneity of everything, such as Seferis saw
In a trance at Engomi, when the antique town
Was opened to the air by archaeologists:
The baker baking, the woman at her loom,
And children having fun beside the vines

Where an old man serenely pruned the shoots—
Something like that, the tenses keyed to 'eternal',
Details may differ,

And after all it was a trance—
Seferis took one step, at once
Inside paradise and out of it.

*

If simultaneity has to include the horrors,
Then paradise remains a latent state of mind
And it eludes the naked force of history.

No wonder there's an Anguish at the gate.
He needs no sword but waves one all the same
To shave the literal-minded of Conceit.

*

Is it at the red raw root
Of a primordial tortoise shout?

Is it manifest in the momentary silver rim
Of a sheet of water blown by the wind
From a lion's mouth of bronze attached
To a village fountain somewhere in the South?

It is not wrong to imagine paradise
Not as a place but as a subtle sound.

*

Sometimes you hear it in a speaking voice:
Vibrance, the floated accents outline every word,
A limpid hint of separation chisels

Word from word, each has a chance to shine

As when who knows who on the air was reporting
The arrest of druglord Lara in Colombia,
And that a car bomb had gone off again,
Killing, this time, eight people—

Her voice woodsmoke
Spilled for its moment out of a paradise.

*

It is a tenuous time, a tenuous space, and it is not
Innocuous vegetation, love, serenity, or pie.
Busily slithering the coiled anaconda Evil,
This way, that way, tilts his head in the right direction,
And prejudice, not knowledge, is what he will advise.

Between the coils, compact as they are,
A time, a space, in which to breathe,
Respire a constellation of sounds more fresh
Than any thought of paradise has the volume for,
Might those be sustainable?

＊

Apparently not. If sense-receptors are the butt ends
Of strings that constitute, they say, the universe,
The image of spirit as a musical instrument
Remains a fiction. If paradise puts a name
To a spiritual attuning, still the fiction
Plays to ear and eye on a polished hollow box.

＊

Go lovely rose into that vacuum.
Anyone can dance away the night.
Anyone can meditate on paradise.
In paradise there might be no more call for meditation.

Sybaritic Elegy

(*Hieronymo Colli tibi gratias ago*)

Who nibble or gobble the candies
Cast so far and wide by the goddess,

Here they are, on a beach, or secluded
In this apartment or that, old folks

Fat or skinny, showing the photographs.
Here, too, is the headland, on good days

Still you see from its belvederes the island
Rooted in blue, and the coves of granite,

Clouds of sulphur, sheep cloud, and golden
Drapes gradually pulled across the heart

Of the universe. Elsewhere, sea-urchins,
Displayed on trays, small, black, and spiny,

They look so radiant: raw you can eat them—
A woman appears with a small knife,

For the price of a telephone call you can eat
Their hearts out, organic innards, with bread

And a drink, extra. Here too there is time,
Spindly time has sprouted out of rock,

Scraped off the surface of electrical waves,
Bank deficits, terrorism, globally

Pulsating market forces, time to breathe
Here in the alley named after the lout Napoleon.

So return from the sea, whose force also
Nobody doubts, when it appears in splendour,

Irresistible as Her Undulance, our genetrix,
Guilty in glory, she catches her breath at

The first ignorant touch of fix-eyed Adam.
Still, forget that, gravestone beaches here

Sport Adam on Adam, Eve swivelling on Eve. None
Of which particularly matters. But time past does

Donate the continuities. Bread as fresh
As it is repetitious, pizza to crunch with cheeses,

And friends visit, those who survive, scribbling
Outraged, else, in the eastern mountains. Where

Might this flotsam land? A waft
Of oregano, rosemary, garlic, sends

Imagination so far into, no, toward
The solitudes of Aphrodite which are stored

Labyrinthine in average human fingertips,
And a place on earth hurts, there is not

Ever enough of what it takes to go, this minute,
All the way to Bethlehem. Dawdlers, read on,

Still in the Eighteenth Century mysteries remain,
Values in Carthaginian coinage, in the storms:

Just open wide your eyes at this bay window,
Here we seem to be safe, airily we can totter

Downhill to Olga's for macerated olives,
Enjoy a choice of doughs and ovens. Dogs bark,

And on tarmac happily drop normal turds,
While we consume the universal airy sunlight

And can articulate it in disputes. Fools might think,
Hoping for change, or for someone to notice them,

That it's dogs who do the fundamental business.
No! Firechiefs perform, the helpful lady at *La Poste*,

And someone else I humour, with her pursed
Oddly angry cupid lips in among the shelves of glass

Where cakes are fragrant, so fastidiously trim,
Chocolate and green, lacework, jellies, twists

Of sugar firming cream into a script—
Every detail of that sort, which we do not forget,

Still vanishes, over the hill. It mattered much
Then, but now precisely what is left of it? A thing

We do not know, hardly can hold in feeling, even,
But speak to sometimes, among friends or alone,

By flourishing only once the flat of your hand,
For there's the thing you live by, die for, enough now.

Elegy of the Flowing Touch

Almost anywhere there's a poem lying around
Waiting for someone to lift it up, dust it off,

For instance, the argument with a neighbour
About a large dog: was it a German shepherd

Or a mutt? Would it jump into the sea hereabouts
To save a child, if a child went overboard?

The argument was conducted in civilized terms,
But we stood in the street, there were distractions,

In spite of which we both felt for the crux:
Does a dog have a will capable of the Good?

Insistent as I was that, however eagerly it swam
Toward the child, a mutt, being untrained,

Might forget the good it had set out to do,
I was brooding on something else—the dignity

Of the dog, whatever it was, standing as we had seen it
There on the prow of a small rubber boat;

That figurehead of a dog, did it know
How dignified it might look to the likes of us?

Who cared if it jumped into the water?
Who cared if it collared a floundering child?

And under the brooding lurked, not yet material,
A poem scheming to coax into focus a local image—

Ten dinghies fluttering tiny peppermint sails,
Each dinghy a nest with two children in it,

Strung out on a cord behind the rubber mother boat,
All the children laughing, waving, and feeling free,

The bursts of song from the children's throats,
And before them, gold against an oceanic blue,

The figurehead dog, ears pinned back by the wind,
His attention to it all, and a great joy in his jowls.

Even then, the scene: and the poem would pivot
On breathlessness, a moment of suspense.

How, it would say, as the procession of dinghies
Headed away from the coast and out to sea,

Either their voices had passed out of earshot,
Or else the children were learning fear.

The silence now as they skim over the water.
The blue of a ravening deep underneath them.

A Ballad of Arthur Rimbaud

That time of year comes round again,
The sea runs high and clouds at dawn
Form hollows like the mouths of hell:
Hollow hearted to the drum
Rimbaud drills, a soldier boy,
Upon the deck of an old Dutch boat:
Rimbaud swimming with a sword.

Switch off awhile your learning gear,
Good folks, unplug your internets,
Imagine something without fear;
It's hard enough to know what's what,
Spy on the globe, agog for secrets,
But harder still is overboard:
Rimbaud swimming with a sword.

He's tired of drilling on the deck,
To Java shores the boat is bound,
No wavering course, so no way out:
Rimbaud thinks—Oh, what the heck,
I chose the ocean, not the ground,
And he goes overboard:
Rimbaud swimming with a sword.

The time of year, a time gone by,
Apples in granny's attic stored,
Shortening days and longer dark,
Cranes overhead and southward fly,
Still Rimbaud's bones inspire a tale
(We know this one's apocryphal):
Rimbaud swimming with a sword.

The children saunter home from school,
Stop to stare at sweets and cakes
Stacked in the luminous window here:
Since Rimbaud jumped, and he no fool,
This boy will be an engineer,
These little girls command republics:
Rimbaud swimming with a sword.

Torpid gaffers lift their cups,
And dream they did a world of good,
Roasted chestnuts go the round,
The mailman comes and in his pouch
Sad news from Jane, from Paul a grouch:
A *petit rouge*, a long *pastis*
And Rimbaud swimming with a sword.

Shake well this medicine of rhyme,
A teaspoon daily, drink, of time,
And then imagine, if you will,
The lurid everlasting sky,
The whole Pacific round him still,
And overboard without one cry—
Rimbaud swimming with a sword.

Envoi

After the Revolution, Doctor Dark
(Doctor of medicine and not a priest)
Was heard on one occasion to remark
That those with most to lose complain the least.

A life of leisure spent in conversation
(So Doctor Dark reflected) frees the mind
From luxury; immune to the contagion
Of mundane troubles, it can play the wind

With dignity, whichever way it blows.
Remember this, when you have lost it all
And stumble after no-one through the snows,
Or lined with comrades up against the wall

You catch a glimpse of someone in a coat
Exchanging chirps with a sparrow in the park,
And recognize the profile, though remote,
Of dependable, clandestine Doctor Dark.

(*Cassis-Istanbul, September-December 1999*)

THE ANTI-BASILISK

1

TABLEAUX I–XX

The Antinomian

Hell is not any crowd you happen to be in,
    Alone, yet not so, feeling a fervour
Attack your marrow, still, in isolation
    Bordering on the profound
Lonesomeness of a damaged animal.
    The fervour of the crowd infects,
It hangs on the hedge of nervous defences
    Heavy impediments like the huge
Static models they make of bacteria.
    But then, for once, you notice
The interstices, holes, crevices, gaps
    In the stems and baubles, hiatus
Happening everywhere; hiatus, the secret
    Long bending corridor of a breath.
It is the crack through which your close-packed
    Fellows have slipped, time after time,
Benign or bestial. Taking their chances,
    Out they stole, to come back in again:
The benign, a breath of fresh air,
    The bestial, out for blood.

This curiously clouded August afternoon
    I mean to celebrate only the generous —
And come to the gap, work skeletal, old hat,
    No closure to it, no comprehensive
Statement such as might make people say
    You have to be smart to say a thing
Like that. But comprehension with closure
    Can be prorogued for now. The grace
Of the hiatus is the fine thing I go after —
    Not escape, not the cop-out,

Simply the gift that can free a body,
    Transmitter of spirit, from all contortion.
Help! The gift, hurting, has to run the gauntlet
    Between packed graves, the solitary givens,
Even between words when, making phrases,
    They are composed as if comprehending
That an antinomian anthropoid, in the hiatus
    Of mouth becoming at last connected,
Found I, without Thou, had no power to speak.

Tableau in the Restaurant

Hairclip a semicircle of imitation tortoiseshell
    To aureole her really uninteresting hair,
She gazed through schoolmarm glasses at a script
    And laughed to see the way her father wrote it.
The matron opposite, more lustre in her soup-spoon
    Than in her ponytail, said little, sat enveloped
In a brown sweater; unlike her pink, spare profile,
    Her thighs, inside a floral dress, and looming
Over the chair's edge, had gone so soon to fat.
    But as the girl laughed, her father tilted
Such delicately modelled features in the halflight:
    At each glance I stole the bony forehead broadened,
Nostrils bronzed by the candle became a tiny double flute;
    Behind deep eye-sockets, in the barbered skull,
The reptile snored, algebra did a dance.
    Florentine his whole allure, yet, utterly forlorn,
He found no way to step back into his picture.
    Somehow, her soda water long forgot, scattered
The ashes of a love she supped on tonight,
    Of that forlorn father she will resolve to tell.

A Lingering Enchantment

Back, what might be found, found intelligible,
    Back, beneath the crusts, beneath
The layering phosphors of antiquity?
    Cropping their hair with flint —
And the toenail, how about that? — the tribal
    Institutions writ in bone marrow,
People it would be no pleasure to live with?
    What compliments might we reciprocate?
We are not mad, these habits, normal, as they come,
    And our unstopped awe amid animals,
Our agility in water, shelter in the stockade,
    Those painted tunnels running tubes
Through Mother, for her own glory and good,
    Not to mention the elaborate
Inventions of our cave speech deliver
    Dreadful truth: the idiot, thou it is;
And all answer of thine speaks brittlish
    Bones; alone thy daintiness
Consigns thy neural node to death.

    Then take a leap, to Mithras,
Occupy for a while the hole through incense
    Dug, and horror, here the blood
Gushes from that bull they wrestle, hoofs
    Clattering on the pinewood planks —
The red stench of this torrent suffocates,
    But born anew, with a huge
Gasp you spring out, into the embrace
    Of white-robed, Greek-speaking,
Tremulous friends: the goddess,
    See now her shimmer, hear it
Pulse in the notes of the double flute
    And re-organize the shattered sea wave
As it was in the beginning and ever shall be.
    Some such folk held the fort
At Montségur. In secret cells others waited

To smell the clear rose of daylight.
Still others chose to haunt, puffing
    Cigarettes, telling the old tales,
A bridge of stone at Visegrad . . .

                        What then,
    What, then, of the circus while Vandals roared
With weaponry sharp, besieging Carthage?
    For in the theatre, wanton as it was,
The applause of spectators mingled, it is said,
    With groans of the dying and amid
The Carthaginian giggle battle cries went ignored.

While of the angel of history it was supposed
    He might like to waken the dead,
To repair what had been broken, still his wings
    Cannot be closed: tempest from paradise,
Caught in his wings, blows only him backwards
    And at his feet ruins amass to the sky,
You open his eyes, your mouth is his, agape,
    You only turn to this teacup, study the leaves.

Washington Fragment

Sunlight ploughshare peeling away from earth,
    Over and over, topsoil darkness, please
Brighten the buzzards at the breakfast table
    When they squat and chuckle: Let us prey.

A Species of Limbo

What might they have done with their long lives,
    These old Turks who sit on the terrace,
Now summer has come and inside the rustic
    Ramshackle tea house it is no cooler?
What might they say that they have not said

A hundred times over, in the noon
Or when twilight hushes the day nightingale,
    And the owl calls from her niche?
What work they ever did, unless their wives
    Did all of it, in the fields,
Hoeing and harvesting okra, aubergine, apricot
    Or far up north the leaves of tea,
Has now gone into the withering of their skin,
    Their crablike hands fondling the worrybeads.
But should a stranger come, they question him:
    Family? Occupation? *Memleket?*
And the stranger has turned away: Their horizon,
    How high? Their carnal compass
How close to the bone? So they sit, hungry for
    Music, exchanging an amiable nod
With a neighbour, who calculates the extent
    To which the other has washed his nose,
Inside his domicile, or Friday at the mosque.
    A swotted fly lands in a tulip,
And the tulip is shaken out, with dregs
    Of tea, the tea-glass being the tulip.
The gentlemen josh one another, now and then.
    The gentlemen live for this *farniente.*
And some are so old they soldiered in Korea,
    Some too numb to sense any sway,
Back and forth, of a lifetime's needle.
    In dark bag trousers, caps of wool,
The gentlemen inhabit a species of limbo.
    They call it the world, *dünya,* just as if
Yesterday it was, the world. Not a single knife
    To be seen in a boot. No visible stir,
If over the potholes a truckload of prisoners
    Hurtles by.
                            Spare for them a thought
Now juvenile swaggering imperialists draw
    Down on themselves again enemy fire,
Now the whole shebang of vain transcendence
    Could go up in smoke (any rapture being
Rancid superstition, atavistic imposture).
    So much for the stone dances of old.
So much for aspiration, taunting the wise . . .

633

Not the Last of Aesthetics

Improvident people, where will they be taken?
    Shots ring out. Into the truck they climb
Over the tailgate. Toby is there, Herb who forgot
    To check his mailbox. Was there a message?
Had they rejected his contribution again?
    In a gust of wind, holding her skirt down,
Megan's ashamed. Someone might see,
    Bitten by Toby, the backs of her legs.
This is the last we see of them alive.
    Seldom under the hammer, Donatello,
Whoever they were, might you have heard
    More true the marble ring.

Prospecting in Sicily, April 1787

I

Disconcerting: such a sorry monk.
    Yet he put the pipe organ through its paces.
Of a reed, the littlest whisper,
    Of trumpet calls, the solidest confabulation;
We never saw who pumped, working the bellows,
    And the swell quite carried me aloft.
Phenomenally intricate couplings wished away
    Fact's grapeshot, blue goodbyes,
The blue goodbye, which does molest our flesh.

II

A blessing that my hat was not blown off today
    Into the crater when I walked around it.
Zeolites picked from cavities in lava,
    Hornstone, basalt, motta
(A significant rock) in my satchel I amass,
    Shells, mosses, and a red, red sedum —
Of Neptune evidence? We'll see about that.
    Sift agates from gravel in a brook; the globe,
Up it goes with the Sicilian lark.

III

Had the roof been blown away? What otherwise
    Woke me? Overhead I saw the best
And brightest star. Of flowers, thick on the road,
    A whiff remembered? Grit needling a shank?
Daybreak: the roof intact, I descried a hole in it;
    And scooping Chance into some not indescribable
Design, that starlight, me in total dark, I reckoned,
    Had passed through my meridian, a rotary design
Which, come the day, with pen and ink, I'll plot.

IV

Gazing on the cast statues at the French Academy
    Megalio thought that form 'included everything.'
'I'm modelling in clay a human foot,' his quill
    Scratched, and now I leave the earth
Of Rome, the moon at full illumines also me.
    So to the light above, atmospheric form, unwarped
The plant aspires. Angelika's garden,
    There I will set a pine-sprout, but in the North
Ego-agonized recall gravity dragging its *Wurzel* down.

The Torture Foreshadowed

    'Hast du wirklich diesen Freund in Petersburg?'
      Kafka, 'Das Urteil'

A door, again a door, and waiting for the door
    To open, through a mica window Aliosha
Discerns the sentinels, motionless, in silhouette
    Against an emerald sky. Poor Tsarevitch!
Enveloped in the odour again of cooking cabbage pie . . .

And Count Andrei, thinking, while the father hugs
    His Aliosha: So the hawk will kiss
The chicken till the last fluff has gone.

Then to Varlaam, not his familiar priest, Aliosha
    Tells his transgressions, every detail
The same as he has told papa, but meekly
    Adding a couple more. Varlaam (was it real
Or fancy?) did seem a trifle agitated; a tremor
    Passes between them, 'fugitive, mysterious . . .'

Tableau X

It might drive anyone to distraction, this hearsay
    That certain souls are formed only for delight,
And music was composed in measures, once,
    Compatible with the plan of Solomon's Temple.
The souls formed for delight, only delight,
    They are unfractured by intent;
The music, to their confusion it was heard
    By citizens in the Cathedral of the Flower.
These rumours only circulate, so the hearsay goes,
    Because a wish wings every thought,
Or else with vanity they are entertained, to reverse,
    At its onset, an inscrutable passion.
So they also circulate when a nation
    Adopts the idea of building itself up,
Only to persist while the pools of blood
    And body parts take back the street.

A Secret-Keeper

Eye on a tennis ball, Henry the Fifth,
    Having raced after who knows what,
Magnifies that kitten, paw sinister lifted
    Haptic on a hollyhock pod, *passant,*
Topaz kitten, tail point foremost
    Flush with haunch, looping a collarbone,
Tensed, now altogether immobile —

Yet this incandescence of a day's end
Fluffs his breast, captive there, it is
    Gloaming you see, eyeballs, both
In a flash reflect it, so intact this cat
    Who knows what his play was discovering —
A Me in the Many, the Singular?
    A kingdom, why not, in the wind.

Narcissus in the Styx

Arms lifting, palm inward, as if a pope or king
    Expected kisses, but no, shoo, shoo!
He says and starts to sweep away, with arms
    Frenetically waving, stories from far afield
Which do not tally right with his conceit,
    Which aim a pin at the skin of his bubble:
Talk other than his, he has divined, is nuts
    And monkeys his interlocutors. French,
His latest claim is that he can speak French:
    Souson, he says, *souson* — even French people
Really do not know what that word means.
    And met with some suspicion he proceeds
To stretch his bones out, on the sofa, trilling:
    If you but knew how I have loved you.

As life in expendable organs desires life,
    Steadily to measure self-love circulates;
Step up the volume to a torrent, torrent exudes
    A choking fume, power being self-abused.
Spawn of democracy in its dotage, such bogus
    Petty despots work their mouths, enthroned,
Each, in a globule of this gas of tin prestige.
    This one, song his talent, and when he sings
The hole in his face displays the dentadura
    Of a jack rabbit — Made in Disneyland.
Room for his bubble. Shocked a moment
    Back to life, stiff in her coffin, yoicks!
It is the mouth of Pushkin's Queen of Spades.

The Signal Officer's Story

Now when I tell you this, what might you be thinking?
    And down to the ships we went, bending
Over my oar I could not see our beaked prow,
    But surely it turned due east. And
Subsequently on that island they threw at us
    Every craft still capable of flight,
The Zeros, not only the Zeros, but crates
    Ill-serviced, every one with a bomb
Strapped underneath, plummeting vertical down.
    The ack-ack shot them up, in mid-air,
You saw the stuff explode, suspended,
    Then shattering, all in a moment.
Pilots, if they jumped in time, them too
    The machine-guns shattered, so bad,
With body parts all dispersed, the parachute
    Deprived of any weight, lost uplift,
Withered, shrank, dropped empty to the ground.
    I tell you, it was something. The cheers
Rose from our pits, savage, for every Jap foe
    Who fell was one step closer to home.
And this perhaps you were thinking, this,
    From his chant, the stodgy old poet,
Composing, prone on his couch, long ago
    Not far, perhaps, from a Mediterranean island?
Anyone with an ego rushes to have or be had;
    Love, to the contrary, is a figure
Relating persons, one free formation bonding
    Erratic particles, timing the growth
A person desires, especially limiting it.
    And I too, it happens, think of that.

The Cubicle

Roll a dice till the side with four dots
    Comes face to face with you,
Then watch. That side like a door opens
    A crack and out slips a dazed
Manikin. Picture him as he grows
    In quite a remarkably short time
To a natural size. Soon a can of beer
    Has unbefuddled him. He speaks:

I must say it's a relief to be back again,
    And none the wiser, so far.
Here the complication is more than enough;
    There I tumbled at high speed
To a tune so old that the latterday
    Pagan Jovius hummed it,
Choosing and changing allegiances
    Compatibly with Sovereign Chance.

Another beer — he flips the little catch
    And sips, and says: I chose
At random, more or less, four images.
    And the four walls on which
I projected them held them in place.
    What was floor, what was roof
Had no part at all in the experiment.

    Did the images blur? I think not.
No, each distinct, each in turn I saw,
    But the velocity of their succession
And my tumbling made attention difficult.

Then he describes (in words, words) the images
    So long the object of his meditation:
All from the welter of things that had been;
    Which one might strike the nerve of history?

Sophie Streatfield, famous for prettily weeping.

Sergeant Bourgogne, veteran of the Grande Armée,
    Through curtains of thick snow he stumbles —
Smolensk, where are you? — hearing behind him
    The elemental moan of organ music.

Bauto the Frank was number three, his Christian
    Faith attested by no more than a singular
Participle in the Latin of Saint Ambrose.

Number four: Dying Hester Thrale, her finger
    Traces an oblong coffin in the air;
So Hester saves the doctor half his trouble.

Had this experiment no upshot whatever?
    What if the images had been
Not images at all, but the real thing?
    The real, raw, unextracted horror?

The man has walked away. His cubicle
    Flies after him, with six doors open.

Spoon, Covered Wagon

The barkeep spoke, fingering a coffee spoon
    (Hush in the bar that night, for some reason):
See the stem, at this end it tapers, but
    Not to a point quite; at the other end,
Lower, only a little lower, here is the scoop.
    Remind you of anything?

        Not much,
We with our red wine said, and he continued:
    The latest thing in design, this; and yet
Almost it is identical with a silver spoon
    Dug from the earth at Roman Cirencester:
No coffee then, but eggs, supposedly.
    Yet where the stem tapered, at that time,

A pretty sharp point stood at the end of it.
    Another difference: the Roman scoop
Was supported by a little silver bridge;
    Soldered it was, soldered on,
Said the barkeep, beneath the narrow throat
    Connecting scoop and stem. But this, this
Absence of a point at the tapering end
    Has been explained by an archaeologist.
The point existed to pierce the shell of an egg.

Such perforation guaranteed that evil demons
    Inhabiting the egg would all disperse.
Dissipated in the atmosphere they could inflict
    Harm no more, no evil on anyone.
Our spoon is not so made as to exert
    A similar effect. An egg spoon
It is not. Are we at a disadvantage?
    That wine, raw, and in our heads afloat
A sombre Jacobaean, no, what he said
    They said of him: *Deep in a dump*
John Ford was alone got, with folded arms
    And melancholy hat, now could not
But remind someone of the brisk tap to top
    Or bottom, aforetimes, of an egg:

One dent in the shell, if it did not disperse
    Foul demons, at least it let the egg
Ventilate. One tap could stop the yellow yolk
    From spreading round itself a blue
Circumference, a demon habitat.

                            Barkeep,
    Event had interrupted here your argument.
Errand took you off. So it began again,
    The patching we do to the spandrils
Which spit grit and creak under the bridge
    Called uneasily culture. Here we are,
America, who take astray your covered wagon,
    Stop the opening lips, then into bluster

Turn treasured objects of people not to be subdued.
    They saw not far, either, but their eyebrows,
Look, how they rise, gracious, how they swoop,
    Look, like bridges, stems of silver spoons.

Theological Fragment

Fearing the invisible
    Might want to make away with you,
Best deny its having any want at all.
    Then backtrack, with your want improvise
An Invisible to have a relation with,
    A relation in the deep, and personal.
Must a God not intervene to frighten off
    Throngs of undependable intermediaries?

Mingling with odium a phobic worm
    Twists ultra-subtle fibres in the skull;
And on the worm enormous robust rhetorics,
    Civilization, fabrics of holy rite
Are mounted.

       When she felt the tremor
    Coming, your girl, so she reported,
Saw vivid animals, safe rooms: the jaguar,
    Giraffe, peacock, strolling;
Rooms luminous, never once too large,
    Yet opening, opening; her animals,
Those depended on her breath to stay alive.

Perhaps the marvel is that, as it foams up,
    The phobia forms crystals of a magnitude
Not to be spoken of. Greed, lusting with hazard,
    Shatters them; odium makes such
Cultures malignant, pulls down on them
    Their curtain. Your girl, unerringly
Over every spike in the crystal, every dome,
    She spans her pirouette.

De Mortuis

The note pad and over it the candle glass
   Spills a shadow. Redder now the candle
Housed in its glass. No red suffusing shadow.

Suddenly there's such a crowd, I can't see
   Over their heads, let alone into them.
I am struck by their muteness, their misty
   Dissolution as they drop, one by one,
Trudging step by step through a wilderness.
   What visions might have made them so
Strangely here at home?

            This mother
   Cadaverous, with pinched lips, atrophied
Yet waiting for her moment still. Her Hubert
   Who tore his colon apparatus out and told
A doctor he had come into the ward to die.
   Johannes, peritonitis picked him off;
Your brother, headache, on a couch, at thirty-one;
   Now John of Brecht, wondering if the cancer
Had it coming to him when he quit two houses,
   Each a rat's nest of old papers, dangerous
Chairs, and the understanding of Anne. These
   First faces blend into Manfred's, comatose,
With drowned Brady's, in sickbay at school he heard
   The owl hoot, me saying one of us must die.

To tell me death dwells in my deep underground
   With speech and all resting on a negative,
Soon to the fore others will surge, soonest
   This one, perhaps. No, put him back
As long as there is time, a little. Otherwise
   He'll gulp your wine, hobnob with you.
Dear dead, who is this not speaking you alive
   And, failing that, fears he stole
Honour off you? Who flightily spoke no word,
   Not one, that speaks to his death

The speaker? All he cared was once to touch,
    Scenting no danger, these blank pages,
Though alone he might die, discovered
    Hosting many maggots, hardest work undone.

Avdagina

Prey they do, each upon another,
    Agglomerated, from beachcomber
To barkeep, full circle.

                    She remembers
    How a heaventree of stars touched her;
When with a tingle in them she leaned
    Her breasts against a wooden window strut,
Vast distance took it back again,
    Rich, limitless, and the wheat,
You could have heard it ripen, so still below,
    And strung along the river, the white town.

How long, this procession of the refugees,
    Huggermugger, white dust on their clothes,
Pots and pans now in saddlebags, the tiny
    Dazed children peering out of baskets.
Singular, in their migration, beaten masses
    Sealed in trucks, then scattered
By howling bombs they still jam the road.

                Here, have another spoon
    Of porridge . . . And in the tea, bromide.

Amaaan! Imdat. Chiquito no tiene cuna.

Datura

At the onset of twilight, Zulf says, you see
    That white datura lily open on the patio;
Against the undivided green of oaks, how white,
    A flourished trumpet, star-gazing.
It does not yearn for anything. It can't resist
    Its time, time to open, for a single night.
You should see the bees come out and visit,
    Bees and moths, working for their lives,
For then it is what they were waiting for.
    No fuss, they flock to the datura,
Taking turns. Space for every one of them,
    Sufficient. Those active insects
Perceive in it a lustrous cavern storing liquor,
    Says Zulf, and if you looked at him
Instead, you saw his dark throat active
    As down it slid, invisible, the wine.

Nobody's Ukelele

Still policed by the poor and hungry,
    Sold for a fair price
Into soup for the politician,
    The sea-turtle, black
Or loggerhead, or green, became
    A species endangered.
Their predators are being told
    Nowadays to desist,
And sure enough, if many can elude
    Monofilament nets
With no sensible discrimination
    Winched aboard factory ships,
The turtles might be coming back.
    Beaches in Japan
To which they travel, beaches
    Californian, Turkish,

Also Greek, where these ancient
    Animals lay eggs,
Have their defenders nowadays.
    Across wet sand
Here comes a young turtle,
    You see her paddles
Indent her heavy body's path,
    Cold glitter, no,
Lustrous her shell, headfirst,
    Imaginably as once
Before time spelled out the human,
    Dash into the foam.

Standing Figure

How long has he stood there, and only now
    He is aware of a warmth, a weight
Encumbering his feet. A small street dog
    Had fallen asleep there. This
Must be the fork in the road, the scene familiar:
    Cosy the strip houses, garden plots,
Unbroken paving stones, this one, that one.
    Yet the figure who waved, the old neighbour
Woman has gone. She had wanted him
    To follow her far up into the hills.
Now not a sight of her. Should he turn back?

    Does he know the way back? The way on
Had its landmarks, as predicted, the ruinous
    Cottage, only weeks ago its brickwork
Intact; the house with the big picture window,
    And in the window those people sat,
Faces uplifted when he had passed by —
    Will they still be there? Will they shout,
Will they ask him to lunch? Not likely,
    For twilight comes and far, far ahead,
The neighbour, had she drawn breath again?
    The air is spreading a terrible hush.

Then he remembers the short cut: a rocky
     Trail that led once, once to the ridge
Where she, the neighbour, must have, by now,
     Almost arrived. A risk, to take it
And stumble, slither into a crevasse, or else
     Limp over the promontory where whitecaps crash
And self evaporates into the cries of birds,
     Might not be the plan. Time,
Besides, has not hesitated. The street dog
     Has trotted away. The little boy
Whose forehead he had mysteriously caressed,
     Only to the boy's disbelief, must have skipped
Back among those thin travellers who stood in the café.

     What could he learn by looking back?
He would go home if he knew, as he turns
     From the crossroads, now, and sees
The way he came, knew where home has gone.
     That bend in the road goes on for ever,
And trees, identifiable once, melt into nebulae
     Disgorging dust, not stars.

2

THE ANTI-BASILISK

> Basilisk. 1. A fabulous serpent,
> lizard, or dragon, whose hissing
> would drive away all other
> serpents, and whose breath, and
> even look, was fatal . . .
>
> 4. A large piece of ordnance,
> generally of brass, and mentioned
> as throwing stone shot of 200 lbs.
>   *Webster*, 1914.

Memoranda

Of birds, whose understanding
Embraces reed, penetrates thicket;

Of its call, a pulse in the skin of light,
The cicada, whose pupa oozes

Just enough juice to speed its labour
Up from the floor of a shaft in earth;

Of magnetic fields, to reap their harvest
How the grey goose responds, how the flamingo;

Of birds again, which do not gash the sky
But wisely judge a storm's commotion,

Much might have been said beside
Things that hid, things too soon forgotten —

Of Quincas ('To the victors the potatoes!');
Of the poteen that simplified the Irish;

Of the oval olive ready on its tree;
Of humble beans that feed for sex the victims;

Of beauty, little beak, tapping inside a shell;
Of that book of stars, empty pages slowly turning.

Marienbad, 1814

A lion, aha, has to have broken loose;
    A boy, he puffs his cheeks; he fingers
Now a flute; picks out a tune,
    With singular glides, while at the fair
(Lodged overnight, for Sunday show)
    An image, advertising fright,
A lion loose, everyone aghast —
    Is not the same as those hussars
Of 1806; we still pick out the marks
    Of gun-butts grooving our front door.

What a porridge! Speak of it
    To nobody. A complex gestates,
Makings of a star, in secret snowballing
    Spacious dusts. Meanwhile *Faustus*;
Done with, sundry loving metamorphoses;
    To Hafiz now the steeps, a distinct
Summit (at my oriental elbow
    Hammerpurgstall prompts *oratio stricta*):
Well, so I scale it. Boozy soldateska,
    Too, I recall, me in my dressing-gown;
I stage an entry, sailing down the stairs;
    For Marshal Ney a bed; quick sharp,
Christiane marched the hoodlums out. How long,
    Lord, how long gestation takes,
Latent lion, latent flute, latent
    Uncle, up he rides with sketches now.
No, plans, that will be more likely,
    Plans of a fort that crowns a hill far off.

And in a room which has a view
He lays them out, explains (a dilettant)
    Details. First, bedrock, a compounded
Permanence; next, vegetation, local foliage
    Evolving; formality at last,
The architecture. We are seeing
    Tower, coign, buttress, the projects
Ego put where Id had been, so was Id
    The story, or Us? Us, an infinitely polar
Plurality; and when the richer concord shatters
    Single vision, what comes next?

Uncle rides in company: the princess
    Who gazed in rapture at the plans;
A gentleman for escort? Through the tiny
    Town they ride: A poster picture
Jumps at them, explained by uncle:
    Lion loose? Hundreds screaming.
Folks are drawn to terror, how?
    Hats off to Goya, he knows, it is alleged,
And serves undistraught the Unconditional.

To see the stuff behind the plans
    On they trot, sort of dreaming. Up hill.
The fort exists. As they approach,
    A puff of smoke, then a bang,
The town explodes? Or something in it?
    We smelled roofbeams in our town,
Blankets, furniture, on fire.
    Peacetime now should mean another smell.
Smoke in the vale, a distant puff,
    A lion loose. But here how else
To let the animal violence in, to tell
    Of human aptitude to foil it?

Now what, if art comes true? Princess
    Has to tremble, uncle is undismayed,
When this way to them very quietly comes,
    Uh-oh, the horror! This can be
No picture. Here or nowhere is
    Africa. What will the lion be thinking?
What is that gypsy doing, what his boy?

Never talk about it, so we tell ourself.
    Little figments, hold quite still.
Hold still while into the wind you lean.
    It crystallizes, in its time; mutable
Gestalt of forest paths, forked, with loops,
    Dovetailed, violence and virgin music;
Strife resolved in a plasticity;
    Can words of ours reach out and twist
Our story round, so to speak it?
    Dispense, dear God, a proper tone,
So let it peak below a viewpoint.

    Forth strode across the turf a boy.
With bloody anklebone, folds of flesh,
    Burrs matting his mane, a lion bewildered.
Should rush at him, and bite?
    A flute upon his lips the boy,
His breath is entering the tube, and out
    Rises a melody that rolls
Over Leo one vast tranquillity,
    A spell, now simple trust is acted on:
(Are we a magpie or a jackdaw?)
    A sharp thing sticks in Leo's lifted paw.

Would this now be the end of it?
    And who built Thebes? Stone
Coheres with stone, though lifting any
    Was labour, terrible, day after day,
Snapping backs, sweat in torrents.
    Flute boy leads on a light string
His lion home and others follow.

    Mustn't be bookish, only enough so
To forestall what ifs; what, for example,
    If civilization has to be ripped whole
Out of savagery, all eyes open, hard
    On any default, on music, on compassion?
A littlest lyric might do
    To end with, as if the flute's
Unheard tune might be syntactical,
    As if it coaxed into the clear a spirit.

Hasn't uncle said enough? He packs
    Probably his sketches up, is off.
Princess, her cheeks at supper, Oh how rosy.
    How long to go? Ripen, words, and let
One day the leaves flip, a tale be told.
    Zuleika, look at me, the bottle empties.

Remembering Mompou's Musica Callada

He makes now the piano notes
Toll a knell.
They toll a knell and it is over.

It is over, all of it, even the agitation,
The minotaurine paisano voice
Howling against the guns.

                    Now children,
You can drop dead at last, one day,
Decorously. The fighters
Disappeared into spider-holes.

How quiet it became, in Catalonia:
There was a town of turrets, of lemon trees.
How still, the sloping alley on its way
Up, up to my keyboard, far off

Here, in Paris, remotely
Still susceptible.
                    The drip
Drip of bright old bells, a languor
Broken only by some last low sunrays,
The faintest thud of donkey turds
Upon this cobble-stone, and that one.

A Short Elegy

In February death
and the ports of March
humming as winds will
the forenames of ladies:

Nostrums withdraw
and georgics follow
a different text —
our poorer whereabouts:

Soon so the tonal glade
opened — a forest,
told — of a river:

Presto, a field of flax
looms on a day near done;
light shimmers over it —
she flips up her ears

O yes the hare hears us

(*mistranslated from Enrique Fierro's poem on a hare*)

A Greek Colonial Bronze (Gordian III)

Bare-headed Hermes, folds of his cloak
Streaming behind him, and in the crook
Of his visible arm the caduceus erect,

Chases Eurydice, she looking back at him,
Arm outstretched. She might be frightened —
Of him? Of the Upper World no more ahead?

For she has turned, surely she must have
Turned; she is running back, back to be dead;
Hermes, she escaping him, quite perplexed,

He has to answer for this, will soon
Sharpen his pace, or so the bronze-smith
Airily imagines, engraving instrument

Poised, to pronounce (a touch) the metal
Muscles, calf and thigh, of his left leg.
How long, besides, since Orpheus absently put

His finish to the bizarre expedition;
Bone-tired from stopping torture with a song,
He could not hold back the rush of his desire

(All he had left): to verify. So he turned his head,
And look, yes, the king had kept his word, then why
Did Hermes break the silence of it, shouting 'No!'?

Of F.M.

Blown off the surge of her mind like fret
The traceries, the racing interfoliated
Designs, ethereal or concrete

And lashings of talk, borne aloft, up vents
Such as riddle limestone, shrill through music
The clustered humours, shock on shock

When towering orthodoxies pancake though Vienna
Hops back on her rocking-horse for another spin —
So Fritzi was not flummoxed by the question:

Was lace the matter tacit in her fashioning
Of language (latent in a body's vault
Aura lives, Noah sends the pigeon out),

Was it lace perhaps, or perforated whalebone?
In wartime the difficult creation of a cake?
Was it, being stroked the wrong way, buckskin?

Those not at all, said she. Head lowered,
Heart pondering — was this the word? and then
Confidently, with surprise, she said it: Steel.

The Black Basalt Tablet

Just a piece of rock, said
The airport security guard,
Just a rock, stowed safe again
In my satchel, distant kin
To the motionless chunk of it
Worshipped by Cypriots until
Radiant foam spelled out her limbs
And ocean, huge with metaphor,
Flavoured the women, just
A slice of the unknown
With signs scudding over it,
A tablet of black basalt,
Writing in five straight lines
Incised latitudinally,
Not Akkadian, not Hittite,
Not Babylonian either, tiny
Guides for tongue and lip,
Five flocks of spermatazoa
In perpetual transilience,
Five tracks for signs to chase along,
Believably a language lost,
Imaginably a music even,
The score, beyond retrieval,
Of a marriage song, a battle dance,
Unearthed as it had been
Obscurely in Anatolia,
Inexplicable still, but not
Perplexing the otherwise
Preoccupied inspector, who
Had weighed the matter to grant
That nothing to be concerned about,
Nothing but rock
Was there to be seen.

A Florida Beach

Hawk and heron come to take
Fledglings from the nest: a brief
Flit overhead, a sudden twist
And all the toil of making egg
Goes down the tube.

First, as yet, the sighting: from
Above, in middle air, the predator
Must hang, and in a wink
The Sarasota tern can spread
A snowy wing: her chick is hid.

Next thing, the hawk
Or heron generates an eye to pierce
Bone and thoughtful plumage.
Next thing, the hen digs deeper in,
Triumphally her abdomen supplies

A Roman arch to shelter
Her offspring. Still blunt
Its orange beak stays mute.

Hurry, dark energy, make soon for her
The egg that hatches while it flies.

Hair Shirt

A pong of roses. A face of liquefied steel. He is baffled. Not a hair's breadth to get out through.

He stands up, a Jacob. He smells the groin, angel meat at the tip of his nose. Who foresaw his appetite? Who divined in his knees, as he knelt, the perplexity of nations?

Now there is a marble, rolling. Flicked by a child's thumb, spirals flashing, it travels; it utters the growl of a doubtful dog until, with a plop, it vanishes between floorboards. And a conch bellows from the lookout: the beautiful tower, urine flushed from the throne room has yellowed its breastworks. A scimitar, made in Sheffield. Horsemen, white and blue cloaks billowing; spit and crack of the flintlocks. Hispania-5 Mozarabia nil.

The crooked generations, how they do bend God, bend him as children bend an apple bough, to make a fist round the stolen fruit. Secret in a household, aye, and cherished, some agile presence transcending imagination, outside the shadows of our deception, this alone enables man or woman to proceed in the joy, in speech upright.

There in the tool shed he sits and sings Lord Have Mercy Upon Us. Slung unsafely under the bellwether, he will grip a slimy pelt, hold his breath, move on out. Then the moon comes over the mountain, no?

Bona Fortuna, Jacopo. Pistols in their armpits, two toadies, refreshed with tequila, rip away the panels and aha, here they are, in their hole, the priests. But Edmund? That brother, by pikemen ringed for security, gratifies the river district dragworms: see the man first hung, then drawn, then quartered. Hear the queen, with curiosity searching past and future, whisper tut-tut.

Infant Patriarch

My rough hand
In its bone hut
Has not mapped
Variably enough
The bay, with inlets,
The wood, with towns.

Around the world
I only suppose
The bay sweeps.
What little I know
Is a flimsy scaffold.
No portable base,
I mean, for a compass.

To be no part, I mean,
But the quick of it, the quick
And the pulse of it.

Here are hawk, pilchard,
Buckeye. Kind to the bugs
Extreme heat in summer.
Here is snow, to fix
And cloud a glass of water.
But sometimes unbidden
From below is ushered up
A quicker breath, clear
Days respond, whole nights

Of, say, grieflessness.
On stones, if I spilt it,
The blood has gone dry.
The animals eat, and gracious,
Quite close to the gods,
Time still is unsatisfied.

The Dead Friends

Who can they have been
In that red car
Going by, so fast, waving
And with a hello so loud
It still hangs in the wind,
Still it softly rings
The compound of my thought?

A Cavity

Long since
I looked
Down deep
Only inches
Wide its
Diameter
The well
Shaft that

September noon
Pump kaputt
And took away
But fortune
Decanted light
And showed
Deep down
A winking pool
A cavity
So crystal
Clear the
New pump
At once
Took prime

And soon with
Our whiskey
We drank
Dragon sweat
Jetted up
From where
We'd never
Ever been
Nor thought
To tell a soul
Of then

A Simple Dinner on the Terrace

A table prepared and not a single
Enemy but myself in sight,
Here again, hungry for language,

Duly on this blank
Rectangle folded four by four
I should commemorate

A wall of stone, a warmth
Still there, unresponsive
Yet in my fingertips conducting

On from here to the promontory,
Looming rock. Record the ten
Old holes that pierce the promontory,

Mouths to caverns, I have heard,
Winding through the rock,
And not forget an earthen dish,

Here outside, the diced vegetables
In the dish, okra, eggplant,
Tomato as they hiss and wink

Fresh from an oven. Another
Blank I have to take and smell
Of mazout the nebula vomited

From the tailpipe of a passing truck,
See the swift whose loop
Now ignites a black firework —

On that bend in the street was not
Aquiline Jerphanion standing once,
And stout Seferis hopping from a jeep?

And such is this plenitude
Tonight in Ürgüp I uneasily
Might go on, the catalogue

Is apt to stretch from the wall
Only in the silver sky
To flicker out. What point

Would there be to all that?
I should finger objects only
Which in their mutation cling

Gaily or gravely to the skin
Of me or my projection. Yet
To despondency no less subject

Than anyone, do not, say I,
Pinchfistedly presume that everything
Encountering me exists

As if it came from me alone.
The real, so dense, so multiple,
Delivers me, as I exist,

From dumb absorbtion in myself.
The wall, the tunnels in the rock
Promontory have to be

Other than mere mediators of
Impressions I construct, and grow
Radiant as they receive

Not an inkling of a gist of self:
I value them but not for me.
That me who gulped his parts of speech,

And had no taste, they say, for death,
I track through hollows, till he smiles:
I eat the eggplant, spare the dish.

Entirely Owlish

Dusk. And washed by a low moon
There it was, a solid
Oblong housing, built

Of railroad ties. Inside it, deep
Down and weedy,
The vegetable patch.

One red pepper took my attention,
Then something else, half-hidden
Underneath a huge

Frond, more bulbous, a squash,
That too, good heavens.
But a flash

Had split the air, small, close
At hand, quick as a screech.
Lightning it was not,

The spirit (was it?) of mother;
Had I dreamed 'written asunder,'
Dreamer quoting dreamer?

What if her ashes
Are scattered here? Still not
Done with my dream I saw

How the screech had split
Mother's fairy shroud, this air:
On which all roads converge

The shrine, at last,
Alas, it was not.
A thread, it must be,

Mothered that moment
By a spider — a car passing,
The high beam hit it.

662

Intimacy

A huge Holstein stallion hauled uphill
An empty wagon; bellows, glowing,
His buttocks, fit to burst, mane aflutter.

Through her new picture window sieved
And cool came sunlight. She turned and said:
The pains of war drove us all, you know,
Deep into idiocy, deeper into corruption.

The hill a good way off, now up it and over
Lumbered the Holstein,
       Creaked the wagon: hackberry
And elm intercept no more our outlook;
We claim the house, intimacy again.

Twin blue cones of air the horse
Had snorted now took on to be, for bed linen,
Shrouds, and writing pads, a field of flax.

Surely not displeased,
       Although for someone else
She'd laid the table, washed the window,
We look not at but through the dark, she said.
And then: I call her Cythera, that horse.
You were mistaken.
       Shall we go bring her in?

Sanctificat

> *His first experience was loving a great luminary*
> *by way of some thin gleam from it.*
>   Plotinus

When a slip of silver foil escaped
At noon from a chocolate bar I broke,
A gust of wind huffing about our kitchen
Whisked the square of silver round and up,

Then let it go. Two breaths, no more,
I drew as down diagonally gliding,
There, on a red medallion of the rug
From far Beluchistan, it landed.

Any old soul might call it futile, this flutter
Of liberation with geometry. Fret no more,
Sainted cat: right royal was the pleasure
You and I could take in such a sign.

The Anti-Basilisk

Some locals now don't even know her name,
Call her a salamander; which she is not.

Nor is she a skink. Go by the book:
Pronounce the e in the name — anole lizard.

Anyway, at 10 p.m. she approaches,
Drawn to the window by a lamp; antique,

Its craning neck springs from an iron base
To crest in a milky shell of glass; perhaps

Downtown in his tobacco shop O. Henry
Electrified a yarn with it. Most peculiar,

The eyes of the anole swivel back, too,
Back they swivel, out into the dark.

Yet with her very sensitive abdomen
And, clinging to the insect screen, her pads,

She captures the light, she must be
Wallowing in it. Indifferent to Mars,

Tonight she brings a friend, or husband:
They share alike, two of them, together,

Brightness. Perhaps the dark torments her.
Or the time of night saddens her unbearably:

Only in the natural daylight, *lumen naturale,*
Can she activate her camouflage and blend

With a brown or green her modesty settles on.
Conspicuous as she is, in the lamplight,

Surely she is most herself in a grotto, climbing,
All perked up, a faun's marmoreal shank?

Might she be tired, even then, of automatism?
It was a thrill to vanish, now it is old hat,

And at her window is this artifice the Hebrew
Of a pentagram prising open nature's trap? —

It will attract a moth, she reckons. See her
In clover apprehend and taste a little tussock.

Suckers for toes, tender belly, flexing her tail,
Hush while she skedaddles clean across

The screen she cannot penetrate, eyesight
Doomed to be beaming out into the dark forever,

You I am in awe of, and see the creature
Undisconcerted ride, though upside down

For anyone whose angle on her sprang apart,
Surfing a huge, mute, hollow wave of life.

Waiting For Harvest Moon

Shadows thrown by people on a wall,
A fragile charm, and they stand upright.

More often the flat shadows, horizontal
On a paving stone. You tread on them.

No, the shadows are not thrown at all.
If it be said that some shadow defined

Significant bodies in a Venetian painting,
Then shadows can be considered transitive.

✻

At a weigh-station on the highroad
Nobody weighs the shadow of a truck.

Weightless, transitive, phrases connect,
In which relief, creation of a human eye

Where nothing's flat, nothing falters,
Airy polygons go at their earthy play.

✻

The shadow secreted in one vocable
Mates with another vocable, and not,

Not with the shadow it secreted:
Fountain. Orphan. Suspect.

Or does the track hereabouts vanish?
Darkest at the point of its inception

The shadow brightens, unless the vocable,
Or body, on this line of sight, bites back

That spasm, and its artificer moves on
And on: to penetrate the carnal.

✻

No again. A body designs to be all in one.
Ashes are illuminated by Acheron,

For the sounds imply a life inseparable,
A drifting net to trawl the shallows

Which, being lifted in, hauls up the herring.

✳

Yet, heavens above, heavens below, how many

Shadow languages not yet extinct abuse
By definition us — and for their sport:

Uncovered on the Gobi floor, an axe
Of jade, but jade, what use had that?

Even if the axe was loot, unriddle it.

✳

Fugitives (in Pindar's canto), *this one,*
What is he? That, whatever is he not?
Men, the dream a shadow had, but then
If ever a radiance, gift of the god,

Illumines them, theirs is a burning
Lamp, and life is pleasing to them.

✳

Alphabets, and not only alphabets drew
From shadow sensual ceremonies. In relief

The terrors and desires of the species
Crystallize in dance, as prescribed

Evidently by angels, obscurely by winds.
On the sand, on marble, on the threshing floor.

✳

And then (stay there, I ask you) if
The systems of the shadows, nurtured only

For the worse by lookers-to-themselves,
By scribes on the defensive, glued to ego,

Peter out, what might be left? Tokens.
Bodily decrepitude. The white lies?

Language like that, the general, expletive,
Endorses only, whole hog, our disaster.

*

They put shadows in the wrong way round,
Sometimes for symmetry, the painters.

Persians put no shadows in at all —
No place for shadow, the divine creation.

Perspectivally the word-penumbras
Make us shiver, hair stand on end;

Flesh creeps back, seeking divinity
As light is caught in the branches of an oak.

For harvest moon to walk upon, a shock
Of wheat unrolls (so to speak) a shadow.

Some Words about Some Silence

I must say it is precious to me nowadays,
The silence collected in the cars outside,
Yes, in every car its own silence,
And with each car itself a shape is made
Of stillness in the shadowy parking lot.

Welcome, altogether, the enormous
Quiet contained at three or four c'clock
Of a summer afternoon. The dog star
Calls air conditioners into action, true,
But this one here, its aspiration

Is not constant. Hush fills the intervals —
No more than a dull drone from the boulevard,
A note or two of popular song far off,
As if someone in Antigua sang them out,
Maybe; shut windows muffle

Even the piccolo call of a Carolina wren;
That crunch a bulldozer pronounces in
The hard-hat zone three city blocks away
Could hardly be mistaken for artillery.
Distance feeds the silence I enjoy

Especially when, for the duration
Of a breath, no more, it has to happen:
Across a mass of foliage there flits
The shadow of a large passing bird;
Across the foliage of hackberries I'm facing

It was the shadow only of a buzzard,
Quick as all the years have been,
The shadow of a buzzard moving, seldom
Noticed in the city — people
Have lost interest in that sort of thing.

I should tell them how free with silence it is,
When such a shadow crosses throngs of leaves
And when the leaves, moving to no measure,
Catch at the shadow, though too late,
Too late, for look, a breath, and it has gone.

Matriarch

Strange thing, in such a hush
It cannot speak: *in-fans*, little face,
Fingers and all, his nest her lap,
So chiselled out of stone,
Peering at an open book.

Her robe hangs, voluminous;
How undulant his mother is.
She flourishes an object, too big
To be a pine cone; her other hand
Helps her infant hold his book.

Rough hewn, says any fancier. And sprung
Clear of time, I say, its claws grooved
That stone garment of hers. Bulls
Ringed in Anatolia her throne, once.
No infant then, no book, till, Catalan

Herself, any mother in the cooling
Twilight, an open door behind her,
Eye on a goat or a geranium,
All of a sudden she stops him
In his tracks, the village mason.

Of that poor devil's tapping, at first,
She would absorb the cicatrices;
So hungrily through the dense
Matter tunnelling, her breath
Did not fog his bright blunt chisel.

Here they are, at first flush
Still intangible, but the open book,
Its Latin lettering
Ordinarily mumbojumbo,
Spells out creation as a feast.

Mater deorum: Dynasty of David.
Infant: a pellet in her slingshot.
Now both are stone,
What might she interject
If back to me he spoke

His word, and if, blent into it,
I heard one single cry
Of all the cries that go
Off earth, so up, to the heart,
And thought no more of it.

An Enigma Commonly Passed Over

True as they possibly are, the graphic details
In Cavafy's poem about the Cappadocian king
Orophernes — that his reign was cut short,
That mixed Asiatic and Greek styles affected
His costume, his jewelry, and his speech,
That he had grown up in Ionia
Good-looking, even distinguished.
And that, deposed, chased back to Antioch,
He gave up lechery and drink for a while,
Though his plot to topple his patron Dimitrios
Was yet another pitiful fiasco —

One feature of that brief kingship
Seems to have escaped Cavafy's notice:
To a silver coin struck for Orophernes he assigns
'The sensuous image of an Ionian boy,' and yet
No such image appears on any of that king's coins.

On a tetradrachm found in Ionia at Priene
The face of Orophernes is that of a clean-cut
And seasoned sort of Australian cricketer.
The 'sensuous image' arrives only fifty years later,
On a tetradrachm of the penultimate king,
Ariarathes the Ninth, who was enthroned
In 93 B.C. at the age of eight, and deposed
By Roman authority at the age of twelve.

Does Cavafy nod, or is the slip deliberate?
Has the name Orophernes perplexed him with echoes?
Can his cool hand have disturbed the layerings
Of history hot and perilous in the Levant,
Feeling for gut strings unsnapped, still taut,
For a dulcet sound, anomalous, beautiful?

Beauty, anomaly. With Ariarathes for a name
Who could ever enjoy being outrageous,
Who fail in his plots, again and yet again?
Who could not, with Orophernes for a name,

Be beautiful, anomalous, an impudent profile
On a slight upward tilt, wavy hair well fashioned,
Cheek of a cupidon, sulky all the same,
Lips full and smiling, the eye at gaze
Engraved by a Cappadocian silversmith?

Acrostic: A Civil Art

Just to occupy the time he's looking on,
A painter pounds from barebone elements,
Neglecting family, colours to be blended.

Voluminous rooms appear, geometrically
Exquisite skirts, fruit of light a figure ripens
Royally aloof, at a keyboard, with a lute, one in a cap
Mastering her quill to indite a comic letter;
Every strawberry brick façade, besides, recites a story
Extracted from proportions deep in Delft, so measured
Really the heavens reach indoors, right here.

The Altar at Vaison

Somebody must have been chipping away
For weeks to make it glow like this;
A polished oblong set an inch below
Its moulded rim, no bigger than a door,
The table stands high on four Corinthian legs.

Some fifteen hundred hurried years ago,
A solid block of marble; then somebody
Made moonlight of it every day for weeks —
Now to sit at it you'd need a barstool;
Shame on you, this never was a nifty place.

Spiralling up from underneath, at the back,
Carved in a darker slab of rock, shoot
Sinuous ligatures close-packed as wheat.
You could figure them as heat rising,
As waves of energy, ripples; from the Gallic

Saint they buried sometime there below
Continuous wellbeing was perhaps expected,
A safe house for good seed, counterthrusting
While predators bombard every village,
Hoggers of harvest perform no sacrifice.

Facts are few. Just as well. Under the altar
Those rippling verticals remember marble's origin;
The mason knew how marble starts in water,
That waters wove marble into its being,
That even the saint, the saint waters the marble.

(*Notre-Dame de Nazareth, Vaison-la-Romaine*)

With a Flap of Wings

With a flap of wings
        and a watery sort of shout
                the heron calls

And calling boosts his lifted
        body, rolls it, with dipped
                paddle wings, this way

Or that, and silent now, unflicked,
        penetrates the twigs.
                Yet with a warble quaintly

Diabolic the belted
        kingfisher calls, his
                harpoon of a voice

Disappears, scaling
        pizzicato off
                one perch to the next:

For what? Each in his turn
        calling, for what? These birds
                are federated also,

Definite in every muscle: Not
        that borders never haunt us,
                position, others, but (say they)

Dispossessed, the minute,
        scrawny and wet, we break
                from shell to daylight

Cry takes, and fierce, a glory
        freaking our costume,
                involved with air

We cling to it. Quit of the cry, so,
        never till I be done,
                till I expel the tune,

I utter it with no alternative,
        no forethought at all,
                as only my kind can.

Hello, for air that whistles
        at detected food, high, low,
                but for a larger trust

In spirit song, from such beyonds,
        you too, molding a breath to lightest
                touch, still you listen.

Memorandum from Gaul

In the second relay, book five, of his epistles
Apollinaris Sidonius of Auvergne (by now
Bishop) insists that Syagrius, the Gaulish
Secretary to the Burgundian king at Lyon,
Sufficiently commands the Germanic idiom,
And those barbarians, respecting his Latin,
Modelled as it is on Cicero and Virgil,
When they approach the desk of Syagrius
Dread his reproof, should he discover
In their expression a taint of barbarism.

That is just as well. Another Apollinaris,
Typically, to King Chilperic was denounced,
Falsely, of course, for favouring the accession
Of Vaison to the Emperor, feeble Julius Nepos.
Now indeed we are independent Gallo-Romans,
Informers all. Our *tribes* (so the original haughty
Apollinaris writes) are on the make. Spiteful
Functionaries attacking every right, we market
Anything, for a price we fix, and anyone,
Stranger or friend or kin, the law itself
We hoodwink. Malice vis-à-vis the antique
Order, where *birth and breeding* signify class
And overshadow us, concocts our game, I say;
Cupidity and rapacity Apollinaris calls it,
Insinuating that our *manners and attire*
Reek of the cloaca, whence our duplicity erupts.

On top of that, sometimes, to our advantage
Hun or Goth, Burgundian or Vandal
Invaders burn the standing grain;
Who kidnaps whom is anybody's guess;
Brigands whose last habitat was the Ravine
Have opened a savings bank in the forum;
While measures of dead rhetoric paralyze
Any schoolboy's eager tongue,
Senators fall silent in their fortified estates.

With junk music blustering for the juvenile
Average citizen, and a lot more spin,
We'll show the old doodads, too, how to manipulate
Language in ways they will not believe.

Some people, unavoidably, are nice, and active:
Lucumon the Merciful Queen, Ecdicius
Defender of Auvergne, and here in Lyon
One saintly, princely bishop, Patiens.

The Secretary takes a nap, every day,
In an adjacent room, at nones.

The stuff we do, still we take pride in it.
What else, nowadays, can a Christian be proud of?

In Ruins

Happily they cut the glorious emperor's throat;
His consort, 'Crumpet Face,' mute at last,
Languishes on the island, hating nuns . . .

This same sun pierced a painter's head,
When long-prepared, all at once,
A wind comes up and scatters
Three plastic chairs, with a crash,
Across the terrace.

      While that other dead woman
Also told her tales, of lust for glory,
Of attitude and language in the Old South,
I cannot hear, high or low, the noise of torture.
As at the sudden crash I jumped,
So seldom is the individual concerted;
Meaning begins again where it should end.

Item: at age fifteen Marcu Maria
Hanged from a tree at noontime in Corsica;
And the barbarian rich draw the bloodbath.
Marcu had no chance to write his book,
Marcu Maria, torn to pieces, in the song.

As for knowing the wholeness of things,
Forget it. Another emperor, glorified . . .

       True, Anna did write hers,
And all aglow, out of the painter's head,
Above a billboard, abolishing azure,
Oddly in order dancing, close-up,
Some celestials sashay.

         Tunc et nunc:
They must communicate with one another,
Voices that haunt the rotunda slowly, slowly
Hurled from this trunk of an old plane tree;
And the song of Marcu was made by fathers.

So the mandarin remembering an oriole
Heard, in disbelief, minute by minute,
       How true to the life truth could not be,
How meaning had to have been created
A matter of legend,
At times to be lived, at none to be known.

The Paradox of Jerome's Lion

Local his discourse, not yet exemplary,
Nowadays he is old, the translator,
So old he is practically transparent.

Good things and otherwise, evils done
Come home to him, too close to the bone
And so little transformed,
Him so transparent,
They float in and out of his window.

Killing fields and the pumpkin patch,
The combat boot putrid in a cherry tree,
Stroke on stroke the mortal build-up,
All the constraint, all the letting go,

So insistent in his attentions
That he needs a breathing block.
For lack of a monitor he might levitate,
The testy old bird, at his window;
He needs an animal, a sure thing,
One to imagine, at last. Speechless
As bedrock, a rough reminder of that.

A dog might be vigilant enough,
Intact, all heart, a yellow desert dog.
Avoirdupoids. A leopard? Markings
Regular, talons to swat
Any hurt away. Knowing
Hunger, not the greed. Sufficient

Unto itself, svelte, clean of limb;
Free through self-discipline, yes,
Yes, through self-discipline free,
And fierce, yet doing no violence
The wild by right he will restore
To a holy place, in time.

For want of that sort of a beast,
He might make do with a frog.

3

Pinkard's Quandary

To fathom a face below the paint,
Study the senator, and the saint.

Over and over the same mistake —
Spirit recoils from temporal shape.

*

'Men of good will,' was once the shout,
'Go clean the Augean stables out.'

A common will kept all in touch;
Disconcerted, overmuch

Consumed by self, by self-conceit
Dwarfed and warped, all flesh is meat . . .

*

Consider the formal prairie flower:
Does it grow grosser by the hour?

Does the bull now shit on everything?
A poisoned globe, Calamity for king . . .

*

So Pinkard broods on evil yet,
This fractional man, he can't forget

What aches: an amputated limb?
Still the abyss bites into him.

What knowledge might transfigure wrath?
What dauntless love disclose his path?

Pinkard Bookish

Prone on a couch, with pillowed head,
Holding with both hands a book,

Pinkard conjectures: Devil take it,
There must be more to life than this . . .

Surprise: crossing his line of sight
As it veers below the edge of the book,

A big bird-spider, all thatch
Of little hairs, has hopped across

A corner of the couch. Pinkard sees
How under the door it inches, to traverse

Invisibly the other room, and scuttle,
Finding a crack, out to the creek . . .

Up there, among the dead peach trees,
Spiders climb from holes in the ground:

The safest way to what they need
Cuts a diagonal through the house.

What tells them 'water'? It's like this
Also with bees, with snails. They know

The way to work, and, done with it,
The straight way back to hive or stone.

Enough explained, Pinkard nods;
Back in his book he finds the hero

Earning a frown: *l'esperienza*
Del mondo senza gente — still,

Where was the world not full of people?
Toys of compulsion. Centipedes.

And now the spider. Passing strange,
The creek is dry in these dog days.

The spider has to find the lake,
For legs so short a long way off

Under the junipers, across the road,
Across the meadow . . . Pinkard gasps:

His knees are hispid, follicles
Consuming him, from head to toe

A jetty thatch, a thirst tremendous.
So Pinkard leaps, to fill a bottle,

Rush, sympathetic, to the rescue.
Outside, pronto, Pinkard stops.

Pinkard recalls the words of Keats,
How he could slip inside a sparrow.

Now unheroic Pinkard squats
And 'picks,' with Keats, 'about the gravel.'

Pinkard's Song in Adversity

My civil owls moult as I sleep;
The nooks they shelter in explode.
Hard as the secret is to keep,
A hole must yawn in every toad.

Ah, this prerogative of consciousness!
At break of day the plumes return,
My civil owls again profess
Reconstitution, yet they burn.

Some sort of demon made it so:
For them a day is night for me.
Go moult, you owls, or stone a crow,
This toad is climbing up your tree.

I took my anger up in fear
For all the owls who love to hoot:
Come, universe, beside me here,
And put your passion to my root.

I'll branch, if buried, from the seed,
I will bear fruit and play with light,
And thank dead stars I never died
But took my chances, walking upright.

My civil owls will know of this —
There is no cage to hold them all;
Then if I go at night amiss,
Their bony wings may break my fall.

Pinkard's Night Thoughts

Something like silliness carries me back to Winterthur,
Carries me back, can it be fifty years, and all
Because of some potatoes in their skins, little
Red potatoes, glowing in their skins, or else
You can take a knife and strip the skins away.

Here goes. But stop. No way back to Winterthur.
New friends, and we ourselves were welcome:
With all the zest of a young and dexterous
Danish wife, Susi prepared, in that cosy room,
A supper of cold cuts, hot potatoes in their skins.

They took their food, like Danes, on wooden platters,
Whereat I did remark, at first: We are not peasants.
The four of us, to be acquainted, this was happiness:
To learn the marital ropes, minute by minute,
Unshackled by skeletons, babies, or infidelity.

Peace was in the world, not yet Cambodia;
Richard explored negatives in fiction; me,
I took delight in the potatoes, yellow, oval,
Golden as they look tonight. The wooden platter, soon,
Dilating on Oetinger the Boehmenist, and William Law,
I could admire the grain in it, and licked it clean.

Those days of pleasure in the pursuit of learning
Give me another Winterthur involuntarily tonight.
Divine exuberance, then you had a hand in it.
Yet Richard went insane and Susi had to cope.
I flitted about; fathering and keen,
I carried a spear for Troy, not for Aldermaston:

Leafing through secret books I could imagine
Kaf's cup, brimming to heaven — so, not otherwise
The holy mountain rose, alchemy in the utterance.
Dupe of vague desire for the sublime exotic
I did scrimp and save, a hangdog hedonist.

Visiting Richard in Lichterfelde once,
I ate nasturtiums from a vase and did a dance
Solo to Brubeck's Rondo à la Turque; I scanned,
At the police presidium, in quest of Dada,
A smoky ledger . . . That *Qualm*, I was the soot in it.

No skindeep shame,
It was, like ours, an ancient sorrow haunted Susi:
What if her daughters might show the signs?
Sorrow bit into her smile, into her posture;
Nocturnally on his volcano Richard went about.

No way back to Winterthur. Rising in the east
A full moon, at my window I believe
The moon itself resembles a majestic potato,
Unskinned, like those I bake, here at home
And with devotion serve across these last horizons,
On an old blue plate, with salt and butter.

Pinkard's Haikus

Grave as Hegel,
Reading a book,
Paulina, smiling
Scatters her clothes.

*

The sign, bipolar:
On its mud, the river,
Turtle still
On that stone.

*

Whoosh and a heron
Flaps away. Human
Footsteps. Who
Broke down my door?

*

Search the stars,
Watchman. So far —
And everlasting night
Still on our tail?

*

684

Safety catches click.
In its clover of contrast,
Mind,
This herd, at peace.

Pinkard Identifies a Lookalike

Those wings I saw, they beat so fast,
Were shadows only, on the tarmac.

Heaps of leaves were not churned up,
Though I'd supposed a mocking-bird,

For once, in sunlight, took a dustbath.
Wrong again. But this, was this

The hell of birds? A parked Toyota
Hid it from me, yet I knew, the peevish

Bird, his claws across the windshield
Skittering, pecked at his reflection.

Dissolute there, at roost in the vanity
Glass on the flipside of the sunflap,

A lookalike mocked the mocking-bird,
A brute (Saddamosamahitlerchingiskahn)

Was hacking signals through his base
Between bamboo patch and telephone pole.

Analogy. Too narrow. Press the pinpoint
Elsewhere, then, on mirrors marvellous —

Pollen of godhood! Their morning beauty
Angels magnify, to stream it raptured

Back into their countenances;
And that bird laughingly can sing

In long cadenzas tunes that take
Your breath away but tell his tale.

Pinkard's Ditty

Since you will needs that I shall sing,
Take it in worth such as I have.
                              Thomas Wyatt

To catch a tulip, yellow out of earth,
Fresh, as it grew, I sloped across a green.
Tulips, two or three, together in my hand
I stoop to catch another, deeper down.

Catch, my word, my hope, and there's a trick:
Pull up a pod sucked halfway underground.
And so I did. As I stood straight again,
Out buzzed a dragonfly, and huge, but hoary

It bristles in my face, so stinging, poison
This tube, a vapid blue, of centuries the rot;
Me bespewed with my own mess of tempers,
That thing will eat the music out of me.

I drop the pod; of innocence I shout.
Nobody hears. Foul into the green
It slithers back, the dragonfly, his palace.
Then I could breathe again, and so could he.

Saul Pinkard on the Fortune of Musicians

Did Samuel Scheidt hit the bottle once too often?
Or did his patrons in the Dutch Baroque decide
That Tafelmusik troubled their digestion?

Since 1610 his music had been popular.
In 1625, whatever might have been the cause,
Scheidt had a fracas with the aldermen.

In 1633, the plague. Forewarned
And holding herbal bags to nervous noses,
The bigwigs in their wagons quit the city.

Humble Scheidt was not forewarned. His wife
And all his offspring perished in the plague.
All his offspring, and his wife, they died.

The boil in the armpit. Sudden agonizing fever.
An old enchanter crazed with helplessness.
And the fresh dead, the handbell, the pushcart.

Scheidt in his compositions could of course
Not tell of this. Music is discreet.
To the smiler Boccherini, to Berwald the Bore

Patrons tender envelopes. However jealous
Syndicated cynics and the gods may be,
While fishier troopers oftentimes cry havoc,

The artist hides underneath his wings
What follies of his own or busy interlopers
Have scored across his back: the stripes.

Saul Pinkard's Tirade

Out there, an oleander whitens in the dark,
For someone, on the fifth floor, fancy that,
A passable musician, playing a violin,

Fills my perception of it to the brim
Almost. The human brute accelerating
Now into the blue cuts a full measure short;

He does not shape, fingering his instrument,
A gaze that seems to trill and milk the earth —
Off-whitens, that is what I should have said,

Fears drain so the colour out of everything.
Burned by the brute, even murk turns bitter.
It is a torpid worm that feeds the roses then.

Nature, graced with art, I wonder when,
Piloted from the brute will a saint. What now
When wilier than ever fat cats in cahoots

With bigots overwhelm the mice of earth?
O picture-fabricators, how you do decompose
The story spelled into experience by time;

You wrench all sentience off like a bottle cap,
Cram slick commodities down yawning throats;
Who militarize, of God, plutonium, and deceit

Smear over rooftops such a glutinous bombast,
Hound from schools or hovels unsteady children,
Then work on some to gun the others down.

Poetry too, you dragged your feet on this.
For one intact imaginary town at most
Your singular felicity still has inhabitants.

How, with your whiff of paradise, could you hope
To break the fiend's teeth, tune a voice to vast
Public atmospheres? Look at you now,

Skimming the pool of language, dowsed at noon,
Clamour without echo, you pick your features out.
While beady-eyed the headlined hogs go rooting

Round that bush, their tusks tear you apart,
Words run for refuge, chatter in the shops;
So at an oleander in the night you flinch

And writhe inside yourself, then eat your mouth.
My knuckles whiten also, on this windowsill.
O arctic oleander, must you be my igloo?

Or might a frozen margarita quench my rage?

Pinkard's Anecdotes

An Iranian Tale (1970s)

He had the cook
Prepare a mountainous pilaff
And there, upon the platter, heaped,
We saw it sparkle; secondly,
A grilled kebap of lamb he laid
With every grace, and then another,
Across the mountain's back.

As we sat down among the lamps,
Thirdly he took from underneath
The knee-high dinner table
A can containing some insecticide.
He sprayed the dish with it, three squirts,
Happy, with a modern smile: 'You see?
No flies will settle on our meat.'

The Village on a Tilt

High on a cliff
Close to the sea
And when in the night
The bell of the church
Tolled, folks
Took fright and quit
Their family beds
Under olive trees
And seeking the reason
Discovered the rope
Dangling over
The cliff, not free —
Down and awash
Mid rocks below,
So intricate is
The fabric of matter,
An octopus tentacle
Pulled on the rope:
Had the octopus fancied
The rope might lead
To an octopa in the sky?
Did the octopus aspire
With a star in mind?
What a tender
Bludgeoned octopus
Brightened their pans,
Perfumed for people
Their sooty kitchens!
Was there a song to sing?
At what perpendicular glittering
Did the song stab?

The House on Fire

Pinkard snatched a book at random
And read before the news at five
How the man, home from a journey,

690

Finds his house on fire, indoors
He knows his children will be playing
So taken by the game
They feel no fire, notice nothing.
The flames would roast him.
He can't go in.

So in a wink the man has found
The time to make
Of toy chariots a team.
One glimpse of their quite perfect
Wooden workmanship, the round
Wheels waiting to spin,
Shafts high for horses,
In beauty on its tilt
An imminent significance,
And out the children rush,
Out they rush for the chariots.
They take them in their hands,
They play with them, delighted.

What parable was this, Pinkard sniffs.
An old parable, therefore chariots.
The chariots, why toys, Pinkard? Which
Might be the playground, which
The burning ground of ritual?
Souls with chariots like these,
Pinkard quips, forgo the mischief
Of their ecstatic game.

An Ominous Circus

(*Rome, A.D. 358*)

Lions and crocodiles from Africa,
Scottish dogs and out of Spain
Horses trained to race, the quickest,
Also ships to carry them
And Saxon gladiators, muscle-men —

Symmachus demanding these
(Pinkard notes) had cost his parent
Many sacks of sesterces:
Appointed praetor at eighteen,
Young Symmachus loves punctilio.

What though gangs of circus agents
Ransack the Imperium,
The crocodiles on hunger strike
(Pinkard winces) must be culled;
From Spain the mares and stallions

Arrive disabled, even dead;
For chariot-drivers (none checks in)
All Sicily is combed in vain;
No comedian dances forward;
Dogs? Nor yap nor Scottish odour.

Old Symmachus recalls the Saxons
(Did only etiquette's abracadabras
Procrastinate the fall of Rome?):
'Before the show,' he writes, 'with all
Their strength they strangled one another.'

Pinkard Brings Hölderlin to the Awareness of Americans

Hölderlin divined the scrappy world as such
To be the only arbiter of truth:
No second Paradise for Fallen Man,
Greek Antiquity a breath of God?
Phut went the speculation of his youth.

The matter distressed Hölderlin so much —
God and Man once cheek to cheek, no rhyme
Or rhythm conjugates them in our time;
Worldlings, parched as we are, in spirit small,
The Fire from Heaven could soon combust us all —

That heading for the road to Bordeaux, France,
He stuffed an Antique Pistol in his pants.

Pinkard's Postscript to Weimar

Possibly he croaked contorted,
Solo, forgotten, but in bed;
And Eckermann, scenting trouble, snorted
'Alter Scheisskerl! Goethe dead?'

With a squeak he strips the sheet off;
Mutters, finding his Poet
Much diminished, 'Is the heat off?
Rigor mortis? No, not yet.'

Meanwhile in Petersburg (the town
Another Athens of the North)
Superintendent Benckendorf
Hounds Alexander Pushkin down.

So Eckermann bends Goethe straight,
Knee and elbow, neck and thighs,
Then pulls a pencil out: The date?
(Who freedom fear, aestheticize):

'I see a zephyr puff the curtain
While the women wash him clean.
He died at peace, you may be certain,
Flesh unblemished, brow serene.'

Five years elapse. Now see how much
The waltzing colonels care who kills!
And, filing past it, thousands touch
The coffin Sasha Pushkin fills.

The Proof and the Pudding

A manifold phenomenon, the baobab.
Its blossoms open only to the moon
And wither on the final stroke of noon.

White, waxy, opening petals house a clutch
Of pistils pumping nectar out for bats
And baobab cats on tiptoe hopping

From their holes. Sun up, a swarm of bees
Arrives to suck the nectar: honeycombs
For storage they construct in other trees.

While, breathless in their pods, the blossoms wait,
Slow to explode at yet another moonrise,
Here comes a hungry lion with his mate.

And there beneath the tree Pinkard the naturalist
Lifts his nose to test one more hypothesis:
Can it be true, or is it only legend

That baobab blossom smells of human flesh
In an advanced condition of decay?
That someone smelling it ends inside a dragon?

Of such doubt, drowsing in a distant lair,
Naturally the lions have taken note.
Now noses animal and Pinkard sniff the air —

Two for their pudding . . . One for his proof.
Under the moonlit baobab's manifold roof
Uplifted, we shall quietly leave them there.

694

4

Translations

From Catullus: Two Travesties

LXVI

I'd rather be the head of hair Berenice combed
    Than stranded here, a star
Yet not exactly stellar: Conon discovers me
    Only as adjunct to some larger
Luminaries you glimpse perhaps at nightfall
    During a certain season of the year.
A head of hair cropped to a single lock
    By legend-builders: wrong, I was her mane,
And Berenice snipped me off, tress by tress,
    So to placate, she hoped, fates that otherwise
Might trim her of a husband in his latest war.
    I crave the warmth of skin that wraps
Berenice's bold immortal skull. Instead
    I have to rise, obligingly, and fall.
I'd even rather be a picture, woolly, woven
    With colours into a coverlet on someone's
Bridal bed, than rise and fall out here.
    Oh well, bleak as I do suppose the outlook is,
It's Peleus and his Thetis who miscegenate
    Under the coverlet, and Berenice's
Husband did come slouching home, unscathed.
    Even then, good folks, a sacrifice, I tell you,
Gains not a whit, unless with Berenice's care
    You disband the passion you put into it.

(*extract, abridged*)

IV

By oars propelled or in full rig
I've skimmed the rough Illyrian deep,
Run loops around the Cyclades,
Propontis then I've penetrated,
Up the Bosphorus come I,
A pinnace, to the Euxine Sea.

East of me, look, the place I was born,
East of Amastris: What a nativity —
High trees, thick on a peak.
Cytorus they call it, not intending
A pun, I think, and pinnace, too,
Was the innocent name bestowed upon me.

Before I was me, I talked the baby
Language of leaf. Fashioned by carpenters,
Boat was the tongue I grew up to speak.
With blade or with sail again
Westward I speed nonstop, to the limpid
Lake of Catullus; though Jove
Blow from astern on both sheets at once,
I soar over deeps and shun the shallows —
Mariners land there, just for a breather,
For being not dead they offer up thanks.

Now I am old, a bit wrinkled, and small,
Retired as I am, to the Heavenly Twins
I offer myself. Anchored, at leisure
Still I can float, just biding my time.

On Hearing of a Death

(*from Rilke's 'Todes-Erfahrung,' 1907*)

This passing-on that we know nothing of
Shares with us nothing. We have no cause
To be surprised at death or show it love
Or hate, oddly distorted as it was

By the tragic mask, mouth twisted in lament.
Still the world is full of roles we play,
And while to please is everyone's intent
Death plays along, displease us though it may.

Yet in the gap where lately you had been,
Reality appeared, a narrow strip, to spill
Across our stage: green really green,
Real the sunlight, and the forest real.

Still we play. Parts we conned in fear,
Strenuously, we recite; now and then
We launch a gesture out. Now not here,
Rapt out of our act, your existence can

Come home to us at moments when we know
That our reality flutters down from yours;
Then till anon the knowledge lets us go
We play our lives not thinking of applause.

Charles Mauron's Poem on Van Gogh (1945)

Let her roll across the hills,
Reflected in the water holes,
That poor madwoman of the moon,
Who frolics with her looking glass.

*

So far, no agony. The beast
Has not as yet begun to howl.
Still, the gateway standing open,
Distant madness gads on by.

*

Now get along: an age ago
Chimeras housed in rock prepared,
Peering down upon the vales,
Tranquillity for this nocturne.

*

Sands of wisdom, there the stalk
Of grass you understood awaits you,
Or the hush, where tall, tall
Cypresses creak in the wind.

On their torches, black and twisting,
You will see the heavens rain
Fires, fruits of many colours,
Of seeds a glittering cascade.

*

If your heavens wheel and wheel,
The reason is that there you winnow
Treasure upturned on the centre
Point where all is at an end.

Robert Desnos

Sonnet

On this brink of an abyss where you will disappear
Consider, still, the rose; listen to the song
You sang, time was, at the door to your house;
Consent to be, a while again, just who you are.

Then you will go, forgotten, back to your ancestors;
O passer-by, with all your seasons over,
In the planet and its harvests you will be lost.
Try not to hope you'll be one day reborn.

A star adrift in the depth of time rejoins
The many points of light, points of darkness
On the river shore where you unlearn to be.

Matter had come, in you, to think about itself;
Remote, now vanish echoes of a love declared,
Pure motion moves for evermore no mind.

5

CODA

The Concord of State

But, I ask you, what was going on —
Long white hairs of the man who vaguely
Chewed on the pommel of a long sword;
And then the lion with an iron collar,
Chains drawn tight, one ran to a rock,
Another vanished underneath the throne?

If no throne, then was this a minstrel?
Left of him, a wedge of bubbles, populous.
Further off, foothills, in the air a tiered
Oval of smoke-rings, elongated, signals.

Then I was getting off my horse, was I?
A boy had run out from nowhere,
He'll grip the reins while I'm dismounting.
Or was I soon to be in the saddle again,
My right leg hoisted over the horse's back?

Ahead, a mass of armoured men, and all
Chaffing, or in dispute, lances tilted.
One of those men, his features partly
An owl, partly a clown, looked perplexed.
What now? The lion, I took a closer look.
His mouth was rounded, not for a roar,
But howling. His brutal head was human.
Between his back and the throng beyond
A chaplet trailed vestiges of ornament —
Tiny emblems: those were clasped hands.

For it was a throng, the wedge of bubbles.
No faces. It was a market, with heads,
Heads for cauliflower, parsnip, and cheese;
Or it was a sea of some description, choppy.

The tree, rooted in the rock, it leaned
Over an armoured man, monumental
On a horse that reared, ready to go.
Lances again, crisscrossed, behind him
Transport the conscience of that cavalier.

But it leaned over, blown that way
Forever by a force of wind, the tree
Leaned, and the wind blew from darkness,
Darkness gathered and hung heavily
Over the force of the helmeted men.

I joined them, or I trotted away;
You can reason well enough, you can
Dissect and even understand these things.
A tempered idea will not be warped in action;
A right idea depends on being proven.
Now, is he still chewing on the pommel
Of his long sword, that indeterminate,
Almost featureless, blear-eyed old man?

December 2004

[*From the oil sketch by Rubens*]

THE TENOR ON HORSEBACK
AND WORK IN PROGRESS

The Part of Gravity

As if to gravity the one were not
   subject enough, the other
like a turtle cosying up

   for coitus but doomed to slip
slants across the exposed
   level surface of it,

two big stones, and both, submerged
   in shallow river water,
must have been made

   substance by fire and a tremendous
pressure, to the start of time
   closer far than yesterday—

Where was I now? calling to mind
   the killed in heaps, and 1848
in Alexander Herzen's ear

   the tocsin clanging from a steeple,
fractured first, then engulfed
   by frenzied act, the fine intention,

then to foresee the microbe of revenge
   drag revolution for the future
ranting to the ground . . .

   Inestimable muck, and little
grains of golden sand, together
   bed the stones, today a flood,

tomorrow all serene, even limpid
   the river, it may welcome
slender craft, where sit

   stooping forward, straining back
to suit their tension to the oars
   they grip, the scullers.

A Pair of Herons

No matter what it means,
I saw a pair of herons.
White, they flew upwind,

Upriver. White, against
A scree of sombre green
Tall trees, rock outcrops,

I saw them flying. If
The wind got brisk and blew
Their breastbone fluff apart

They reeled, sideslipping.
Then each would caracol,
To luff at any lull.

I saw them reeling, each
Easily righting itself
And flying, flying on.

So contraries collide,
For when I saw that pair
My worm writhed in their rose,

But vanishes like a nose
Now I, interpellated,
Imagine them still there.

A Sonnet of Nice Goats

Daredevil skateboard boys, they
   Scoot along a sidewalk.
And of a vacant floodlit tunnel
   They conceive, of whirling, heavens,

706

Across the roof. When a shot
    Rings out from the ghost house,
Who else has now surpassed
    Quietus with a bare bodkin?
Wind-chimes, far enough off,
    Yet mellower wind-chimes
In the porch we never stopped at,
    Become bells on billygoats,
Nannies too, on a rosemary slope
    Grazing, out of harm's way.

The Tenor on Horseback

As the tenor on horseback was,
    In mid-aria, carried backstage
And the hurriedly hired circus horse
    Soon reappeared, for the next
Bar of the aria, only to resume his
    Circuitry, so my thought, too seldom now,
Brings back into focus the old reasons given
    For worldly being, for ways
Unspeakable pain might be made sense of.

    Surely they were wise, in their robes of cotton,
And never distracted, those midnight men,
    Those who pondered the laws of creation,
Who saw, behind the rotation of the stars,
    Not nothing at all but love with a design?
Of what now is known they knew little,
    Of where feelings come from, of chemical
Reaction in the brain, of chromosomes,
    They knew not a thing.
Yet spelling it out, time the fugitive,
    Vanity liquidating every place desired,
Memory doomed as an ostrich gobbling,
    Instead of water, stray bullets,
Hadn't they told it like it was?

Yes. There is *kellipot,* the shattering:
Something began, but pulverized its vessels:
 They could not contain the tremendous ray
Shot from the head of Ein-Sof, alias Adam Kadmon,
 And the task of reconstitution, writ,
Writ it is in holy books, no poppycock.

 Even then I wonder if, much as they meant
Well and told of truth as they surprised her,
 It was authority alone that they pursued—
Mobile men on camel or horseback,
 Some next to naked, observing the buffalo,
Dared to command the rough and the tumble,
 Mind's bow measuring its pitch of tension,
Then letting fly its projectile power.

 Privy to secret tunes, vibration
Fathomless in a supposedly divine
 Cosmogonic harp, whose tonalities
Happened as heaven and haunted as riffs
 The blood of us who ache in the pit,
Surely their pursuits refined the liberty to question:
 They combed great glowing spaces for fresh disbelief.

Job, in the stories told of him, was he confident
 Of working a change in Jehovah's attitude?
Of peeling away an immutable mask? In true tales
 Of justice, hollow model and stale god dissolve:
Creations, subjecting their creators to change,
 Gather around them present pain, to relieve,
A little, sour delusions fixing the scowl or grin.
 Slowly, unperceived, a new design will enter
These mutant mobile geometries of species, hurting—
 Or else, for want of variation, all is dispersed.
Agony abides, look, listen, even if people,
 People change, and smile.

Expressionless the Vast:
To fly in its face, to contradict it, midnight men
    Composed imagination; each, his manifold
Travelling deep design, soul to the cut stone,
    He grounded in earth, sidereal or not;
And as a mason scoops, then trims the mortar,
    He toils with time and the blade of his trowel.

The First Portrait

Then she went and died on us,
Just like that. And her face, extinct.
We saw nothing move in it, trouble it,
Or rest content, or yawn, or give her smile,
Or even scowl, for us to laugh at.

*

Then we watched while the knife man
Cut off her head. We watched
And took out our loudest voices,
And twisted them in hoots, yelps,
Groaning as the scoop went in;
Spring water washed away the gunk;
Till that was done we howled.

*

Then came the woman with her clay
And stuffed the skull with it,
And made her face again, the face
We could not bear to never see.

*

A clay face for her, any moment now
See its motions; so for her alone
We copied, breathless, the big silence.

*

But to give her all the credit,
Body and head we buried together.
Her clay face had to belong down there.
Our underground is memory of her,
For her the memory is part of us
Who anyway forget. How else
To undo our division?

*

Gossips will say an ostrich
Invented such a funeral custom.
We hope her clay-featured egg,
Not popping so its eyes of sea-shell,
Will hatch and she return to us,
Or with her glance encourage others,
Good kin, who drink at Jericho
The waters of our spring.

(Note: A man's skull with the face modelled in clay [Natufian, Proto-
Neolithic, c.B.C.7500] was excavated at Jericho. See Grahame Clark,
World Prehistory: An Outline, 1962.)

Orbiana

I could never help uttering a light soupir,
Just one, whenever the times
Were hard; today
Just one more, it hardly passed my lips,
But murdered they were, such news,
Murdered near Mayence, those two
Who sent me here, to Leptis Magna.

The emperor was never up to it, really,
In peace or war. She governed, Julia Mamaea,
Selecting me for him. So when she found,
To her astonishment, that I, a tiddler,
Had it in me to influence Alexander,

She packed me off, with his consent—
Nobody knew where. Nobody, either, now
Will inquire where I come from, nobody
Will know which city in Africa
Took me in, so I have disappeared.

But the shopping is quite splendid.
In this great new city of arcades,
Several temples to various divinities,
A triumphant arch, the amphitheatre
And almost superfluous fortifications,
There are nice people to listen to
And black weavers who manufacture
Singular objects to recline or to stand on.

Yes, for the Christians Mother had a soft spot;
From Syria once she had a cavalry escort sent
To save that tyke, whatever his name was.
It starts like mine with O and R.
I like to beachcomb. It attracts,
Ha ha, I mean the beach attracts provincials.
And yet, and yet . . . From Rome
And from Pamphylia come

Real artists with guitars, who chant
Devotedly of ocean, even to the moon—
I never had children, what a shame,
And the years of loving, few, complicated
By Mother, them I've forgotten now.
The shopping gets, by the way, a bit
Monotonous. Funds I was allowed
Exhaust themselves, somehow,
Even though I did, if I remember rightly,
Stir up a nasty fracas, insist
On statutory imperial support.

I feel behoved to say (don't ever quote me
On this) that I am not yet negligible,
Negligible enough to mark the passage
From finite to infinite. I was not one to wheedle,

But those officiants, what rot they talk—
Into the atoms they ship their designated
Sacrifices, not into some dock of heaven.
Where bodies tasted chance, they make a waste.

You should see me glimpse, now and then,
Into the shrinking bijou bag under my bed.
The wind cooling profuse vegetation
And the display of stars at nightfall
Are supposed to console. They don't.
Disease, at least, is hereabouts minimal.
What a mercy my destination was not Mauretania.
That's such a long, long way west.
And Mauretanians, they do say,
Are a scruffy lot. Please write
To your little friend, Orbiana.

Imagine Mallarmé

Imagine Mallarmé with a long and vaporous
Periphrasis buttonholing, at his desk, the mayor
Of Mézy-sur-Seine in 1890, imploring him
To rid the neighbourhood of a herd of pigs,
Which he politely called, of course, *messieurs*.

The matter bothered for a while, at least,
Eugène Manet and Berthe Morisot.
They loved the summer house they'd rented,
But rainy days and then the pig noise
And pig smell from a neighbour's yard

Reduced their pleasure and her chance to paint.
Meanwhile, from Giverny, not far away,
Monet wrote: *My canvases, I ruin them,*
Scraping out whatever I've accomplished.
What I achieve is beneath anything.

The Manets and Mallarmé in a carriole
Took off to visit Monet in Giverny.
After lunch, on Sunday, July 13, 1890,
Monet, to compensate for having failed
To do for Mallarmé a promised illustration,

Told the poet to take a picture home.
Mallarmé didn't dare to choose the one
He liked the most, but soon, persuaded
By Berthe herself to take it, he did so.
Then going home to where the pigs were stinking,

Oink oink in the distance, Mallarmé declared,
His painting luminous across his knees
While the carriole jogged through the twilight:
It makes me happy, just to think now
I'm living in the same age as Monet.

Chekhov at Sumy

First to go, the right lung;
Then, at intervals, unanticipated
Spates of spitting blood.

Devotedly at work, the iridescent
Stories; unhopeful
"Doctoring in my spare time;"
Focus on fact, on detail, all those letters.

1890: by boat the long haul to Sakhalin,
The prison swamps, and duly eye-opening
His report. Somewhere else
He builds a school, takes charge

Of a cholera outbreak. Kropotkin
Quotes his dictum with approval:
We need desire most, force of character
To banish "whining shapelessness."

Nightingales had nested in the open window
At Sumy, Summer 1888. While he slept,
One lung, or both, might have whistled
So entertainingly, the light-winged
Dryad of the woods joined in.

Not a remnant, left to erode
In acidic debate,
He purposed and accomplished
The utmost he had known —

Sixteen more years above the dust.
In two, from Ukleyevo, Lipa, Lipa,
Her baby scalded, and her scream
Building,

Complete as now his pleasure is
To see "slip from their shells
The children of the nightingale."

Judge Bean

Of him or her who placed it there, and why,
No one knew anything.
   Thomas Hardy

Judge Roy Bean of Long Ago
Beheld once in a magazine
The face of Lily Langtry,
And in the twilight often
Judge Bean upon his porch
Rocked in a rocking chair,
Upon his porch he'd rock,
And dream and dream of her.

A distant blue, how it pulls
The flesh to Long Ago
And far away, although
Judge Bean had hopes:
Lily Langtry just might come,
Passing through, and sing to him.

Not far from where the judge
Had sat and rocked and hoped
There was a tree festooned
With bottles that were blue.
Over the tips of many twigs
Somebody had been slotting
Milk of Magnesia (Phillips),
His empties, by the dozen.

Well-water there is hard;
Deep canyons through the rock
The Rio Grande, a trickle now,
Had had long since to carve.
There too the mountains host
Various flocks of birds,
Yet not a one would choose
To nest in such a tree.

The tree, so dead its twigs
That pronged the bottles, have
They in the meantime broke?
A striking sight against the sky,
An image not to be forgot,
So many bottles of blue glass
And sips of milk drunk up,
It still explodes to mark
Dimensions in the mind,
A horizon in the heart.

Long before the twigs had pronged
Blue bottles for my sight,
Like Tao it had for sure
No name at all, that place
Where Judge Bean rocked;
But Lily Langtry's face
Nothing airy in his mind,
Not despairing of his dream,
One stormy day he took his pen
And wrote:

Now Langtry is its name.

Felo de se

When he had pulled upright his jingle-jangle cart,
he said he hoped he would not be disturbing me.
He unpacked his kit from the cart and lost no time
but baited his lines with worms from a box of dirt
and made a long cast for the lead to plop in mid-river.

When he says he is Tex-Mex but spoke as a child
no Spanish, he explains that he took himself soon
to school, learning the way they speak it in Spain.

When he was little his father died, says he.
So he helped in the house, cleaning and sweeping,
cooking the beans, washing dishes for mother.

When he had a family of his own, two boys
and a girl, he told them, one by one, as they grew,
there'll be no lazy nobodies in my house,
told them when it was time to grow up
and that it won't be easy but here's your support,
grow up to be somebody with an education:

Now there's my boy in the marines (this war, it makes
no sense) but then his line is aviation, the mechanics,
in law-school the girl, the other boy in medicine,
and all three speak Spanish as well as they do English.

When he's set to make a cast with his third rod,
he says his father-in-law's funeral cost ten thousand,
but his own uncle's was cheaper for he was cremated.

And when he has cast with a fourth rod far out
into mid-river, he says that he'll be tonight
in Marble Falls where the catfish bite better,
that because of the funeral he has a week off.

But when he went to Mexico he didn't like it,
didn't like the Mexicans, a crooked lying crowd,
says he, they look down on us, call me a gringo.

Me, I'm a carpenter, he says, I can build you
a pretty house, restore, where wood has gone to rot,
repair, adapt, install any kind of cabinet:

anything to do with wood, I can do it with finish,
fishing is just a pastime when you're needing it,
and it has clouded over now, the fish like that.

Yes, he says, any kind of wood, I can handle it,
and we were standing under a water-cypress,
a very tall tree that has gone brown by March,
the tangle of its roots ran in long looped
cylinders out under water, while he talked,

wearing a cobalt gimme cap with NY in a monogram,
an olive-green tabard (pockets in place of emblems),
drainpipe trousers and spongy-soled suede boots,

yet all I had asked was if he knew perhaps
the meaning of *felo de se,* supposing it Spanish.
Not theft, he said, thieving is *robar, robo;*
what you said, might that be in a book?

Senex

Hearing at night the first Fall Norther
I think no more of Artaud's tantrums;
No more of Ungern-Sternberg's magnificent beast;
Of balance perfect in the form of a pear
I think, then poof it goes, the Buddha temple.

That wall: it is the rock face of a mountain.
Fumbling for a handhold, slowly slowly
I step sideways, the ravine at my heels
Deepens, unsteadily I must step sideways.

Nose to nose with my mountain wall,
The path no wider now than a foot's length,
How will it end, where then shall I go?

I had to limber up, to risk a look:
And what I'd thought was not, was not—
But was a plain, immense, and it was shaping
Soon to become a fair field of folk.
Still it wanted curvature for a horizon,
Still it hid its dells and lakes and alps;
Now in it rose, I see, putting them there,
Many many footholds I had mistaken
For brushes quicker than a breath, contacts
Of clothes in the café, in a shop—
Yet people, singly, clusters, were appearing,
All distinct, each face rich in expression:
Scowling, perplexed, then relief, the smile
Brief or broadening, and grim if in revenge.

Every single glance grew thriftily from the stem,
Unmistakeable, inexchangeable, the body.

And by the balls the horror of it got me:

There was no way to make good
Wrongs of my doing. With one quick breath,
No way, to chuck the humbug; to be done

718

With dithering; understand at least
A secret dread; so to bring crashing down
As vapour only, absorbed back into earth,
The tabernacle cant, enforced conformity,
Those violations that had shrunk my time,
And to annul in me the predator,
Root out of me the pest, indifference.

Oh well, so much abstract projection
Still is, tooth and nail, a hanging-on.
Symmetry I did perceive, agile in faces,
Stormy, or in suspense, it might promise
Value, though passion rushed, then halted. Stooping
You could glimpse the star, absurd, it was afloat
Where the well-shaft had no end.

Then I was touched.
                    Then I was free.
I turn, how else, alone again, to the mountain.

Ancient Emigré (Irish)

Once only I've heard in (of all places)
This candybar town, where songs
Are composed by the dozen, composed
In the beds, on the porches,

A person singing at work. (Ten years back,
Must I recall, I passed on a street
In the outskirts a fellow who sang
For joy, while walking, a popular song.)

Among cabbages, this nineteenth
Of November, 2005, I noted, yes,
Among cabbages, celery, spinach,
Heaps of arugula, vegetables from

Half the world over, a young caballero
Singing, and it was 'Molly Malone'.
Sweeping the floor, fresh-faced he was,
With a daredevil forelock, and as he sang

That song of the streets, some broad,
Some narrow, I pictured rooftops,
Flat rooftops in Corsica, women sing there,
Soon after sunrise, answering songs

Sung by their neighbours, at work
Hanging the laundry out. On broccoli,
Snap beans and cauliflower dwelled
This morning the eyes of shoppers, all

Attentive to tasks having today to be done.
That Molly Malone could have sunk
So deep in the people who pushed their carts
Hither and thither, heaping the produce up,

The shaft of her glance, startled them with
Obstreperous beauty (rough, into the bargain,
From counting the pennies, privation, abuse);
Could they marvel, I ask, at nothing at all?

My cart hummed with its wires, my kilo
Of strawberries trilled, *conamore* the praties,
Onward wheeling the work with a song,
Did it? Briefly. Midnight. Now I inhale

And smell in this paper I scribble on
Molly, her skin. Her wheelbarrow is parked,
My cap's falling off as, friendly-like,
In a bombarded garden, she comes to be mine.

From the Cat

The niyam woe is westergone,
The slavit with a shrill,
Betone the ghast, obese the lid,
Alack the cock until.

Crumb forks to pick a winsome up,
One plays the yoick, and then
Another dove into the first,
Or snubs a gentlemen.

You think a looky star will strike,
A wolverine will spin?
Pot nest you snugly, Mister Toph,
But critter risk a grin.

Then if he chews to blow a scowl
Much bitter oft you be—
Since revoluzzers busted ope,
Wobbly the One-in-Three.

Full up your gourd, swot wide away
The chumps that bite behind,
For on the muse left at your door
Red meat you still may find.

In Memory of W.G. Sebald

A bipolarity remark, native to the species.
Observe ecstasy in acts of laying waste.
Consider your apprehensions at the sight
Of a bone pulled out of an avalanche.
How ecstasy and apprehension skip, consider
Next, the supervision of intellect.

A noise not stopping, very loud, destruction:
Heed the skeleton's poise—as if to speak.
Amnesia, aphasia, anaesthesia remark:
While fleets of souls, all twittering, take off,
A blank occupies pained heart, or vandal head.
One who came through, clutching a god—
Contemplate the god who took away his speech.

Thorny species, a Kalahari shrub,
Shrunk by heat at day's end, contrives
Nocturnally to unwind, seasonally to sprout.
As if that sound were what a desert listens for,
Heed, during a breath or two of cool at night,
The rustle when a thorn, a lucky leaf, expands.

There'll be prognoses printed out, decades in advance
And on a scale so vast that guesswork is eliminated;
Surely with some device we'll temper any rising heat;
Banish the blank from this heart or that head;
Bury the hatchets, for people of tomorrow
Cultivate sensibly earth, all the nursed grudges
Volatilized behold, reformed into the rose
We give to those whom fear set free to think.

The Laundress

Bothering us for a long time,
This laundry woman: Beneath
A blue segment of sky she is
All brown and profiled against
A cliff so laboriously hewn
That it resembles a rampart.
Like a baby mask her face,
Black crescent moons for eyebrows
And greys to streak her bodice,
But yellow or brown the rampart
Towers behind the woman, as if
Its gravity propelled her—darkly

Her combed hair clings to the head
She launches forward, stooping.
Awkward skirts impede her,
Surely now she has to be hurrying
Somewhere. A little daughter
Runs at her left side, one foot
Lifting off the shadowy ground,
Hurled stooping foward she
Mimics her mother, and the labour
Extracted from the mother, that
She will inherit too. Still,
Goya's glimpse of them has put
Happy family bonding into question:
Are they running to the fountain
Or to the river at all? Are they
Running away from something
Hidden? Their velocity
Must have to do with bread. Yet
Won't they have had to scoot,
In those times, across the picture,
Basket on the mother's haunch
Bumping up and down on it, because
Shirts coiled in the wickerwork
(Where bristles dashed, dripping
White, the profile of a billygoat)
Had been stiff with blood, or wet?
The next up for execution
Needed snowy linen, so the French
Bullets could be met with decent
Spanish gestures, death be dignified,
You now conjecture, whereupon
Some villagers in bleached
Apparel sign to us how best not
To die, if only, in Bordeaux,
Goya, to assuage despair, stands
Candle-crowned for half the night,
Imagining, him, in grief and detail,
Horrors he had likely never seen.

Of the Belovèd Someone

Confused about that which
Touches nothing, without which
There would have been nothing,

Attend to it a moment,
Attend: as it retrieves,
On this day like no other,

A joy, once to have felt in it
Nothing to be acknowledged,
From an impact uplift, at the utmost

A breath, when close, a touch
Of the belovèd someone—
Immediately wide-awake to it

Now, perceiving it diffused
Among new leaves, old spines
Of books perhaps, the moment

There is here again, the time
All felt afresh, not to be redeemed,
For so, only so, in this hive

Where entombed it wanders, this body,
Not a word for it can ego there pin down,
Rare the trope, moonlit vapour of

Syntax or instrument agile, agile
Enough to convey its tremor, still
Opening Memory first

It begins Forever, even, briefly,
When, with a light, a distant laughter,
The Door has closed.

NOTES

Our Flowers & Nice Bones

The title of this book comes from a letter written by Kurt Schwitters to Raoul Hausmann (c. 1946), in which he described an event of 1922 in Utrecht: "In Utrecht they came on the scene, presented me with a bunch of dry flowers and bloody bones and started to read in our place . . . Nelly lighted a cigarette and cried to the public, that as the public had now become quite dada, we would be now the public. We sat down and regarded our flowers and nice bones" (*Pin:* London, Gaberbocchus Press 1962, quoting Schwitters's original English).

'Found Poem with Grafts 1866' and 'A Concert 1866' come from *Hand-Book of French Conversation: Consisting of Progressive Dialogues on Ordinary and Familiar Subjects,* by M. de Rouillon (New York 1866). The grafts in the first of these poems are extracted from Henri Perruchot's life of Cézanne (translated by Humphrey Hare: New York 1961). The misprint in 'A Concert 1866' comes from the source. The found poem about Tommy Phelps came from *The New York Times* in 1967.

The Lonely Suppers of W. V. Balloon

In Balthazar's Village. Written in Le Barroux (near Carpentras): Balthazar is the patron saint of the village. The next five poems concern other southern French and Spanish regions.

Mandelstam to Gumilev 1920. The first six lines allude to a poem addressed by Gumilev to Mandelstam; the remainder is a version, based on a translation by Paul Celan, of Mandelstam's reply.

Opoponax. The word is Greek ('all-healing juice'); the object in question — a small bottle of lavender essence from the Vaucluse. Molly Bloom's drawers were 'redolent of opoponax, jessamine, and Muratti's Turkish cigarettes'. The word occurs in the *Physicus* of Dioscorides (cf. Hugh Kenner, *The Pound Era*, 1971, p. 42); D. may have been phy-sician to Antony and Cleopatra.

The Monk of Montaudon. Imitation, based on Kasimir Edschmid's Ger-man versions of this late 12th century troubadour (*Die Aktion*, 1917).

Football Players U.S.A. Sources: CBS TV, and Henri Rousseau's paint-ing 'Les joueurs de foot-ball' (1908). The poem was written for Hans Bender, to confirm his perplexity.

The Ulcinj Postcards. Ulcinj is the last Montenegrin coastal town be-fore the Albanian frontier (itself a study in negative imagination).

Chanel Always Now: The text is a montage of phrases from a memoir by the painter Sir Francis Rose.

The Fossil Fish, 14. Clay trumpets were excavated during the building of a meteorological station on the top of Mont Ventoux.

Luberon Story. The place in question is Fort de Buoux (12th century); events — the persecution of Catharists and Vaudois, throughout this and more western regions, 13th–16th centuries.

Idiocy of Rural Life (Variant 2). '. . . easily destructible . . .' from Günter Eich's *Botschaften des Regens* (1955) — the blue book reflected in the windowpane.

Mérindol Interior. Place: Mérindol-les-Oliviers (Drôme, France). 'Sun-burst of petrol': from a press photo of Vietnamese children.

Title. As I was walking out of Mrs Robinson's on Guadalupe Street at night, the name W. V. Balloon occurred to me, falling suddenly out of some other sky; and then, attached to the name like a string, a phrase — 'the lonely suppers'. Mrs Robinson's is a place with a 1912 décor where people eat everything but air. W. V. Balloon, like other Balloons, and like poems, eats nothing but air. *Poiesis:* a defining of enigmas.

Patterns. Cf. Gilles Deleuze, *Proust and Signs* [1964], 1972: '. . . a work whose object, or rather whose subject, is Time . . . concerns, brings with it fragments which can no longer be restored, pieces which do not fit into the same puzzle, which do not belong to a preceding to-tality, which do not emanate from the same lost unity. Perhaps that

726

is what time is: the ultimate existence of parts, of different sizes and shapes, which cannot be adapted, which do not develop at the same rhythm, and which the stream of style does not sweep along at the same speed. The order of the cosmos has collapsed, crumbled into associative chains and non-communicating viewpoints. The language of signs begins to speak for itself . . .' (translated by Richard Howard, G. Braziller, New York, 1972).

Austin (Texas), December 1973

Carminalenia

Most of the poems in this book take their bearings from actual or imaginary spaces in or around people.

In 'Night Blooming Cereus' the student who reflects upon the making of a poem (by Georg Trakl) is set end to end with the flower of the title as the flower itself comes into the fore-ground. And the epigraph in the background of 'Razzmatazz' reads (Loeb translation): 'May the field of fruit trees receive increase from gladsome Dionysus, the pure sunshine of the fruit time.' The book's design does not, however, stop at the relative orders of things to which words are made to point. For instance, 'Night Blooming Cereus' formally triangulates its two areas of reference by moving through a third area, which is the text itself as a poem about poesis. This text and others conspire to levitate the world's body and construct a poetic space.

Trees: various trees occur, with modulations, *e.g.,* 'Ginestra,' 'The Winter Poplars'. Even if one cannot reverse Brecht's plaint (in 1938) that in such times it is almost a crime to converse about trees, my context goes further back, beyond the eloquent chapter in Norman Douglas's *Siren Land,* to Pliny. Who knows if Pliny knew about the Bo Tree, or of fabulous trees in old Siberian, Semitic, and Asiatic cosmologies, like the Vedic upside-down tree *nyagrodha.* He took to heart, even then, a tree's good sense as a vector in the realm of practice and in the spaces of imagination, triangulating the homes, the ships, and the unseen:

The trees and forests were supposed to be the supreme gift bestowed by Nature on man . . . These first provided him with his food, their foliage carpeted his cave and their bark served him for raiment . . . We use a tree to furrow the seas and bring the lands nearer together; we use a tree for build-

727

ing houses; even the images of gods were made from trees (Natural History, trs. Rackham).

'Anasphere: le torse antique': it might seem to be invoking itself in the guise of the poem it avows it is not. Yet the real absence of the ultrapoem is so felt that this negative turns out to be chromatic, not blank. Some negative emotions and public terrors are positively sensitive to the vacuum which steadily absorbs self-shattering human value systems. The pages of a book may not be spattered with blood, but tensions in the poetic space resist the dodo syndrome, or they twit those general ideas which are despotically sired upon indifference by the literal mind.

The title comes from Propertius: *Carmina mansuetus lenia quaerit Amor*. A kind of lexical fan, carminalenia when folded says only itself as English (two dactyls, the *le* spoken as *lay*); several words suggest themselves anagrammatically, including 'criminal,' *pace* Brecht. Or the word is, like the poetic space, a palimpsest: in 'Razzmatazz,' 4, appear traces of Seferis's poem 'Our Sun,' in 'Ibeji' traces of Yeats's 'The Statues'.

Two Horse Wagon Going By

'Jacob's Hat' is based on the mural by Delacroix in the church of St. Sulpice, Paris. 'Halicarnassian Ghost Dialogue' is about Herodotus. 'In Memory of Peter Szondi': the "beech wood" detail derives from the German context — *Buchstabe* = letter, and runes were originally made of beechwood sticks (*Buche* = beech). Buchenwald = Beech Wood. The scholar Peter Szondi was actually released from Auschwitz early in the 1940s while still in his teens, but the experience marked him for life. His suicide by drowning followed soon after that of his friend Paul Celan. 'Cabaret de la Canne, January 1855' is based on Alfred Delvau's report of an encounter with Gérard de Nerval (unbeknownst) shortly before his suicide. 'People in Kansas, 1910' elaborates on a postcard photograph, hence the postage stamp toward the end. I'm grateful to Sally Sullivan for letting me use her unpublished draft version of the 11th–12th century original as a basis for 'Shih-Ch'u's Magic Letter'.

728

I called the second of the two collections in this book *Apocrypha Texana* because the poems in it are anomalous in the frame of writing by native or settled Texans about their immense and varied habitat. Some poems allude to other parts of North America, but the terrain for many is Travis County, South Central Texas.

The preliterate idiom of 'Woden Dog' modulates from quasi-Old English through quasi-Black to a compound of Black and Western Apache English patois. It was a female voice I was hearing when I wrote the poems (Berlin, Winter 1978).

Twenty Tropes for Doctor Dark

Lucile / MA 632883. The title gives the name of the 'blue boat' registered at Marseille. Lines 19–21 from William Law: 'Man, wandering out of Paradise, a Colony of Heaven, was taken Captive by the Stars and Elements . . .' (*The Way to Divine Knowledge*, 1752, pp. 37–8).

Charles Meryon. French artist in eauforte (1821–68). After his years in the French navy, he settled in Paris. Tenuous human figures appear in only a few of his images of buildings, bridges, streets. Quotations in the third sonnet come from Baudelaire's articles and letters. Meryon's prodigious work was done during the dozen or so years before he went insane.

The Moon from a Box of Lokum. The story amplifies (and warps) an anecdote about Nicolai Gogol, during the mid-1840s.

The Digging. 'Chinks in a forest', from the end of Auden's poem 'Nones'. 'Words that taunt . . . ,' cf. *Beowulf,* line 1105 (cf. also lines 2057–9).

Envoi. Line 4 comes from Alfred de Vigny's prose work *Stello* (1832). Docteur Noir in that text, a rational and considerate, if secretly luciferian physician, together with traces of Gogol and of de Nerval's *'le ténébreux',* prompted the invocation here of an elusive 'compound ghost'. The reader may decide whether the doctor also appears, behind a dragoon's moustache, in 'Cassis, October 23, 1999.'

The Anti-Basilisk

Notes to *Tableaux I–XX*

A Lingering Enchantment
Samuel Dill, *Roman Society in the Last Century of the Western Empire* (1898).
Ivo Andric, *The Bridge on the Drina* (1945; English translation, 1957).
Walter Benjamin, 'Geschichtsphilosophische Thesen'.

A Species of Limbo
Memleket = native country. Dünya = world. Dün = yesterday.

Prospecting in Sicily, April 1787
Various details from Goethe, *Italienische Reise*. Megalio was the name bestowed on Goethe at his induction into the Arcadian Society in Rome.

The Torture Foreshadowed
Details from Dmitri Merejkowski, *Peter and Alexis* (English translation, 1905).

A Secret-Keeper
Henry the Fifth: cf. Shakespeare, *Henry V*, Act 1, Sc. 2.

Spoon, Covered Wagon
John Ford: quotation from Peter Quennell, *The Singular Preference* (originally Cyril Tourneur?).
Eyebrows: notable in daguerreotypes and ambrotypes.

The Signal Officer's Story
World War II (Pacific Theatre) details communicated by Donald L. Weismann.
De Mortuis
'. . . resting on a negative': cf. Hegel, *Phenomenology* cap. 1, and commentary by Giorgio Agamben, in *Le langage et la mort* (1982, French translation, 1991).
'. . . speaks to his death . . .': cf. W.S. Graham, 'The Nightfishing,' part 3 (1955).

Avdagina
Ivo Andric, *The Bridge on the Drina.*
Last line: Aman. Imdat = Ah! Help! (Turkish). Chiquito no tiene
cuna: from an old Spanish copla ('the little boy has no cradle').

Nobody's Ukelele
Marks scuffled in wet sand by the turtle resemble the alternating
flush and indented lines of Roman elegiacs (photograph by H.H.
Huey, *National Wildlife,* August–September, 2003).

Notes to '*The Anti-Basilisk*'

Marienbad, 1814. As late as March 1828 Goethe was still 'touching up'
(in proof) the *Novelle* he had been incubating at intervals since 1797.

A Greek Colonial Bronze (Gordian III). The coin, dated c.240 C.E., is
reproduced as No. 789 in the Classical Numismatic Group catalogue
for January 13–14, 2004 (Triton VII'). Other prompting came from
Boethius: 'For whososever is overcome of desire, and turns his gaze
upon the darkness . . . (*The Consolation of Philosophy,* 3, Mat.xii)

Memorandum from Gaul. Details (but not the murder plot) from Samuel Dill, *Roman Society in the Last Century of the Western Empire* [1898],
1921. Cf. Georg Forster's remarks in a letter to his wife from Paris,
July 8, 1793 '. . . here I discern with a special shudder, in the instance of
many heartless, enlightened, and supposedly nice people, that knowledge and thought, when applied exclusively to shedding the yoke of
prejudice, and not accompanied by inner nobility of soul, produce
the most repulsive moral monsters.' (*Georg Forster, Das Abenteuer seines
Lebens,* ed. Peter Kunz. Ebenhausen bei München: W.Langewiesche-
Brandt, ND.)

The Paradox of Jerome's Lion. A number of painters chose a lion to be
St. Jerome's animal; in one drawing, Carpaccio introduces a charm-
ingly astonished little dog.

Notes to *'Pinkard's Anecdotes'*

An Iranian Tale. Personal communication from Gerrit de Mol.

The Village on a Tilt. Details from a letter by D.H. Lawrence, from Lerici, Italy, December 1913.

An Ominous Circus. Details from Samuel Dill (see above).

The House on Fire. As recounted from the Lotus Sutra in Andrew Schelling, *The India Book,* O Books, 1993 (no place of publication).

On Pinkard: he ought to be distinguished from schismatics who bestrode the Twentieth Century solo: Barnabooth, M. Teste, Robert Walser's Helbling, Prufrock, Lichtenstein's Kuno Kohn, Ehrenstein's Tubutsch, Anna Blume, Mauberley, Bibi la Bibiste, Plume; later — Tulipan (Meckel), Manig (Lettau), Lucas (Cortázar). They variously had their fates. Pinkard, the unexterminated Gnostic, prefers not to have one today. He'll figure instead as the fool, in silhouette.

Notes to *Translations*

Catullus. The numbering of the texts follows the Loeb edition [1913], 1931.

Charles Mauron's Poem on Van Gogh. The original is in Provençal and appears together with a French version in Mauron's *Van Gogh: Etudes psychologiques* (Paris, José Corti 1976.)

Sonnet. The rhymed original is one of the extraordinary Surrealist Desnos' last poems. He died of typhus on June 8, 1945, after captivity in Auschwitz and Terezin.